Proceedings of the Estonian Institute
of Historical Memory 1 (2018)

Eesti Mälu Instituudi toimetised 1 (2018)

Proceedings of the Estonian Institute of Historical Memory 1 (2018)

Eesti Mälu Instituudi toimetised 1 (2018)

Sovietisation and Violence: The Case of Estonia

UNIVERSITY of TARTU
Press

Edited by Meelis Saueauk and Toomas Hiio

Translated into English by Alias Translation Agency, Tiia Raudma,
Refiner Tõlkebüroo and Peeter Tammisto

Copy editor Peeter Tammisto, proofread by Olaf Mertelsmann

Layout: Kalle Paalits
Cover design: Asko Künnap

On the cover:
Representatives of the Estonian SSR Academy of Sciences at the demonstration
marking the 43rd anniversary of the October Revolution in Tallinn in 1960.
Source: Estonian National Archives Film Archives

ISBN 978-9949-77-824-9 (print)
ISSN 2613-5981 (print)

ISBN 978-9949-77-825-6 (pdf)
ISSN 2613-621X (pdf)

University of Tartu Press
www.tyk.ee

Contents

6

Abbreviations

AUCP(B)	All-Union Communist Party (Bolsheviks) (Vsesoiuznaia kommunisticheskaia partiia (bol'shevikov), VKP(B)), the name of the CPSU in 1925–52
CC	Central Committee
CPSU	Communist Party of the Soviet Union
ECP	Estonian Communist Party (Eestimaa Kommunistlik Partei, EKP)
ECP(B)	Estonian Communist Party (Bolsheviks), the name of the ECP in 1940–52
ERM KV	Estonian National Museum, Archives (Eesti Rahva Muuseum, Korrespondentide vastuste arhiiv)
ESSR	Estonian SSR, Estonskaia SSR (Eesti NSV, ENSV)
GARF	State Archive of the Russian Federation (Gosudarstvennyi Arkhiv Rossiiskoi Federatsii)
GULAG	Main Camps' Administration (Glavnoe upravlenie lagerei)
KGB	Committee for State Security (Komitet gosudarstvennoi bezopasnosti)
KM EKLA	Estonian Literary Museum, Estonian Cultural History Archives (Kirjandusmuuseum, Eesti Kultuurilooline Arhiiv)
MGB	Ministry of State Security (Ministerstvo gosudarstvennoi bezopasnosti)
MVD	Ministry of Internal Affairs (Ministerstvo vnutrennykh del)
NKGB	People's Commissariat for State Security (Narodnyi komissariat gosudarstvennoi bezopasnosti)

NKVD   People's Commissariat for Internal Affairs (Narodnyi komissariat vnutrennykh del)

OBB   Department for anti-bandit combat (Otdel po bor'be s banditizmom)

OGPU   Unified State Political Administration (Ob"edinjonnoe gosudarstvennoe politicheskoe upravlenie)

RA   Estonian National Archives (Rahvusarhiiv)

RGANI   Russian State Archive of Contemporary History (Rossiiskii Gosudarstvennyi Arkhiv Noveishei Istorii)

RGASPI   Russian State Archive of Socio-Political History (Rossiiskii Gosudarstvennyi Arkhiv Sotsial'no-Politicheskoi Istorii)

RSFSR   Russian Soviet Federative Socialist Republic (Rossiiskaia Sovetskaia Federativnaia Sotsialisticheskaia Respublika)

SNK   Council of People's Commissars (Sovet narodnykh komissarov)

SSR   Soviet Socialist Republic (Sovetskaia Sotsialisticheskaia Respublika)

SSSR   Union of Soviet Socialist Republics (Soiuz Sovetskikh Sotsialisticheskikh Respublik)

TÜA   University of Tartu Archives (Tartu Ülikooli Arhiiv)

USSR   Union of Soviet Socialist Republics

Foreword

Dear Reader,

You have before you the Estonian Institute of Historical Memory's first collection of articles that deals with the violent phase in the establishment of Soviet power in the Baltic states, including Estonia. The authors are researchers from the Estonian Institute of Historical Memory and the Institute's cooperation partners.

The seizing of new territories and the establishment there of regimes, termed Communist, was rendered possible for the Soviet Union due to the Nonaggression Pact and its secret protocol, which was concluded with Hitler's Germany on 23 August 1939. The first victim was Poland – followed by an ultimatum to Estonia, then to Latvia and Lithuania. The next was Finland, which however resisted the demands by taking up arms, thereby preserving its independence. In 1940, it was the turn of the Baltic states and Bessarabia, which had been part of Romania, to be occupied and annexed. Violent Sovietisation began in all these territories.

There were distinctive features in the Sovietisation of the Baltic states and the accompanying terror. Firstly, the aggression by the Soviet Union in these countries preceded German occupation, which was an important influence on the attitude of the people regarding the various occupation regimes. When re-sovietisation followed in 1944–45, the local population was unable – for more than 40 years – to freely discuss their historic experiences. Secondly, although 'Sovietisation' is generally understood as the establishment of Soviet-style regimes in Eastern and Central Europe, then – in the Baltic states' context (as in the areas taken from Romania and Finland) – it meant the complete destruction of the independence-period's state and social systems, and their replacement by the systems in place in the Soviet Union, both in content and form. Thirdly, the wave of total terror crashed here 3–10 years later than the Great Terror in the Soviet Union. It was only in mid June of 1941 that the so-called 'troikas' and 'mass operations' appeared here. We can see that the largest numbers of political arrests occurred only after the re-occupation of this region in 1945, and the largest mass deportations in scale took place in 1948–49 (Lithuania) and 1949 (Estonia and Latvia). During the March 1949 deportations, and in the course of just a few days, over 20,000 people were taken from Estonia to Siberia, but deportation files had also been compiled for another 10,000 persons. The number of Estonians in the GULAG was largest in 1952, when more than 27,000 Estonians were held in imprisonment at the camps and colonies. In total, around 75,000 Estonian residents were murdered, imprisoned or deported by the authorities of the Soviet Union. In absolute numbers, this is low on the world scale, but considering that in 1939 Estonia had a population of just 1,134,000, it is more than 6,5 per cent of the population. All this became firmly fixed in the national psyche, and formed the image of the Soviet regime as a violent foreign power. Although the situation eased somewhat after the death of Stalin so that by the beginning of the 1960s most of those who had survived imprisonment and forcible exile were permitted to return to their homelands, the Soviet regime did not weaken its actual control over either Eastern Europe or the Baltics, continuing to harshly supress any strivings for freedom amongst the populations.

The violent establishment of the Soviet system won the attention of political scientists and Sovietologists, and also historians, immediately after the Second World War. A major contribution in scholarly research was provided by the exile communities of the Baltic states and Ukraine. Over the recent three decades there has been new attention shown to analysing the Sovietisation topic as a whole, and this also in Estonia. At the time of the disbanding of the Communist Party and the local KGB authorities in 1991, only a part of the documents was handed over to the Baltic states. Nevertheless, these documents that are held in the national archives have been available to researchers since the mid-1990s, and have enabled the quality of the research to be raised to a new level. In recent years, the attention of researchers has been widened to the fuller context of the entire Soviet period, and also beyond the repressions. Research has been carried out on how the state system functioned as a whole, the nomenklatura of those in power, the economy, the relationship of the state with religious communities, Soviet propaganda ranging from journalism to primary schools and kindergartens, and much more.[1] There are still many aspects of the subordination of society to Communist rule, however, that require more thorough research and new researchers. This can be done today through extensive cooperation, which covers both international research projects and inter-disciplinary studies, as well as the joint activities of 'archival historians' and those who have during the last decade become a centre of focus: the researchers of historical memory.

In Estonia, research of the Soviet period has been concentrated in the units of the University of Tartu and Tallinn University that deal with the study and teaching of history, but not only there. The work of identifying the victims of repression has been carried out for almost 30 years by the Estonian Repressed Persons Records Bureau, working as part of the Memento organisation that unites former deportees and political prisoners.[2] An intermediate result, a 'White Book', was published in 2005 by the Estonian State Commission on the Examination of the Policies of Repression, which was set up by the Parliament in 1991.[3] The non-profit organisation

---

[1]   A selection of relevant collections: *Vom Hitler-Stalin-Pakt bis zu Stalins Tod: Estland 1939–1953*, ed. Olaf Mertelsmann (Hamburg, Tallinn: Bibliotheca Baltica, 2005); *Eesti NSV aastatel 1940–1953: sovetiseerimise mehhanismid ja tagajärjed Nõukogude Liidu ja Ida-Euroopa arengute kontekstis* [Soviet Estonia 1944–1953: Mechanisms and consequences of Sovietisation in Estonia in the context of of Soviet Union and Eastern Europe], ed. Tõnu Tannberg (Tartu: Eesti Ajalooarhiiv, 2007); *Eesti ajaloost nõukogude võimu perioodil = Studies in the history of Estonia during the soviet rule*, ed. Tõnu Tannberg – Ajaloolise Ajakirja teemanumber (Tartu: Ajalookirjanduse Sihtasutus Kleio, 2009); Olaf Mertelsmann, *Die Sowjetisierung Estlands und seiner Gesellschaft* (Hamburg: Verlag Dr. Kovač, 2012); *Behind the Iron Curtain: Soviet Estonia in the era of the Cold War*, ed. Tõnu Tannberg (Frankfurt am Main: Peter Lang Edition, 2015); *Nomenklaturisüsteem Eesti NSV-s = The nomenklatura system in the Estonian SSR*, ed. by Tõnu Tannberg – Ajaloolise Ajakirja teemanumber (Tartu: Tartu Ülikooli Kirjastus, 2015); *The Baltic states under Stalinist rule*, ed. Olaf Mertelsmann (Köln: Böhlau, 2016).

[2]   The Office of the Register of Estonian Victims of Repression has published several books with the names of the victims of political murder, arrest and deportation, see: https://www.memento.ee/trukised/memento-raamatud/, 1 June 2018.

[3]   *The White Book: losses inflicted on the Estonian nation by occupation regimes 1940–1991*, eds. Vello Salo et al. (Tallinn: Estonian Encyclopaedia Publishers, 2005).

S-Keskus, which was set up in 1998, has published two collections on the period 1940–1941, and a number of volumes are ready for publishing.[4] In 1998, the Estonian President Lennart Meri called for the establishment of the Estonian International Commission for the Investigation of Crimes Against Humanity, where the result of the research was a collection of articles covering the first Soviet occupation in 1940–1941, the German occupation in 1941–1944, and also the beginning of the second Soviet occupation, up until the death of Stalin in 1953.[5] In 2008, President Toomas Hendrik Ilves called for the establishment of the Estonian Institute of Historical Memory on the basis of the research team of the Estonian International Commission for the Investigation of Crimes Against Humanity. The Institute works as a partner to the many similar institutions that have been established, or re-formed, in Eastern European countries at the beginning of the 21st century, but it primarily continues research of the Soviet era, concentrating on the period 1944–1991. The task of the Estonian Institute of Historical Memory since 2016 has also been the establishment of the international museum of the crimes of communism and an academic research centre, in the former Central ('Patarei') prison in Tallinn.

The Editors

---

[4]   *Sõja ja rahu vahel. I köide, Eesti julgeolekupoliitika 1940. aastani* [Between War and Peace. Vol.1, Estonian security policies to 1940], editor-in-chief Enn Tarvel, ed. Tõnu Tannberg (Tallinn: S-Keskus, 2004); *Sõja ja rahu vahel. II köide, Esimene punane aasta: okupeeritud Eesti julgeolekupoliitiline olukord sõja alguseni* [Between War and Peace. Vol.2, The first 'red' year: security situation in occupied Estonia, to the beginning of the war], editor-in-chief Enn Tarvel, ed. Meelis Maripuu (Tallinn: S-Keskus, 2010).

[5]   *Estonia 1940–1945: reports of the Estonian International Commission for the Investigation of Crimes Against Humanity*, eds. Toomas Hiio, Meelis Maripuu and Indrek Paavle (Tallinn: Estonian Foundation for the Investigation of Crimes Against Humanity, 2006); *Estonia since 1944: reports of the Estonian International Commission for the Investigation of Crimes Against Humanity*, eds. Toomas Hiio, Meelis Maripuu and Indrek Paavle (Tallinn: Estonian Foundation for the Investigation of Crimes Against Humanity, 2009).

Preface

Norman M. Naimark

This volume contains important new and reprinted contributions to the historiography of the Soviet takeover of the Baltic states. In this collection, scholars associated with the Estonian Institute of Historical Memory explore in depth and with nuance the processes by which Moscow incorporated Estonia, Latvia, and Lithuania into the Soviet Union. The articles take excellent advantage of the overall maturation of the historiography of the post-communist period in the Baltic states, along with the possibilities of research in fresh archival sources from the Soviet period, including the Republic KGB collections, located in Tallinn and elsewhere in the region. The post-1991 proliferation of published and unpublished memoirs of Estonians and others about the Soviet period, especially in connection with the deportations, and answers to questionnaires collected by the Estonian Institute of Historical Memory about the Soviet occupation, provide additional fascinating material for reconstructing the ways in which the men and women of the region faced the unknown future under Soviet rule.

By its very nature, the Soviet takeover of the Baltic states was a violent process that involved the use of the 'repressive organs' of the Soviet state – the NKVD, the MGB, and the judicial system. Above all, the ability of Moscow to establish the state's control of violence, combat groups of 'Forest Brothers', and infiltrate and crush the political opposition determined the outcome of the struggle for the Baltic area. Frequently, the Soviet organs of repression were combined under the control of senior Soviet intelligence specialists who would direct the campaigns against opponents and alleged political enemies. The role of the intelligence services was not just one of the application of violence and the threat of violence. They also involved themselves in cultural politics and publishing activities, in part to influence the indigenous population of the Baltic region, but also to undermine the unity of purpose of émigré organisations. Especially after the death of Stalin, the repressive organs also co-opted psychiatric installations, which served as another police method of quashing dissent and persecuting political opponents. One of the most nefarious characteristics of the repressive policies of the Soviet authorities was the attack on family members of the accused, who were often also sentenced to harsh terms of prison or exile.

The establishment of Soviet power in the Baltics belonged quintessentially to the realm of politics. Control of Estonia, Latvia, and Lithuania required a massive reorientation of the political character of the region. This included the assertion of communist party domination and its ability to control the most important appointments to administrative offices, universities, and cultural and economic institutions through the nomenklatura system that was supervised by the Cadres Administration of the Central Committee. The development of indigenous Baltic cadres was crucial to the successful emergence of Soviet republics in the region, though when necessary, as the 1950–52 'Estonian Case' demonstrated, Moscow was ready to dismiss local cadres in favour of importing leaders from the Soviet Union.

In short, the Baltic states were to be Sovetised under any circumstances, and this meant the transferal of Soviet institutions, assumed in every case to be superior to 'bourgeois ones',to the region. Sovietisation also meant that the Baltic states would be forced to partake in the militarisation of the population of the region, joining the Soviet Armed Forces, which became a particularly contentious issue in the dozen years before the fall of the Soviet Union. This also meant the building of Komsomol and Trade Union organisations, the development of networks of informants for the KGB, and the participation of the Baltic peoples in Soviet sports, cultural, educational, and scientific organisations. Moscow demanded conformity to Soviet models and frequently to specific Soviet demands regarding such matters as who would win literary prizes or who would be appointed to particular positions in the respective societal organisations.

New documentation and published memoirs available to Estonian researchers have also made possible new insights into the everyday travails of the Baltic peoples as they faced deportations, the incessant rumours of deportations, and the possibilities during and immediately after the war of leaving their homelands for the West. The decision to leave was sometimes thwarted by simple quotidian considerations: what to do with the animals on the farm, how to deal with elderly relatives, how long to put off leaving before it was too late. Chance often dictated whether those who sought to flee made it safely out of the country or not. Many people of the region were certain the West would not allow their countries to be incorporated into the Soviet Union. So the tendency was to hesitate. Frequently, the situations that the refugees met when they went to the West were less than ideal. The camps in Germany were especially crowded, hungry, unsanitary, and unfriendly to the Baltic internees.

From a January 1949 document reproduced and analysed in this book, we know that Stalin and the Soviet leadership ordered the deportations of the spring of 1949 from the Baltic republics and that Lavrenti Beria was assigned the task – which he had already frequently carried out throughout the Soviet Union – to disperse the deportees throughout Siberia and the Gulag. But the idea for the deportations came from the Baltic communist leaders themselves, anxious to 'de-kulakise' their own republics along the model of the Soviet 1930s. From the 'ego-documents' collected by Estonian historians, we also know that many locals were able to hide from Beria's teams and avoid deportation altogether. Rumours about deportation kept everyone on edge; but this also meant that many people of the region were ready to hide when the deportation teams came to their villages.

The history of the incorporation of the Baltic states into the Soviet Union is reminiscent of the fate of Eastern Europe in the same period. The role of the Soviet intelligence services was very similar. Their job was to smash the opposition and to infiltrate and control their 'friends'. They built up indigenous intelligence services in the East European countries, but their successes were limited, as each country in the region had its own problems with adopting Soviet models. Thus Soviet officers were constantly monitoring local police and secret police operations. This persisted into the period of the East European purge trials, 1950–54, when Soviet operatives oversaw the elimination of alleged opponents in and outside the communist parties. Indigenous communists were encouraged to engage politically and take control of their respective political systems, though, like the Baltic states, the number of communists was generally quite small at the outset and it took many years before the local communists who came to power could accurately anticipate Moscow's wishes.

Particularly in the period of the Stalinisation of Eastern Europe, 1948–1953, the incessant propaganda of the superiority of the Soviet system infused the life of East Europeans, much as it dominated the Baltic region. The difference, of course, was that the East Europeans were able to maintain a modicum of sovereignty. After all, they were not integrated the Soviet Union as some local communists had advocated, nor were they intended to be, even in the period of high Stalinism. The Baltic states, despite the vain hopes of their peoples to the contrary, did indeed become constituent republics of the USSR. They were forced to adapt to the new system in ways that violated many of their most precious values, including those of independence and self-determination. The East Europeans, at the least, could rule their own countries. They were forced to Sovietise, but there were limits and those limits proved crucial in the maintenance of a sense of national dignity and autonomy. Yet, the peoples of the Baltic region maintained their own private hopes and dreams of a better life free of Soviet rule. Sovietisation in the region also had its limits and was incomplete. When they could seize the chance, the Baltic peoples, like the East Europeans, opted for freedom and sovereignty.

How to Define Sovietisation?

*Olaf Mertelsmann**

Introduction

It is not easy to define the term 'Sovietisation', because the actual implementation of the process varied from country to country. In addition, over time the content of this term underwent slight changes. If we examine only one country, such as Latvia or Estonia, we risk overlooking the larger context.[1] Thus this discussion of 'Sovietisation' starts by looking at the history of the term.

The word 'soviet' (*sovet*) means 'council' in Russian and was used in the Russian Empire as a politically neutral term, as in Council of Ministers (*Sovet ministrov*). In the context of the February Revolution in 1917, across the empire workers' and soldiers' councils were established, often elected, and played a role in the revolution. They turned into a parallel power structure vis-à-vis the institutions of the provisional government, especially because the remnants of the old administration began to dissolve and lacked legitimacy in the eyes of the population. In most workers' and soldiers' councils, it was not the Bolsheviks who dominated but other

* An earlier version of this paper was published under the following title: 'What is Sovietization?', – Olaf Mertelsmann, *Everyday Life in Stalinist Estonia* (Frankfurt: Peter Lang, 2012), 9–25.

[1] After the 1989–1991 collapse of socialism, many studies based on extensive archival research were published concerning Sovietisation in individual countries. By covering only one country, these studies neglected often the broader perspective. In this context, broader cooperation across the borders of national historiography is necessary to enable comparisons and combat the assumption that developments in one's own country were unique.

socialist parties such as the Mensheviks and the Social Revolutionaries. The 'trick' used by Lenin and the Bolsheviks during their coup d'état, also known as the October Revolution, was to seize power in the name of the workers' and soldiers' soviets under the slogan 'all power to the soviets'. The long-term goal of the coup d'état, the establishment of a one-party dictatorship headed by Lenin, was hidden. Workers' and soldiers' councils played a certain role locally in developments, especially in the unfolding civil war. But step by step, the Bolsheviks pushed aside all other political groups, including the left-wing Social Revolutionaries, which whom they had initially formed a coalition. Likewise, workers' control of factories survived only briefly after the putsch. Workers' control was never completed, meaning the workers' councils never really directed the enterprises, and they were pushed aside over time by appointed commissars, communist-dominated trade unions and state institutions such as agencies of planning and the war economy.

On closer examination, then, the terms 'Soviet power', 'Soviet Russia' and 'the Soviet Union' were misnomers, because soviets were usually not elected democratically, and their influence and authority declined rapidly. The meetings of those soviets increasingly turned into a staged performance for the acclamation of the regime, and they had nothing to do with democracy. Consequently, until the 1960s, a number of Western researchers spoke of 'Bolshevik Russia' when referring to Soviet Russia or the Soviet Union.[2]

After the Bolshevik coup d'état and during the civil war, the term 'Sovietisation' (*sovetizatsiia*) first appeared. It was used by the Bolsheviks to mean the application of the Bolshevik model of governance and organisation in one region or country. Thus, for example, Lenin spoke in September 1920 about the Sovietisation of Lithuania.[3] The first Sovietised areas were those conquered by the Bolsheviks during the civil war. Initially the term possessed mainly a political meaning. Over time the meaning grew broader. Turning a non-Soviet society into a Soviet one meant not only taking political power but restructuring the economy, everyday life, society and culture. In the end, virtually everything could be 'Sovietised',

---

[2]   For example, Georg von Rauch, *Geschichte des bolschewistischen Rußland* (Wiesbaden: Rheinische Verlagsanstalt, 1955).

[3]   Lenin's speech from September 20, 1920, cited in *The Unknown Lenin*, ed. Richard Pipes (New Haven-London: Yale University Press, 1996), 95–115.

including the music on a radio station, as one source states.[4] In the 1940s the term 'Sovietisation' was still used, but in the 1950s it disappeared from Soviet sources, as a result of the word's use in Western research and media since the early Cold War.

Before World War II, some Soviet publications even contained passages about the future Sovietisation of neighbouring countries. Soviet military theoretician Vladimir K. Triandafillov (1894–1931) published the classic textbook on the subject in 1929: *The Nature of the Operations of Modern Armies (Kharakter operatsii sovremennykh armii)*. It is quoted below extensively, because the textbook was written for future officers, and it quite openly elaborates how Sovietisation should unfold in the framework of a military conquest. The author used his background experience from the Russian Civil War, and there are striking similarities between the description in the book and the events in the territories occupied and annexed in 1939 and 1940. The smaller states mentioned were, of course, Estonia, Latvia and Lithuania:

Enormous work involving Sovietisation of regions captured from the enemy will fall to the political apparatus. Major successive operations, given favourable conditions, may over a period of three-four weeks lead to liberation of territory with frontage and depth of 200–250 kilometers. If small states are involved, this signifies that one must cope in a short time (two-three weeks) with Sovietisation of entire states. This could mean three-four weeks of Sovietisation of extremely large areas if larger countries are involved. Of course, complete Sovietisation of such territories is a long-term concern, but deployment of a Soviet apparatus must take place within the aforementioned periods. Here, from the very outset, one must achieve a high-quality and reliable apparatus dedicated to the ideals of Soviet power, people capable in demonstrating to the population of newly captured areas the difference between the Soviet and the capitalist system must be put in place.

It will be very hard to count on local assets when organising revolutionary committees because the enemy will undoubtedly destroy all local revolutionary organisations in the area of the front. Only part of the technical apparatus and the most responsible workers will be found locally. All responsible workers and even some of the technical personnel must be

---

[4]   Meeting of the Bureau of the Central Committee of the ECP(B), 20 June 1946, RA, ERAF.1.4.360, 151–152.

brought in. Of course, they will and, if the capability exists, must be taken from among the local workers, who fled from the Whites. The number of these workers required to carry out the Sovietisation of newly captured areas will be enormous. [...] The Sovietisation mission, of course, cannot be handled without wide use of local workers, local revolutionary organisations. Strengthening the Soviet system and the Soviet apparatus wholly depends on the rate of reestablishment of revolutionary social organisations such as trade unions, poor peasant committees in villages, and so forth. The Soviet system in captured areas will be finally strengthened only when their own peaceful Communist Party is created.[5]

After the October putsch, the Bolsheviks tried to ignite revolution in nearby states, most notably in Germany, Poland, and Hungary, but also in other countries. Weapons, ammunition and money were brought in and used to start local insurrections. After the failure of the last uprising – the December 1924 attempt to seize power in Estonia – the Bolshevik leaders finally understood that revolutions in the West would not succeed without the direct support of the Red Army.[6] This meant a change in the Soviets' policy towards their neighbours. Tobias Privetelli has demonstrated convincingly in his unpublished thesis that Stalin became a cautious expansionist. When the time was ripe, after the August 1939 signing of the German-Soviet Treaty of Non-Aggression and its secret protocol, the Soviet Union invaded eastern Poland in September and Sovietised the region according to a rough plan drawn up mainly by Andrei Zhdanov, one of Stalin's lieutenants. The plan resembles Triandafillov's ideas. The Soviet army occupied eastern Poland, and special plenipotentiaries came in. Sham elections; incorporation into the USSR; and the restructuring of the administration, society, economy and culture started within weeks.[7] Eastern Poland later served as a rough model for the events in the Baltic states, following a similar time frame.

---

[5]   V. K. Triandafillov, *The Nature of the Operations of Modern Armies* (Ilford-Portland: Frank Cass, 1994), 164–165.

[6]   Tobias Privetelli, 'Irredentism, Expansion and the Liberation of the European Proletariat: Stalin's Considerations on How to Bring Communism to the Western Neighbors of the Soviet Union, 1920–1941' (PhD thesis, University of Berne, 2008), 68–72.

[7]   *Ibid.*, 318–326.

The Bolsheviks felt the Sovietisation of other states was ideologically justified and did not constitute imperialist expansion. According to the doctrines of Marxism-Leninism-Stalinism, socialism was superior to other political systems, and its victory in the long run was historically inevitable. The population of the Sovietised territories would be freed from the ills of capitalism and could look forward to a brighter future. This explains why Triandafillov and others could write so openly about the Sovietisation of neighbouring countries during a military occupation. Only after cooperating with the Western Allies during World War II and then in the Cold War did the Soviets conceal their plans for expanding their territory and sphere of influence and portray Sovietisation as a result of genuine local processes and the wishes of the local populations. To this end the Soviets created the myth of a revolution, which many socialist historians later echoed in books and articles.

In international media and the language of some foreign diplomats, the term 'Sovietisation' appears as early as the interwar period, but it spread more widely after the war. By then, the Western media and historians used the term to describe the changes in the Soviet-controlled territories of Central and Eastern Europe. Often the word was used by refugees from those regions.[8] The restructuring of all aspects of everyday life, economy, politics, society and culture was called 'Sovietisation', and the term had a highly negative connotation. There were local varieties, such as the East German, Czechoslovak or Polish model. In the Federal Republic of Germany, the term was widely used to describe developments in the eastern part of the divided country. The West German federal government sponsored an entire series of publications.[9] Further works followed, often

---

[8]   For example, Endel Kareda, *Technique of Economic Sovietisation: A Baltic Experience* (London: Boreas Publishing Company, 1947).

[9]   The West German Ministry for All-German Questions published, for example, the following volumes: *Die Sowjetisierung der deutschen Länder Brandenburg, Mecklenburg, Sachsen, Sachsen-Anhalt, Thüringen* (Bonn: Bundesministerium für gesamtdeutsche Fragen, 1950); *Die Sowjetisierung der Landwirtschaft in der Sowjetzone* (Hamburg: Bundesministerium für gesamtdeutsche Fragen, 1951); *Bibliotheken als Opfer und Werkzeug der Sowjetisierung* (Bonn: Bundesministerium für gesamtdeutsche Fragen, 1952); *Das Erziehungswesen der Sowjetzone: Eine Sammlung von Zeugnissen der Sowjetisierung und Russifizierung des mitteldeutschen Schulwesens* (Bonn: Bundesministerium für gesamtdeutsche Fragen, 1952).

imbued with the spirit of the Cold War.[10] The late 1950s saw the publication of a groundbreaking overview, cited to this day, on developments in
East-Central Europe.[11] Outside the Federal Republic of Germany, the term
was not as popular.[12] With new developments in Soviet studies, especially
in the English-speaking world—such as revisionism—the use of the term
'Sovietisation' declined. It conjured up the rhetoric of Cold War hawks.
In addition, some Western experts were themselves Marxists and did not
reject socialism per se. Only the collapse of socialism led to a revival of
the term, and today it is used in a more neutral way.[13]

---

[10]   Marianne Müller and Egon Erwin Müller, '... *stürmt die Festung Wissen-
schaft!' Die Sowjetisierung der mitteldeutschen Universitäten seit 1945* (Berlin:
Colloquium-Verlag, 1953); Bartho Plönies and Otto Schönwalder, *Die Sowjetisierung des mitteldeutschen Handwerks* (Bonn: Bundesministerium für gesamtdeutsche Fragen, 1953); Robert von Benda, *Die betriebswirtschaftlichen Auswirkungen der Sowjetisierung auf die Landwirtschaft Nordosteuropas* (Hamburg:
Agricola-Verlag, 1955); Helmut König, *Rote Sterne glühn: Lieder im Dienste der
Sowjetisierung* (Bad Godesberg: Voggenreiter, 1955); Andrivs Namsons, 'Die
kulturgeographischen, wirtschaftlichen und soziologischen Auswirkungen der
Sowjetisierung Lettlands' (PhD-thesis, Technische Hochschule Stuttgart, 1958);
Anthony Adamovich, *Opposition to Sovietization in Belorussian Literature,
1917–1957* (Munich: Institut zur Erforschung der UdSSR, 1958); Ādolfs Silde,
Die Sowjetisierung Lettlands (Bonn: Bundesinstitut für Ostwissenschaften und
Internationale Studien, 1967).

[11]   *Die Sowjetisierung Ost-Mitteleuropas*, eds. Ernst Birke and Rudolf Neumann
(Frankfurt: Metzner, 1959).

[12]   The number of books using the term in the title was definitely smaller: *The
Sovietization of Culture in Poland*, ed. Mid-European Research and Planning
Centre (Paris: Mid-European Research and Planning Centre, 1953); Jurij Bo-
rys, *The Sovietization of Ukraine 1917–1923* (Edmonton: Canadian Institute of
Ukrainian Studies, 1980); Janis Labvirs, *The Sovietization of the Baltic States:
Collectivization of Latvian Agriculture, 1944–1956* (Gladstone: Taurus, 1989).

[13]   Wladimir Berelowitch, *La soviétisation de l'école russe 1917–1931* (Lausanne:
L'Age d'Homme, 1990); *Sowjetisches Modell und nationale Prägung: Kontinuität
und Wandel in Ostmitteleuropa nach dem Zweiten Weltkrieg*, ed. Hans Lem-
berg (Marburg: Herder-Institut, 1991); *Amerikanisierung und Sowjetisierung in
Deutschland 1945–1970*, eds. Konrad Jarausch and Hannes Siegrist (Frankfurt:
Campus-Verlag, 1995); Rüdiger Kühr, *Die Reparationspolitik der UdSSR und die
Sowjetisierung des Verkehrswesens der SBZ* (Bochum: Universitätsverlag Brock-
meyer, 1996); Donald O'Sullivan, 'Die Sowjetisierung Osteuropas', *Forum für
osteuropäische Ideen- und Zeitgeschichte* 2 (1998): 109–160; *Sowjetisierung und
Eigenständigkeit in der SBZ/DDR (1945–1953)*, ed. Michael Lemke (Cologne:

The first Sovetised territories, as mentioned above, formed part of So-viet Russia. At first, the Bolsheviks had to secure power in the territo-

Böhlau, 1999); John Connelly, *Captive University: The Sovietization of East Ger-man, Czech, and Polish Higher Education, 1945–1956* (Chapel Hill: University of North Carolina Press, 2000); Ruth Büttner, *Sowjetisierung oder Selbständigkeit? Die sowjetische Finnlandpolitik 1943–1948* (Hamburg: Dr. Kovač, 2001); Elena Zubkova, 'Fenomen "mestnogo natsionalizma": "estonskoe delo" 1949–1952 go-dov v kontekste sovetizatsii Baltii', *Otechestvennaia istoriia*, no. 3 (2001): 89–102; Erwin Oberländer, 'Instruments of Sovietization in 1939/40 and after 1944/45', – *The Soviet Occupation Regime in the Baltic States 1944–1959* (Riga: Institute of the History of Latvia Publishers, 2003), 50–58; *The Sovietization of the Baltic States, 1940–1956*, ed. Olaf Mertelsmann (Tartu: Kleio, 2003); *Sovietization in Ro-mania and Czechoslovakia: History, Analogies, Consequences*, eds. Flavius Solo-mon and Al Zub (Bucharest: Polirom, 2003); *Sowjetisierung oder Neutralität? Op-tionen sowjetischer Besatzungspolitik in Deutschland und Österreich 1945–1955*, ed. Andreas Hilger (Göttingen: Vandenhoeck & Ruprecht, 2006); Katrin Boeckh, *Stalinismus in der Ukraine: Die Rekonstruktion des sowjetischen Systems nach dem Zweiten Weltkrieg* (Wiesbaden: Harrassowitz, 2007); David Feest, *Zwangs-kollektivierung im Baltikum: Die Sowjetisierung des estnischen Dorfes 1944–1953* (Cologne-Weimar: Böhlau, 2007); *Eesti NSV aastatel 1940–1953. Sovetiseerimise mehhanismid ja tagajärjed Nõukogude Liidu ja Ida-Euroopa arengute kontekstis* [Soviet Estonia 1944–1953: Mechanisms and consequences of Sovietization in Estonia in the context of of Soviet Union and Eastern Europe], ed. Tõnu Tan-nberg (Tartu: Eesti Ajalooarhiiv, 2007); Juliette Denis, 'Identifies les 'elements ennemis' en Lettonie: Une prioriteé dans le processus de resoviétisation', *Ca-hiers du Monde russe*, no. 49 (2008): 297–318; Elena Zubkova, *Pribaltika i Kreml' 1940–1953* (Moscow: Rosspen, 2008); *The Sovietization of Eastern Europe: New Perspectives on the Postwar Period*, eds. Balázs Apor, Péter Apor and E. A. Rees (Washington: New Academia Publishing, 2008); Indrek Paavle, *Kohaliku hal-duse sovetiseerimine Eestis: 1940–1950* [Sovietisation of local administration in Estonia 1940–1950] (Tartu: Tartu Ülikooli Kirjastus, 2009); Felix Ackermann, *Palimpsest Grodno: Nationalisierung, Nivellierung und Sowjetisierung einer mit-teleuropäischen Stadt 1919–1991* (Wiesbaden: Harrassowitz, 2010); Olaf Mertels-mann, *Die Sowjetisierung Estlands und seiner Gesellschaft* (Hamburg: Dr. Kovač, 2012); Małgorzata Ruchniewicz, *Das Ende der Bauernwelt: Die Sowjetisierung des westweißrussischen Dorfes 1944–1953* (Göttingen: Wallstein-Verlag, 2015); Meelis Saueauk, *Propaganda ja terror: Nõukogude julgeolekuorganid ja Eestimaa Kommunistlik Partei Eesti sovetiseerimisel 1944–1953* [Propaganda and Terror: Soviet Security Organs and the Communist Party of Estonia in the Sovietisa-tion of Estonia in 1944–1953] (Tallinn: SE&JS, 2015); *Jahrbücher für Geschichte Osteuropas* 64:3 (2016): special issue 'Reframing Postwar Sovietization: Power, Conflict, and Accommodation'; Jamil Hasanli, *The Sovietization of Azerbaijan: The South Caucasus in the Triangle of Russia, Turkey, and Iran, 1920–1922* (Salt Lake City: University of Utah Press, 2018).

ries they controlled militarily and politically, and afterwards they had to integrate the many areas conquered during the civil war.[14] Right from the start, *sovetizatsiia* implied more than mere political takeover—it also meant social, economic and cultural restructuring according to the ideas of those in power. The basic pattern would also be used later with different variations: oppression and terror against real or invented 'enemies', the nationalisation of private property, measures taken against the market and private enterprise, state control of prices, remoulding the social structure, strict censorship, political agitation and propaganda and the support of one particular way of culture. Parallel to this was the offer to integrate certain social strata of limited means, which encouraged their accommodation to the new regime. Often the offer of integration involved upward social mobility and privileges.

Tsarist Russia and its successor, the Soviet Union, constituted a multiethnic and multicultural empire. This means that, in different regions, the process of Sovietisation happened in the framework of different cultures and even civilizations. Stalin initially worked out the basic concepts of the Soviet nationalities policy under the influence of Austrian Social Democrats. The policy was summed up in the slogan 'national in form, socialist in content'. As a result, the young Soviet state had a very different face from region to region. As we know from studies on the Caucasus and Central Asia,[15] the Bolsheviks formed the strangest coalitions with religious or national minorities, with a clan or a tribe, playing one group against another. In one place they were modernisers or supported a national awakening and nation-building, while in other places they behaved like colonisers or brutal oppressors. Thus there was not one uniform method of Sovietisation within the Soviet Union but many local varieties of one basic model.

Stalin's cultural revolution, the forced collectivisation of agriculture and the start of the campaign of industrialisation in the late 1920s and

---

[14] On the revolution and the civil war, see Richard Pipes, *The Russian Revolution*, 3 vols. (New York: Knopf, 1990–1993); Orlando Figes, *A People's Tragedy: The Russian Revolution 1891–1924* (London: Jonathan Cape, 1996); Helmut Altrichter, *Russland 1917: Ein Land auf der Suche nach sich selbst* (Paderborn: Ferdinand Schöningh, 1997); Geoffrey Swain, *Russia's Civil War* (London: The History Press, 2000).

[15] Oliver Roy, *The New Central Asia: The Creation of Nations* (London-New York: Tauris, 2000); Jörg Baberowski, *Der Feind ist überall: Stalinismus im Kaukasus* (Munich: Deutsche Verlagsanstalt, 2003).

early 1930s, together with the 'Great Terror' in 1937–1938, including the attack on 'enemy nations', brought a certain degree of unity to the Soviet empire. In addition, the number of languages accepted for instruction in the native tongue at 'national' schools sharply declined, which also led to more uniformity.[16] The end of the New Economic Policy (NEP) and the restructuring of the economy, everyday life, society and culture, together with repression and terror, might be seen as a continuation of the Sovietisation of the USSR. Only then did the Bolsheviks control the countryside, where the vast majority of citizens lived, and agriculture, where most of the population was employed. Other parts of the economy were placed under tighter state control than in the 1920s. For a long time, the Soviet economy was seen as a planned economy, but new research finds it to have been a command economy.[17]

The 1930s saw the establishment of the USSR's main structures, which were to persist until the collapse of the state in 1991. The Soviet Union was a house built by Stalin on the foundation laid by Lenin. Stalin's successors attempted to make some renovations to this house but tried not to touch the foundation. Certainly one of the most important reforms was the end of state terror and open oppression in the 1950s, not for humanitarian reasons but because mass terror was too costly in economic terms. The foundations of Stalin's house were rocked by Mikhail Gorbachev in the late 1980s, causing the structure to finally collapse.[18]

---

[16]   On the Soviet nationalities policy, see Gerhard Simon, *Nationalism and Policy toward the Nationalities in the Soviet Union* (Boulder, CO: Westview Press, 1991); Terry Martin, *The Affirmative Action Empire: Nations and Nationalism in the Soviet Union, 1923–1938* (Ithaca: Cornell University Press, 2001); Francine Hirsch, *Empire of Nations: Ethnographic Knowledge and the Making of the Soviet Union* (Ithaca: Cornell University Press, 2005); Daniel Müller, *Sowjetische Nationalitatenpolitik in Transkaukasien 1920–1953* (Berlin: Köster, 2008); Friedrich Dönninghaus, *Minderheiten in Bedrängnis: Sowjetische Politik gegenüber Deutschen, Polen und anderen Diaspora-Nationalitäten 1917–1938* (Munich: Oldenbourg, 2009); Grigol Ubiria, *Soviet Nation-Building in Central Asia: The Making of the Kazakh and Uzbek Nations* (London: Routledge, 2016).

[17]   Paul R. Gregory, *Behind the Façade of Stalin's Command Economy: Evidence from the Soviet State and Party Archives* (Stanford: Hoover Institution Press, 2001); idem, *The Political Economy of Stalinism: Evidence from the Soviet Secret Archives* (Cambridge: Cambridge University Press, 2004).

[18]   See Robert Service, 'Stalinism and the Soviet State Order', *Totalitarian Movements and Political Religions*, no. 4 (2003): 7–22.

The Export of the Soviet Model

After the German-Soviet Treaty of Non-Aggression in August 1939, the opportunity to export the Soviet model arose (the first attempts were made in Mongolia in the 1920s). Where did Sovietisation happen?[19] We must distinguish among four groups of countries:

- The territories occupied and annexed by the Soviet Union in 1939 and 1940 with a population of more than 20 million inhabitants:
  - Eastern Poland was invaded in September 1939 and later incorporated into the Belarussian and the Ukrainian SSR.[20] The Vilnius region became part of Lithuania. The Kresy or border region was the least developed part of Poland. Soviet and German terror, population transfer and ethnic cleansing during and after the war changed the area more profoundly than it did the Baltic states.[21] The incorporation into existing Soviet republics involved a deeper restructuring, too.
  - Estonia, Latvia and Lithuania had been independent states and were turned into Soviet republics. This meant that measures of oppression and terror notwithstanding, there was more room for local decision-making and more continuity than in eastern Poland.[22]
  - Bessarabia, the least developed province of Romania, was occupied and annexed and became, after 'unification' with the Moldavian ASSR, a Soviet republic. Because Romania was among the poorest countries in Europe, some leftist circles viewed in-

---

[19]   There is not enough space to list the vast literature on Sovietisation for each separate country. Thus only a few titles are mentioned.

[20]   See Jan T. Gross, *Revolution from Abroad: The Soviet Conquest of Poland's Western Ukraine and Western Belorussia* (Princeton: Princeton University Press, 1988); Krystina Kersten, *The Establishment of Communist Rule in Poland, 1943–1948* (Berkeley: University of California Press, 1991).

[21]   See also Timothy Snyder, *Bloodlands: Europe between Hitler and Stalin* (New York: Basic Books, 2010).

[22]   *The Sovietization of the Baltic States; The Baltic Countries under Occupation: Soviet and Nazi Rule 1939–1991*, ed. Anu Mai Kõll (Stockholm: Department of History, 2003); *The Baltic States under Stalinist Rule*, ed. Olaf Mertelsmann (Cologne-Weimar: Böhlau, 2016).

corporation into the USSR as, in a sense, progressive. The republic was placed under strict central control, and the first party secretary was often an ethnic Russian. A Moldavian nation was constructed.

- North Bukovina, formerly part of Romania, was incorporated into the Ukrainian SSR.
- The territories gained from Finland after the Winter War were already evacuated.

- Territories newly acquired in 1945–46:
  - In the northern part of East Prussia, some of the German population fled, died of famine or was killed or deported; the remainder were expelled. The population transfer was nearly complete, and the region—now inhabited by Soviet settlers—was transformed into the Russian province of Kaliningrad.[23]
  - The population of the formerly Japanese Kuril Islands was deported or displaced.
  - The eastern part of Slovakia, Carpathian Ruthenia, was incorporated into the Ukrainian SSR, but large population transfers did not take place. Carpathian Ruthenia was a remote mountainous region and had been the least developed part of Czechoslovakia.

- The people's democracies of Central and Eastern Europe and the Soviet zones of occupation: in those countries and regions, the start of the Cold War and the division of Europe was an important turning point, as was the increasing political pressure.
  - In the countries supposedly 'liberated' but, in fact, controlled by the Red Army, the first governments to be established were usually people's fronts. Several political parties existed and some free elections were even held. Restructuring, such as land reform or nationalisation of private property, began slowly. By the end of the 1940s, socialist parties were in power. In some places, other parties were forbidden; in other countries they were tolerated but controlled. Developments were different from country to country and were guided by local politicians who were dependent on Moscow and Soviet advisors. What initially seemed to be a

---

23   *Als Russe in Ostpreußen: Sowjetische Umsiedler über ihren Neubeginn in Königsberg/Kaliningrad nach 1945*, ed. Eckhard Matthes (Ostfildern: Edition Tertium, 1999); Ruth Kibelka, *Ostpreußens Schicksalsjahre 1944–1948* (Berlin: Aufbau-Verlag, 2000).

'national path to socialism' turned into Sovietisation with increasing centralising tendencies due to the Cold War.[24] We might differentiate between Germany's former allies, such as Hungary or Romania, and German-occupied countries. In Poland, for example, the Catholic Church was able to preserve its influential position, collectivisation of agriculture remained incomplete, and censorship was less strict. In all cases Sovietisation involved the use of violence, including party purges. Violence was later used later, as in 1956 and 1968, when a country threatened to leave the Soviet bloc.

– In Yugoslavia and Albania, communist partisan leaders established their own socialist dictatorship, which was initially supported by the USSR. These regimes were inspired by the USSR and were initially fairly Stalinist. In the long run they broke with the Soviet Union and followed their own path to socialism, Yugoslavia in 1948 and Albania in 1961.

– In the Soviet occupation zone in Germany, a satellite state—the German Democratic Republic—was established in 1949, deepening the partition of the country.[25]

– The Soviet occupation zone in Austria experienced some cautious measures of Sovietisation but was not turned into a socialist state. Given Austria's geographic location, the USSR preferred a neutral and unified state. The Austrian State Treaty of 1955 defined the status of Austria, and thereafter, the occupation ended.[26]

---

[24] T. V. Volokitina, 'Stalin i smena strategicheskogo kursa Kremlia v kontse 1940-kh godov', – *Stalinskoe desiatiletie kholodnoe voiny: fakty i gipotezy* (Moscow: Nauka, 1999), 10–22.

[25] On the Soviet policy towards East Germany, see, for example, Wilfried Loth, *Stalins ungeliebtes Kind: Warum Moskau die DDR nicht wollte* (Berlin: Rowohlt, 1994); Gerhard Wettig, *Bereitschaft zu Einheit in Freiheit? Die sowjetische Deutschland-Politik 1945–1955* (Munich: Olzog, 1999); *Stalins großer Bluff: Die Geschichte der Stalin-Note in Dokumenten der sowjetischen Führung*, ed. Peter Ruggenthaler (Munich: Oldenbourg, 2007).

[26] See *Die Rote Armee in Österreich: Sowjetische Besatzung 1945–1955: Beiträge*, eds. Stefan Karner and Barbara Stelz-Marx (Graz-Vienna-Munich: Verein zur Förderung der Forschung von Folgen nach Konflikten und Kriegen, 2005).

- Other communist or socialist states and the Third World:
  The Soviet Union supported revolutionary movements and the establishment of socialist dictatorships all around the world. Nevertheless, the Chinese, North Korean, Cuban, Angolan or Vietnamese path to socialism, not to mention that of Cambodia's Khmer Rouge, was in many ways different from the Soviet model. In this context it seems difficult to speak of full-scale Sovietisation, even when there were a few similarities with the USSR.

  For a time, the Soviet Union served as a model for a number of former colonies, such as India or Egypt, in their first years of independence. Soviet advisors were invited in, and some elements of the Soviet model were adapted to local conditions. In particular, the command economy seemed an attractive way to overcome economic backwardness. This perception proved wrong. In those countries we might speak of a certain influence of the Soviet model. Afghanistan was a special case because of the Soviet occupation.

The list of states and regions that can be considered Sovietised, or thoroughly influenced by the Soviet model, is long and diverse. Certain components such as one-party rule, purges or a nationalised economy were similar, while developments often turned out differently. Another factor seems important: there was no detailed master plan to follow. Instead, considerable improvisation occurred, and as a result, local solutions influenced by cultural traditions were found. This was particularly true of states that remained sovereign and were not annexed to the USSR. A couple of states even managed to leave the Soviet camp and to declare that they were taking their own path to socialism. The first, violent phase of Sovietisation under military protection was usually followed by a second, less violent phase. As part of the Soviet Union, the affected states were in a permanent metamorphosis; the regime accommodated to changing conditions but stood firm on certain basic issues. Whenever the very foundations of the Sovietised state were touched, the regime would break apart, as in 1989 and 1991 in Central and Eastern Europe.

Attempt to Define Sovietisation

In the introduction to a volume on the early history of the German Democratic Republic, Michael Lemke defines Sovietisation thus: 'The term Sovietisation [...] stands for structural, institutional, spiritual-cultural processes of transfer and adoption of the Soviet model with the aim of adjustment of non-Soviet societies to the social and political conditions in the USSR.'[27] Gerhard Simon writes that Sovietisation included instruments of annexation and integration of newly acquired territories used by the Soviets.[28] In his case study on the Sovietisation of East German, Czech and Polish universities, John Connelly concludes that essential ideas of transfer of the Soviet model were developed on the spot.[29]

In the author's opinion, the term 'Sovietisation' refers to a complex network of processes of adoption, transfer and imposition of elements of the Soviet model of power and social structure. These processes included the institutional and structural change of society, economy and state, and the restructuring of culture and education and of everyday life. Aside from enforcement measures and direct pressure, incentives were used to integrate part of society into the new project. The precise course of those processes of transfer and adoption was dictated by the local political, economic and cultural conditions, the policies of those in power, the attitude of advisors and direct interventions by the center. While institutional restructuring took only a couple of years, the restructuring of society and culture took much more time. The population had to be 're-educated'. The long-term goal was an adjustment to conditions in the Soviet Union. A violent phase was followed by a second phase fortifying the already reached and continuing changes.

The author thinks that 'Sovietisation' is the term best suited to describe socio-political restructuring in those territories directly incorporated into the USSR. Nevertheless, the Soviet model was not static and changed in

---

[27]   Michael Lemke, 'Einleitung', *Sowjetisierung und Eigenständigkeit*, 11–30, here 13–14.

[28]   Gerhard Simon, 'Instrumente der Sowjetisierung in den annektierten westlichen Gebieten der Sowjetunion', *Sowjetisches Modell*, 13–20, here 13.

[29]   Connelly, *Captive University*, 21.

the framework of its possibilities. In research the term 'Stalinisation' is sometimes used to characterise the first, violent phase of Sovietisation.[30]

Sometimes the Americanisation of Western Europe and the Sovietisation of Eastern Europe is dealt with in a rather similar way.[31] But Americanisation happened mostly voluntarily and not under the pressure of a dictatorship. In addition, Americanisation is often seen as a cultural or economic phenomenon, and many issues mentioned in this context are actually the results of globalisation, modernisation or democratisation.

Some people see Sovietisation as equivalent to Russification.[32] Particularly in the territories incorporated into the USSR, a certain degree of Russification was one aspect of Sovietisation, stressing Russian language and Russian culture. Nevertheless, this tendency toward Russification was restricted by another element of Sovietisation, the Soviet nationalities policy or *korenizatsiia* (taking root). To take root, the Soviet system needed the help of national cadres, languages and cultures.

Sketching a 'Typical' Sovietisation

The first step of Sovietisation is securing political and military control. In a country occupied by the Soviet army, the army possesses a near-monopoly of force. Other armed units such as the local military, police or border guards have to be brought under control and often have to hand over their weapons. Because of this, communists or their puppets take over the Ministry of the Interior and the Ministry of Defence. It makes sense to act under the cover of legitimacy; sham parliaments or puppet governments are helpful. For the new authorities to secure power, they must arrest or eliminate potential rivals and parts of the country's former elite.[33] The new regime's next aim is to control justice.

---

[30] Andreas Malycha, *Die SED: Geschichte ihrer Stalinisierung 1946–1953* (Paderborn: Schöningh, 2000); Hua-Yu Li, *Mao and the Economic Stalinization of China, 1948–1953* (Lanham: Rowman & Littlefield, 2006).

[31] *Amerikanisierung und Sowjetisierung.*

[32] The author composed a questionnaire for the Estonian National Museum in which he asked among many other things for a definition of Sovietisation. Many people replied that this simply meant Russification.

[33] According to Zhdanov's outlines from 1939, the Sovietisation of a territory was to be led by three Soviet plenipotentiaries: one responsible for politics, one

To maintain the façade and prevent resistance from going public, censorship and propaganda soon begins. This allows the regime to take over the media, control published expressions of opinion and influence the population. Propaganda provides the backdrop for restructuring. The reconstruction of the existing state apparatus is the next step; key positions are assigned to trustworthy personnel while, in less important fields, the old civil servants remain in office.

Education and culture require control and long-term restructuring and must be forced to take the official line. This happens in stages and might include consideration of local circumstances. It helps to use a compromise tactic acknowledging the population's national feelings or to present the new regime as the best guardian of national values, as was done in Poland or Hungary.[34] In the economic sphere the new regime first seizes control and then begins nationalisation. In the beginning, industry and large enterprises are the main target of change; later small enterprises and agriculture are also targeted. The formal establishment of a planned economy rounds out the takeover of the economy.[35]

Because the social order in the affected country is different from that in the Soviet Union, social engineering and the 'cleansing' of society from real or potential 'social alien' or 'enemy elements' are necessary.[36] In the event of resistance or uprisings, those measures might be repeated. One problem is that 'cleansing' and terror often lead to resistance or increase opposition. A spiral of violence might result.

This is the repressive side of Sovietisation, but if a society puts up active and passive resistance, power cannot be established sustainably or be

for the military and one for security (or cleansing). Privetelli, 'Irredentism, Expansion and the Liberation', 319–320.

[34]   On the context of communism and nationalism, see David Brandenberger, *National Bolshevism: Stalinist Mass Culture and the Formation of Modern Russian National Identy, 1931–1956* (Cambridge, MA: Harvard University Press, 2002); Martin Mevius, *Agents of Moscow: The Hungarian Communist Party and the Origins of Socialist Patriotism* (Oxford: Oxford University Press, 2005).

[35]   André Steiner, *Von Plan zu Plan: Eine Wirtschaftsgeschichte der DDR* (Munich: Deutsche Verlagsanstalt, 2004).

[36]   Gerd Koenen, *Utopie der Säuberung: Was war der Kommunismus?* (Berlin: Fest, 1998); Peter Holquist, 'State Violence as Technique: The Logic of Violence in Soviet Totalitarianism', – *Stalinism: The Essential Readings*, ed. David L. Hoffmann (Oxford: Blackwell Publishing, 2003), 133–156.

consolidated without the use of large-scale violence. Thus the regime must reach out to certain strata of society. The destructive aspects of Stalinism are well-known, but Stalinism was also able to integrate. How can parts of society be encouraged to participate or collaborate?

Ideology might be one factor: local communists or socialists might work for the regime out of conviction, while others have to be persuaded. Younger people might be recruited through youth organisations like Komsomol. Still, this author thinks that ideology played only a minor role. More important seems to be the prospect of upward social mobility and privilege. Because the socialist economy is an economy of shortages and the regime distributes the scarce resources, the communists can win some support by distributing material benefits, such as through land reform. The regime can ask for loyalty in exchange for education and career opportunities. Sometimes, those with stains on their record cleave to the new regime in order to stay employed. In a shortage economy, when the state is the most important source of goods, nearly everyone depends to some extent on the state's benevolence. Sovietisation included carrots and sticks.

In the long run, the population might accommodate to Sovietisation after a phase of resistance, especially when there are temporary hopes for political change. People attempt to arrange their lives within the new socio-political framework. Propaganda, education, cultural policy and the realities of life lead to partial acceptance of the values of the regime. The passing of time inevitably leads to greater acceptance. Even when the new order is rejected and there are alternative sources of information such as foreign radio broadcasting and an idealised memory of the pre-Soviet period, the Sovietisation process continues.

This outline focuses on developments in Central and Eastern Europe, but it should be made clear that there were huge differences within the region. Local conditions differed, regional peculiarities were acknowledged in some way, and the new elites possessed some room for manoeuver. Nevertheless, the centre, Moscow, always had the possibility to interfere and to replace the local power elite, as happened in the late 1940s (to a limited extent) in Central Europe, in 1950 in the Estonian SSR and in 1959 in the Latvian SSR.

The 'typical' chain of events of Sovietisation presented here is, of course, simplified and ignores a couple of problems accompanying the complex process. For this reason, the author presents some hypotheses concerning Sovietisation.

Hypotheses on Sovietisation[37]

- Sovietisation was characterised not by a complete break with the past overnight but by continuous change and a certain degree of continuity. There was personal continuity as the integration of a small part of the former elite and the cultural framework persisted.

- While external restructuring and institutional change happened comparatively quickly, internal restructuring and social change occurred much more slowly. Because most of the affected societies later freed themselves of socialism, Sovietisation was never completed, not even in Russia.

- Sovietisation in the initial phase went hand in hand with mass violence: arrests, deportations, executions, and cleansing of society. The new regime deemed those measures necessary to intensify the grip on society and to reconstruct it thoroughly through cleansing.[38] Nevertheless, the regime was also able to offer a certain compromise policy towards certain groups.[39]

- The socialist system lacked legitimacy because it was obviously introduced from the outside; initially there was a lack of local cadres; for a long time, the economic situation was worse than in pre-socialist times, and in the beginning Sovietisation was accompanied by fierce oppression and terror.

---

[37]   Most of those hypotheses are from my earlier project, supported by the German Research Foundation in 2004–2006: 'The Sovietization of Estonian Society'. Some of these hypotheses I have already presented in individual articles mentioned here.

[38]   Olaf Mertelsmann and Aigi Rahi-Tamm, 'Soviet Mass Violence in Estonia Revisited', *Journal of Genocide Research*, no. 11 (2009): 307–322; Olaf Mertelsmann, Aigi Rahi Tamm, 'Estland während des Stalinismus 1940–1953: Gewalt und Säuberungen im Namen der Umgestaltung einer Gesellschaft', *Jahrbuch für Historische Kommunismusforschung* (2012), 99–112.

[39]   Olaf Mertelsmann and Aigi Rahi-Tamm, 'Cleansing and Compromise: The Estonian SSR in 1944–1945', *Cahiers du monde russe*, no. 49 (2008): 319–340.

- The population might initially take a wait-and-see approach. Later the prevailing attitude might be passive resistance or silent non-consent, or in individual cases even active resistance. Only when hopes for regime change or liberation from the outside were finally quelled did the majority come to terms with the socialist system. In Central and Eastern Europe this occurred in the late 1950s after the unsuccessful uprisings in the GDR, Poland and Hungary.

- In contrast with the difficult socialist reality, there was often an idealised picture of the pre-socialist period, which only slowly faded from collective memory. This image, as well as listening to foreign radio broadcasts, reading forbidden books, hearing rumours, and the existence of resistance and later of dissidents, led to questioning of the Soviet model.

- The gap between the level of development of the Sovietised countries and the 'old republics' of the USSR was sometimes huge. For example, Estonia and Latvia remained for decades the most developed union republics of the USSR. In addition, cultural differences necessitated different strategies of adaptation.

- Social change and the implementation of a new set of values also led to unintended consequences. For instance, austerity and mismanagement in the command economy led to the decline of work discipline and the increase of corruption, *blat'* (mutual favours) and petty theft.[40] Discontent with the new conditions led to an increase in alcohol consumption[41] and other socially destructive patterns of behaviour, which represented an erosion of moral values.

---

[40] Olaf Mertelsmann, 'Mehrdimensionale Arbeitswelten als Überlebensstrategie während der stalinistischen Industrialisierung am Beispiel Estlands', – *Mehrdimensionale Arbeitswelten im baltischen Raum*, eds. Burghart Schmidt and Jürgen Hogeforster (Hamburg: DOBU Verlag, 2007), 94–106; 'Living on a Stalinist Kolkhoz: Peasant Survival Strategies in Estonia', *Humanitāro Zinātņu Vēstnesis*, no. 15 (2009): 83–94.

[41] Olaf Mertelsmann, 'Der Zusammenhang von Sowjetisierung und Alkoholmissbrauch aus der Sicht der estnischen Bevölkerung', – *Estland und Russland: Aspekte der Beziehungen beider Länder*, ed. Olaf Mertelsmann (Hamburg: Dr. Kovač, 2005), 275–288.

- One important method of stabilising the new order was the expansion of education starting in the 1950s, allowing for upward social mobility and the professionalisation of state institutions.[42]

- Even in 'extraordinary times' (Sheila Fitzpatrick) there was a 'normal' cultural life and traditional leisure activities with sport clubs, choirs or voluntary fire brigades, which were an element of continuity but could be instrumentalised by the regime. Despite all measures to level and homogenise the formerly non-Soviet societies, many structures and social networks remained intact.[43]

- In the newly acquired territories of the USSR, the process of Sovietisation was accompanied by large-scale immigration, raising the national question. One unintended consequence might have been the construction of a new 'image of a national enemy', the Russians or the Soviets.[44]

- Secularisation, expansion of education, urbanisation and a rise in industrial employment accompanied Sovietisation. Thus many processes of change were influenced by 'socialist modernisation'.

- Ideology offered those in power a worldview and a framework for decision-making. Still, many decisions were pragmatic and designed to fulfill short-term aims.

- The affected societies were indeed Sovietised but were able to retain their own character. The term 'unfinished penetration of society' seems appropriate.

- The new, Sovietised national elites identified themselves increasingly with the particular interest of their state or Soviet republic, which

---

[42]   Olaf Mertelsmann, 'Die Ausweitung von Kultur und Bildung als Stütze des sowjetischen Systems in Estland', *Vom Hitler-Stalin-Pakt bis zu Stalins Tod: Estland 1939–1953*, ed. Olaf Mertelsmann (Hamburg: Bibliotheca Baltica, 2005), 251–265.

[43]   Olaf Mertelsmann, 'The Private Sphere in Estonia during Stalinism', *Problemy istorii, filologii, kul'tury*, no. 18 (2007): 58–81.

[44]   Olaf Mertelsmann, 'How the Russians Turned into the Image of the "National Enemy" of the Estonians', *Pro Ethnologia*, no. 19 (2005): 43–58.

made it easier for them to opt for democracy or nationalism during the collapse of socialism.[45] This also explains, to a certain degree, the continuity of elites in the post-socialist states.

Conclusion

Sovietisation is a very complex development of different processes influencing one another. Accounting for this complexity and for regional differences of Sovietisation requires a differentiated analysis that relies on a variety of perspectives. Historical memory, economic problems and the use of violence were crucial factors curbing the acceptance of the Soviet model and of Sovietisation. We have to differentiate between intended consequences, such as the restructuring of the state, economy, culture and society, and the results, which might have been partly unintended. Because the Soviet model was based on a utopian ideology and could never have been realised,[46] one does not wonder about unintended consequences. Among historians the debate over the importance of ideology in the politics of socialist states has not yet ended. This author tends to think that pragmatism was more important than ideology.

The Sovietisation of one state should not be seen in isolation from developments in other Sovietised countries, and we should not ignore the international framework. For example, Elena Zubkova sees a clear relation between the outbreak of the Cold War and the course of Sovietisation in the Baltic republics.[47]

Finally, 'Sovietisation' seems to be the best way to conceive of the multifaceted processes of restructuring and remoulding in the countries under consideration. This author has not found a more suitable term.

---

[45]   Gerhard Simon, 'Entkolonialisierung in der Sowjetunion: Die neuen nationalen Eliten in den sowjetischen Unionsrepubliken seit den 1950er Jahren', – *Deutschland, Rußland und das Baltikum: Beiträge zu einer Geschichte wechselvoller Beziehungen: Festschrift zum 85. Geburtstag von Peter Krupnikov*, eds. Anton Florin and Leonid Luks, (Cologne: Böhlau, 2005), 277–289.

[46]   Martin Malia, *The Soviet Tragedy: A History of Socialism in Russia, 1917–1991* (New York: Free Press, 1994).

[47]   Elena Zubkova, 'Estland unter sowjetischer Herrschaft 1944–1953: Die Moskauer Perspektive', – *Vom Hitler-Stalin-Pakt bis zu Stalins Tod*, 266–81, here 268.

The Baltic Question in the Kremlin in the Last Months of 1944: How to Combat the Armed Resistance Movement?

Tõnu Tannberg[*]

Introduction

During the Second World War, the Baltic question was on the Kremlin's agenda from a military, diplomatic as well as domestic political point of view. The issue became urgent at the end of 1943 and the beginning of 1944 when the Red Army was approaching the borders of the Baltic countries and the military campaign for re-invading Estonia, Latvia and Lithuania was approaching. At the same time, the Great Powers were actively involved in organising the issues of the post-war world structure, including the fate of the Baltic countries.

The diplomatic aspect of the Baltic question became topical in 1940 when the three Baltic countries had been occupied by the Soviet Union and the questions of a possible response by the Western countries and of recognising the invasions perpetrated by Moscow became an issue. After war broke out between the Soviet Union and Germany in 1941, it became one of Moscow's main aims to make the Western countries recognise the Soviet Union's western border as it had been on 22 June 1941. Therefore,

---

[*] The current article is based mostly on earlier published materials that have been adapted and supplemented: Tõnu Tannberg, 'Wie bekämpft man die Waldbrüder? Die baltische Frage im Kreml Ende 1944', *Forschungen zur baltischen Geschichte*, no. 4 (2009): 190–209. See also in Estonian: Tõnu Tannberg, 'Balti küsimus Kremlis 1944. aasta lõpukuudel: kuidas võidelda relvastatud vastupanuliikumisega?', *Tuna: ajalookultuuri ajakiri*, no. 4 (2009): 50–66.

Moscow sought recognition of its invasions from 1939–1941, including the annexation of the Baltic states. The Western countries did not recognise the occupation of the Baltic countries *de jure* but they accepted it *de facto*.

The most complicated aspect for the Kremlin was definitely the domestic political dimension of the Baltic question, since after the invasion a systematic Sovietisation process had to be launched in order to secure the new regime and make it function long-term. This had to be preceded by a substantial system of control mechanisms, an ideological levelling of society, and a rapid suppression of any resistance to the new regime.

At the end of October and in November of 1944, the Kremlin's top brass discussed the Baltic question. The Organisational Bureau of the Central Committee of the All-Union Communist Party (Bolsheviks) adopted decisions on the 'errors and shortcomings' in the work of the Party organisations of the three Soviet Baltic republics, where besides the problems of restoring the economy, etc. the fight against 'bourgeois nationalism' was given priority.[1] Hence, gaining ideological control of the newly invaded territories was one of Moscow's main aims. The Kremlin had previously used the same scenario in Ukraine and Belarus.

The above-mentioned decisions were without any doubt extremely important in the political circumstances of all three Baltic countries in the coming years, and the Kremlin put together the basic documents for the Sovietisation of Estonia, Latvia and Lithuania. These documents were interpreted similarly by the then leaders of the Soviet Baltic republics.[2]

The contents and the circumstances of adopting these documents have been fairly thoroughly discussed in research. The studies of Elena

---

[1] See: Decision of the Organisational Bureau of the AUCP(B) CC 'On Shortcomings and Tasks of Political Work of the ESSR Party Organisation', 30 October 1944, RGASPI, f. 17, o. 117, d. 459, 1–4. A similar decision was adopted on the Lithuanian SSR on 1 November 1944 (see the text: RGASPI, f. 17, o. 117, d. 460, 8–11) and on the Latvian SSR on 3 November 1944 (RGASPI, f. 17, o. 117, d. 464, 16–18); Tynu Tannberg, *Politika Moskvy v respublikakh Baltii v poslevoennye gody (1944–1956), Issledovaniia i dokumenty* (Moscow: ROSSPEN, 2010), 196–215; Meelis Saueauk, *Propaganda ja terror: Nõukogude julgeolekuorganid ja Eestimaa Kommunistlik Partei Eesti sovetiseerimisel 1944–1953* [Propaganda and Terror: Soviet Security Organs and the Communist Party of Estonia in the Sovietisation of Estonia in 1944–1953], (Tallinn: SE&JS, 2015).

[2] Nikolai Karotamm began his 'letter of repentance' to Stalin in 1950 with the notion that the directions of 30 October 1944 still remained unfulfilled. See: N. Karotamm's letter to Stalin, 17 February 1950, RA, ERAF.1.46.6, 1.

Zubkova[3] and her monograph on Moscow's politics in the Soviet Baltic republics in 1944–1953[4] published in 2008 are worth pointing out. The author of the current article has written a lengthy study of Moscow's control mechanisms.[5] So far, historical research has paid much less attention to the Kremlin's suppression of resistance in the initial phase of Sovietisation in 1944 when the Red Army's invasion triggered large-scale armed resistance to the Soviet occupation in Western Ukraine and Western Belarus, as well as in the Baltics. The question of how to suppress the growing resistance became increasingly urgent for the Kremlin in the autumn of 1944.

Moscow officially named it anti-bandit combat. In Soviet terminology, a clear distinction was made between criminal banditry and 'bandit-insurgent activities' or 'political banditry', handled by Soviet authorities as an activity of a 'bourgeois-nationalist element'. As a result of this distinction, Estonia, Latvia, Lithuania, Western Ukraine, Western Belarus and the other Eastern European areas invaded by the Soviet Union in 1939–1940 formed a separate zone. The Soviet State Security divided the resistance movement into two separate levels: The People's Commissariat for State Security (NKGB) was responsible for eradicating the higher level resistance or secret organisations, while the People's Commissariat for Internal Affairs (NKVD) was responsible for destroying the armed groups of resistance. To complete this task, departments for anti-bandit combat

---

[3]   See e.g.: Elena Zubkova, 'Moskva i Baltiia: mehanizmy sovetizatsii Latvii, Litvy i Estonii v 1944–1953 godakh', – *Trudy Instituta rossiiskoi istorii. Vypusk IV* (Moscow, 2004), 266–283; Elena Zubkova, 'Fenomen "mestnogo natsionalizma": "Estonskoe delo" 1949–1952 godov v kontekste sovetizatsii Baltii', *Otechestvennaia istoriia*, no. 3 (2001): 89–102; Jelena Subkowa, 'Kaderpolitik und Säuberungen in der KPdSU (1945–1953)', – *Terror. Stalinistische Parteisäuberungen 1936–1953*, ed. Hermann Weber and Ullrich Mählert (Paderborn: Schöningh, 1998), 187–236; Elena Zubkova, 'Estland unter sowjetischer Herrschaft 1944–1953', – *Vom Hitler-Stalin-Pakt bis zu Stalins Tod. Estland 1939–1953*, ed. Olaf Mertelsmann (Hamburg: Bibliotheca Baltica, 2005), 266–281.

[4]   Elena Zubkova, *Pribaltika i Kreml, 1940–1953*, (Moscow: ROSSPEN, 2008).

[5]   Tõnu Tannberg, 'Moscow's Institutional and Nomenklatura-based Control Mechanisms in the Estonian SSR during the Post-War Years', *Tuna. Special Issue on the History of Estonia* (Tartu: Rahvusarhiiv, 2009): 197–229; Tannberg, *Politika Moskvy*, 13–61.

(OBB) with internal troops and destruction battalions at their disposal were formed under the NKVD.[6]

The aim of this article is to analyse Moscow's activities in the suppression of armed resistance in Estonia, Latvia and Lithuania in the last months of 1944, including the institutional framework and methods for suppressing resistance, the results of the suppression of armed resistance, and to what extent the principles of suppressing resistance set in 1944 functioned in the following years.

In seeking answers to the above-mentioned questions, previously conducted research on armed resistance in the post-war Baltics is available.[7]

---

[6]   Dzheffri Burds, 'Bor'ba s banditizmom v SSSR v 1944–1953 gg.', – Sotsial'naia istoriia. Ezhegodnik (Moscow: ROSSPEN, 2000), 169–190.

[7]   References to some more recent studies: *The Anti-Soviet Resistance in the Baltic states*, ed. Arvydas Anušauskas (Vilnius: Du Ka, 1999); Valdur Ohmann, 'Eesti NSV Siseministeeriumi institutsionaalne areng ja arhivaalid (1940–1954)' [The Institutional Development of the ESSR Ministry of Internal Affairs and Archival Documents (1940–1954)], (MA Thesis, supervised by Tõnu Tannberg, University of Tartu, 2000); Pearu Kuusk, *Nõukogude võimu lahingud Eesti vastupanuliikumisega: Banditismivastase Võitluse Osakond aastatel 1944–1947* [The Soviet Regime's Struggle against the Estonian Resistance Movement. The Department of Anti-Bandit Combat in 1944–1947] (Tartu, Tartu Ülikooli Kirjastus, 2007); Pearu Kuusk, 'Julgeolekuorganite võitlus Eesti vastupanuliikumisega sõjajärgsetel aastatel: Banditismivastase Võitluse Osakond (1944–1947)' [The State Security Organs' Struggle against the Estonian Resistance Movement in the Post-War Years: the Department of Anti-Bandit Combat (1944–1947)], – *Eesti NSV aastatel 1940–1953: sovetiseerimise mehhanismid ja tagajärjed Nõukogude Liidu ja IdaEuroopa arengute kontekstis* [The Estonian SSR in 1940–1953. Mechanisms and Consequenses of Sovietisation in the Context of Developments in the Soviet Union and Eastern Europe], ed. Tõnu Tannberg (Tartu: Eesti Ajalooarhiiv, 2007), 225–272; Meelis Saueauk, 'Riikliku julgeoleku rahvakomissariaat (NKGB) Eestis 1944–1946' [The People's Commissariat for State Security (NKGB) in Estonia 1944–1946], *Tuna*, no. 3 (2008): 33–57; Elena Zubkova, 'Lesnye brat'ia v Pribaltike: voina posle voiny', *Otechestvennaia istoriia*, no. 2 (2007): 74–90; no. 3, 14–30; Aleksandr Kokurin, 'Organy NKVD-NKGB SSSR po bor'be s vooruzhennym natsionalisticheskim podpol'em (Zapadnaia Ukraina i Belorussiia, Latviia, Litva i Estoniia) (1939–1953)', – *Trudy obshchestva izucheniia istorii otechestvennykh spetssluzhb*, 3 (Moscow: Kutchkovo pole, 2007), 254–276; Tillmann Tegeler, *Der litauische Partisanenkampf im Lichte sowjetischer Akten* (München: Osteuropa-Institut München, 2001); Björn M. Felder. '"Tod dem Roten Terror!" Antikommunismus, gesellschaftilicher Konsens und Widerstand in Lettland 1943 bis 1946', – *Jahrbuch für Historische Kommunismusforschung 2007* (Berlin: Aufbau Verlag, 2007), 137–159.

So far, no thorough research has been conducted on the events of the last months of 1944 from Moscow's point of view.[8] This article will attempt to fill this gap on the basis of materials from the Estonian National Archives and the source publications recently published in Russia.[9]

Implementation of Anti-Bandit Combat

The development of the organisational structure of anti-bandit combat began in the early spring of 1941. In February of 1941, the security forces were separated from the USSR People's Commissariat for Internal Affairs and a separate People's Commissariat for State Security was formed. Later, in April of 1941, a separate Department of Anti-Bandit Combat (OBB) under the NKVD Main Directorate for the Militia was formed in order to step up the struggle against 'all types of political and criminal banditry' in the territory of the Soviet Union. After war broke out between the Soviet Union and Germany in the summer of 1941, an emergency reorganisation of security forces was conducted: the People's Commissariat for Internal Affairs and the People's Commissariat for State Security were merged into the USSR People's Commissariat for Internal Affairs.[10] The OBB initially remained under the jurisdiction of the Main Directorate for the Militia, but the decree issued by the USSR People's Commissar for Internal Affairs

---

[8]   See: Mikhail Krysin and Mikhail Litvinov, *Organy gosbezopasnosti protiv natsionalistov Pribaltiki* (Moscow: Veche, 2017); Iuliia Kantor, 'Resovetizatsiia Pribaltiki', – *Velikaia Otechestvennaia voina. 1944 god: Issledovaniia, dokumenty, kommentarii*, ed. V. S. Hristoforov (Moscow: GBU 'CGA Moskvy', 2014), 399–416; Iuliia Kantor, *Pribaltika: voina bez pravil (1939–1945)* (SPb: Zvezda, 2011).

[9]   See: *Lubianka: Stalin i NKVD-NKGB-GUKR 'Smersh': 1939–mart 1946: dokumenty*, comp. V. N. Haustov, V. P. Naumov and N. S. Plotnikova (Moscow: Materik, 2006); *Organy gosudarstvennoi bezopasnosti SSSR v Velikoi Otechestvennoi voine, T. V, Kn. 2: Granitsy SSSR vosstanovleny (1 iiulia–31 dekabria 1944 g.)*, comp. V. P. Iampol'skii (Moscow: Obshchestvo izucheniia istorii otechestvennykh spetssluzhb, Kuchkovo pole, 2007); *NKVD-MVD SSSR v bor'be s banditizmom i vooruzhennym natsionalisticheskim podpol'em na Zapadnoi Ukraine, v Zapadnoi Belorussii i Pribaltike (1939–1956): sbornik dokumentov*, comp. N. I. Vladimirtsev and A. I. Kokurin (Moscow: Ob"edinennaia redaktsiia MVD Rossii, 2008).

[10]   AUCP(B) CC Politburo decision on uniting the commissariats for internal affairs and state security, 21 July 1941 – *Lubianka: Stalin i NKVD*, 298–299.

on 30 September 1941 established an independent Department of Anti-Bandit Combat as an operative agency under the jurisdiction of the People's Commissariat in order to liquidate and pursue all 'bandit formations', to destroy 'single bandits' and catch their helpers throughout the entire territory of the Soviet Union. Another major task of the OBB was confiscating weapons from the population in co-operation with the militia. Sergei Klepov,[11] a State Security Major, was appointed head of the USSR NKVD OBB. He was succeeded by Aleksandr Leontyev. Corresponding branches of the USSR NKVD OBB had to be formed in all Soviet republics and oblasts. By the time the above-mentioned decree was published, the Germans had occupied the Baltic countries and it was no longer possible to set up these departments in 1941.

The breakout of extensive armed resistance after the Soviet invasion of the western parts of Ukraine, Belarus and the Baltic states resulted in the reorganisation of the NKVD Department of Anti-Bandit Combat within the Main Directorate on 1 December 1944. Leontyev continued as head of the Main Directorate with seven departments under his command, with some separate departments and the Secretariat of the Main Directorate. The functions of the departments were distributed according to geographical location. The Baltics were allocated to 2nd Department (headed by State Security Lieutenant Colonel Veniamin Karlin and staffed by 21 people) with a view to co-ordinating the struggle against anti-Soviet underground organisations and armed resistance in Belarus and in the three Baltic states. The department level tasks were allocated so that the underground organisations in Belarus were the responsibility of the 1st Department, the underground organisations in the Baltic countries were the responsibility of the 2nd Department, and the 3rd Department was responsible for suppressing resistance in Belarus as well as in Estonia, Latvia and Lithuania. In addition, the 6th Department co-ordinated the operations of the destruction battalions.[12]

The ESSR NKVD OBB became active in March of 1944 in Leningrad. Its first task was to 'process' the estonians in the Soviet rear and to try to recruit agents in the Estonian border areas, in the district of Kingissepp. The department possessed information on Estonian forest brothers and

---

[11] USSR People's Commissar for Internal Affairs Beria's decree no. 001414, 30 September 1941 – *NKVD-MVD SSSR v bor'be*, 474.

[12] *NKVD-MVD SSSR v bor'be*, 431.

by the beginning of July, 1944, at least two agents under the code names Kotkas and Mets had been sent to infiltrate the German rear area.[13] In January of 1944, Konstantin Kolk, a State Security Captain, was appointed head of the ESSR NKVD OBB but in August he was replaced by Vladimir Glushanin, a State Security Lieutenant Colonel.[14] In July of 1944, Lieutenant Colonel Nikolai Slepnev became head of the Lithuanian SSR NKVD OBB. He was later replaced by State Security Lieutenant Colonel (later Colonel) Aleksandr Gussev. In March of 1944, State Security Major Karl Bedik became head of the Latvian SSR NKVD OBB and he continued in this position until he was wounded at the end of April (he died later from his injuries).[15] The following table presents the sizes of the personnel of the OBBs of the three Soviet Baltic republics in October of 1944.

Table 1. NKVD OBB personnel in the Soviet Baltic republics as of 13 October 1944.

Soviet republic	Size of personnel		Total
	In central apparatus	In the periphery	
Estonian SSR	31	46	77
Latvian SSR	23	63	86
Lithuanian SSR	20	75	95
Total	74	184	258

Table compiled by: *NKVD-MVD SSSR v bor'be*, 436, 444.

According to the table, the OBB departments in the Soviet republics were small-size structural units that were definitely unable to successfully suppress growing resistance in the late autumn and winter of 1944. In the

---

[13]   USSR NKVD BVVO 6th Department Head Golovlev's Report, 6 July 1944 – *NKVD-MVD SSSR v bor'be*, 164. The structure of the ESSR NKVD OBB has been thoroughly studied by Pearu Kuusk in his research: Kuusk, *Nõukogude võimu lahingud*, 28–42; Kuusk, 'Julgeolekuorganite võitlus', 322–325.

[14]   Kuusk, *Nõukogude võimu lahingud*, 28, 31. Glushanin remained in this position until October of 1946.

[15]   *NKVD-MVD SSSR v bor'be*, 436, 444.

Soviet Baltic republics, the anti-bandit combat structural units retained their status as departments, whereas in Ukraine and Belarus, where the resistance movement was much more extensive, the local OBB departments were reorganised into main directorates, leading to significant increases in personnel.[16]

Joint Operations of Internal Troops and State Security

Moscow had realised by the early autumn of 1944 that the people's commissariats of the Soviet republics could not manage the suppression of the resistance movement on their own. Hence the importance of co-operation with the people's commissariats for state security was emphasised in every possible way. In October of 1944, Vsevolod Merkulov, the USSR People's Commissar for State Security sent detailed guidelines to the State Security organs of the Lithuanian SSR, stating unambiguously that regardless of the general principle of the NKVD being responsible for 'anti-bandit combat', the NKGB should not be excluded. According to Merkulov, State Security organs were obliged to provide any possible assistance to the NKVD to 'secure the elimination of gang formations via certain operative-agency measures'. Merkulov's motivation of 'gangs formed by Germans' in Lithuania being 'anti-Soviet in their essence' is quite remarkable.[17] Handling anti-Soviet organisations was the task of State Security. Without any doubt, similar guidelines were forwarded to the Estonian SSR NKVD and the Latvian SSR NKVD.

The first output of this forced co-operation was the joint operations of the People's Commissariat for State Security and the People's Commissariat for Internal Affairs, initiated by Moscow in October of 1944, based on the decrees issued jointly by the People's Commissariat for State Security and the People's Commissariat for Internal Affairs. The first decree of this kind was adopted for co-ordinating operations in Ukraine, followed

---

[16]   See: *NKVD-MVD SSSR v bor'be*, 431, 435–437.

[17]   USSR People's Commissar for State Security Merkulov's guidelines to the Lithuanian SSR NKGB, 4 October 1944 – *Organy gosudarstvennoi*, 399–400.

by similar decrees on 12 October 1944 concerning the Belarussian SSR and the Lithuanian SSR.[18]

In general, the measures for suppressing the resistance movement, initiated and designed by Moscow, can be divided into organisational and operative-tactical measures.

The organisational measures that were to secure the successful implementation of anti-resistance measures can be demonstrated via the example of the Lithuanian SSR. Overall responsibility was delegated to the People's Commissar for Internal Affairs Juozas Bartašiūnas. The People's Commissar for State Security Aleksandras Guzevičius was appointed his deputy, and the commander of the 4th Division of NKVD internal troops, Major General Pavel Vetrov, was appointed his second deputy. The above persons were authorised to immediately redeploy units of internal troops in the Soviet republic.[19] In the regions 'more severely infected by banditry', three to five-member OBB detachments had to be formed by the NKVD, and the permanent staff of the Lithuanian SSR NKVD OBB had to be increased by 15. In order to reinforce the personnel of the bodies of NKVD and NKGB, 35 experienced operatives from Moscow and other areas were deployed on a mission to Lithuania for three months. The border guard units located in the Lithuanian SSR were given orders to clear the border zones of 'anti-Soviet and bandit-espionage elements'. Operative-pursuit based on anti-diversion activities on railways needed to be stepped up: the head of the 14th Division of NKVD railway troops guarding the railway was provided with an armoured train and a training armoured train with a 100-member manoeuvre unit at his disposal, in addition to 150 cadets from the NKVD signal troops school of sergeants, and two operative-pursuit units from the 3rd Directorate of the USSR NKGB were deployed as additional resources. To increase the manoeuvring capability of the NKVD internal troops deployed in the Lithuanian SSR, 30 lorries, 24 'Belka'-type radio transmitters with specially trained operators were sent to Lithuania, and two 'Willis'-type off-road vehicles were placed at the disposal of the overall leader of the operation. In order to improve

[18]   USSR People's Commissar for Internal Affairs Beria's and People's Commissar for State Security Merkulov's joint decree on stepping up anti-resistance combat in the Lithuanian SSR, 12 October 1944 – *Organy gosudarstvennoi*, 454–457.

[19]   The 4th Rifle Division of the NKVD internal troops has been deployed to the Lithuanian SSR from the Northern Caucasus, the 5th Rifle Division was moved from Latvia, and the 63rd Rifle Division was located in Estonia.

the efficiency of the interrogation of the arrested persons, the standard personnel of the investigation department of the Lithuanian SSR NKVD was increased by seven. Information of operative interest obtained during interrogations had to be instantly forwarded to the relevant officers in order to take action. Party authorities had to be kept constantly informed as well.

Operative-tactical measures included detailed guidelines for acting against the resistance movement. It was necessary to find and eliminate the armouries, ammunition, food storages, duplicators, etc. that were at the disposal of the resistance. It was crucial to provide timely protection for anti-resistance military-Chekist operations: with the help of ambushes and similar methods to cut off possible escape routes for forest brothers in order to secure the total destruction of the enemy. The plans for eliminating armed 'gangs' had to be carefully planned and systematically and gradually implemented, meaning primarily the securing of the non-entrance of any new forest brother units after the elimination of one unit troop or the 'cleaning' of the area. For that reason, small battle-capable garrisons had to be formed or ambushes set in settlements and on the expected routes of forest brothers. In the elimination of underground organisations and armed units, the local population needed to be involved, possibly on a large scale, forming groups of 'honest Soviet citizens' as auxiliary units – primarily family members of Red Army soldiers, local Soviet representatives and Party activists, and people who had suffered from the activities of forest brothers.

The joint operations of the internal forces and state security agencies that had commenced in October of 1944 in the western regions of Ukraine and Belarus and in the Lithuanian SSR expanded to the territories of Latvia and Estonia in 1945. Nikolai Slepnev, the ex-chief of the Lithuanian SSR NKVD OBB, arrived in Estonia at the beginning of 1945 with a mission to implement the new measures.

The Role of Moscow State Security Emissaries in Implementing the Purge in the Baltics

Regarding the joint operations that began in the autumn of 1944, a few significant aspects should be pointed out once again. First, they were so-called unified measures that were applied in a more or less similar manner in the western regions of Ukraine and Belarus as well as in the Baltics. No local or regional variations were really taken into consideration. Secondly, the recruited executors of the joint operations were mostly Chekists commissioned from Moscow, Leningrad and other interior regions of the Soviet Union. Chekists with some earlier anti-resistance experience were exceptionally highly valued.[20] The even more remarkable fact that at the end of 1944, the chiefs of the USSR NKVD and NKGB visited Estonia, Latvia and Lithuania in person should not be neglected; the aim of their visits was to co-ordinate the anti-resistance struggle and to be in charge of the execution of the 'purge'.

Under the supervision of Merkulov, the USSR People's Commissar for State Security, an operative group from Moscow operated in Tallinn in November and December of 1944. Both the ESSR NKGB and NKVD were subordinated to that group. On 22 September 1944, the Red Army invaded Tallinn and as early as 5 October, all housing had been inspected in accordance with plans that had been drawn up in advance.[21] The operation conducted by Colonel Denissov, the commandant of Tallinn, involved 1,486 people. During the operation, 401 people were arrested and 205 of them were set free after being checked. The paperwork regarding the arrested persons was transferred to the SMERSH Department of the Leningrad Front. Major General Ivan Pankin, the commander of NKVD troops of the rear area of the Leningrad front, provided military manpower for that operation.[22]

A possible reason for Merkulov's visit, who arrived in Tallinn on either 5 or 6 November, was the 'exposure' of Otto Tief's government by the ESSR NKVD. Otto Tief's government had been formed just before the fall of Tallinn.[23] For executing the purges, the territory of the ESSR was divided into seven operative sectors (Tallinn, Rakvere, Pärnu, Vil-

---

[20] By October of 1944, over 3,800 Chekists from other regions of the USSR had been deployed in the western oblasts of Ukraine and Belarus and in Lithuania. When counting Latvia and Estonia, the total was much larger.

[21] See: Plan for checking the population of Tallinn, not dated, RA, ERAF.17SM.4.9, 239.

[22] Saueauk, 'Riikliku julgeoleku', 43.

[23] The formation of Otto Tief's government was an attempt to restore Estonia's independence after the withdrawal of German troops and before the Red Army's invasion.

jandi, Tartu, Haapsalu and Saaremaa) where groups consisting of a total of 70 operatives were deployed and managed by Chekists exclusively from Moscow or Leningrad. In order to secure county level NKVD personnel, another 50 operatives were summoned to the ESSR from Moscow and other regions.[24] The local NKVD and NKGB drew up the lists of people to be arrested. The plan for the whole operation had to be signed by Boris Kumm, the ESSR People's Commissar for State Security, Aleksander Resev, the People's Commissar for Internal Affairs, and Leonid Raikhmann as Moscow's representative, who at that time was the vice chief of the 2nd Main Directorate of the USSR People's Commissariat for State Security.

The implementation of the operation and the arrest of the people on the lists was the task of 'troikas' comprising a representative of the NKVD, a representative of the NKGB and a military officer from the 260th NKVD Regiment. A separate group was formed for drawing up orders of arrest. No prosecutor's sanctions were needed for arrests. Separate groups were also formed for receiving the arrested persons in prisons and for conducting investigation procedures. The so-called reception group's responsibilities included searching the arrested persons and placing them in cells, making sure that people who knew each other would not end up in the same cell. The reception group was always accompanied by an NKVD officer who was responsible for registering the items confiscated from the homes of the arrested persons and for making sure that they were transferred to investigators.[25]

During the purges of 6–14 November, the state security authorities arrested 1,116 people in Estonia, including 575 in Tallinn. Extensive efforts were made to catch the members of the Omakaitse (Home Guard)

---

[24] USSR People's Commissar for State Security Merkulov's report to the USSR State Committee of Defence on the organisation of operative-agency work in the ESSR, 14 November 1944 – *Organy gosudarstvennoi*, 588.

[25] Plan for capturing anti-Soviet and espionage elements in Tallinn, November 1944, RA, ERAF.17SM.4.9, 228–231. On the operation of 12 November 1944 in Tallinn, see: Saueauk, 'Riikliku julgeoleku', 43–44; Pearu Kuusk, 'Vabastajad või vallutajad? Siseasjade Rahvakomissariaadi Tartu Linnaosakonna tegevusest 1944. aastal' [Liberators or Invaders? On the Activities of the People's Commissariat for Internal Affairs Department of the City of Tartu in 1944], *Tuna*, no. 3 (2008): 25.

organisation.[26] The majority of the arrested people were men who had served in the German armed forces and men who had avoided Red Army conscription.[27] The cases of more important people, primarily the members of Otto Tief's government who had been arrested by the ESSR NKVD, were transferred by Merkulov's orders to the ESSR NKGB for investigation.[28]

Battles were still raging in the southern part of Saaremaa (Sõrve Peninsula was captured by the Red Army on 24 November 1944 – the last area of Estonia to be taken) when on 17 November 1944, State Security Lieutenant Colonel Pavel Pastelnyak arrived as a representative of Moscow, since he had been appointed chief of that operative sector. People in these positions had practically unlimited authority. Eight operative groups were formed for arresting people in Saaremaa, also involving the local militia. On 20 November, People's Commissar for State Security of the Soviet Union Merkulov made a personal appearance in Saaremaa. In official correspondence, the extremely important role of well-planned co-operation between the NKVD and the NKGB in anti-resistance combat was emphasised.[29]

High-ranking emissaries were also sent from Moscow to Latvia and Lithuania to suppress the armed resistance. In November of 1944, USSR Deputy People's Commissar for Internal Affairs Sergei Kruglov was dispatched to Lithuania accompanied by 'a group of workers of responsibility'.[30] Merkulov, the USSR People's Commissar for State Security, arrived in Latvia after his visit to Estonia. In January of 1945, Merkulov and his entourage were in Riga, engaged in implementing 'urgent organisational measures to strengthen the Chekist organs of Latvia

---

[26]   By then, State Security has arrested 421 members of the Home Guard (local auxiliary police force during the German occupation).

[27]   Kuusk, 'Vabastajad või vallutajad', 25.

[28]   See: ESSR NKVD report for the 4th quarter of 1944 to USSR People's Commissar for Internal Affairs Beria, January 1945, RA, ERAF.17SM.4.7, 84–98; Saueauk, 'Riikliku julgeoleku', 44.

[29]   Head of the ESSR NKVD Saaremaa Department to head of the ESSR NKVD OBB Glushanin, 1 December 1944, RA, ERAF.17SM.4.3, 31; Kuusk, 'Vabastajad või vallutajad', 24; Saueauk, 'Riikliku julgeoleku', 44.

[30]   Beria's report to Stalin and Molotov, 1 December 1944 – *NKVD-MVD SSSR v bor'be*, 211. At the same time, Bogdan Kobulov, the USSR Deputy People's Commissar for State Security, was appointed to Belarus.

for better organisation of operative-agency work'[31] – the model implemented in Estonia was launched in Latvia. The territory of the Latvian SSR that was under Soviet control (Courland remained under the control of German troops until Germany's defeat in May of 1945) was divided into six operational sectors ruled by 'qualified operatives'. The units of internal troops were distributed between the sectors as well. The extra personnel deployed from Moscow was assigned to the county and rural municipality branches of the People's Commissariats for State Security and Internal Affairs to consolidate their human resources. By January of 1945, 40 Chekists from Moscow and other regions had arrived in Latvia, then another 100 operatives were summoned. Between 8 and 20 January 1945, the NKVD and NKGB arrested 1,396 people. Starting from July of 1944, a total of 5,223 people had been arrested in Latvian territory. Among the arrested persons were eight German residents of Riga who were sent to prison camps without any delay. Hence the preparations for deporting Germans were underway in January of 1945.[32]

State Security was seriously seeking to gain control of the churches. Beria's report to Stalin states that preparations for arresting the head of the Latvian Lutheran church were underway in order to be able to replace him with 'our agent', who would be respected by the population as well as the clergy.[33] By then the leading clergy of the Latvian orthodox and catholic churches had already been arrested. Beria finished his report in traditional style: 'work on purging the territory of the Latvian SSR of hostile elements continues'.[34]

The results of the actions for suppressing resistance in the Baltic states, launched in the late autumn of 1944 by high-ranking state security emissaries (Merkulov and Kruglov) from Moscow, are summed up in the following table.

---

[31] Beria's special report to Stalin, Molotov and Malenkov on the results of the purge of Latvian territory, 26 January 1945 – *Lubianka: Stalin i NKVD*, 487.

[32] In the ESSR, the deportation of Germans was carried out in the summer of 1945. See: Aigi Rahi-Tamm, 'Deportation und Verfolgung in Estland 1939–1953', – *Vom Hitler-Stalin-Pakt*, 211–237.

[33] Beria's special report to Stalin, Molotov and Malenkov on the results of the purge in Latvia, 26 January 1945 – *Lubianka: Stalin i NKVD*, 488.

[34] *Ibid.*, 490.

Table 2. Preliminary results of the purge by State Security in Estonia, Latvia and Lithuania in November 1944 – January 1945.

Categories of arrested persons	In the Estonian ESSR as of 14 November 1944	In the Latvian SSR as of 20 January 1945	In the Lithuanian SSR as of 1 January 1945
Intelligence agents and members of counter-revolutionary organisations	48	625	449
Collaborators of intelligence agencies and counter-revolutionary organisations	97	379	26
Members of nationalist organisations	421	479	1,007
Traitors and collaborators of the Germans	206	2,721	5,456
Members of forest brothers groups and *their supporters	-	376	543
Any other 'anti-Soviet elements'	344	643	992
Total	1,116	5,223	12,449

Table compiled by: Beria's special report to Stalin, Molotov and Malenkov on the results of the purge in Latvian territory, 26 January 1945 – *Lubianka: Stalin i NKVD*, 486; USSR People's Commissar for State Security Merkulov's report to USSR State Defence Committee, 14 November 1944 – *Organy gosudarstvennoi*, 589; Lithuanian SSR People's Commissars for State Security and Internal Affairs Bartašiūnas and Guzevičius's report to USSR People's Commissar of Internal Affairs Beria, 5 January 1945 – *NKVD-MVD SSSR v bor'be*, 230.

The extensiveness of the anti-resistance movement is characterised by the number of prisoners. While ESSR NKVD prisons held 202 inmates on 10 October 1944, Estonian prisons were packed by the beginning of 1945 after the 'massive detention of counter-revolutionary elements' in the last months of 1944. On 1 January 1945, Estonian prisons held a total of 4,218 detainees, out of whom 2,378 people were imprisoned in Tallinn Prison with its actual capacity of 1,300 people. Tartu Prison with its capacity of 415 inmates held 855 people. While prisons in the entire Soviet Union were operating at 134% of their capacity at the beginning of 1945, then these indicators were 141% and 198% in the prisons of the Lithuanian SSR and the Latvian SSR (accordingly, 9,578 and 3,193 detainees) and in the Estonian SSR it was 137%. The total number of prisoners in the three Baltic countries was 16,989, accounting for 6.2% of the total number of detainees in the Soviet Union.[35] According to the available data, the State Security arrested a total of 7,059 people in the three Baltic countries in the last months of 1944, including 2,962 in Estonia, 2,584 in Lithuania and 1,513 in Latvia.[36]

This vivid data on prisoners is a good indicator of their so-called administrative origin (see Table 3). The data clearly demonstrates which administrative units were engaged in purging society and what their share was in the execution of repressions. While in the Estonian SSR and in the Latvian SSR, the main executor of repressions of the last months of 1944 was primarily the NKGB, then in the Lithuanian SSR it was the NKVD.

The participants in launching anti-armed resistance actions and in achieving preliminary results were rewarded with high state awards. A total of 4,327 Chekists received awards for contributing to the suppression of resistance movements in Ukraine, Belarus and the Baltics in 1944 and the beginning of 1945.[37]

---

[35] Aleksandr Kokurin, 'Tiurmy NKVD Latvii, Litvy i Estonii (1944–1953 gg.)', – *Padomju okupācijas režīms Baltijā 1944.–1959. gadā: politika un tās sekas: Starptautiskās konferences materiāli, 2002. gada 13.–14. jūnijs, Rīga*, Latvijas Vēsturnieku komisias raksti, 9. sēj. (Riga: Latvijas vēstures institūta apgāds, 2004), 188–189; ESSR People's Commissar for Internal Affairs Resev's report to USSR People's Commissar for Internal Affairs Beria, January 1945 (not accurately dated), RA, ERAF.17/1SM.1.8, 97–98.

[36] Oleg Mozokhin, *Statisticheskie svedeniia o deiatel'nosti organov VChK - OGPU - NKVD - MGB (1918–1953 gg.)* (Moscow: Algoritm, 2016), 241–249. It must be pointed out that the most massive arrests took place in 1945 when a total of 20,647 people were arrested in the Baltics, including 6,569 in Estonia, 6,958 in Lithuania and 7,120 in Latvia.

[37] See: *NKVD-MVD SSSR v bor'be*, 438, 448–452.

Table 3. The administrative origin of the detainees in the prisons of the Soviet Union and in the Baltic countries as of 1 January 1945.

Administrative origin and other characteristics of prisoners	Soviet Union	Lithuanian SSR	Latvian SSR	Estonian SSR
NKGB	19,675	2,227	1,221	2,860
SMERSH	3,077	167	55	163
NKVD	22,564	4,246	579	204
Militia	34,358	330	96	126
Prosecutor's office	4,844	562	319	218
Courts	26,227	298	181	102
NKVD Troika	6,296	80	26	1

Table compiled by: Kokurin, 'Tiurmy NKVD', 188.

State Security Commissioners of Moscow

State Security (NKVD and NKGB) commissioners were central figures in Moscow's significant control authorities formed in 1944 – the Soviet Republican Bureaus of the AUCP(B) Central Committee. In Estonia, these positions were held first by Lieutenant General Nikolai Sazykin (starting from 22 November 1944), followed by Lieutenant General Nikolai Gorlinski.[38] The appointment of high-ranking figures by the central administration of NKGB and NKVD to the positions of commissioners of the Bureaus clearly demonstrated that Estonia was far from being a secondary region for Moscow. No doubt, Sazykin's and Gorlinski's previous experience was to be implemented in the Sovietisation of Estonia. Sazykin had been the People's Commissar for State Security of the Moldavian SSR in the summer of 1941, overseeing a mass deportation there. During the war, he was the head of the Special Department of the Southern Front and thereafter the head of the 3rd Department of the USSR NKVD.

---

[38]   See the biographies: Nikita Petrov and Konstantin Skorkin, *Kto rukovodil NKVD 1934–1941: spravochnik* (Moscow: Zven'ia, 1999), 372–373.

Gorlinski's experience came from Ukraine where in 1938–1940 he was the Deputy People's Commissar for Internal Affairs. Then he worked for the central administration of the State Security. Sazykin as well as Gorlinski were Beria's confidants. After Stalin's death they became heads of central departments of the unified Ministry of Internal Affairs in 1953. Prior to that, for a short while – from February to April of 1949 – Gorlinski had been Minister of State Security of the Lithuanian SSR, carrying out the mass deportation there. Then he proceeded to the position of head of the State Security of Leningrad. He was also one of the key figures in the 'Leningrad Affair'. A purge of Communist Party and government officials in Leningrad in 1948–1950. The fall of Beria ended the careers of both men. Aleksei Babkin, Security Commissioner of the Latvian Bureau of the AUCP(B) Central Committee starting from 10 March 1945, also had earlier experience as a minister, having worked as the People's Commissar for Internal Affairs and State Security of the Kazakhstan SSR in 1940–1943 and as the head of the NKGB of Chelyabinsk oblast in 1944–1945. Babkin held the position of Security Commissioner at the Latvian Bureau from March of 1945 to April of 1946.[39]

The task of the NKVD and NKGB commissioners was to manage the suppression of the resistance movement, to purge society from 'hostile elements', and to co-ordinate the activities of the NKVD and NKGB in the Soviet republics. The commissioners also had to keep their eye on the administration in the Soviet republics and to forward relevant information directly to Moscow. The activities of Ivan Tkatchenko, the NKVD and NKGB Commissioner by the Lithuanian Bureau of the AUCP(B) Central Committee,[40] provide an excellent example of how in June of 1945 he notified Beria of the situation in the administration of the Lithuanian SSR, including details on diligence levels and, more significantly, how sluggishly and grudgingly the struggle against 'anti-Soviet elements' was proceeding. Tkatchenko complained that the administration in the Soviet republic had been holding meetings behind closed doors without inviting 'Russian comrades', meaning primarily the Second Secretary of the

---

[39] Petrov and Skorkin, *Kto rukovodil NKVD*, 97.

[40] Mikhail Suslov, head of the Lithuanian Bureau had brought Tkatchenko with him from Stavropol, where he had been the head of NKGB.

Lithuanian Communist (B) Party Aleksandr Issachenko.[41] Tkatchenko also pointed out that the head of the Lithuanian Bureau Mikhail Suslov 'worked little' and was often spotted 'reading literature' during working hours. Furthermore, he had mostly been in Moscow and only managed a couple of trips to the actual countries.[42]

Summary

The Kremlin's top brass aspired toward the rapid suppression of armed resistance in the western regions of Ukraine and Belarus and in the Baltics in 1944 and the following years for reasons regarding domestic and foreign policy. After re-establishing itself in 1943–1944, the Soviet regime could not feel secure until resistance had been completely suppressed. Its persistence was a significant obstacle to the Sovietisation of the newly annexed territories. It was also necessary to demonstrate the unity of the Soviet Empire to the outside world. Hence the standpoint of historiography, stating that the Kremlin was not paying much attention to the anti-resistance struggle in the Baltics at the end of 1944 and in the first half of 1945, is not correct.[43] The Kremlin's top brass was extremely well informed about the events taking place in the Baltics through a number of relevant reports arriving on Stalin's desk every week. Moscow's special interest in the matter is demonstrated by the deployment of the highest ranking leaders of the State Security – people's commissars and their first deputies – to Estonia, Latvia and Lithuania in order to carry out the purges essential for suppressing armed resistance and, no doubt, to obtain useful information on location. This style of top level 'counselling' was not applied by Moscow in the Sovietisation of other areas.

---

[41]   Member of the Lithuanian Bureau of the AUCP(B) CC and the NKVD and NKGB commissioner for Lithuania Tkatchenko's special report to Beria, 19 June 1945 – *Lubianka: Stalin i NKVD*, 528–532.

[42]   NKVD and NKGB commissioner in Lithuania Tkatchenko's special report to Beria, 19 June 1945 – *Lubianka: Stalin i NKVD*, 528–532. On Tkatchenko's activities, see: *Lietuva 1940–1990: okupuotos Lietuvos istorija*, ed. Arvydas Anušauskas (Vilnius: Lietuvos gyventojų genocido ir rezistencijos tyrimo centras, 2007), 272–274, 283, 305, 350.

[43]   Zubkova, *Pribaltika i Kreml'*, 224.

In the interpretation of the Soviet State Security, the resistance move-ment operated on two separate levels. In 1944, the struggle against the 'nationalistic underground' as well as the 'gangs bound to it', in other words armed resistance, commenced according to this notion in Estonia, Latvia and Lithuania: the task of the NKGB was to eradicate the higher level of resistance, in other words underground organisations, and the task of the NKVD was to liquidate the armed resistance created or guided by them. At the same time, Moscow did not trust the anti-bandit combat departments of the People's Commissariats for Internal Affairs in the So-viet republics and forced them to co-operate with the State Security. One of the results of co-operation was the joint NKGB and NKVD operations carried out under the leadership of security emissaries dispatched from Moscow. This model had been launched in the Lithuanian SSR in 1944. In 1945, this method was implemented in Estonia as well as in Latvia. This method was by no means specific to the Baltics; it was an extension of the method practised earlier in the western regions of Ukraine and Belarus. The forced co-operation created competition and mutual accusations be-tween the NKVD and the NKGB. Considering a longer perspective, we can say that as early as 1944, the NKGB gradually began taking over the functions of the suppression of armed resistance from the NKVD, leading to the incorporation of the Departments of Anti-Bandit Combat into the NKGB in 1947.

Moscow distrusted local personnel and a large number of state security operatives from Moscow, Leningrad and other regions of the Soviet Union were dispatched to the NKVD and NKGB of Estonia, Latvia and Lithuania in 1944. Under the guidance of these people, the measures essential for the suppression of armed resistance were actively implemented. Although the majority of those deployed operatives returned to their previous po-sitions, some of them were kept in leading positions of the NKVD and NKGB of the three Baltic Soviet republics. They took on leading roles in the post-war repressions. The local representatives from Moscow in secu-rity matters were the appointed NKVD and NKGB commissioners at the republican Bureaus of the AUCP(B) CC, established in the Soviet republics in 1944. Until 1947, when the Bureaus were closed down, the people's com-missars for internal affairs and the people's commissars for State Security (ministers starting in 1946) were subordinated both formally and practi-cally to the State Security commissioners from Moscow and they had to co-ordinate their activities with them.

The main direction of the Soviet regime defined in 1944 aimed at suppressing the resistance movement through repressions and violence was long-term. The main method was the execution of military-Chekist operations. It was implemented for the suppression of armed resistance in the Baltics, as well as in the western regions of Ukraine and Belarus. Until 1953, the authorities were solely committed to violence. Considering a longer perspective, the choice made in 1944 turned out to be a failure and never achieved its stated goals. The primary goal of eradicating resistance in 1945 turned out to be unachievable and the confrontation persisted for years, leading to large numbers of casualties. Committing to violence was later accepted as a mistake by the Kremlin. After the new direction was launched after Stalin's death in 1953, the policies of suppressing resistance in the western regions of the Soviet Empire were revised under the guidance of Beria.

Misapplication of Enforced Psychiatric Treatment in the Soviet Union – a Few Examples from Estonia

*Peeter Kaasik**

Introduction: Ideological-Medical Foundation of Enforced Psychiatric Treatment

In a totalitarian system psychiatry that actually is a means of therapy to relieve suffering, obtained the characteristics of a punitive method. One of the peculiarities of a totalitarian society is the assessment of dissidence based on psychiatric criteria. The doctrine of totalitarian ideology embraces total economic wellbeing, respect of human rights and absence of international tensions. The person doubting the doctrine was supposed to be consciously malicious or suffering from a psychic disorder and so many dissidents were labelled delusional bearers of sick ideas and convictions.[1] Thus one of Soviet punitive methods applied for a suspect or, actually, an anti-Soviet person was closing him or her in a psychiatric hospital, where he could be treated forcefully with drugs influencing his psyche. This treatment could cause changes like spiritual degeneration, resignation, weak-willingness, subsidence or a hypnotic condition, the result of which could be a psychic and moral travesty of personality.[2]

---

* First published: Peeter Kaasik, 'Psühhiaatrilise sundravi kuritarvitamisest Nõukogude Liidus', *Tuna: ajalookultuuri ajakiri*, no. 4 (2011): 79–96.

[1] Shimon [Semen] Gluzman, 'Totaalne psühhiaatria: lagunev kindlus [Total psychiatry: a crumbling fortress]', *Vikerkaar*, no. 12 (1989): 50.

[2] Heino Noor, 'Tervisele tekitatud püsikahjud' [Permanent damages to health] *Valge raamat: eesti rahva kaotustest okupatsioonide läbi 1940–1991* [The White

Soviet psychiatry was not entirely separated from international practice and thus it operated with universally accepted terms and categories. That is why we must deal with its misapplication in the Soviet Union within the general framework, not separated from customary practice.

Several specific matters should be considered when we observe somebody's hospitalisation in a special psychiatric ward for religious or political reasons. Dissident Semen Gluzman[3] has formulated these concerns as follows:

1. Was the victim really hospitalised for political or religious reasons?
2. Did he/she have any symptoms of a psychic disorder before?
3. What were the psychic aberrations like (i.e. were they socially dangerous, or were they a danger to the person himself/herself or to the community)?
4. What was the usual world practice in these cases?
5. What was the common procedure of criminal trials in the Soviet Union?
6. Was every case like that a misapplication of psychiatry or was there something that needed psychiatrists' attention indeed?
7. Was it possible that a mentally healthy person could suffer from psychic disorders due to the enforced treatment or repression?

For an objective research of the subject matter one would need all the documents concerning the inquest and medical treatment. Psychiatrists of these hospitals should express their views too. Discussions are not easy to hold as both parties lack the patience that is needed. The repressed still

---

Book: losses of the Estonian nation through the occupations in 1940–1991], editors Ülo Ennuste, Enn Tarvel et al. (Tallinn: Okupatsioonide Repressiivpoliitika Uurimise Riiklik Komisjon, Eesti Entsüklopeediakirjastus, 2005), 56–57.

[3]   Semen Gluzman was born in 1946. He graduated from the Kiev Medical Institute in 1970. In connection with Major General Piotr Grigorenko's case he was arrested in 1972, spent seven years in the GULAG and later three years in exile. P. Grigorenko (1907–1987) was a Soviet army officer, who served as the division chief of staff at the end of the Second World War. In 1945–1961 he was a lecturer in the M. V. Frunze Military Academy. In 1959 he had been promoted to the rank of Major General and became the head of military cybernetics department. In 1961 he joined the dissidents and spent some time at special psychiatric hospitals. In 1977 he was permitted to go and visit his son in the USA and when he was there he was deprived of his Soviet citizenship.

believe that psychiatrists invented their case histories and they could only hit the doctors' all round defence that hides the functioning mechanisms of the system. The doctors explain and excuse their silence with the patients' confidentiality clause.

It should be pointed out that the role of a psychiatrist in repression cases was always secondary. The psychiatrist was not the initiator of the expertise opinion. Whatever his personal views, he had to observe the medical aspect only. In case the doctor was an orthodox communist or a merely obedient citizen, the psychiatric repression of dissidents must have clashed with his physician's ethics. However, there are always people whose moral principles and professional ethics can be easily bent.

In case of the dissidents we should also consider the evaluation of their political or religious convictions. Generalising, we have to admit that the ideas one makes a big deal of can become a paranoia-like condition. And hence the question – were there people with psychic disorders among the dissidents indeed? Obviously there were, like in any other social group. Whether the symptoms justified closing them in a special hospital is another matter.[4]

The aim of 'political psychiatry' was not only to separate political dissidents from the society. Another, and probably even more important aim was to 'break them spiritually' and let the society think that they were, indeed, mentally ill. Andres Lepik who was detained in Chernyakhovsk Special Psychiatry Hospital in the 1970s has described the procedure as follows –

Pursuant to the reputation of the establishment one can find all sorts of figures here.[5] There are certainly some "normal lunatics" who are more or less realistic and only sometimes suffer from seizures, and there are even under-age lads. The company is profuse and motley but intelligent faces shadowed by the SYSTEM can be noticed immediately. For example a writer (FORMER member of the Writers' Union) who has great self control in his present expression. The paradox of this hospital is just that among the numerous self-made generals, writers, Nobel-prize winners and others are the

---

[4]   Gluzman, 'Totaalne psühhiaatria', 50–52.

[5]   According to A. Lepik murderers were in the majority but there were rapists, embezzlers (who could not remember what had happened to the stolen property). There were few political prisoners, some border violators included.

real live ones. Having recklessly underestimated the essence of the SYSTEM we are in danger of soon getting mixed up with the others... The self-made writer can join forces with the real one and nobody cares or notices. In five years one's OWN sight disperses and this, the worst possibility for the patient, is evidently the purpose. Chemistry – the enforced doses from the "pharmacists" – is certainly a great help, like punitive injections and secret treatments.[6]

The following will not pretend to be a medical analysis – specialists should take care of that. Mechanisms of the enforced treatment of dissidents have remained unclear but they had to have some sort of medical foundation. Like in any other state, the punitive policy of the USSR was directed at those who endangered the society. The basis for criminal policy established –

Any act committed or neglected can be considered endangering the society if it is anti- Soviet or violates the juridical state of the workers and peasants' power before the time the changeover to communism occurs [...][7]

Thus everything anti-Soviet was the most severe crime of all as the state's interests were the priority. Enforced treatment was established in the criminal code. This makes forensic psychiatry a part of the repressive system that was subjected to the general principles of the criminal policy. Disturbances with anti-Soviet symptoms had to be explained somehow in medical terms and this important ideological-medical task was given to Moscow Forensic-Psychiatry Institute named after Serbsky.[8] The special

---

[6]   Memoirs of Andres Lepik, *Vikerkaar*, no. 2 (1990): 56–57.

[7]   See: *VNFSV kriminaalkoodeks: muudatustega kuni 1. detsembrini 1938: ametlik tõlge* [The Criminal code of the Russian SFSR (1926) with amendments until 1 December 1938: Official text] (Tallinn: ENSV Kohtu Rahvakomissariaat, 1940), § 6.

[8]   The official name for the establishment was 'The Central Red-Banner of Labour Institute of Forensic Psychiatry Research named after professor Vladimir Petrovich Serbsky of the USSR Ministry of Healthcare' (*Tsentral'nyi Ordena Trudovogo Krasnogo Znameni nauchno-issledovatel'skii institut sudebnoi psikhiatrii im. professora V. P. Serbskogo MZ SSSR*). Vladimir Serbsky (1858–1917), was a Russian psychiatrist, founder of the Russian forensic psychiatry. Graduated from the natural science department at the University of Moscow. Defended his doctor

department – Fourth department – responsible for political dissidents' case histories, first of all invented them and later also confirmed them.

Dissidents were defined in various ways. One of the main conclusions of A. Kassatchov's dissertation 'Clinical and forensic psychiatric evaluation of paranoiac psychopaths' was that enforced treatment should be carried out also in case of persons who continuously protest and present 'reforming ideas'. To be exact, one of the diagnoses for the 'reformers' was 'protesting paranoia as a revelation of schizophrenia'. An example of the latter could be the article by Soviet medical research fellows A. Taltse, Iu. Landau and L. Tabakov – 'Criteria for prescribing enforced treatment for patients with paranoiac syndrome schizophrenia' (1981). The article was based on the case histories of 90 schizophrenics who had 'reforming delusions':

Their assessments and interests, side by side with their paranoiac combinations, are on the level of common conjunctures, they do their habitual duties, their formal orientation within their environment has survived. [...] Enforced treatment in a general type psychiatric hospital can be recommended to these schizophrenics who have become passive, whose words and acts are not in correlation, who do not have any background for mood rises and who are indifferent to their fate.[9]

To make it clearer – the patients who had been tamed could continue treatment in general psychiatric clinics and hospitals. Religious beliefs that did not correlate with the official atheist doctrine belong to a topic of their own. It was hardest of all for the so-called sectarians who were difficult to control as their organisations were decentralised (differently from the Russian Orthodox Church that was almost totally under the control of the KGB). So, for example, D. Lunts and L. Elmonov wrote in their article 'Some peculiarities of forensic psychiatry in case of criminal sectarianism' (1961) –

Activities of sectarian groups like Pentecostals (or as they themselves like to be called – Evangelical Christians – that had needed forensic-psychiatric

---

of medicine thesis on psychiatry in 1891. In 1892–1911 he taught forensic psychiatry at the law and medical schools of the University of Moscow, in 1902–1911 Professor extraordinary.

[9]   Gluzman, 'Totaalne psühhiaatria', 53

expertise, have been described in press. [...] Before we start discussing prob-
lems that belong to the field of experts, it is necessary to enlighten these
psychically traumatic situations that are connected with the Pentecostals'
cult and rituals.[10]

Already the headline of the article shows that the authors consider the cult
psychically traumatic and its activities a religious fanaticism.

Everybody who was concerned knew very well what was going on and
while it was declared to be a 'wrong diagnosis', the statements were published again in science journals. So, for example, professor N. Timofeyev
had to admit –

We were often convinced that diagnosing the person who had violated the
law for religious reasons as a paranoiac psychopath, the experts misunder-
stood his affective reactions and did not have any knowledge about his views
that were totally opposed to our reality and the expert's own system of views.

Professor D. Lunts who gave many dissidents 'the wrong diagnosis' in
1960–1970 has even described the reasons for them:

One reason for the "wrong diagnosis" is the behaviour of the psychopaths
we observed and the conditions in which this behaviour was revealed. There
certainly were coinciding features reminiscent of schizophrenia. The errone-
ous diagnosis in these cases can be explained with neglecting the influences
of environmental and social-psychological matters. Unaccustomed lifestyle,
extirpation of the healthy environment, use of intoxicating drinks, incompre-
hensible tendencies of the modern western art, philosophy and literature –
discussions of these topics are unjustly considered to be acclimatisation to
a schizophrenic mind.

It is quite noteworthy that a reputable psychiatrist directs the fire at himself and, speaking about the erroneous diagnosis does not even hint at the
role of the KGB and the court. However, we can also detect the opinion
that there is but one short step from literature, art, music and philosophy
that have not been officially approved up to schizophrenia.[11]

---

[10]   Gluzman, 'Totaalne psühhiaatria', 55.

[11]   Gluzman, 'Totaalne psühhiaatria', 53–56. See also: Vladimir Bukovskii
and Semen Gluzman, 'Posobie po psikhiatrii dlia inakomysliashchikh', http://

Basis for Enforced Treatment in Soviet Legalisation

The so-called punitive medicine existed already in the first months of the Soviet regime.

The Russian dissident Aleksandr Podrabinek[12] hints at the temporary instruction of the People's Commissariat of Justice on 23 July 1918, recommending that the adversary should be closed in a 'punitive medical establishment'.[13] So it was openly said that it was a punitive establishment where some treatment could be given. A judicial body or the 'revolutionary military tribunal' could decide who had to go. This instruction does not even mention any expertise, everything was based on the 'revolutionary conscience', that is the discretion of the decision-maker (or the order of some higher institution). Typically of the anarchist period, a few interesting diagnoses were invented, such as 'counter-revolutionary psychosis', for instance.

These establishments did exist and such punishments have been known since February 1919. It was used against the political rivals who were not shot or imprisoned. One example, for instance, is the leader of Socialist Revolutionaries Maria Spiridonova.[14]

The Russian SFSR Criminal Code from 1922 and the Code of Criminal Procedure Code from 1924 gave a more exact definition of the enforced

---

antology.igrunov.ru/authors/bukovsky/psychiatr.html, 1 July 2018.

[12] A. Podrabinek (born in 1953) worked in emergency medicine. He was one of the initiators of 'Psychiatry in the service of politics' research commission at the Moscow - Helsinki group. He is the author of *Punitive Medicine* (Aleksandr Podrabinek, *Karatel'naia meditsina* (New York: Hronika, 1979). Was arrested on 14 May 1978 and imprisoned for five years in Irkutsk oblast.

[13] In Russian – *Karatel'no-lechebnye zavedeniia dlia pomeshcheniia arestantov s zametno vyrazhennymi psikhicheskimi defektami* (Punitive and medical treatment establishments for inmates with clearly expressed psychic defects).

[14] M. Spiridonova was arrested in January 1919 and hospitalised in the Kremlin clinic, from where she managed to escape in April 1919. She managed to hide herself until October 1920 when she was caught and sent to a mental hospital, where she was kept until November 1921. When she was released she had to promise never to deal with politics again. She was arrested again in 1923 when she attempted to escape abroad. The rest of her life was spent in prisons and prison camps until she was sentenced to death and shot in 1941.

treatment.[15] In the latter we can already find the term of specialised psychiatry to be used for removing extremely dangerous patients from society.[16] Both codes were complemented in 1926. The emendatory issues were more exact in defining the means of social protection of compulsory-corrective character. These were enforced treatment and hospitalisation to separate the patient from the society.[17]

With the directive of the Russian SFSR People's Commissariat of Justice from 17 February 1935 the article was complemented and the enforced treatment as 'a means of social protection of medical character' could be sentenced only by court. That means the formal interdiction of prosecution bodies to dictate enforced treatment. The enforced treatment could be applied to persons who had committed a crime in a fit of insanity, were mentally ill at the time of the trial or to the persons who were taken ill during their detention.[18]

Articles 142 and 148 are also significant for the enforced treatment as according to them the hospitalisation in a psychiatric clinic of a person with a sound mind for the personal gain or for any other reason, could bring up to three-year imprisonment. Inflicting intentional bodily harm or injury that caused a mental disorder brought imprisonment up to two years.[19] Today these articles could well be measuring-sticks for the activities of the psychiatrists responsible for hospitalising persons in an absolutely sound mind.

---

[15]   See the Criminal Code of the Russian SFSR §§ 17, 24, 46 and the Russian SFSR Criminal Procedure Code § 457, *VNFSV kriminaalprotsessi koodeks: ametlik tekst muudatustega kuni 1. aug. 1944. a. ühes paragrahvide järgi süstematiseeritud materjale sisaldava lisaga: ametlik tõlge* [The RSFSR Criminal Procedure Code. Official text with amendments up to 1 August 1944 together with the supplement arranged according to articles: Official translation] (Tartu: Teaduslik Kirjandus, 1947).

[16]   Podrabinek, *Karatel'naia meditsina,* 19–21.

[17]   *Ugolovnyi kodeks RSFSR (1926). Ofitsal'nyi tekst s izmeneniiami na 1 iiulia 1950 g i s prilozheniem postateino sistematizirovannykh materialov* (Moscow: Gosudarstvennoe izdatel'stvo iuridicheskoi literatury, 1950), §§ 11, 24.

[18]   Directive of the Russian SFSR Peoples' Commissariat of Justice, 17 February 1935 – *VNFSV kriminaalprotsessi koodeks,* 125–126.

[19]   *Ugolovnyi kodeks RSFSR,* §§ 142, 148.

The criminal procedure code elaborated on the procedure. The inquest was to be stopped in case the person interrogated had a mental disease.[20] The inquest was stopped until the interrogated recovered or was declared to be mentally ill. In the second case 'the means of social protection' were applied, i.e. the person was hospitalised.[21] The time spent in the mental hospital was included in the sentence.[22]

The possibility of the mental disease was ascertained by an expertise. Later on this article was specified and the forensic-medical experts had to ascertain the persons' mental state. The experts were subjected to the medical system and had to observe the criminal code, the criminal procedure code and the respective directives, instructions and decrees of the ministries. The forensic-psychiatric expertise was formal and carried out at the order of investigation bodies, the court or when demanded by the detention establishment. Expertise could be carried out in stationary or ambulatory conditions, in special cases even in absentia.[23] The expert assessment was presented as an official act. First of all there was to be the introduction (the personal data of the observed, the time and performers of the expertise, the name of the establishment that had asked for it, and a brief survey of the crime committed). The data about the previous life of the observed was the next, description of the mental and physical-neurological condition and conclusions (recommendation for the medical treatment included) followed.

---

[20] *VNFSV kriminaalprotsessi koodeks*, § 202.

[21] *Ibid.*, § 203.

[22] *Ibid.*, § 457

[23] This was indeed also done in absentia. For example on 9 October 1957 Helmut Valgre (an agent of the KGB 4th department, alias 'Kuusk') escaped from the trade union officials' tourist group in the port of Ålesund, Norway. The criminal case was started immediately. Oskar Kuul, the chairman of the collective fishery named after Kirov, who had been in the same group, testified and a forensic-psychiatric expertise was set up although Valgre was not present. The Republican Psycho-Neurological Hospital commission (Vsevolod Grünthal, A. Andreyeva, Bella Rosenfeld) declared Valgre *non compos mentis*. The Serbsky Institute commission cancelled this absurd in absentia judgement and the ESSR Supreme Court sentenced Valgre in absentia for a 10 year imprisonment. See: Jaak Pihlau, 'Eestlaste põgenemised Läände: ärahüppajad III' [Estonians' Escapes to the West: Defectors III], *Tuna*, no. 3 (2003): 78–87.

In case either the court or prosecuting body found the expertise faulty or not acceptable, another expertise was allowed. Especially complicated cases were to be transferred to the Moscow Serbsky Forensic-Psychiatric Institute of the USSR People's Commissariat/Ministry of Healthcare.

Permanent forensic-expertise commissions at medical establishments performed ambulatory assessment. These commissions consisted of three members appointed by the local healthcare department. If any complications occurred, they could transfer the case to stationary expertise that was performed at institutes, hospitals and clinics of psychiatry. The observed were accommodated in the special departments of these establishments and if there was none, in the general department, where they had to be isolated. The three members of the expert commission were the chief physician or the head of the medical department of the establishment (chair), the head or somebody else with special training of the forensic-psychiatric department and the doctor that had examined the observed. The assessment had to be completed within 30 days but when the decision was not made, more time was provided.[24]

The Russian SFSR Criminal Code and Criminal Procedure Code were in force on Estonian territory until 1 April 1961 when the Estonian SSR Criminal code became effective. There were no principal supplements as far as the enforced treatment was concerned, some things were more precisely defined only. According to the code only an imputable person could be prosecuted. There were two kinds of characteristics for irresponsibility – psychological and medical ones. In the first case the person was unable to understand either the act or its consequences nor describe and report it. The medical characteristics were divided into chronic mental disease, temporary mental disorders and imbecility. The person was declared irresponsible if both, psychological and medical characteristics were present.

The expertise assessment could not declare the observed imputable or irresponsible. This was the responsibility of the judicial organs that based their decision on the expertise assessment.[25] After recovery the observed was taken back to the former place of detention.[26]

---

[24]   RSFSR Criminal Procedure Code, § 63.

[25]   *Eesti NSV kriminaalkoodeks: kommenteeritud väljaanne* [Estonian SSR Criminal Code with commentaries], comp. Ilmar Rebane (Tallinn: Eesti Raamat, 1972), § 11.

[26]   *Ibid.*, § 52.

The 'forced medical means' were not called punitive. They could be used until recovery (the time in the psycho-neurological hospital was equalised with that in the place of detention) or until the person could be trusted to the care of the family (a doctor's surveillance included). The enforced treatment was justified when the person could be a danger to the society. The court decided whether to hospitalise the mental case in a special psychiatry establishment (especially dangerous persons), a general psychiatric clinic (not so dangerous, could be treated in the common way) or in an establishment for chronic mental patients (surveillance excluded the danger they could present).[27]

Technical details of the enforced treatment were defined in the criminal procedure code. Forensic-psychiatric expertise was the basis for hospitalisation.[28] The inquest could be stopped when the accused was seriously ill (or was suspected to be ill, mental illness included).[29] The time spent under treatment was included in the sentence.[30]

The suggestion to conclude the inquest and pass it to the court was made by the prosecutor.[31] The trial had to decide whether the defendant had committed a crime that endangered the society, if the defendant was not answerable or whether the illness occurred after committing the crime and whether 'medical means of enforced character' had to be applied. The decision could be appealed.[32]

In case the 'medical means of enforced character' were no more necessary, the hospital could suggest that the treatment should be concluded.[33]

Thus the hospitalisation for enforced treatment consisted of several steps and included various establishments like committees of inquiry, the prosecutor's office and court instances. Doctors were used as experts, whose assessment was not exactly the basis for enforced treatment but

---

[27]   *Ibid.*, § 59.

[28]   Eesti NSV kriminaalprotsessi koodeks: ametlik tekst muudatuste ja täiendustega seisuga 29. mai 1970 [Estonian SSR Criminal Procedure Code. Official text with amendments and complements up to 29 May 1970] (Tallinn: Eesti Raamat, 1970), §§ 58, 156–162, 281.

[29]   *Ibid.*, § 163.

[30]   *Ibid.*, § 333.

[31]   *Ibid.*, §§ 281, 282.

[32]   *Ibid.*, §§ 283–287.

[33]   *Ibid.*, §§ 288–289, 336–337.

could have some influence on the court's decisions. The court did not have to take the experts' assessment into account but it could consider it partly. For instance – the experts recommended a general psychiatric hospital but the court decided on the special one (see further: the case of S. K.). Or vice versa. It is not known who decided to send dissidents of sound mind to a special psychiatric hospital and how exactly it was done. The forensic psychiatrists had their right to appeal as well and unusual cases could be transferred to the Serbsky Institute that had quite close connections with the KGB.

The Serbsky Institute was founded in 1927. They did research work, too, not only psychiatric expertise. Their responsibility was to work out methods and the ideology for forensic medicine. Officially the institute was subjected to the USSR Ministry of Healthcare, but many of its staff were MVD or KGB officers. A high concrete wall surrounded the territory of the institute that was guarded by a quasi-military unit. According to several memoirs the 'political' patients were in department 4 (also called a special department) that contained three wards 'for especially dangerous anti-state mental patients'. Each of these wards could accommodate 30 patients and there was also an isolation ward for five patients.[34]

Specialised Psychiatry Hospitals

The Criminal Code and the Criminal Procedure Code let us understand that for especially dangerous mental patients there were prisons-psychiatry hospitals that later were renamed specialised psychiatry hospitals. They were subjected to the People's Commissariat of Internal Affairs, from 1946 to the Ministry of Internal Affairs. Psychiatric hospitals of general type were subjected to the USSR People's Commissariat of Healthcare

---

[34]   Reference about the Serbsky Institute of Psychiatry, 31 July 1956, RGANI, f. 6, o. 6., d. 1684, 1–19; *Kaznimye sumasshestviem. Sbornik dokumental'nykh materialov o psikhiatricheskikh presledovaniiakh inakomysliashchikh v SSSR*, eds. A. Artemova, L. Rar and M. Slavinskii (Frankfurt am Main: Posev, 1971), 187–188, 12–13; Podrabinek, *Karatel'naia meditsina*, 88–101; Kalju Mätik, 'Kuidas ma tegin sundekskursiooni Serbski-nimelisse Kohtupsühhiaatria Instituuti' [My Forced Excursion to the Serbsky Forensic-Psychiatric Institute], *Kultuur ja Elu*, no. 2 (2008): 58–63.

(since 1946 Ministry of Healthcare)[35] Although the victims of 'political psychiatry' were hospitalised also at psychiatric hospitals of general type, the main form of detention was 'treatment' at a MVD specialised psychiatric hospital, were especially dangerous patients, among them serial killers and rapists, were kept.

Initially this sort of an establishment was only in Kazan. There were, however, closed psychiatric departments and wards within several hospitals and prisons, the data about which is scarce. Memoirs have mentioned the Butyrka prison in Moscow (the President of Estonia Konstantin Päts was detained there for some time), others in Vladimir, Gorky (Nizhni-Novgorod). At the state farm *Chekist* in Tomsk region was a prison-hospital for patients with mental illness and the so-called malingerers and there were evidently several more that were neither prisons-psychiatry hospitals nor specialised psychiatry hospitals in the true sense of the word. In 1953 there were three establishments of that type – in Kazan, Chistopol (Tatarstan) and Leningrad.[36] Later there were more specialised hospitals in Blagoveshchensk (upon the Amur in East Siberia), Sytchevska in Smolensk region, Oryol (opened in 1970), Chernyakhovsk (in Kaliningrad region that used to be Insterburg in East Prussia, 1966), Dnepropetrovsk (1968), Smolensk, Minsk (1966) and others.[37]

These hospitals, like prisons and prison camps, were guarded by MVD troops.[38] The specialised psychiatric hospitals had two administrations – the military and the medical one. The head of such a hospital was a military and the chief physician was usually a military doctor, too. The latter might have graduated from a military medical school or he might have been transferred to the army system from the civic sector (in the Soviet Union all students of university medical schools had to pass the basic military surgeon's training and as conscripts were officers in reserve).

---

[35] *Psikhatricheskaia tiuremnaia bol'nitsa.*

[36] Aleksandr Kokurin, 'Tiuremnaia sistema 1934–1960', – *Sistema ispravitel'notrudovykh lagerei v SSSR 1923–1960: spravochnik*, comp. M. B. Smirnov (Moscow: Zven'ia, 1998), 538–539.

[37] *Kaznimye sumasshestviem*, 140–172.

[38] Some of the troops in the Soviet Union were under the command of the Ministry of Internal Affairs. The Internal troops were mainly used for guarding prisons and prison camps but they might have had other duties as well. Most of the prisons and camps and other places of detention were guarded by youngsters doing their compulsory army service.

Generally the regime of these hospitals was not different from that of prisons. So, for example, the wards had lights on at night, the toilets were either in the rooms or in the corridor. One had to ask for permission to use the corridor toilets. Bed sheets were to be changed in every ten days according to the instruction. The food was scant and even from that meagre fare a big part was stolen by doctors, nurses, nurses' aids and guards.

It was possible to get food parcels – not heavier than five kilograms. Just like in Soviet prisons, part of these parcels went to the staff and part to the other patients, depending on the interior hierarchy and the patient's ability to protect his property. Two letters a month, only in Russian and to the family, could be sent. All the correspondence was censored, no mention of the detention or 'treatment' was allowed. More often than not, the letters were not received, may-be because of censorship but quite possibly due to the generally dominating chaos and sluggishness of the administration.

Immediate family could come visiting once a month for two hours. Those families who lived far away from the prison-hospital were allowed four hours every two months. The meetings were watched by a guard or guards and certain topics of conversation, like living-conditions and treatment, were prohibited.

Labour-therapy was carried out in various workshops like sewing-, cardboard- and others and even some pay – ten roubles for a month – for the completed product was provided. Only those who really could not be made to work were free of the obligation, others could not refuse. The ones who dared to protest were quickly 'put on their place' by nurses' aids who were usually prisoners with a criminal charge.

As everybody else in the Soviet Union, a patient in such kind of an establishment was also given political instruction. It was mostly formal and depended on the administration and place but quite a common form of it was watching films. These were mainly films of Soviet propaganda but sometimes a feature film might have been shown. The idea of libraries was similar. Theoretically it was possible to subscribe even to newspapers. 'For security reasons' Russian-language journalism was preferred. Depending on the place and time the patients were sometimes forced to do sports and participate in amateur activities that could be rather grotesque in the outcome.[39]

---

[39]   Podrabinek, *Karatel'naia meditsina*, 85–88; *Kaznimye sumasshestviem*, 5–220.

A few specialised psychiatric clinics had a separated part for criminals who were used as nurses' aids and to do various maintenance chores. They were hospitalised for the same reasons as the mental patients but had a less strict regime. One can easily imagine what their attitude to their patients was like. Andres Lepik has described the 'calming down' process as follows –

I remember a case with a senile patient: at that time I was for the first night in a ward under close observance when in the early hours somebody started to bawl, "Guard! Guard!" Well, the guards, of course, came in and gave him and the EVIL SPIRIT in him a thorough beating with fists and everybody except me was surprised at the bawling that did not die down but got louder and louder. His limbs were wrested and twisted, it did not help. The nurse with an immense syringe did not help either. Somebody was trying to squeeze the bleeding body into a straightjacket when other militiamen and officers on duty arrived from their room that for the old man's misfortune happened to be nearby. They seemed angry to have been disturbed but eager to participate in the beating. The department head happened to hear about it somewhat later and all the participants were called into his office one by one and evidently scolded – tchort poberi![40] –Why couldn't you be less noisy?[41]

It is difficult for a layman to describe the treatment methods and the drugs, but in the memoirs it is mentioned that the medicaments turned the patient something totally inefficient, unable to think or act. Long treatment brought along permanent mental damage even for those who were hospitalised in sound mind and body.[42]

So, for example Ivan Ikkonen,[43] a Roman Catholic, writes about his treatment (not in a specialised psychiatric clinic, but the methods were the same.)

---

[40]   Blast you! (in Russian).

[41]   Andres Lepik's memoirs, 58–59.

[42]   See in greater detail Bukovskii and Gluzman, 'Posobie po psikhiatrii'.

[43]   Ikkonen, a conscientous objector of military service, was called up to the Military Commissariat on 19 April 1978, where it was discovered that he was religious, a Roman Catholic. He spent four months and 11 days at Tartu Psycho-Neurological Hospital. Having been released he spread his memoirs first among

Already on the first day I was forcefully tied up and injected – it was such an injection that did not let me even pray. [...] A talk with Dr. Michelson followed and he declared me ill because I believe in God. Then some nurses gave me an electric shock to release me from my religion. In a week's time Michelson showed me to a group of students and asked me to talk about my religion. I did but the students were only grinning. A little later I was called to Dr. Adamsoo, who was together with some other doctors. They peppered me with questions like "Why is religion necessary? What will arrive first, Paradise or communism? Why do you believe?" After this talk another electric shock was given, but my belief persisted. The medical commission decided to treat me with insulin. [...] On 3 August my insulin therapy ended, after which I thanked the God that this had not taken my belief either. My treatment continued with pills and some liquid that made me unable to speak and eat. Michelson and other doctors talked to me after the insulin therapy and they all asked me only about my religion. I was told that I was still ill and had to be sent to a home for the disabled persons but before that they had still to cure me from my religion. They decided that the religion disturbed my life and gave me another electric shock. [...] A nurse brought me "Scientific atheism" to read and I refused. [...] On 31 August I was released. [...] This year I am not able to go to a technical school as my head simply cannot get round anything after all this "therapy". [...] The doctors still consider me ill because I have not given up my belief in spite of everything done to me. All in all I received five electric shocks and 60 insulin comas.[44]

As a special psychiatry hospital was still a place of detention, the regime in it was fixed. For the violations of this regime the patients could be 'calmed down', procedures were more-or-less like described before – a straight-jacket or an injection. There were other punishments at the discretion of the medical staff and the guards. It did not matter whether the patient was mentally disturbed or not, the stick and the carrot-method was popular: either curbing or enforcing the right for walks and work, cancelling the right to get and write letters, receive parcels, have meetings, smoke, use

---

the religious people and later, thanks to the self-print periodical *Lisandusi mõtete ja uudiste vabale levikule Eestis* [Supplement to the unhindered spread of thought and news in Estonia] this material reached Sweden and via that into the world.

[44]   Ivan Ikkonen, 'Üks lõik minu elust [A passage of my life]', *Lisandusi mõtete ja uudiste vabale levikule Eestis*, vol. 1, 1–7: 1978–1980 (Stockholm: Eesti Vangistatud Vabadusvõitlejate Abistamiskeskus, 1984), 39–40.

the library or watch TV. The worst was transfer into the department of the 'unstable' or reconsidering the decision about the patient's release.[45]

The release from a special psychiatry hospital was rather haphazard and happened at the discretion of the doctors or the commission. The aim was to suppress the patients whether by attitude or 'therapy'. In case the patient could stay calm and leave that impression, he could be released if he was lucky or he could be sent to a general psychiatry hospital with a bit more lenient regime and that was an establishment of treatment. When the detainee did not show any signs of having given up his ideas, he could be detained in a special psychiatry hospital indefinitely. The commission who made the release decision played a significant role, they made the proposal to the court that made the final decision. According to the law the commission had to make their decisions in every six months. The only chance for the dissidents was to hide their real thoughts and viewpoints, only then might they have a chance to be released.[46]

Some Examples of the Practice of 'Political Psychiatry'

Rearrangements after Stalin's Death

Data about this form of psychiatry in Stalin's time is rather scarce but it is known that it was used widely enough, especially in case of 'counterrevolutionary mental patients' neither shot nor arrested. This was a general practice that the so-called contra revolutionaries (basically those who had been arrested according to § 58 of the Russian RSFR Criminal Code) were considered to be much more dangerous than those who had committed severe crimes concerning other people. Dissident Vladimir Gusarov,[47] for example, spoke about a woman, who was kept at the Kazan specialised psychiatric hospital in 1934–1954 because she had thrown a stone at Lenin's mausoleum in 1934. After Stalin's death the punitive system was relieved and this also concerned the special psychiatry. Sergei Pisarev could be considered the initiator for the move as he wrote a letter

---

[45]   Podrabinek, *Karatel'naia meditsina*, 92, 95.

[46]   Bukovskii and Gluzman, 'Posobie po psikhiatrii'.

[47]   Vladimir Gusarov (born in 1930) was arrested in 1953 and spent the next year at the Kazan specialised psychiatry hospital. Later he was several times detained for political reasons in general psychiatric hospitals.

to Stalin in 1953 and attempted to draw attention to the MGB falsification of documents in the so-called 'Doctors' Plot'. On the day of Stalin's death, 5 March 1953, he was arrested and detained in the Butyrka prison, from where he was transferred to Leningrad prison-psychiatry hospital. After his release in 1955 he attempted to launch an investigation about the staff of the Leningrad prison-psychiatry hospital and the Serbsky Forensic-Psychiatric Institute but did not succeed at first. He appealed to the Central Committee of the CPSU and was finally heard – a commission was appointed and the investigation started.[48] It was ascertained that the expertise assessments of the Serbsky Institute were not and could not be proved. It was also ascertained that the Institute was closely connected to the security organs whose commissions it fulfilled, diagnosing persons of sound mind to be psychopaths, schizophrenics, paranoiacs and so on. A destructible assessment was also given to the specialised psychiatric hospitals and it was ascertained already at the time of the investigations that the people detained were innocent and most of them had no mental disorders either.[49]

A few things did get better, but most changes were merely cosmetic. Russian dissidents consider the year 1961 the beginning of a new era in 'political psychiatry'. This happened when the USSR Healthcare Ministry, the USSR Prosecutor's office and the Russian SFSR Ministry of Protection of the Social Order confirmed the instruction for 'Special hospitalisation of persons who are a danger to the society'. What is especially noteworthy about this instruction is that there was no need for a court decision any more, a special commission of three could make the decision. The instruction contained also five points that should help to ascertain the 'unusual case', but the term became even more vague as the characteristics of a mental disease were rather indefinite. The instruction was nothing special actually and there was no mechanism to check how it was followed but a little later some principles of the instruction were put into practice.[50] It is difficult to estimate how many people were sub-

---

[48]   Sergei Pisarev had belonged to the Communist Party since 1920. See in greater detail: *Kaznimye sumasshestviem*, 187–188.

[49]   Certified statement of J. Kalashnik, assistant director of the Serbsky Forensic-Psychiatric Institute, 21 June 1956, RGANI, f. 6, o. 6, d. 1684, 1–19, 22–24.

[50]   Instruction for Special hospitalisation of persons who are a danger to the society, 10 October 1961 – Podrabinek, *Karatel'naia meditsina*, 180–181.

jected to enforced treatment without the court's sanction.[51] In principle it was not in concord with the USSR laws, especially the criminal and criminal procedure codes.

Beginning from the 1960s special psychiatry was extensively applied to dissidents and fighters for human rights. Detention in specialised hospitals and special camps was widely used. The peak period was the end of the 1960s and the beginning of the 1970s. These hospitals were responsible to law enforcement authorities and the medical staff did not have much say. While the detainee had at least some kind of legal protection at prison camps, the patient at a specialised hospital was absolutely at the mercy of the staff – that is, a mental patient was mad and his protests could be ignored. When the period of detention was determined by a term at camps, the patient could be kept at a hospital as long as the authorities wished (it was only a formality that they had to re-examine every case once in six months). In addition the means and methods that were used to 'calm the patients down' were such that could easily lead to mental instability.[52]

Six cases of 'political psychiatry' connected with Estonia follow. The selected cases differ from each other and not all of them are connected with dissidents. The reader has probably heard most about the case of Konstantin Päts, who was detained for years in confined psychiatric hospitals and prisons. He was detained for a bit different reasons than the other victims of 'political psychiatry'. Two of the cases (those of H. K. and S. K.) definitely concern dissidents and spreading self-print materials. J. L. was a legendary escapee whose wish to get out of the Soviet Union was so overwhelming that the authorities finally decided to give him a mental disease diagnosis. The last case is a good example of fabrication in the evidence materials and of how a person could be confined in a hospital

---

[51]   Rein Randmaa has recalled his arrest in November 1977. He was accused of spying, nationalism, planning to escape to Sweden, anti-Soviet ideas etc. As he refused to admit to any of these accusations he was forcibly hospitalised at the Tallinn Psychiatry Hospital. Randmaa said he was a 'voluntary' patient, actually the KGB forced Randmaa's wife to admit just this. Randmaa spent four months at the hospital and his case history bears the mysterious words 'reactive state'. See: Rein Randmaa 'My Flight over the Cuckoo's Nest', *Eesti Aeg*, 23 March 1994.

[52]   *Dissidentlik liikumine Eestis aastatel 1972–1987: dokumentide kogumik* [Dissident movement in Estonia in 1972–1987], comp. by Arvo Pesti (Tallinn: Rahvusarhiiv, 2009), 27.

without any proof of his anti-Soviet ideas and activities. The sixth case is not connected with any anti-Soviet activity but shows how psychiatry could be used to conceal some bigger problem.

The Case of Konstantin Päts

The first president of the Republic of Estonia who was deported together with his family in the summer of 1940 was at first exiled in the town of Ufa. When the war with Germany broke out, he was arrested on 26 June 1941 and accused of connections with the German espionage and military and diplomatic circles. He was also accused of anti-Soviet activities when he was president. And even after deportation he had used anti-Soviet expressions. It goes without saying that these were fabricated accusations that were necessary to complete the order of arrest.[53]

Päts was interrogated continuously already in Ufa, the last interrogation took place on 25 August 1942.[54] On 28 August he was transferred to Moscow and the 3rd department of the NKVD continued interrogating him.[55] According to the decision of the Deputy People's Commissar for Internal Affairs Merkulov, interrogations ceased on 23 February 1943 up to a special order.[56] Beginning from March 1943 K. Päts was detained at the Kazan prison-psychiatry hospital as 'prisoner no. 12'. He was never officially tried or declared guilty.

The chief physician of the MVD Kazan prison-psychiatry hospital, major of Medical Service Major Kh. Erzhov signed a certificate about K. Päts' medical state in April 1950. The diagnosis was senility (*starcheskii psikhoz*).[57] As there is no expert assessment this statement may be considered the document replacing the latter and the basis for the enforced treatment, although this kind of form was contrary to the criminal procedure code.

---

[53] Order for arrest, 26 June 1941, RA, ERAF.198SM.1.28796.

[54] Record of interrogation, 25 August 1942, RA, ERAF.129SM.1.28796(A).

[55] Decree of the Bashkir ASSR NKVD intelligence department, 18 September 1942, RA, ERAF.129SM.1.28796(A).

[56] Decree of the USSR NKVD 3rd department, 22 February 1943, RA, ERAF.129SM.1.28796(A).

[57] Statement of the USSR MVD Kazan prison-psychiatry hospital chief physician, Medical Service Major Kh. Erzhov, 13 December 1950, RA, ERAF.129SM.1.28796(A).

Interrogations were opened again on 5 April 1952. The decree has a note that as Päts had been declared irresponsible, the posterior decision had to legalise his detention in a mental hospital.[58]

According to the summarised prosecution's closing speech on 7 April 1952, Päts was an active participant in anti-USSR activities, had contacts with German espionage and when exiled in Ufa, used anti-Soviet expressions. As experts had ascertained Päts' mental disease, he had to be hospitalised in a psychiatric hospital.[59] The USSR MGB Special Board made the necessary decision on 29 April 1952.[60]

After Stalin's death in 1953 during the rehabilitation and amnesty procedures the cases of the three former Baltic republics' leaders were also discussed. These men had been arrested and/or deported together with their families in 1940–1941 and detained in camps, special prisons or psychiatric hospitals. Among them were President of the Republic of Estonia Konstantin Päts and the Commander-in-Chief, General Johan Laidoner (who died in the Vladimir prison a week after Stalin, on 13 March 1953). On 1 June 1954 the chairman of the KGB at the Council of Ministers Colonel General Ivan Serov and the USSR Chief Prosecutor Roman Rudenko sent a memorandum to the CPSU Central Committee. It ascertains that the investigation on the leaders of the three Baltic countries[61] had been closed at a special order during the Second World War. As proposed by the MGB, the USSR Council of Ministers made the decision to transfer the cases to the USSR MGB Special Board on 4 February 1952. Every one of the leaders still alive was sentenced to 25 years of imprisonment and Päts' diagnosis of a mental disease was confirmed. That justified his detention in the Kazan specialised psychiatry hospital. Rudenko and Serov proposed

---

[58] Decree for separating documents from the file, 5 April 1952, RA, ERAF.129SM.1.28796(A).

[59] Prosecution's closing speech on 7 April 1952, confirmed by USSR Deputy Minister of State Security Affairs Ryaznyi, 8 April 1952, RA, ERAF.129SM.1.28796(A).

[60] Excerpt of report no. 32 on the Special Board at the USSR Minister of State Security, 29 April 1952, RA, ERAF.129SM.1.28796(A).

[61] Next to Päts and Laidoner the memorandum mentioned also Konstantin Päts' son Viktor, Johan Laidoner's wife Maria, the former Minister of War of Latvia Jānis Balodis (with wife), the former Minister of Foreign Affairs of Latvia Vilhelms Munters (with wife), the former Lithuanian Prime Minister Antanas Merkys (with wife and son) and the former Lithuanian Minister of Foreign Affairs Juozas Urbšys (with wife).

that the cases should be reviewed and the convicts released on condition they would not live in Estonia, Latvia and Lithuania or in the towns under special regimen.[62]

The Politburo of the CPSU CC seems to have agreed with the decision and the KGB chairman Serov confirmed the decree to release Konstantin Päts from the special psychiatry clinic and transfer him to a general psychiatric hospital but not in the so-called regime towns or Baltic republics.[63]

A posterior forensic-psychiatric act was also composed. It was dated 28 September 1954 and signed by the Kazan specialised psychiatric hospital chief physician Balashev and two department heads. According to the expertise the detainee was sometimes calm but then again restless, did not let anybody close to him, heard voices and talked to himself. Recently (i.e. in 1952–1954) he had been peaceful, did not show any interest to anything and kept generally quiet but sometimes talking to the doctor he could be garrulous. He had problems with memory. The expert assessment was that Päts was a 'calm, inactive chronic mental patient, his detention in a specialised psychiatric hospital is not necessary'.[64] It is difficult to ascertain or confute the diagnosis. Considering Päts' age (born in 1874), the imprisonment that had lasted over 10 years already and his isolation, it might even have been true, although opinions on the contrary have been expressed.[65] His last letters that were written either in 1953 or 1954 at the Kazan special psychiatric hospital and smuggled out by two Lithuanians could actually be a proof of his sound mind. Antanas Keblys had evidently

---

[62]   Roman Rudenko and Ivan Serov's memorandum to the CPSU CC on political prisoners, former Estonian, Latvian and Lithuanian leaders – *Reabilitatsiia. Kak eto bylo. Dokumenty Prezidiuma TsK KPSS i drugie materialy. V 3-kh tomakh. Tom 1. mart 1953 – fevral' 1953 – fevral' 1956*, comp. A. Artizov et al., ed. A. N. Iakovlev (Moscow: MFD Materik, 2000), 153–154.

[63]   USSR KGB decree, 29 July 1954, RA, ERAF.129SM.1.28796(A). Confirmed by the KGB Chairman Serov.

[64]   Act of the forensic-psychiatric expertise on mental patient Konstantin Päts, 28 September 1954, RA, ERAF.129SM.1.28796(A).

[65]   Heino Kään, 'Konstantin Pätsi elu lõpuaastad' [The Last Years of Konstantin Päts' Life] and Hilda Kaudre, 'Mälestusi Konstantin Pätsist Jämejalas' [Memoirs of Konstantin Päts in Jämejala], – *Alasi ja haamri vahel: artikleid ja mälestusi Konstantin Pätsist* [Between the Anvil and the Hammer, Articles and Memoirs about Konstantin Päts], ed. Anne Velliste (Tallinn: MTÜ Konstantin Pätsi Muuseum, 2007), 160–177, 274–275.

urged Päts to write these letters and Kestutis Stepšys smuggled them out. Keblys got these letters in his hands later and his cousin of the same name who lived in Montreal and managed to visit Lithuania in 1977 took them sewn in his underwear from Vilnius to New York. Two of these letters were addressed to the General Secretary of the United Nations and to his compatriots, the third and the longest letter described the conditions of eighty-year-old Päts' detention and the injustice he had to endure. Already the same year, 1977 the letters reached Ernst Jaakson, the Consul General of Estonia to New York.[66] The content of the letters does not allow us to suggest that Päts would not be of sound mind but the expertise proved that the handwriting was not his. The signatures, however, were. It might be possible that his condition did not allow him to write the letters himself and he dictated them.

The proposal of USSR Deputy Military Prosecutor, Judicial Lieutenant Colonel Krisko was dated on 19 October 1954 and suggested that the former decision of the Special Board should be changed and the patient should be sent to a general psychiatric hospital.[67] On 15 November 1954 the same kind of decision was reached by the central commission for reviewing the cases of counterrevolutionary crimes of the detainees in camps, prison colonies and in exile.[68]

On 8 December 1954 the chief physician of the Kazan specialised psychiatry hospital, A. Khalfin, reported to the KGB accounting-archive department and the chief of the MVD prison department Kuznetsov that Päts was to be released from his hospital and should be sent to Estonia. There he should be first placed in ESSR MVD prison no. 1 and from there to be transferred to the Jämejala psychiatric hospital.[69]

---

[66]   Before the Second World War Estonia had no legation in the United States, the highest representative was the Consul General in New York.

[67]   USSR chief military prosecutor's summary of the prosecution's closing speech, 19 October 1954, RA, ERAF.129SM.1.28796(A).

[68]   Extract of the statement no. 27 on revision of cases of detainees found guilty of counterrevolutionary crimes who are in USSR MVD prisons, camps and colonies or in exile, 15 November 1954, RA, ERAF.129SM.1.28796(A).

[69]   Report of the Kazan special psychiatric hospital's chief physician Major A. Khalfin to the USSR KGB accounting-archive department and the USSR MVD prisons department chief Kuznetsov, 8 December 1954, RA, ERAF.129SM.1.28796(A).

From 18 December 1954 to 29 December 1955 Päts was at the Jäme-jala mental hospital near Viljandi in Estonia. Due to extensive public attention he was transferred to Burashevo psychiatric hospital in Kalinin (Tver) oblast.[70] Witnesses say that Päts was of sound mind but had some peculiarities due to his age. According to Heino Noor, a legal aid consultant, Päts was 'burdened with long psycho trauma, followed by stress and senility'.[71] The first president of the Republic of Estonia died in Burashevo on 18 January 1956.

H. K.'s case

The criminal case was opened on 4 August 1961 due to H. K.[72] having been 'anti-Soviet and with national attitudes, spreading respective leaflets'. When his home was searched, written texts were found, e.g. 'Message no. 4 to Devoted Estonian!' that starts with the words, '[...] on the 16th of March the Estonian people are going to be asked again whether they approve of the present politics or want changes. Every Estonian has to watch the present politics with open eyes and ears in order to be able to vote for or against.'[73]

---

[70]   See the note of the ESSR KGB chairman A. Pork to the head of the USSR KGB 10th department Major General S. Seryogin on 24 April 1954, RA, ERAF.129SM.1.28796(A), Surveillance file 3, 12–14.

[71]   Noor, 'Tervisele tekitatud püsikahjud', 57.

[72]   H. K. was born in 1904 and graduated from the law school of the University of Tartu in 1932. He worked as an assistant of attorney-at-law in Tallinn and in 1939–1940 as accountant of St John's parish congregation in Tallinn. In 1940/41 he was accountant of the sports society *Dynamo*. He was mobilised into the Red Army in the summer of 1941 and taken to the ship *Eestirand* that was wrecked off the Estonian coast. So the mobilised and the prisoners escaped being sent to the Soviet rear. During the German occupation H. K. lived on his father's farm and managed to escape the German mobilisation in 1944. In 1944–46 he worked as a fire fighter in Nõmme, in 1946–49 lived on his father's farm again. In 1949–61 he was accountant, later a furnace- and watchman at the furniture factory *Standard*. In 1961–63 he was under enforced treatment, in 1963–66 worker at the metal plant *Vasar*. He retired in 1966. Died in 1992.

[73]   RA, ERAF.130SM.1.4271, 79.

He slipped his messages into people's letterboxes. They were signed either 'Rescue committee' or 'Group of honest citizens' or 'Estonian principal socialists'.

Vigilant citizens took some of these messages to the KGB, of course. So, for example, E. Kuslap who sent the message to the KGB on 2 February added a note,

'I received the enclosed anonymous letter with an anti-Soviet content that begins with the words – "The brave people, keep and save our messages!" As the letter is anti-Soviet I pass it on to you.'[74]

There are several letters of the kind in the file.[75] It was not always the addressees' loyalty to the system or vigilance – quite often the people were evidently afraid of a provocation that was one of the items of the KGB control over the population.

At the interrogation K. explained his views as follows,

'I am a principal supporter of socialism. I am for all the right principles of socialism like, for example those –

1. *Every nation must have a right for freedom and happiness.*
2. *Every nation has to be the master of their country.*
3. *An end must be put to the colonisation of other people's lands.*
4. *Everybody must have the right to live free and happy in his/her land.*[76]*'*

At the next interrogation that was carried out by the KGB Senior Lieutenant Kasak explained his letters and leaflets as follows,

'I have been making similar messages since 1957, spreading them by post. [...] I do not admit that they are anti-Soviet, only national and socialist in content. What makes me dissatisfied is the fact that so many Russians migrate to Estonia, and that, as I understand, would make Estonians a minority in their own country and a minority cannot be the master of his country.'[77]

---

[74] E. Kuslap to the ESSR KGB, 2 February 1961, RA, ERAF.130SM.1.4271, 53.

[75] E. Kuslap to the ESSR KGB, 2 February 1961, RA, ERAF.130SM.1.4271, 53.

[76] Explanation of H. K., 4 August 1961, RA, ERAF.130SM.1.4271, 53.

[77] Interrogation report of H. K., 5 August 1961, RA, ERAF.130SM.1.4271, 20–21.

There was actually nothing wrong in his utterances, but KGB still made a conclusion that he was mentally unbalanced and should be taken to psychiatric expertise.[78]

The Tallinn State Psychiatric Hospital presented the expertise act signed by chief physician Udo Luts, department head Risto Reala and department chief physician Ellen-Erika Härma on 24 August 1961. The experts ascertained that K. 'propagated bourgeois nationalism, hatred between nations, slandered Soviet reality and the policy of the CPSU, behaved in a peculiar way during the interrogations, giving illogical explanations that were unrealistic and naïve for a person of his age and education'. Due to the expertise it became clear that his unbalanced mental state became apparent in his ideas about socialism that declined from the party line. The expertise assessment was that K. was irresponsible and the diagnosis was 'psychopathic personality chronic mental activity disturbance paranoiac development'.[79]

Although he was neither a (political) criminal nor a mental case and might have been only an eccentric, they could not let him be free and that is why he was detained for enforced treatment. The latter was worded by the ESSR Supreme Court (presiding judge was Hilda Uusküla) on 29 September 1961. His criminal case was closed and he was declared irresponsible.[80]

He was transferred to the special psychiatry hospital in Leningrad. A new expertise on 13 March 1963, with S. Torubarov from the Serbsky Forensic-Psychiatry Institute presiding, decided that the treatment must continue (with small doses of insulin, labour therapy, psychotherapy etc.).[81]

Based on the expertise before, the ESSR Supreme Court decided on 22 April 1963 that the patient may be transferred to the residential psychiatric hospital and the enforced treatment was concluded the same year.[82]

---

[78] ESSR KGB investigation department regulation, 21 August 1961, RA, ERAF.130SM.1.4271, 101–103.

[79] The forensic-psychiatric ambulatory expertise assessment act of the Tallinn State Psychiatric Hospital, 24 August 1961, RA, ERAF.130SM.1.4271, 104–106.

[80] Minutes of the session of the ESSR Supreme Court, 29 September 1961, RA, ERAF.130SM.1.4271, 114–114v.

[81] Act of the forensic-psychiatric expertise, 13 March 1963, RA, ERAF.130SM.1.4271, 118–118v.

[82] Decree of the ESSR Supreme Court, 22 April 1963, RA, ERAF.130SM.1.4271, 123–124.

Juhan Lapman's case

Juhan Lapman's story is considerably more adventurous. He had migrated to the USA in 1937. In January 1940 he returned home and in 1941 he was the chairman of the Nõva Parish Soviet of Workers' Deputies Executive Committee. Together with the rest of 'soviet active cadres' he was evacuated into the Soviet rear. In 1942 he was caught when he attempted to cross the border in the vicinity of Motovabad, Central Asia. He was accused of espionage but he was soon released. He was not mobilised due to ill health. In 1945 he was caught again on board of the British ship *Empire Peacemaker* in Archangel. In 1947 he, under the name of Oskar Kuuse, was sentenced to eight-year imprisonment. This time the State Security did not discover his real name. In 1948 he escaped the Gnesbekost camp (in the Komi ASSR). After a hazardous journey he managed to get back to Estonia.

He managed to hide himself for some time at his home village in Nõva. There he built a sailing boat of twigs, a trench coat and other available materials and sailed towards Finland in November 1948. As he had no compass he sailed straight into the Soviet naval base in Porkkala. At the beginning of the interrogations he called himself Henry Parker, born in New York and living in Stockholm without a Swedish citizenship. He could not conceal his true identity for long and at the interrogation on 29 November he admitted to his 'real' name Oskar Kuuse and said where he lived.[83] This was reason enough to arrest his sister and uncle. On 20 July 1949 Lapman was sentenced for 25 and his helpers for 10 years of imprisonment.[84] Lapman was released in 1958.

But all this did not put an end to his wish to escape from the USSR. In 1972 he made a new attempt. In a motorboat he managed to reach about the centre of the Baltic Sea, where a Danish fishing trawler picked him up. Unfortunately, his boat had been sighted from the Latvian trawler *Kutum*,

---

[83]   Records of interrogating detainee Henry Parker, 18 November 1948, 29 November 1948, 28 December 1948, RA, ERAF.130SM.1.9126 (I), 33–36, 58–68v, 122–125; Certificate of the interrogation and detention materials concerning a demarcation line violator, compiled by Major Shkurko, deputy commander of unit no. 70085 intelligence department, 11 April 1949, RA, ERAF.130SM.1.9126(V), 133–136.

[84]   Excerpt from record no. 39 of Special Board at the USSR Minister of the State Security, 20 July 1949, RA, ERAF.130SM.1.9126(III), 153–155.

the crew of which reported about it to their base in Ventspils. Several Soviet border guard ships started to pursue the Danish trawler. Although the captain of the latter denied any escapee's presence on board, the Soviet border guard attacked the Danish trawler in international waters and took Lapman away.[85]

At the interrogation on 12 September Lapman admitted that he had been aware of his location and activity but all the info that he had, belonged to the competence of the CPSU CC. To the question why he had been on board of the Danish fishing trawler he answered that he had lost his bearings in the dark and having no proper map had had no opportunity to turn back. At the 14 September interrogation in the military border guard unit that had captured him, he admitted that he had been arrested after the war but did not remember for what and for how long he had been detained. As he did not want 'his sister to know that he was spending money on trifles' he registered the boat on the name of a local boy, Aare Hagus. He said that he had spent most of his August vacation in the boat on the inland rivers and lakes and the coastal waters off Pärnu, Riga and Haapsalu. He said he did not remember how he left the coastal waters behind and got lost. He had encountered the Danish trawler quite by chance and as the weather had changed and he was short of fuel, he decided to board the trawler. The Danes had promised to take him to Gotland and Lapman agreed. The question why there had been such an amount of water and food on board he answered that this was fixed in the rules in case you get shipwrecked. He answered the question about his personal belongings with an explanation that he was afraid of burglars during his absence from home. Actually, there was nothing strange in his story, perhaps only his demand that he wanted to be connected to the CPSU CC and the USSR Council of Ministers in order to discuss the publication of his theoretical work on economy.[86]

His last workplaces, the V. Klementi Garment Factory and the experimental mechanical plant *Mehis,* gave the locksmith Lapman character

---

[85]   Record of J. L.'s arrest, 8 September 1972; Record of the search of personal belongings, 14 September 1972, RA, ERAF.129SM.1.29052 (I), 8–16v, 18–55.

[86]   Records of the suspect's interrogation, 12, 14, 15 and 20 September 1972, RA, ERAF.129SM.1.29052 (I), 71–101v.

references of 'a diligent, modest, introvert but friendly person who did not take an active part in social life'.[87]

Several people were interrogated but it does not become clear whether anybody was aware of Lapman's plans to escape. Some witnesses, though, hinted at a possibility of such plans. So, for example, the captain of the yacht that belonged to the V. Klementi Garment Factory said that once, half-jokingly, Lapman had asked to be taken to Sweden. The provisions in the boat had also been a proof of the wish to escape. It seems that Lapman's past became the pointer of balance. There were no direct accusations against him. The formal reason for sending him to have psychiatric treatment might have been his manuscript 'Anatomy of Economy' that contained a few apolitical pointers how to fight the economic crises.[88] The character reference given from the Klementi Factory also mentions that economy was Lapman's hobby but that he never bothered anybody with his opinions and did not have any supporters either.

According to the decree of the KGB investigation department on 4 October 1972 Lapman was sent to the forensic-psychiatric expertise. It was decided that as Lapman was interested in the theory of economy and had tried to escape from the Soviet Union for several times, he must have been mentally ill. Lapman had also got therapy for his radiculitis in the Tallinn Psycho-Neurological Hospital in 1961.

The forensic-psychiatric commission that consisted of Udo Luts, Regina Kon and Vsevolod Grünthal reported the results of the expertise on 26 November 1972. The case history started with the statement that Lapman was psychically disturbed and needed treatment. A survey of the patient's' biography and his attempts to escape from the Soviet Union follow. The therapy for radiculitis at the psychiatric hospital was mentioned, too. The patient's physical condition was declared normal, in his psychic assessment it was mentioned that he understood very well, where he was and that his conversation with the doctors was tense, the patient was watchful and suspicious. He did not answer the questions immediately, he first thought them over and then replied briefly. He refused to say anything about his life and advised the doctors to ask that from the secu-

---

[87]   Character references of J. L. from the V. Klementi Garment Combine and the experimental mechanic plant *Mehis* at the ESSR Ministry of Food Industry, September 1972, RA, ERAF.129SM.1.29052 (I), 63–65.

[88]   'Anatomy of Economy', RA, ERAF.129SM.1.29052 (II), 36–100.

rity authorities. Making an 'inadequate' joke, the patient mentioned that his conversation with the doctors was exactly on par with that he had had with the KGB officers. He considered himself an expert of economy but he had only six-year education. This was the only reproach as the doctors were not interested in the article itself. Obviously it was concluded that a six-year education would not allow him to assess economic problems.

The conclusion was that Lapman was schizophrenic and not able to be responsible for his actions. The act of expertise does not show what exactly was schizophrenic in Lapman's conduct. It may be concluded that the whole assessment was a political commission, as there is nothing in the case history that would show that the patient might be a danger to himself or to other human beings. However, he might have been dangerous to the society, as he had tried to escape from the Soviet Union for several times. Besides, it was not proper for unauthorised persons to doubt the state's economic-political foundations.[89]

The decree of Captain Pimenov, senior investigator of the Estonian SSR KGB investigation department, is dated on 8 December 1972. ESSR prosecutor Karl Kimmel confirmed the document on 11 December and the case was transferred for trial.[90] The ESSR Supreme Court criminal chamber's judge H. Uusküla decided to send Lapman for enforced treatment in a specialised psychiatric hospital on 19 December 1972.[91]

In March 1973 Lapman was sent to the Chelyabinsk specialised psychiatric hospital where he was detained until August of 1976. Then the enforced treatment was concluded and the patient was to be transferred to a general psychiatric hospital. On 24 August 1976 he was registered as a patient in the Tallinn Psycho-Neurological Hospital. On 17 May 1977 a forensic-psychiatric assessment concluded the enforced treatment. The assistant chief physician Endel Päll, department chief physician Helve Gofman and department chief physician Leili Cherkasova signed the expert assessment. The commission ascertained the following about Lapman who had spent years under enforced treatment –

---

[89]   Act of the stationary psychiatric expertise no. 160, 28 November 1972, RA, ERAF.129SM.1.29052 (II), 200–203.

[90]   Decree on transferring to court the case of a person who has committed a socially dangerous crime in order to force him to be medically treated, 8 December 1972, RA, ERAF.129SM.1.29052 (II), 206–209.

[91]   Minutes of the ESSR Supreme Court criminal chamber's session and the court's decision, 19 December 1972, RA, ERAF.129SM.1.29052(II), 215–218v.

He is single, lived alone. Is said to have coped with his life. The beginning of the mental disease is impossible to determine. Was restless already in childhood, had lots of fantasy. Later became interested in various philosophical problems. He attempted to cross the border on poetic motifs.[92] *As can be seen from the material gathered in the special hospital, he behaved well there, worked properly and his delusional production decreased. Having been at the present hospital since August 1976, he has behaved well. He goes to work at the therapy workshops and has not violated the regime. His mental processes seem complicated and are hard to observe. Has disturbances in the thought process, his concentration ability has diminished. A few single paranoiac delusions have appeared but they have lost their actuality. He does not write any more. Emotional-intentional level has lowered, he is numb and insensitive. His critical ability has subsided. He goes to work regularly and takes care of himself. Aggressiveness and antisocial thoughts have not occurred.*

Conclusion – Suffers from chronic mental disease in the form of schizophrenia. It was established that Lapman was not a danger to the society any longer. On 23 May the proposal to put an end to the enforced treatment was sent to the Estonian SSR Supreme Court.[93]

The Estonian SSR Supreme Court's criminal chamber presided by Asta Tooming decided that the forensic-psychiatric assessment expertise was justified and should be granted. To be more exact – to conclude the enforced treatment and continue in a general psychiatric hospital on general basis.[94] Later Lapman was sent to the Võisiku (in Central Estonia) care home as a person without active legal capacity and told not to leave the place. In 1989 Lapman managed to get a certificate that annulled without active legal capacity and declared him responsible. On 20 September 1989 the expert commission of the Tartu Psychiatric Hospital (the chief physician A. Adamsoo, H. Ligi and department head H. Lepp) decided that 'accordingly to his psychic condition J. Lapman is able to live alone and

---

[92] Expertise assessment – 'Had been compiling an economy collection in his free time and wanted to go abroad to publish it in Switzerland'.

[93] Act of the stationary forensic-psychiatry expertise no. 92, 17 May 1977, RA, ERAF.129SM.1.29052 (II), 230–231.

[94] Decree of the ESSR Supreme Court criminal chamber, 6 July 1977, RA, ERAF.129SM.1.29052 (II), 245–246.

participate at the trial'. On 11 October 1989 the Jõgeva People's Court decided that J. Lapman was 'with active legal capacity' and the guardianship was annulled. On 28 October he was released from the Võisiku 'hostel'. In 1989 at the Hotel *Viru* J. Lapman managed to get acquainted with an American journalist John Hamer, who provided him with an invitation to the United States. Juhan Lapman took off in the Leningrad-New York plane on 11 October 1990 and thus finally, after numerous attempts, he managed to leave the Soviet Union.[95]

S. K.'s case

The Estonian SSR KGB opened a criminal case against S. K. based on the accusation of Ats Suvisild on 23 December 1974. It started from a parcel that had been addressed to Heiki Sähka that the latter had to pass to Ats Suvisild. Suvisild and Sähka became curious, opened the suitcase, found two texts with anti-Soviet content and handed the suitcase over to the KGB.[96] On 31 December S. K. was interrogated and admitted that he had started to write articles critical of the Soviet Union under the name of Lev Gorn in the 1960s but had never spread them anywhere.[97]

S. K. had been working as a manager in the Pärnu Drama Theatre named after Lydia Koidula. His flat and workplace were searched on 24 December[98] and on 20 January 1975 he was arrested.

[...] *in 1967–1973 composed the texts 'For not bureaucratic socialism' and 'What the Russian people are going to do now?' in order to spread them*

---

[95]   Certificate of the Republic of Estonia Prosecutor's Office department head M. Tibar, 19 November 1990, ERAF.129SM.1.29052 (II), 254; Jaak Pihlau, 'Lehekülgi Eesti lähiajaloost. Merepõgenemised okupeeritud Eestist' [Pages from Estonian Latest History. Escapes over the Sea from Occupied Estonia], *Tuna*, no. 2 (2001): 76–80.

[96]   ESSR KGB investigation department's decree about opening a criminal case and procedure, 23 December 1974, RA, ERAF.130SM.1.11181 (I), 1–2.

[97]   Record of S. K.'s interrogation, 31 December 1974, RA, ERAF.130SM.1.11181 (I), 15–17.

[98]   Search warrant from the ESSR KGB investigation department from 23 December and records of the search on 24 December 1974, RA, ERAF.130SM.1.11181 (I), 8–14.

and weaken the soviet power. The texts contain slanderous and denigrating expressions about the state and social order. He kept these texts at his place of residence until 1973, when he passed them to a person, not ascertained, for copying.[99] *In the summer of 1947 he got 44 complete and 27 incomplete copies together with a duplicator from that person.*[100]

The charge was based on Estonian SSR Criminal Code's § 68, section 1 (i.e. anti-Soviet agitation).[101] At the interrogation K. admitted that he had written the texts but emphasised that there was nothing anti-Soviet or disparaging the social system in them. Thus they could not weaken Soviet power and he was not guilty.[102] What he thought about the Soviet system was as follows –

I began to write texts including critical remarks about the soviet social order I 1964, By that time I was convinced that our society did not operate properly, in my opinion. I found that although the personal cult period had been publicly condemned, not all the political and economic errors of the period had been liquidated. In my opinion the soviet citizens have yet not been granted all the rights the international conventions foresee. Among other rights the right for freedom of speech and the right to leave the Soviet Union freely.[103]

---

[99]   According to S. K.'s own testimony given during the interrogation this person was a German named Wolf, 50–60 years of age, a sturdy man who spoke Russian fluently. On 22 January 1975 he confessed that he copied the material himself when he was the manager of the Pärnu information and computing centre and had access to the necessary technology. He had copied the texts in his own bathroom and used his washing machine's roller. As for Wolf, he really existed and K. knew him, but never gave his texts to Wolf.

[100]   Decree of the indictment of the accused, 20 January 1975; decree on applying the deterrent, 20 January 1975, RA, ERAF.130SM.1.11181 (I), 18–19, 23–25.

[101]   Decree of the indictment of the accused, 20 January 1975; decree on applying the deterrent, 20 January 1975, RA, ERAF.130SM.1.11181 (I), 18–19, 23–25.

[102]   Record of S. K.'s interrogation, 20 January 1975, RA, ERAF.130SM.1.11181 (I), 20–21.

[103]   Record of S. K.'s interrogation, 20 January 1975, RA, ERAF.130SM.1.11181 (I), 20–21.

This was the reason for having written the before-mentioned texts. When he was in Moscow in August 1974, he put about 20 texts in Russian translation[104] into some letterboxes in the Arbat region. About the same number of texts were spread in Leningrad on Vassili Island and on Nevsky Prospect. A few copies that he could not spread were in the above-mentioned suitcase and got into the KGB hands thanks to vigilant citizens.[105]

At the interrogation on 30 January 1975 S. K. said more about his activities on 2 – 18 January 1975. He had asked his friends to forward his letters to the Estonian SSR Council of Ministers, the KGB and the ESSR Writers' Union. In these letters he had described his situation and said he had given up his Soviet citizenship and wanted to leave the country. A little bit different letters were addressed to writers Uno Laht and Aadu Hint, to the elder of the Tallinn Baptist congregation Osvalt Tärk, to Mikhail Bronshtein from University of Tartu and some others.[106]

All his workplaces – the Pärnu Information and Computation Centre, the Pärnu Council of Workers' Deputies Executive Committee and the Pärnu Drama Theatre gave him rather good character references. He was said to have been a dutiful and polite colleague who sometimes neglected some smaller things in management.[107]

Quite possibly the enforced treatment decision was caused by his check-up at the Tallinn Psycho-Neurological Hospital in April 1970. It does not become clear in the file, why the check-up was needed.[108]

Witnesses' interrogations led the investigation department to the conclusion that S. K. is 'remote from life and tries to express his thoughts in written form that has left a strage impression on people'. On 7 March 1975 the deputy head of the Estonian SSR KGB investigation department

---

[104] Ahto Siig, S. K.'s acquaintance, translated the texts and his criminal case was opened as well.

[105] Record of S. K.'s interrogation, 22 January 1975, RA, ERAF.130SM.1.11181 (I), 38–42.

[106] *Ibid.*, 43–44v.

[107] S. K.'s character references from the Pärnu Information and Computing Centre, Council of Working People's Deputies Executive Committee dwelling management and Pärnu Drama Theatre, 24–28 January 1975, RA, ERAF.130SM.1.11181 (I), 31–37.

[108] Certificate of the Tallinn Psycho-Neurological Hospital chief physician U. Luts and department head A. Augla, 8 January 1975, RA, ERAF.130SM.1.11181 (IV), 153.

Nikitin confirmed the expert assessment that sent S. K. to psychiatric expertise.[109]

The expert commission consisting of Udo Luts, V. Jänes and Regina Kon presented their assessment on 7 May 1975. It included composing and spreading of manuscripts, mentioned the check-up in the Psycho-Neurological Hospital and also recalled S. K.'s parents who had been declared 'people's enemies'. His father had died during his detention in Siberia in 1950 and his mother had emigrated in 1944. The expert assessment considered his ability to read at an early age and his interest in politics. His contemplation of the issues of philosophy and social life was rebuked as he 'did not have corresponding education'. The final conclusion of the commission was that S. K. was mentally ill and needed to be treated in a hospital subjected to the Ministry of Healthcare.[110]

On 26 May 1975 the ESSR prosecutor Karl Kimmel confirmed the KGB investigation department's decree, according to which

The stationary forensic-psychiatric expertise act shows that S.K. (full name given in the original) has been suffering from a chronic mental disease in the form of schizophrenic paranoia since childhood. During the actions incriminated to him, he was irresponsible, i.e. he could not control himself or understand what he was doing. At present he is not able to accept the criminal responsibility and needs enforced treatment in a general psychiatric hospital.[111]

The Estonian SSR Supreme Court presided by judge Hilda Uusküla still decided on 3 June 1975 to send S. K. to the USSR MVD specialised psy-

---

[109] Expert assessment 7 March 1975, recorded by ESSR KGB investigation department's First Lieutenant Veinberg, RA, ERAF.130SM.1.11181, 154–156.

[110] Act of stationary forensic-psychiatric expertise no. 92, 7 May 1975, RA, ERAF.130SM.1.11181 (IV), 160–166.

[111] Decree on transferring to the court the criminal case of a person who has committed a socially dangerous act, imposing the medical enforced treatment, compiled by ESSR KGB investigation department's First Lieutenant Veinberg, RA, ERAF.130SM.1.11181 (IV), 130–135.

chiatry hospital.[112] He never got there as he committed suicide in the preliminary confinement prison on 8 August 1975.[113]

L. K.'s case

On 22 July 1971the *Dvigatel* plant director Boris Kuznetsov and the secretary of the party committee A. Lazarev addressed a complaint to the KGB. The complaint was about the electrician of the plant, L. K. who was said to be anti-Soviet and had behaved outrageously. He had made anti-Soviet propaganda and disfigured the Soviet reality, simultaneously praising Israel, the USA and the Federal Republic of Germany.[114]

L. K. was arrested on 22 October 1971 (for anti-Soviet agitation) according to the ESSR Criminal Code § 68 section 1. Evidently even more significant was the complaint of Viktor Kanosh to the KGB on 22 September 1971. K. had asked him for 'dynamite in order to explode the *Dvigatel* powerhouse'.[115] Another criminal episode that was ascertained was K.'s anonymous letter to the editor of the newspaper *Birobidzhaner Shtern* B. Miller in the Jewish Autonomous Region. The letter contained expressions that were 'anti-Soviet and Zionist'.[116]

After the interrogations of K. and the witnesses it was decided to send L. K. to forensic-psychiatric expertise and the decree about that also con-

---

[112] Record of the session of the ESSR Supreme Court (Uusküla, Lall, Prokof'eva) on 3 June 1975; criminal case no. KI-041 1975, decree, 3 June 1975, RA, ERAF.130SM.1.11181(IV), 186–187.

[113] Notice of the ESSR Ministry of Internal Affairs no. 1 to the ESSR KGB investigation Department, 1 September 1975, RA, ERAF.130SM.1.11183 (IV), 196. See also: *Dissidentlik liikumine Eestis,* 201–219; Jaak Pihlau, 'Eesti demokraatlik põrandaalune ja kontaktid Läänega 1970-1985' [Estonian Democratic Underground and Contacts with the West 1970–1985], part 4, *Tuna,* no. 1 (2005): 104–105; *Lisandusi uudiste ja mõtete,* vol. 1, 19–20.

[114] Complaint of the *Dvigatel* plant director B. Kuznetsov and secretary of the party committee A. Lazarev to the ESSR KGB, 22 July 1971, RA, ERAF.130SM.1.10558, 4.

[115] Record of opening and processing a criminal case, 12 October 1971, RA, ERAF.130SM.1.10558, 2–3, 183–184.

[116] Photo-copy of the anonymous letter addressed to the assistant editor of *Birobidzhaner Shtern* and Decree of adding a material evidence to the file, 27 December 1971, RA, ERAF.130SM.1.10558, 249–250.

tains what he was accused of. He had been making anti-Soviet propaganda among his friends and colleagues already for years, he had denigrated the state system of the USSR, the Communist Party etc. The expertise discovered and used it against him that he had had several unpleasant events in his private life, at school and at work (He had studied at the Tallinn Polytechnic Institute but by the time of the interrogation he was not a student any more). He also admitted that at the age of 13 he had fallen from horseback and lost consciousness. When he was conscripted for service in the border guard troops in 1962–1963, he had had headaches and been hospitalised. All this was used later in the expertise act, just like his diary that contained anti-Soviet expressions. The investigator concluded that K. was psychically unstable and transferred the case to the Tallinn Psycho-Neurological Hospital with the questions if K. had been mentally ill when he committed his 'crime' and if he needed psychiatric help. K. was placed in isolation ward no. 1.[117]

The forensic-psychiatric expertise act from the psychiatry hospital bears the date 6 January 1972. The chief physician Udo Luts, the deputy Vsevolod Grünthal and the head of the forensic-psychiatry department Regina Kon had signed the act. The chief psychiatrist of the ESSR Ministry of Healthcare and psychiatry professor of the University of Tartu Jüri Saarma, also participated in the expertise assessment. The patient's physical condition was said to be good. His former life has been described; a worker, uncompleted higher education, no criminal record, etc. The headaches and fall were mentioned. His studies at the institute had been rather promising, although economy did not interest K. much. He was more interested in art and it was his hobby also in his free time after work at the *Dvigatel* plant, where it caused a conflict with the administration. He must have had more disagreements with the party functionaries. Among other things he had defended the activities of Israel [in the 1967 war. *Author's remark*] against the official standpoint of the USSR (K. was Jewish.) Already at the institute he had wanted to discuss the same issue. This seemed to be his biggest expression of anti-Soviet ideas and the expertise goes into details about his Zionism.

It seems that his loquacity during the assessment was fatal for him and it was used to make up the diagnosis of a mental illness. He had said he was an artist but he had not had any training for it. He had a very bad

---

[117] Decree on forensic-psychiatric expertise, 1 November 1971, RA, ERAF.130SM.1.10558, 28–29.

opinion of the administration of the plant and did not keep it to himself. He did not seem to worry about his future and did not care whether he would be sent to prison or an asylum. His opinion that he was a 'political detainee' was taken as one of the symptoms of his illness. (Actually, he was, as he was detained on § 68.) He hoped he would be able to continue and finish his studies in the future and also get education in art. All the 'symptoms' were taken into consideration and the commission made the conclusion that they had been dealing with a 'paranoiac schizophrenic', who had had the disease already since he was 19 years old.

The dossier does not make it clear what in all these symptoms was anti-Soviet and the experts did not evidently pay much attention to it. The final conclusion was: Owing to his psychic condition K. is not able to be responsible for what he does and when committing his crime, he was *non compos mentis*. The commission recommended hospitalisation in a MVD specialised psychiatric hospital.[118]

It is not clear how such conclusions were made but some hints suggest that the doctors had used also the diary and correspondence of K. The KGB has recorded confiscated materials and their 'analysis' of them – some phrases out of context have been presented as evidence etc. His diary from 1964–1967 was taken as a significant find as it contained several expressions of dubious value. For example – 'Freedom, oh how sweet it smells but I cannot sniff it yet'; 'Goods are expensive, food is expensive. One hears how they live there [in capitalist countries. *Author's remark*] and thinks, why the Soviet citizen suffers. Perhaps because he is stupid?' [119]

It is difficult to understand from all these documents why the commission decided to send K. to a specialised hospital for very dangerous lunatics. None of the documents show that he could have been a danger to the society. Even his character reference from the *Dvigatel* plant director B. Kuznetsov, party committee secretary A. Lazarev, trade union committee chairman M. Kozyrev and the young communist league secretary V. Bodrenkov does not make it any clearer. They mention a few violations of discipline (e.g. art hobby in his free time), some conflicts with the authorities. As for his anti-Soviet activities they mention only that K. did not

---

[118] Act of the stationary forensic-psychiatric expertise no. 1-71, 6 January 1972, made up by the commission consisting of Udo Luts, Vsevolod Grünthal and Regina Kon, RA, ERAF.130SM.1.10558, 30–35.

[119] Record of document observation, 2 November 1971, RA, ERAF.130SM.1.10558, 42–46.

participate in the 1970 and 1971 elections. (Hereby we should remember that according to the Soviet constitution participation in the confidential elections was a matter of conscience. So, if it really became an open secret that L. K. had not participated, it could not have been a point of accusation. As a soviet citizen he had the right not to participate.) The character record contains one sentence about K. having praised democracy and gave the USA, Israel and the German FR as good examples of it.[120]

On 11 January 1972 the KGB investigation department passed the decree on starting the enforced medical treatment to the Estonian SSR deputy prosecutor Karl Kimmel, who confirmed it on 12 January and the case was transferred to the Estonian SSR Supreme Court for final decision. The decree was based on the expertise commission's (presided by Udo Luts) act that made the conclusion about K. as an 'haughty and quarrelsome person, inclined to engage in intrigues'.[121]

The 27 January 1972 session of the Estonian SSR Supreme Court, presided by H. Uusküla declared K. irresponsible and decided he should be hospitalised in a special psychiatric ward for especially dangerous patients.[122] He was sent to the Chernyakhovsk special psychiatric hospital from which he was released on 17 July 1975.[123]

The story has an epilogue. During the *perestroika* and *glasnost* in the second half of the 1980s several cases of persons unjustly tried and sentenced we re-examined, among them were the misapplications of enforced psychiatric treatment. L. K. protested the expertise and his hospitalisation in 1989. What turned out when his protest was processed is quite a good evaluation of Soviet forensic psychiatry the assessments of which were made to order. On 23 October 1989 the legal representative of L. K. Leon Glikman from Tallinn Legal Consultation Office No. 1 presented a surveillance appeal to the Estonian SSR prosecutor. The appeal gives a brief

---

[120] Character reference of L. K., 19 November 1971; Decree of starting the legal proceedings in order to apply enforced medical treatment for the person who has committed a crime endangering the society, compiled by Major Silkin, 11 January 1972, RA, ERAF.130SM.1.10558, 299–300.

[121] *Ibid.*, 310–311.

[122] ESSR Supreme Court record, 27 January 1972, RA, ERAF.130SM.1.10558, 322–330.

[123] Request of Ü. Roots, assistant prosecutor of the Estonian SSR to the Presidium of the ESSR Supreme Court concerning archive criminal case no. 29049 about L. K., RA, ERAF.130SM.1.10558, 342.

survey of the case, the result of which was that K. was dismissed from his job, removed from the list of extramural students of the Tallinn Polytechnic Institute and was sentenced to have enforced medical treatment as an especially dangerous mental patient. The appeal stresses several judicially dubious measures and actions that were applied. So, for example, the attributes of a criminal case (anti-Soviet activities) were missing. The most significant witness statement (Kanysh's claim about the diversion being prepared) had not been proved. Kanysh did not appear at the trial and the court proceeded from the statements given during preliminary investigation that the court did not check. Besides, Kanysh was the person whose witness statement should have been suspected as he had no opportunity to get any explosives and he had no confidential relationship with K. Was Kanysh an instigator used for fabrication of pieces of evidence? We cannot prove it and the investigation records usually do not show it either. K.'s Zionist views had not been proved either and even if they had, Soviet legal practice did not foresee punishment for that.

The expertise act was more than questionable in Glikman's opinion –

The forensic-psychiatric act provokes doubt. It shows neither paranoiac-schizophrenic characteristics nor the clinical overview. The illness is mainly based on K.'s (in the file here and further on the full name is given) ideology. His non-standardised ideology and way of thinking are by no means characteristics of a mental disease. [...] The conclusions the forensic-psychiatric expertise made provoke suspicion also because it is said that K. has had schizophrenia since he was 19. At that time he was in service in the border guard troops, after having passed the medical commission.[124] At the time of this supposed illness he studied[125] and also worked at the Dvigatel plant. [...] The expertise act does not show, why enforced treatment in a specialised hospital was recommended. The court decision does not have any motif for that either.

---

[124] When young men were conscripted into the border guard troops that were subjected to the KGB, the medical check up was much more severe than usual.

[125] At the admission to higher educational establishments one had to present a special medical certificate (form 286) from the previous medical check up. At least theoretically this certificate should have avoided admitting persons sick and unable to study.

The request was concluded by the appeal to cancel the Estonian SSR Supreme Court criminal college's decree from 27 January 1972 and concluded the criminal case proceedings as there are no necessary elements of a criminal offence.[126]

The Estonian SSR Prosecutor's Office renewed the process on 25 November 1989 and commissioned a new forensic-psychiatric expertise.[127] The ambulatory forensic-psychiatric expertise was made in the Tallinn Psycho-Neurological Hospital, the assessment act was presented on 15 February 1990. Psychotherapists Airi Värnik, Elmar Karu, Innar Tergem, Anu Kasmel, Jaanus Mumma, Endel Päll and forensic psychologist Tiina Kompus signed it. The final conclusions are significant:

1. L. K. was not mentally ill in 1971–1972.
2. L. K. is not mentally ill at the moment (at the beginning of 1990).[128]

Having received the act of expertise, the Estonian SSR prosecutor's office presented the Estonian SSR Supreme Court Presidium with a protest. They advised to declare the enforced treatment of L. K. unjust and the decree of the ESSR Supreme Court on 27 January 1972 null and void, fully rehabilitating L. K. The decision was made on 26 March 1990.[129]

M. K.'s case

The last case is not connected with dissidents or punitive medicine but describes one facet of the disorder in the Soviet army and the misuse of psychiatry for concealing its faults and drawbacks.

---

[126] Surveillance request of the defence lawyer from Tallinn Legal Consultation Office No. 1 to the Estonian SSR Supreme Court criminal cases college on 27 January 1972, on enforced medical treatment case, 23 October 1989, RA, ERAF.130SM.1.19558, 344–347.

[127] Decree of the ESSR assistant prosecutor A. Tooming on renewing the criminal process in connection with a new forensic-psychiatric evidence in archive criminal case no. 29049, 24 November 1989, RA, ERAF.130SM.1.19558, 358.

[128] Act no. 96 of ambulatory forensic-psychiatric expertise, 15 February 1990, RA, ERAF.130SM.1.19558, 348–357.

[129] Certificate of rehabilitation, 26 March 1990, by the ESSR Supreme Court Presidium Vice Chairman V. Litvinov, RA, ERAF.130SM.1.19558, 359–361.

The relationships with their hierarchies among the conscripts in the Soviet Army reminded those in Soviet detention establishments. Everyday life in the army was subjected to the *dedovshchina* – a phenomenon that ensured at least part of the discipline and was quietly approved both by the higher military and party command. Its most-spread form was the arbitrary conduct of the older servicemen over the younger ones. (The infantry troops were conscripted for two years, the navy for three. So new youngsters were brought into the unit every half-year.) Persecution did not depend only on the age of the victim – it could well be for national reasons or something else. It was rather a public secret as so many young men were conscripted and many of them talked but only with the *perestroika* did it become truly public through the press. It was a great shock when Lithuanian Antanas Sakalauskas who had been victimised physically and psychically for a long time shot eight of his fellow conscripts. Sakalauskas' case was certainly not the only one, it had happened before that the victimised youngster killed his torturers, committed suicide or broke entirely spiritually and mentally. The army was a closed structure and such cases were only rumoured. On the pretext of 'keeping the military secrets' the conscripts had to keep quiet also after the service. During the *perestroika* though, by and by such cases became public.[130]

In case of M. K. the events connected to special psychiatry began in the Turkestan Military District, Kazakhstan, in April 1989. He served with the internal troops at Chimkent, unit no 6506. On 17 May 1989 an application arrived at the registration department of the Estonian SSR Supreme Soviet Presidium and the check-in registration card has the following message –

M. K. was conscripted on 30 June 1987. On 26 April 1989 at 10 p.m. he shot a volley (eight bullets) into the commander of the guard's chest. The first sergeant[131] was killed. His name was F. and he came from Krasnodar. [...] My son was very nervous and wrote already earlier that he was being victimised and if it won't get better he would shoot somebody. The applicant

---

[130] Kristjan Luts, 'Eestlased nõukogude armees 1968–1991' [Estonians in the Soviet Army in 1968–1991], *Ajalooline Ajakiri*, no. 1/2 (127/128) (2009): 266–267.

[131] The first sergeant – *starshina* – was the highest rank for a non-commissioned officer in Soviet Army and as such the top of military career for those who did not go to cadet schools. To get to this rank in two years was quite rare.

pursues for a permit to meet the son who is in preliminary confinement prison (isolated cell).[132]

As the family did not get any information about their son, they appealed to the local deputies for help. On 1 September 1989 people's deputy Toomas Varek made an inquiry to the USSR chief military prosecutor, Judiciary Lieutenant Colonel Vladimir Chermakov.[133]

The answer came on 2 October 1989 and showed that the hushing up had started. According to the reply M. K. was on the guard on 26 April 1989. During their free shift he played chess with another conscript in 'the Lenin room' and did not notice that the commander of the guard, senior sergeant F. had entered. The latter reprimanded them for not standing up and avoiding the military salute. Both players were sent 'to do the rooms'.[134] Checking the results of their work F. said it had been badly done and they should do it again the next day. Going back to the guard unit M. K. got the automatic gun and 'being dissatisfied with the punishment' decided to kill F. He shot eight bullets in F.'s direction, wounding him fatally. The Chimkent garrison's military prosecutor completed processing the case on 25 July 1989 and transferred it to the Military Tribunal of the Turkestan Military District. On 21 August the same year the military tribunal sent the defendant to the Moscow Serbsky Forensic-Psychiatric Institute for stationary expertise assessment. The said 'victimisation' of the defendant had not been proved and the military prosecutor's office did not consider criminal proceedings expedient.[135]

On 7 September 1989 M. K.'s mother applied to Aleksandr Grienko, the commander of the MVD troops' political administration, describing the violence and victimisation her son had suffered under the main initiator of it, the shot F. The inquest had continued the violence. On 22 August

---

[132] Check-in and registration card of the reception at the ESSR Supreme Soviet Presidium, 17 May 1989, RA, ERA.R-3.10.318, 1.

[133] Letter of USSR people's deputy T. Varek to the USSR chief military prosecutor Lieutenant Colonel of judiciary Vladimir Chermakov, 1 September 1989, RA, ERA.R-3.10.318, 8.

[134] This is euphemism for the toilets, that A. Korotkov did not mention.

[135] Letter of A. Korotkov, the USSR military prosecutor's office's, investigation department assistant head to the USSR people's deputy T. Varek, 2 October 1989, RA, ERA.R-3.10.318, 9–10.

when the family got permission to visit M. K. he had a blue eye and several minor injuries.[136]

The reply of the MVD troops Central Asia and Kasakhstan region department of political administration commander Generalov, on 16 October 1989, declared all the hints at violence 'a malicious slander'.[137]

A hide-and-seek game followed. The family did not know where M. K. was detained. On 3 November 1989 the secretary of the Estonian SSR Supreme Soviet Presidium Arno Almann wrote to the USSR chief public prosecutor informing him that there was no person as such in the Serbsky Institute and wanted to know where he was.[138]

On 20 November 1989, A. Korotkov replied that M. K. would be transferred to the Serbsky Institute only in 1990. Up to then he would be detained in the isolation cell of the Chimkent region MVD investigation department.[139] He got into the Serbsky Institute at the beginning of 1990. On 2 February 1990 the Chairman of the Estonian SSR Supreme Soviet Presidium Arnold Rüütel sent a letter to the director of the Serbsky Forensic-Psychiatric Institute G. Morozov and asked permission for one of the ESSR State Psychiatric Hospital specialists to be present at the expert assessment. The letter also mentioned that M. K. could not speak Russian well.[140]

The second time it was tried to take M. K. to court was in June 1990 but again he was hospitalised in a psychiatric ward.[141] The parents did

---

[136] Application of M. K.'s mother to the commander of the MVD troops board of political administration, A. Grienko, 7 September 1989, RA, ERA.R-3.10.318, 25.

[137] Letter from Generalov, the commander of the MVD troops in Central Asia and Kasakhstan region, department of political administration, to the mother of M. K., 16 October 1989, RA, ERA.R-3.10.318, 27.

[138] Letter of A. Almann, Secretary of the Presidium of the ESSR Supreme Soviet to the USSR Chief public prosecutor, 3 November 1989, RA, ERA.R-3.10.318, 11.

[139] Letter of A. Korotkov, the assistant head of the investigation department at the USSR Military chief public prosecutor's office to A. Almann, 20 November 1989, RA, ERA.R-3.10.318, 12.

[140] Chairman of the Presidium of the ESSR Supreme Soviet A. Rüütel to Director of the Moscow Serbsky Forensic-Psychiatry Institute G. Morozov, 2 February 1990, RA, ERA.R-3.10.318, 14.

[141] Military Tribunal of the Turkestan Military District, Decree of the trial, 5 June 1990, RA, ERA.R-3.10.318, 66–68.

not have any information about their son for several months.[142] The third time the Turkestan Military District Military Tribunal convened was on 19 February 1991 and it again concluded with no other decision than to send M. K. to the Moscow Serbsky Institute.[143]

On 21 February 1991 the Estonian Committee presented a declaration to support M. K. that summed up the whole case as follows:

Victimisation, beating, blackmail, derision and humiliation from the other conscripts made M. K. repeat the desperate act of the Lithuanian Arturas Sakalauskas. […] The forensic-psychiatric expertise declared M. K. irresponsible and sentenced to open-ended detention in specialised psychiatric hospitals. In the course of the revelations the public has learned about the disorder and violence in the Soviet army. The warmongers still attempt to preserve their status and distort the real situation, covering up what has happened. That is why we cannot consider the military prosecutor's conclusions trustworthy. The same is true for the Moscow Serbsky Forensic-Psychiatric Institute's expertise assessment made obviously to order. The institute is notorious for declaring political dissidents mentally ill and there is no guarantee that they would recently have reversed their practice.

The Estonian Committee made a suggestion that the Estonian SSR Supreme Soviet Presidium should demand a complementary investigation with independent investigators who would consider all the circumstances.[144]

The matter is clearly revealed in the ESSR Supreme Soviet Presidium reception room's check-up and registration card from 15 April 1991 –

26 April 1989 M. K., who was conscripted to the MVD troops in Kazakhstan shot his platoon commander. He has been detained in psychiatric wards for several times to ascertain his mental condition and due to that the court has

---

[142] Lääne-Viru County administration's decision about transferring the Soviet Army conscript M. K. for treatment in the Estonian Republic, 27 March 1991, RA, ERA.R-3.10.318, 20–21.

[143] Military Tribunal of the Turkestan Military District, Decree of the trial, 19 February 1991, RA, ERA.R-3.10.318, 69–71.

[144] Declaration of the Estonian Committee, 21 February 1991, RA, ERA.R-3.10.318, 17.

not made its decisions yet. Today we do not know where our son is. Estonian doctors who participated in the expertise assessment in the Serbsky psychiatric institute consider it necessary to ascertain the beatings that brought about the shooting by M. K. That is why the Supreme Soviet Presidium requests help for opening a criminal case that has been requested for three times already but with no success.[145]

As the impartiality of the forensic-psychiatric expertise was suspected and the matter seemed to be hushed up, it was repeatedly suggested that the person investigated should be brought to Estonia. It was also stressed that the parents should be told where their son was and kept informed about the developments.

The last known expertise act from the Serbsky institute (attended by two psychiatrists from Estonia – H. Gofman and V. Bogdanov) made the conclusion that the treatment up to that moment had had no results and the patient should be transferred to a general psychiatry hospital at the place of his residence. The institute made the proposal to the Turkestan Military District's Military Tribunal.[146] As they suspected information leaks the military district was not approachable. The last document concerning the case dates from 30 January 1992 – i.e. the Soviet Union had already disintegrated. It shows that there was no solution yet and M. K. had been taken to the Chimkent prison. What the conclusion was, the author could not find out. There is no information either about the mental state of M. K. when he committed his crime and during the investigation. Evidence that was collected from other conscripts shows the situation that led to the manslaughter and characterises the prevailing conditions in Soviet Army rather well.

Conscript H. P. from the same squad wrote in his statement to the Turkestan Military Tribunal on 10 March 1990 –

M. K. was badgered and pestered all the time like most of us. It was quite normal in our company, when you are hit it finally starts getting on your nerves. M. K.'s relationship with F. was not good. M. was a quiet lad and

---

[145] Check-up and registration card of the ESSR Supreme Soviet Reception room, 15 April 1991, RA, ERA.R-3.10.318, 4.

[146] Letter of A. Rüütel, Chairman of the ESSR Supreme Soviet Presidium to Lääne-Viru County administration, 6 May 1991, RA, ERA.R-3.10.318, 23.

F. made use of it. He commanded and forced M. K. in whatever way he liked and usually he had these moods at night. I do not remember the date but it was in February or March when F. told M. to clean the floors in the company in the dark at night. It was after one of these feasts that happened quite often at night. […] Now I would like to say something about 26 April 1989. At eight o'clock my shift started. I went to the guard, had supper and dealt with my own business. M. was cleaning the lavatories and I asked why he was doing it and he answered that F. had told him to as he had not stood up when F. entered the room. We never stood up when some of our own lads entered.[147]

R. H. from the same company –

In February 1989 M. K. had a conflict with Zh. And he lost consciousness. The reason was that F. quietly told Zh, "Beat him!" […] When we were in the guard we often had to wash F.'s clothes and he usually selected the Estonian to do it. M. frequently washed F.'s underwear, sewed on his collar and ironed his pants. […] Even more, it turned out that F. confiscated M.'s food parcels and money the family sent him. F. became violent when he had used drugs or alcohol, then he did not even choose who to beat up.

Several other conscripts said the same.[148] These statements were not taken into consideration and no investigation was opened.

Conclusions

Semen Gluzman's application to the emergency session of the Assembly of the World Association of Psychiatry on 17 October 1988 is an excellent summary to the essence of the 'political psychiatry' –

The psychiatric legislation in force at present on the territory of the USSR has no regulations that would grant the patient a chance to fully defend

---

[147] H. P.'s statement to the Turkestan Military Tribunal, 10 March 1990, RA, ERA.R-3.10.318, 23.

[148] R. H.'s statement to the Turkestan Military District Military Tribunal, 3 October 1990, RA, ERA.R-3.10.318, 44–45.

himself. In court the citizen has no right to defend himself from enforced treatment in a hospital. [...] The USSR Ministry of Healthcare would not pay any heed to facts that reveal the systematic misapplication of psychiatry published in press, these facts are not investigated. The medical staff who has committed this abuse is not condemned or punished. [...] In secret psychiatrists have given their "political patients" a clean bill of health and in some cases no medicaments have been used at all. The doctors of special hospitals have even got a slang term for such treatment – "wall therapy", i.e. the only treatment is detention within the walls of a specialised psychiatric hospital. At the same time psychiatric medicaments are extensively and devastatingly used, even shock therapy is applied when the patient protests against hospitalisation or the conditions of treatment. [...] The fact that misapplication of psychiatry in the USSR is not accidental but has become systematic can be proved by group diagnoses, that is the diagnoses that have been declared by phone without examining the patient.[149]

The world was aware of the 'political psychiatry' applied in the USSR.

On 5 January 1977 a psychiatry task group was established at the Moscow Helsinki group (A. Podrabinek, F. Serebrov, V. Bakhmin and others), the aim of which was to observe the application of psychiatry for meeting political demands. The group had lawyer S. Kalistratova and psychiatrist A. Voloshanovic as consultants. The commission was active for four years, by that time all the members had been arrested. They had managed to compose 24 information bulletins.[150]

The dissident activities finally led to the condemnation of the abuse of psychiatry for repressive purposes in the USSR. At the 1977 world congress of psychiatrists in Honolulu it was officially condemned.[151] The chief psychiatrist of the ESSR Jüri Saarma participated in the congress and having returned home, he began to justify the conduct of Soviet psychiatrists in press and radio (see, e.g. the newspaper *Kodumaa*, 5 October 1977).

---

[149] Statement of Shimon [Semen] Gluzman to the emergency session of the World Assembly of the Association of Psychiatrists on 17 October 1988, *Vikerkaar*, no. 4. (1990): 77–78.

[150] *Dissidentlik liikumine Eestis*, 28, 37.

[151] A. Podrabinek, 'Politicheskie aspekty sovetskoi psikhiatrii', *Puti obnovleniia psikhiatrii. Materialy s"ezda*, ed. Iu. Savenkov (Independent Psychiatrists' Association, 1990), 147.

These performances urged one of the leaders of Estonian dissidents, Mart Niklus, to write public appeal to J. Saarma –

It is depressing and sad to learn that at the world forum you had no cour-age to condemn the violation of physician's professional ethics that occurs in your homeland, [...] What a great pity that you used your talent and reputation so that the suffering of the innocent repressed may go on; what concerns your scientist's courage and citizen's honour you could never be compared to the Nobel Prize Winner A(ndrei) Sakharov. I also think that if this sore issue is stubbornly avoided and not discussed, it will return at the next, the seventh congress – however unpleasant it may be for the USSR delegation.[152]

Professor Saarma did not like Niklus's letter at all and on 10 November 1977 he sent it to the KGB Tartu Department for 'taking a stand', calling the appeal 'slander and fabrication' about the basis of healthcare and prin-ciples of psychiatric help in the Soviet Union.[153] Considering this conduct we may conclude that psychiatric abuse was no problem for Professor Saarma.

However, it seems that some conclusions were still made and a few cos-metic improvements were introduced. So, for example, the USSR MVD suggested in June 1978 that the specialised psychiatric hospitals should be transferred into the healthcare system and after that they were not places of detention any more but medical care establishments. The minister of internal affairs said that there was no legal act about these hospitals that had been established in 1939 from the USSR NKVD prisons psychiatric wards and departments. He also hinted that the existence of these special-ised hospitals is made use by the 'anti-Soviet element' in their propaganda against the Soviet Union, although they were 'merely ordinary medical establishments'. It is said that the USSR MVD had been trying to pass the specialised psychiatric hospitals to the Ministry of Healthcare but the lat-

---

[152] Public appeal of Mart Niklus to Professor Jüri Saarma, 1 November 1977 – *Dissidentlik liikumine Eestis*, 244–245.

[153] The letter of the USSR Academy of Medicine corresponding member Profes-sor J. Saarma to the ESSR KGB Tartu department, 10 November 1977 – *Dissi-dentlik liikumine Eestis*, 243.

ter did not agree to take them. The same letter reveals that in June of 1978 7,420 patients were detained in specialised psychiatric hospitals. There seems to have been no problem with the transfer in the ESSR MVD.[154]

Niklus occurred to be a prophet in this occasion. Saarma's colleagues abroad could not share his views and the USSR Psychiatrists and Narcologists' Union was expelled from the World Psychiatrists' Association (WPA) in 1983.[155] In the second half of the 1980s when the *perestroika* had started in the Soviet Union, many cases of psychiatric misapplication were revealed.[156] In 1988 in Athens the congress of the association reinstated the USSR Psychiatrists' umbrella group. However, it did not go easily. The reinstatement was decided backstage. A declaration was made up for the USSR delegation that the representative of it read. The USSR was conditionally admitted to membership but the vote was mostly given to support Gorbachev's *perestroika* policies.[157] It did not mean, though, that the 'political psychiatry' had come to its end yet. Even in 1988 the KGB was not ashamed to threaten the dissidents with enforced therapy. So, for instance, they suddenly took an interest in the mental health of Vello Salum, Pastor of Pilistvere Parish congregation. In February 1988 he began to receive messages from the Jämejala Psycho-Neurological Hospital.[158] On 23 February an ambulance was sent to his home with a doctor and a militiaman who wanted to take him for an 'examination'. The pastor happened to be out and the family managed to convince the uninvited guests that he was sound and healthy. Representatives of the local administration and militia arrived at the divine service the next day. It is not clear what the sense of all this was. They might have wanted to isolate the pastor from the society

---

[154] USSR MVD special psychiatric hospitals being transferred to the USSR Ministry of Healthcare subordination. Letter of the USSR minister of internal affairs N. Shtshelokov to the USSR Council of Ministers, 8 June 1978, RA, ERA.R-1.5. 1001, 205–206.

[155] Podrabinek, *Karatel'naia meditsina*, 140.

[156] See, e.g. Ia. Karpovich, 'Stydno molchat'', *Ogonek*, no. 29, 15 July 1989.

[157] Shimon [Semen] Gluzman, 'Kuidas meid Ülemaailmsesse Psühhiaatria Assotsiatsiooni (WPA) vastu võeti' [How we were admitted to the WPA], *Vikerkaar*, no. 4 (1990): 74–78.

[158] Pastor Vello Salum had had encounters with the Soviet authorities already at earlier times. The bothersome pastor was arrested in Tallinn in 1980 and taken to the Jämejala mental hospital 'to recuperate'. See: Viktor Niitsoo, *Vastupanu 1955–1985* [Resistance 1955–1985] (Tartu: Tartu Ülikooli Kirjastus, 1997), 115.

but it might also have been only a threatening gesture.[159] The case of M. K. shows that that the same measures were used until the total disintegration of the Soviet Union.

---

[159] Information bulletin no. 13, March, 1988 – *MRP-AEG Infobülletään 1987– 1988: kogumik* [Info bulletin of the MRP-AEG 1987–1988], comp. Eve Pärnaste and Viktor Niitsoo (Tallinn: SE&JS, 1998), 332–333.

Family Members of 'Exploiters' and 'Enemies of the People' in the Fetters of the Soviet Regime

*Eli Pilve**

Introduction

Throughout their history, Estonia's inhabitants have repeatedly had to experience the sudden change of political power, sometimes even several times over the course of one lifetime. Although the changes in political power that took place in 1940, 1941, 1944 and 1991 can broadly and generally be considered cultural traumas, they are not by any means comparable. In all of these cases, people invariably had to adapt to changed conditions. Often, but not in all cases, political attitude coincided with linguistic divisions. In 1940 and 1944, the Estonian-speaking population, with a few exceptions, was shocked and in opposition to the new regime, and was forced at least outwardly to replace its former convictions with new ones. This, in turn, conditioned the development of an odd parallel consciousness where people learned to carefully monitor when, where and to whom they could divulge their real thoughts, when to present the imposed ideology, and what to keep secret altogether. It was prudent to keep information secret that nowadays can be considered entirely innocent, such as speaking of the occupation of one's parents, because in the spirit of the Soviet ideology of class struggle and by virtue of Soviet methods of repression, the declaration of one family member as an enemy of the ruling regime marked the entire family in a negative light. Large numbers of memoirs

* First published: Eli Pilve, '"Kurnajate" ja "rahvavaenlaste" perekonnaliikmed Nõukogude võimu kammitsais', *Tuna. Ajalookultuuri ajakiri*, no. 1 (2017): 58–73.

are deposited at the Estonian National Museum and the Estonian Literary Museum describing how people have had to suffer because of their social origin through being deprived of education or employment. It is also easy to gather oral heritage in researching this topic. There is, however, little documentary evidence because the repression of family members was covered up by the authorities. In reference to the Communist Party platform of 1919, Lenin clearly stated that the bourgeoisie had to be suppressed, but the way to accomplish this was not prescribed at all.[1] Thus persecution due to one's origin became standard Soviet practice, where documents did not reflect reality, or the connection was very much distorted. For instance, the reason given in decisions on the exmatriculation of university students who had been deported was failure to attend lectures. Similarly, the reason for firing someone from their job could be presented as failure to satisfactorily fulfil his work duties, even though the actual reason for dismissal was the employee's unsuitable social background. This is why it is methodologically difficult to research the setting up of obstacles in everyday life due to social origin since in most cases, documents were not drawn up concerning such procedures, at least not the kind that would be accessible nowadays to Estonian historians. There is, however, a relatively large number of recollections concerning such hindrances, but they are not always entirely reliable. It is human to blame circumstances that are independent of us for our failure to fulfil our ambitions. By comparison, there are examples of people whose parents were not 'socially suitable' yet who were accepted to universities even during the Stalinist era, such as the former President of Estonia Lennart Meri. It would be unfair to suspect them all of agreeing to compromises with the authorities, even though this is at first glance one of the possible explanations.

Class Struggle and the Dictatorship of the Proletariat

According to Karl Marx, private property was what enabled one person to exploit another and thus it had to be liquidated in order to do away with antagonism.[2] In the Soviet Union, however, class struggle was not at all

---

[1]   Vladimir Lenin, *Valitud teosed II* [Selected Works II] (Tallinn: Poliitiline Kirjandus, 1946), 364.

[2]   Henn Käärik, *Klassikaline ja nüüdisaegne sotsioloogiline teooria* [Classical and Modern-Day Sociological Theory] (Tartu: Tartu Ülikooli Kirjastus, 2013), 38–40.

restricted to private property. The aspiration was to liquidate all manner of dissent along with the people involved in dissent. During the first year of Soviet rule, the Communist Party suppressed even the slightest sign of resistance with the help of the Red Army, favouring public terror in this endeavour. The creation of the so-called classless society took place within the framework of the 'dictatorship of the proletariat', which in reality, however, created a far more rigid class society. Thereat, the use of any kind (*sic!*) of restrictions on liberty was permitted for suppressing exploiters. According to the official rhetoric, this was a temporary measure, and the Party platform promised that as the possibility for one person to exploit another disappears, so the need for violence would also disappear.[3] Until then, however, according to the statutes of the Communist International, the proletariat was supposed to intensify class struggle in order to retain power, making the struggle particularly widespread, acute and merciless. Representatives of the bourgeois class were to be dislodged from their jobs even more resolutely than before, even by replacing them with incompetent workers if necessary if the new workers could be relied on ideologically.[4]

When the Russian Social Democratic Workers' Party adopted the party's first platform at its second congress in 1903, the principles for joining the party were also regulated. Lenin demanded that the party should systematically and persistently cultivate people little by little who would be suitable for the party's central body so that he could see the entire activity of each candidate for a higher post like the palm of his hand and familiarise himself even with their individual peculiarities. A party member had to belong to a single party organisation, meaning that he was not permitted to be in several elementary organisations simultaneously. The reason for this requirement was that in this way, it was possible to make sure that the party had strong central control over the activity of every member and

---

[3]   Richard Service, *Seltsimehed: Maailma kommunismi ajalugu* [Comrades: the History of World Communism] (Tallinn: Varrak, 2010), 97–98.

[4]   *Kommunistlise Internatsionaali resolutsioonid ja põhikiri : Wasta wõetud Kommunistlise Internatsionaali teisel kongressil 17. juulist 7. augustini 1920. a* [Resolutions and Statutes of the Communist International: Adopted at the Second Congress of the Communist International from 17 July to 7 August 1920] (St. Petersburg: Kommunistlise partei Eestimaa keskkomitee Kirjastus, 1920), 5, 7.

that this activity was guided firmly.[5] The same requirement remained in effect in the Communist Party program that was adopted in 1961.[6]

Party members and candidate members were indeed kept watch over as if they were in the palm of the hand. For instance, the acceptance of Arvid Laatsit into the Party was discussed in 1945. Laatsit had fought in the ranks of the Red Army in the Second World War and had been decorated with two medals but he was deleted from the list of candidates for party membership as a random person who had ended up on the list by mistake because his father had served in the Estonian Police and his sister and brother had belonged to the Naiskodukaitse (Women's voluntary defence organization) and Kaitseliit (Defence League) respectively.[7] This is one of many examples that characterise the situation at that time, where on the one hand, people were solicited to join the Party, and evasion of the Party or being left out of it caused problems. On the other hand, when one was already in the Party, expulsion from the Party marked a person, and this in turn could cause him to lose his job and made it more difficult to find a new one, to say nothing of making it impossible to climb the ladder of social position. Of course, as always, there were exceptions here as well.

The same kind of practice was also implemented outside the 'more responsible governmental positions', as they were referred to in the statutes of the Communist International.[8] The cadre department that had already been established at the University of Tartu in January of 1941 can be pointed out as an example. Its job was to staff the university's personnel with lecturers who would be competent both in their specialty and ideologically. Since it was difficult to fulfil both requirements in Estonia in 1941, the latter became decisive. The cadre department kept personal files on lecturers containing characterisations, political complaints, anonymous letters and statements obtained behind people's backs. Under

---

[5]   B. N. Ponomarjov et al., *Nõukogude Liidu Kommunistliku Partei ajalugu* [History of the Communist Party of the Soviet Union] (Tartu: H. Heidemanni nimeline trükikoda, 1975), 57, 597.

[6]   *Nõukogude Liidu Kommunistliku Partei põhikiri: Kinnitatud NLKP XXII kongressi poolt, osalised muudatused sisse viidud NLKP XXIII kongressi poolt* [Constitution of the Communist Party of the Soviet Union: ratified by the CPSU XXII Congress, partial amendments introduced by the CPSU XXIII Congress] (Tallinn: Eesti Raamat, 1966), 13.

[7]   Minutes no. 88 of the ECP(B) CC Bureau, 25 February 1950, RA, ERAF.1.4.931, 90.

[8]   *Kommunistlise Internatsionaali*, 7.

such conditions, many lecturers considered it wiser to resign on their own initiative before being fired.[9]

A massive purge of cadres began when the Soviet occupation was restored in 1944. The university's cadre department was required to submit proposals to the Party Bureau for purging the university professors and lecturers with anti-Soviet attitudes, along with university students and postgraduates from the families of kulaks, merchants and businessmen, and persons who had served in the German Army. Over 700 students were exmatriculated from the University of Tartu during the first post-war year, often on the pretext of failure to attend lectures. The actual reason may have been the concealment of biographical data, service in the German Army, escape to the West, or also deportation in 1949.[10]

Repressions of students became more frequent when the former head of university cadres Jenny Nõu was replaced by Helene Kurg. The personal file became the primary means for making staffing decisions. Anti-Soviet attitudes or unsuitable information that could among other things reflect social origin that did not meet requirements were inferred from the personal files of employees. Control was extended to also include the university's technical employees and auxiliary staff.[11]

The greater portion of teachers at general education schools was also replaced. So-called bourgeois teachers were fired or forced to leave 'of their own accord'. They were sometimes arrested and replaced with reliable cadres that oftentimes did not even have secondary education, to say nothing of specialised professional training.[12] One example of many is the proposal made by the ECP(B) Tartu County Committee secretary to Comrade Pärt, who served at that time as head of the education department of the Executive Committee of the Tartu County Soviet of Deputies of the Working People, to dismiss from school two female teachers whose

---

[9]   Lembit Raid, *Tartu Ülikool kommunistlikus parteipoliitikas aastail 1940–1952* [The University of Tartu in Communist Party Politics in 1940–1952] (Tartu: Tartu Ülikooli Kirjastus, 1995), 12–13.

[10]   *Ibid.*; Karl Siilivask and Hillar Palamets, *Tartu Ülikooli ajalugu III, 1918–1982* [History of the University of Tartu III, 1918–1982] (Tallinn: Eesti Raamat, 1982), 201.

[11]   Raid, *Tartu Ülikool kommunistlikus*, 94.

[12]   Väino Sirk, 'Haritlaskond osutus visaks vastaseks' [Intellectuals Proved to be a Tenacious Opponent], *Tuna*, no. 1 (2010), 61–63.

unsuitability for the vocation of teaching lay in the fact that the father of one teacher and the husband of the other had been imprisoned for 25 years as 'henchmen of the Germans'.[13]

Loss of employment due to social origin was a threat in every walk of life. In 1946 for instance, ECP(B) Tartu County Committee Secretary Peeter Tiido demanded that the head of the Tartu County Communications Office fire an employee of the Tabivere post office because that employee's social origin did not meet requirements: 'Herewith we inform you that citizen Karin Põder, who works at the Tabivere post office is from the family of an enemy of the people. Her mother has been arrested and banished from our SSR. Why do you employ such persons? You are to report what you have undertaken to staff the communications apparat with reliable cadres.' Five months later, a handwritten note was added to this notice: 'Citizen Põder has been dismissed effective immediately. Basis: a telephone conversation with Comrade Cherbanov, head of the Communications Office'.[14]

Liquidation of the Exploiting Class

According to the resolutions passed at the 2nd Congress of the Communist International in 1920, there were three main tasks for the achievement of socialism as the first stage of communism. The first of these contained within it the overthrow of 'exploiters' and the bourgeoisie. Mustering the entire working class under the ideas of the Communist Party was only the second task. Thirdly, the suspicious position of the smallholders and small entrepreneurs between the bourgeoisie and the proletariat, between bourgeois democracy and Soviet power, had to be liquidated. The only measures that could bring about the complete achievement of the first task were the forcible overthrow of the bourgeoisie, the expropriation of all private property, the annihilation of the bourgeois state apparat, and

---

[13]   ECP(B) Tartu County Committee Secretary Kurvits to Comrade Pärt, head of the Educational Department of the Executive Committee of the Tartu County Soviet of Deputies of the Working People, confidential, 8 January 1947, RA, ERAF.12.7.24, 33.

[14]   ECP(B) Tartu County Committee Secretary Tiido to the head of the Tartu County Communications Office, 10 December 1946, RA, ERAF.12.7.24, 52.

the banishment of the most dangerous and tenacious exploiters from the state or their internment in prison camps.[15]

At a conference of agrarian Marxists in 1929, Stalin said that the time was ripe to switch from the policy of restraining the exploitative tendencies of the kulak class to a policy of liquidating the entire class. Kulaks were not to be allowed to join the kolkhozes under any circumstances.[16] There were allegedly 5,618,000 kulaks in total, including their family members, in Russia in 1928.[17]

Probably in the spring of 1950, the head of the ECP CC Agriculture Department Aleksandr Sokolov gave a speech about kulaks, nationalists and other enemies of the people who had secretly wormed their way into the kolkhozes. He also briefly mentioned suspicious persons who were suspicious only because they were related to 'anti-Soviet elements'. Among other things, connections to anti-Soviet elements also proved to be fateful for Milla Palu, a member of the Võimas Jõud (Mighty Force) kolkhoz belonging to the Kureküla village soviet, whose husband Osvald had been arrested. A general meeting was held at the kolkhoz on 4 March 1952, where Comrade Tiits, the chairman of the board, raised the question of Osvald Palu, whether he is still fit to belong to the collective of the kolkhoz or whether he should be expelled from the kolkhoz. Thereafter people took the floor to condemn Palu's crime and to admonish the participants in the meeting to give the matter careful consideration before making their decision. Thereat, someone named Glass made the proposal to expel Osvald Palu's wife Milla from the kolkhoz as well for the offences of her husband, and that is indeed what transpired: 'There are no objections and the general meeting decides without any opposing votes to expel the kolkhozniks Palu, Osvald, son of Jaan, who is already arrested, and his wife Palu, Milla, daughter of Kusta, for hiding a wanted robber-murderer

---

[15]   *Kommunistlise Internatsionaali*, 2–3.

[16]   Jossif Stalin, *NSV Liidu agraarpoliitika küsimustest. Kulakute kui klassi likvideerimise poliitika küsimusest* [On Questions of the Soviet Union's Agrarian Policy. On the Question of the Policy of Liquidating Kulaks as a Class] (Tallinn: Punane Täht, 1948), 23–27.

[17]   Pavel Tšeremnõhh, *Kuidas tekkisid klassid ja miks toimub klassivõitlus* [How Classes Were Formed and Why Class Struggle Takes Place] (Tallinn: Eesti Riiklik Kirjastus, 1954), 54–55.

in their household.'[18] Milla Palu managed to find work at the Kureküla sovkhoz, the chairman of which was an Estonian who had come from Russia named Anton Konijärv, who consented to hire her. This is a vivid example of the fact that where humaneness remained, it was possible to conceal dangerous social connections.

The Second Stage of Class Struggle

Stalin's personality cult was condemned at a secret session of the XX Congress of the Communist Party of the Soviet Union held in 1956 but at the same time, it affirmed that the Party's policy up to that point had been correct.[19] The decision was passed at the XXI CPSU Congress held in 1959 that socialism had achieved complete victory in the Soviet Union and that the process had reached the era of the extensive building of communist society. The same claim was made in the CPSU's third program adopted in 1961, which also repeated that continued progress needed to be made towards communism, which was to be a classless society where the common public ownership of the means of production and the social equality of all members of society are in effect.[20] Class struggle as the destruction of the stratum of exploiters was no longer mentioned. Instead, the program preached that the remaining classes were approaching one another. A new wording of the Party program was adopted in 1986. It stated that overcoming the differences between classes and the creation of a classless society meant the disappearance of differences between cities and the countryside, the ever increasing similarity between the lifestyle of the peasantry and the way of life of the working class. It meant doing away with differences between life in the city and in the countryside, and the ever more organic alignment of physical and intellectual workers in

---

[18] Minutes no. 4 concerning the general meeting held at the Elva rayon Kureküla village kolkhoz *Võimas Jõud*, 4 March 1952, RA, EAA.T-794.1.48, 102–107.

[19] Ponomarjov et al., *Nõukogude Liidu Kommunistliku*, 563.

[20] *Nõukogude Liidu Kommunistliku Partei programm (vastu võetud NLKP XXII kongressi poolt)* [Program of the Communist Party of the Soviet Union (ratified by the XXII Congress of the CPSU)] (Tallinn: Eesti Riiklik Kirjastus, 1961), 4–5, 19, 58.

production activity.[21] This is essentially the same thing that Lenin had said in 1919 when he asserted that it was necessary to abolish all manner of private property, to do away with differences between cities and the countryside and also between those who did physical and intellectual work.[22] The peasants and workers, and persons who did intellectual and physical work were indeed presented as classes in the platform of 1986.[23]

The Party's first platform had promised that according to how the possibility for one person to exploit another disappears, the need to use temporary measures, in other words various violent coercive measures, would also disappear, and the Party would strive to limit them and cast them aside altogether.[24] By the 1980s, the massive violation of human rights had indeed decreased but political liberties, the right to freely express one's opinions, actual religious freedom, the equal treatment of citizens, freedom of movement, and other such rights, cannot be considered to have existed in the Soviet Union until its collapse.

Legal Basis for Repression of Family Members

Examples of how people were punished for the fact that persons connected to them had been convicted as opponents of the state by the Soviet Union's court system have already been described above. Legally speaking, direct repressions carried over initially to the family members of military personnel, thereafter extending to civilians as well.

According to the RSFSR Criminal Code, adult family members of military personnel could be punished by imprisonment for five to ten years in the event that the member of the armed forces in question had fled

---

[21] *Nõukogude Liidu Kommunistliku partei programm: Uus redaktsioon: Vastu võetud NLKP XXVII kongressi poolt* [Program of the Communist Party of the Soviet Union: New Version: ratified by the XXVII Congress of the CPSU] (Tallinn: Eesti Raamat, 1986), 36–37, 50–51.

[22] Tšeremnõhh, *Kuidas tekkisid klassid*, 78–79.

[23] *Nõukogude Liidu Kommunistliku partei programm: Uus redaktsioon*, 58–60.

[24] *Wenemaa Kommunistlise (enamlaste) Partei programm: wastu wõetud partei VIII kongressil Moskwas, 18–23. märtsil 1919* [Russian Communist (Bolshevist) Party Program: ratified at the Party's VIII Congress in Moscow, 18–23 March 1919] (St. Petersburg: Kommunistlise Partei Eesti Keskkomitee Wenemaa Büroo, 1919), 8–9.

abroad and his family member had assisted him in this or had known of it but failed to alert the authorities. Thereat, those adult family members who had lived with an escaped member of the armed forces at the time that the crime was committed or were being supported by him lost their voting rights and they were banished into exile to the most distant rayons of Siberia for five years.[25] When war broke out between Germany and the Soviet Union, provisions for punishing the family members of military personnel were augmented. According to the directive issued on 16 August 1941 by the General Staff of the Supreme Command, the family members of commanders and political instructors who had been taken prisoner were to be arrested. The same sort of practice was implemented during the Second World War in Germany as well according to the so called *Sippenhaftung* (kin liability) principle, where the punishment of political opponents extended to their families.

Family members of Soviet soldiers and non-commissioned officers who had been taken prisoner were in danger of being deprived of state handouts and means of assistance, which was a severe punishment in the starving wartime rear area under conditions of nonexistent supplies for civilians.[26]

The penalties applicable to the family members of civilian 'traitors of the homeland' were gradually made more severe. For instance, according to the AUCP(B) CC Politburo decision issued on 13 May 1939, the spouses of 'especially dangerous' persons who had been convicted of treason were to be sent to prison camps.[27] The Politburo decision issued on 17 August

---

[25] *VNFSV Kriminaalkoodeks: muudatustega kuni 15. novembrini 1940* (RSFSR Criminal Code: with amendments through to 15 November 1940] (Tallinn: ENSV Kohtu Rahvakomissariaat, 1941), § 58^{1v}.

[26] Peeter Kaasik, *Nõukogude Liidu sõjavangipoliitika Teise maailmasõja ajal ja sõjajärgsetel aastatel: Sõjavangide kinnipidamissüsteem Eesti näitel ja hinnang sõjavangide kohtlemisele rahvusvahelise õiguse järgi* [The Soviet Union's Prisoner of War Policy during the Second World War and the Postwar Years: Detention System of Prisoners of War Using the Example of Estonia and Assessment of the Treatment of Prisoners of War According to International Law] (Tallinn: Tallinna Ülikool, 2012), 221.

[27] Decision of the AUCP(B) CC Politburo on wives of the traitors of the Homeland, 13 May 1939 – *Lubianka: Stalin i NKVD-NKGB-GUKR Smersh: 1939–mart 1946: dokumenty*, comp. V. N. Khaustov, V. P. Naumov and N. S. Plotnikova (Moscow: Mezhdunarodnyi fond Demokratiia, Materik, 2006), 81.

1940 extended this to all family members.[28] USSR People's Commissar for Internal Affairs Lavrentiy Beria sent Stalin a special notice in December of 1940 in which he said that previous lenient measures, according to which the family members of persons who had fled abroad were not subject to repression if they had not known about the escape, had not produced the desired results. Thus Beria proposed to bring criminal charges against the family members of all persons who had fled abroad and give the NKVD jurisdiction over deciding the punishments for such cases.[29] The Politburo handed down the decision on 7 December 1940. According to this decision, the family members of persons who had fled from the Soviet Union were subject to banishment into exile for three to five years together with the confiscation of all their property. If aggravating circumstances came to light, the family member of the 'traitor of the homeland' was subject to arrest. The NKVD Special Board handed down such verdicts.[30]

The parents, husband/wife, children, brothers-sisters, mother-in-law and father-in-law of a 'traitor of the homeland' were considered to be his family members in the event that they lived together in a single household. If there were no aggravating circumstances, they were subject to deportation to the northern regions of the state. The NKVD Special Board handed down the verdicts on banishment into exile and people were to be sent into exile under escort by a convoy of guards. It was not permitted to separate underage children from adults. The underage children of family members of arrested traitors of the homeland were not sent to prison but rather were placed in orphanages. The property of family members who were banished into exile was subject to confiscation.[31]

The USSR State Defence Committee decision issued on 24 June 1942 stressed that this applied to both military personnel and civilians. Family members of 'traitors of the homeland' who had been convicted by the NKVD Special Board in accordance with Section 58[1a] (espionage, defection, service in German penal or administrative organs, attempted trea-

---

[28]   Decision of the AUCP(B) CC on traitors of the Homeland, 17 August 1940 – *Lubianka: Stalin i NKVD*, 184.

[29]   AUCP(B) CC to I. V. Stalin, 4 December 1940– *Lubianka: Stalin i NKVD*, 202–203.

[30]   Decision of the AUCP(B) CC Politburo, 7 December 1940, – *Lubianka: Stalin i NKVD*, 201–204.

[31]   *Ibid.*

son, and other such offences) were subject to internment and banishment into exile for five years. The NKVD Special Board handed down the verdict concerning banishment into exile. Parents, husband/wife, children and brothers-sisters, who lived in the same household together with the so-called traitor of the homeland at the time when the crime was committed, were considered to be family members. Those family members of the 'traitor of the homeland' who were themselves Red Army soldiers or partisans were not subject to repression.[32]

The provisions of the criminal code and the above-mentioned decisions were nevertheless not completely implemented. The different categories of 'traitors of the homeland' and their family members included millions of people across the Soviet Union and the investigation and punishment of all these cases was physically not within the means of the NKVD, NKGB and Red Army counterintelligence. Thus punishment was to a great extent random. It is not possible to give the exact numbers of arrests of family members.

Socially Alien Elements

In addition to banishment into exile, several groups of society that were qualified as 'socially alien elements' to the new socialist society were publicly pilloried, deprived of civil rights and liberties, work and places to live, and demoted in the social hierarchy. People from all walks of life who for some reason did not fit in with the new society that was to be created suffered in the revolution against capitalism and in the class struggle.[33]

A population group existed in 1918–1936 that on the basis of the Constitution of the Soviet Union had been deprived of voting rights (*lishennye izbiratelnykh prav*) and started being known as *lishentsys*.[34] They were people who (formerly) 'lived off of income not acquired by way of work',

---

[32]　Decison of the State Defence Committee on the Members of the families of the traitors of the Homeland, 24 June 1942 – *Lubianka: Stalin i NKVD*, 350–351.

[33]　Stéphane Courtois et al., *Kommunismi must raamat : kuriteod, terror, repressioonid* [Black Book of Communism: Crimes, Terror, Repressions] (Tallinn: Varrak, 2000), 173.

[34]　*Wenemaa Sotsialistlise Föderatiwse Nõukogude Wabariigi põhjusseadus (Konstitutsion)* [Constitution of the Russian Socialist Federal Soviet Republic] (Petrograd: 13th State Publishing House, 1918), § 65.

whose income accrued from landed property, business, capital, and other such sources. This stratum included merchants, clergy, tsarist era policemen, particularly employees and agents of the gendarme corps and secret police (*ohranka*), members of the tsar's family, but also the mentally ill, wards and persons that had been punished for certain crimes. From the latter half of the 1920's onward, persons who not only currently used hired labour but also those who had done so prior to the revolution were added to the category of deprived persons. In the latter half of the 1920's, former officers of the tsarist army, whose voting rights had in the meantime been restored, were once again deprived of those rights. These former officers were seen as potential internal enemies in the event of war. At the same time, in order to carry out the collectivisation that had begun, kulaks were defined as a social stratum that was stripped of all civil rights and liberties in addition to voting rights. Their property was confiscated and they were forcibly resettled. In the 1930's, even organists who were responsible for some other tasks associated with the religious ceremony in addition to playing the organ for church services were deprived of their voting rights.[35]

The declaration of one family member as an enemy of the regime marked the entire family, and the members of the families of such persons were also reduced to deprived status. At the turn of the years 1929 and 1930, 3.7 million people were classified as deprived persons. Family members under the age of 18 accounted for 44% of this group. By 1932, deprived persons together with their families numbered seven million.[36]

---

[35]   S. A. Krasil'nikov, *Na izlomakh sotsial'noi struktury: Marginaly v poslerevoliutsionnom rossiiskom obshchestve (1917–konets 1930-kh gg.)*, http://zaimka.ru/soviet/krasiln1.shtml, 1 June 2018; *Istoriia stalinskogo Gulaga: konets 1920-kh-pervaia polovina 1950-kh godov = The history of Stalin's Gulag : late 1920s–early 1950s: sobranie dokumentov v semi tomakh. Tom 5, Spetspereselentsy v SSSR*, ed. T. V. Tsarevskaia-Diakina (Moscow: ROSSPEN, 2004), 42; Letter from the People's Commissar of NKVD N. Jezhov to the Prosecutor of USSR Vyshinski et al., January 1937, – *Istoriia stalinskogo Gulaga*, 236–237; Reference of the GULAG OGPU about the legal status of the exiled persons, 4 February 1931 – *Politbiuro i krest'ianstvo: vysylka, spetsposelenie, 1939–1940: v 2 knigakh. Kniga 2*, ed. N. N. Pokrovskii et al. (Moscow: ROSSPEN, 2006), 509–511; Explanations for the Instruction of the USSR Central Election Committee on the re-elections to the soviets, *Pravda*, no. 345 (1930), http://www.oldgazette.ru/pravda/16121930/text2.html, 1 June 2018.

[36]   *Ibid.*; Courtois et al., *Kommunismi must raamat*, 178.

The group of deprived persons was formally done away with when the constitution of 1936 went into effect, but there were exceptions. The rights of kulaks who had been banished into exile were restored but regardless of this, they were allowed to change their place of residence only within the region that they had been exiled to. They were not considered equal to the owners of passports with unrestricted rights to movement within the borders of the state.[37]

Deprivation of voting rights was used to stigmatise one part of society and the importance of having voting rights did not lie in its literal meaning but rather in not belonging to that branded group of people. Setting aside the mentally ill, wards and criminals, representatives of the 'former exploitative classes' and ideological enemies of the Bolsheviks formed the nucleus of the deprived persons.[38] Reduction to the status of deprived persons brought with it the loss of one's job, deprivation of medical care, expulsion from trade unions and cooperatives, which under the conditions of the ration card system in effect in 1929–1935 also meant loss of the right to purchase staple goods, including food, at state prices. In the course of their eviction from municipal housing and apartments, and the 'purging' of large cities, deprived persons were also driven out of the larger cities. Their tax rates were increased and additional taxes were imposed on them.[39]

The deprivation of their parent(s) of voting rights was grounds for the expulsion of their children from educational institutions. The principle of class selection also had to be strictly observed when mobilising conscripts into the army. Only working-class persons were to be accepted into the army. Kulaks and other 'parasitic elements' had to be sent to special labour battallions.[40] In 1930–1937, the sons of deprived persons who were at the age for military service were sent to rear area defence (*tyloopolchenie*)

---

[37]   The new places of residence of forcibly resettled kulaks were known as *trud-poselenie* in the early 1930's and this term also came to refer to the banishment of kulaks into exile in general. Smaller scale resettlements had taken place earlier but the use of resettlement of people on a large scale in the name of fulfilling the regime's security, ideological, economic, demographic and other objectives began with the kulaks.

[38]   Krasil'nikov, *Na izlomah* etc.

[39]   *Ibid.*; Courtois et al., *Kommunismi must raamat*, 178.

[40]   Ponomarjov et al., *Nõukogude Liidu Kommunistliku*, 276.

units that were established separately for them. This was in turn accompanied by the imposition of war taxes on their parents because their sons were left out of the Red Army. Although the members of labour battalions were not exactly outlaws, the rest of society perceived their defencelessness and lack of rights. Superiors often treated them more brutally. There were cases where men recruited as independent manpower, so to speak, took the credit for work done by labour battalions. They were fed more poorly than independent manpower and a great deal of labour accidents occurred due to the fact that the attitude towards the occupational health and safety of members of the labour battalions was indifferent.[41]

Voting rights were restored successively and in the mid-1920s, the voting rights of some deprived persons were restored as part of a campaign. In 1930, the restoration of the voting rights of adult offspring who were not living with their parents was allowed. This bore the aim of generating conflicts between generations through the creation of a new society and the destruction of the old. Additionally, the voting rights of men who served in the labour units were restored after three to four years of working, and of former officers and officials of the white armies who had served in the Red Army and actively participated in defending the Soviet Union. The remainder were allowed to apply for the reinstatement of their voting rights five years after the deprivation of their rights.[42] Stigmatisation continued more covertly by the addition of a question in questionnaires concerning previous loss of rights.[43]

Proving Social Origin

A questionnaire system was set up in occupied Estonia immediately in 1940 for verifying social origin. A comprehensive questionnaire concerning the respondent himself and people in his household had to be filled out when taking a job or enrolling in school, applying for some sort of permit or financial support, etc. For instance, the Ministry of Internal Affairs demanded information from police prefects in August of 1940

---

[41] Krasil'nikov, *Na izlomah* etc.

[42] *Ibid.*

[43] Facsimile copy of the NKVD questionnaire, http://commons.wikimedia.org/wiki/File:Анкета_СпН_НКВД.jpg?uselang=ru, 1 July 2018.

concerning among other things the social origin of police commissars, deputy commissars and constables, and warned that '[...] inclusion of incorrect notifications in the information will bring serious complications for the official filling out the declaration'.[44] When the police apparat was liquidated once and for all in September of 1940 and the militia of workers and peasants was formed, militia candidates also had to submit their *curriculum vitae* when applying for work, indicating their social origin, previous membership in political parties and/or organisations, financial status and other such information.[45] The same kinds of questionnaires also had to be filled out by teachers, who were warned against submitting incorrect or incomplete information: 'Thereat the Administration of Rural Schools asks you to warn and direct the serious attention of persons filling out this questionnaire to the fact that the information given must correspond completely to reality and that not a single question should be left unanswered nor should any answer be partial or incomplete for the purpose of deviating from reality.'[46]

School pupils and university students also had to submit questionnaires concerning themselves and their family. The Soviet Union declared the availability of education for all, which was nevertheless accomplished with reservations. According to the temporary regulation issued in 1940 governing the work of ESSR secondary schools, the parents or guardians of pupils wishing to enrol in secondary school were required to submit an application to the school principal indicating the pupil's education, personal status and social origin and including a certificate indicating the financial status of the parents.[47] The same sort of requirement also applied to enrolling in university. A certificate issued by the local government indicating which social stratum a person belonged to and that person's financial status prior to 21 June 1940 had to be submitted for both the candidate himself and his parents. Preference was given in uni-

---

[44] Tallinn-Harju prefecture to the police commissar of the Keila police station, 8 August 1940, RA, ERA.27.3.2812, pages not numbered.

[45] Peeter Kaasik, 'Eesti politsei' [Estonian Police] – *Sõja ja rahu vahel II* [Between War and Peace II], ed. Enn Tarvel (Tallinn: S-keskus, 2010), 384–386.

[46] Circular from the Viljandi County Government Department of Education, 14 September 1940, RA, ERA.R-967.1.103, pages not numbered.

[47] *ENSV Teataja* [ESSR Official Gazette], 1940, 3, 27, Temporary regulation for organising the work of secondary schools, 3 September 1940.

versity enrolment to representatives of workers, the poorer sort of peasants and working intellectuals.[48] Hans Kruus, who was appointed rector of the University of Tartu in 1940, has recalled that the aim was to enrol more children of workers and peasants as far as possible and that perhaps the requirements for the children of intellectuals were somewhat more demanding, to say nothing of the offspring of the petit bourgeois.[49] The comprehensiveness of the questionnaires changed over time. In 1954 for instance, applicants for a place at the University of Tartu had to submit a detailed overview of the activities of their parents prior to 21 June 1940, giving notice among other things of the former social position of their parents, their primary field of activity, whether they owned land and livestock and if so, how much, whether they used hired manpower and if so, how much, whether they owned an industrial enterprise and if so, then which one, how many workers it employed, etc. Additionally, notification had to be given whether any of the applicant's relatives had served in the German Army or was living abroad. The same kind of questionnaire had to be filled in concerning the applicant himself, who also had to answer the question of whether the person submitting the information harboured any doubts regarding the implementation of the Party line.[50] This sort of questionnaire regimen lasted until the end of the 1960s, when the authorities started requiring university applicants to fill out questionnaires covering only the most important personal data. More thorough background checks were shifted to the time when people were starting their working lives or entering postgraduate education.[51] In 1976 for instance, university applicants had to give notice of only the place of employment and place of

---

[48]   *Riigi Teataja* 1940, 97, 957, Regulation concerning the acceptance of students to universities, 6 August 1940.

[49]   Jüri Ant and Toomas Hiio, 'Tartu ülikool esimese Nõukogude Liidu okupatsiooni ajal 1940–1941' [The University of Tartu during the First Period of Soviet Occupation 1940–1941], – *Universitas Tartuensis 1632–2007*, eds. Toomas Hiio and Helmut Piirimäe (Tartu: Tartu Ülikooli Kirjastus, 2007), 428.

[50]   Student's personal statement no. 50231, 13–15p, Personal questionnaire for registering cadres, 21 December 1954 TÜA, 9/56-318, Student's personal statement no. 50231, 13–15v.

[51]   Toomas Hiio, 'Ülikooli asend Nõukogude Liidu valitsemissüsteemis' [Position of the University in the System of Governing the Soviet Union], – *Universitas Tartuensis*, 460.

residence of their parents.[52] There are no differences in the questionnaire for 1983, though admittedly it now had to be filled out in duplicate, meaning in both Estonian and Russian.[53]

In the post-Stalin period, working class youth status became increasingly more important than social origin since the Party was annoyed by the fact that the university student body was comprised more and more of young people who were not of working class origin. While previously, favourable social origin and active political participation in the activities of the Komsomol could help gain acceptance to university even if the results of the entrance examinations were not the best,[54] starting in 1957 according to regulations for accepting students to university, those applicants who after completing secondary school had worked in manufacturing or served in the armed forces started gaining preference in acceptance to institutions of higher education. Otherwise, that working experience had to be acquired in institutions of higher education alongside one's studies.[55] The social status of one's parents was no longer of such importance if they did not happen to belong to a group that was under the particular scrutiny of the regime, such as the clergy.[56]

Credentials Committee

In addition to the questionnaire and certification of financial status, a so called credentials committee was set up in all institutions of higher

[52] Declaration to the rector, 9 July 1976, TÜA, 4-k, 10453, 1–1v.

[53] Student's personal file no. 83056, declaration to the rector, 23 August 1983, TÜA, 4-k, 21623, Student's personal file no. 83056, pp. 2–2v.

[54] Hiio, 'Ülikooli asend Nõukogude', 461.

[55] Anu Raudsepp, *Ajaloo õpetamise korraldus Eesti NSV eesti õppekeelega üldhariduskoolides 1944–1985* [Organisation of the Teaching of History in General Education Schools in the Estonian SSR where Estonian was the Language of Instruction], (Tartu: Tartu Ülikooli Kirjastus, 2005), 35.

[56] Väino Sirk, 'Stalini-järgsete aastate haritlaspoliitika kahest tahust' [On Two Aspects of Policy Concerning Intellectuals in the Post-Stalin Years], *Tuna*, no. 4 (2004): 52.

education.[57] Its task was to ascertain the background of each individual applicant in cooperation with the state security organs. The credentials committee consisted of the head of the corresponding institution of higher education, a Communist Party organiser, a trade union representative, an ECP Central Committee representative, and others. The committee met with applicants and questioned them before deciding on each individual candidate whether to allow them to take the entrance examinations. Thus the records of Tartu State University from 1955 include a list of persons who were to be allowed to take the entrance exams 'if they provide information concerning their father'.[58] The same sort of comments are also found in the records of the admissions commission of Tallinn Polytechnical University.[59] Information on both parents was sometimes required.[60] Applicants were often asked to appear before the commission a second time, but entries concerning repeat meetings are no longer found. With some rare exceptions, it is likely that generally speaking, denial of permission to take the entrance exams was not reflected on paper. The decision on Matti Päts[61] is written in black and white in the records of the Tallinn Polytechnical Institute's admissions commission: 'Not to be allowed to take the exams. The admissions commission finds that he is unsuitable to be a TPI student due to his origin.'[62]

Professor Enn Tarvel recalls that in the course of his conversation with the credentials committee in 1950, he was asked three times if his father

---

[57] It is currently unclear whether the credentials committee was separate from the admissions commission or if it was another name for that same admissions commission. The term 'admissions commission' is used in written sources, while oral sources speak of the credentials committee. Thus, both terms are used in this article according to the respective source.

[58] Minutes no. 13 of the Tartu State University student admissions commission, 30 July 1955, RA, ERA.5311.2.9, 65–76.

[59] Session minutes no. 3 of the Tallinn Polytechnical Institute student admissions commission, 4 July 1952, RA, ERA.R-1834.3.246, 7; Session minutes no. 4 of the Tallinn Polytechnical Institute student admissions commission, 11 July 1952, RA, ERA.R-1834.3.246, 10.

[60] Session minutes no. 5 of the Tallinn Polytechnical Institute student admissions commission, 16 July 1952, RA, ERA.R-1834.3.246, 13.

[61] Grandson of Konstantin Päts, former president of the Republic of Estonia.

[62] Session minutes no 6 of the Tallinn Polytechnical Institute student admissions commission, 18 July 1952, RA, ERA.R-1834.3.246, 16.

had served in the Omakaitse (Home Guard) during the German occupation. Tarvel answered this question in the negative each time. In answering the same question for the third time already, he added that they did not want his father since he was too old! Tarvel's admission to university was remarkable because his brother had served in the German Army, was taken prisoner in Czechoslovakia, and subsequently served in a labour battalion, and his uncle Peeter Tarvel, a history professor at the University of Tartu, had been imprisoned and sent to Vorkuta prison camp. The members of the commission could not have been unaware of this.[63]

A search of the archives has thus far failed to locate any decision concerning the termination of the activity of the credentials committee, but sources support the claim that this system was done away with in the mid-1950s. While even as late as 1955, the Communist Party Committee at Tallinn Pedagogical Institute reprimanded the school at one of its meetings because the credentials committee had not spoken with all candidates for admission in the previous year, and demanded improvement in this work in the future,[64] the question of admissions was not on the agenda even once at Party committee meetings in 1956, and the same also goes for the University of Tartu.[65] As a certain substitute for the credentials committee, characterisations from school Komsomol organisations started being required from university applicants by 1959 at the latest.[66] The reduction of background checks opened the doors of the university to quite a few people for whom they had hitherto been shut.

School Education 'Free of Charge'

School education was allegedly supposed to be available to everyone and without restrictions in the Soviet state, but nevertheless, that same state

---

[63] Author's interview with Enn Tarvel, 14 February 2012.

[64] Minutes of the closed meeting of the Party Organisation of the Tallinn Pedagogical Institute, 8 June 1955, RA, ERAF.7068.1.73, 51–59.

[65] Minutes of the Partburo, 6 January–26 December 1956, RA, ERAF.7068.1.73 and Minutes of the meetings of the Partburo, 23 January–11 December 1956, RA, ERAF.7068.1.305.

[66] Session minutes of the Tallinn Polytechnical Institute student admissions commission, 1959, RA, ERA.R-1834.3.562.

immediately set about discriminating between classes among pupils and along with this discrimination restricting the availability of education, using tuition fees as one possible means.

On 25 September 1940, the ESSR Council of People's Commissars passed a decision to do away with tuition fees in secondary and vocational schools,[67] yet on 15 October of that same year, tuition fees were once again levied on those students in secondary schools and institutions of higher education whose parents supported themselves 'by income acquired without work'.[68] Depending on the educational institution and the social status of the student or his parents prior to 21 June 1940, tuition fees prior to monetary reform ranged from 140 to 600 kroons per year.[69]

In 1946, tuition fees were restored in all secondary schools and institutions of higher education from the eighth grade upward, ranging from 150 to 500 roubles per year.[70] Recipients of all manner of pensions were

---

[67]   *ENSV Teataja* 1940, 14, 137, decision issued by the ESSR Council of People's Commissars, 25 September 1940.

[68]   *ENSV Teataja* 1940, 27, 311, Estonian SSR Council of People's Commissars ordinance concerning the establishment of tuition fees for the children of citizens who live off of income acquired without work in the senior grades of secondary school and in institutions of higher education, and the establishment of scholarships for university and technical school students whose parents do not live off of income acquired without work, 15 October 1940.

[69]   *ENSV Teataja* 1940, 27, 315, Instructions for doing away with tuition fees for the children of workers, working peasants and working intellectuals and for assigning tuition fees for those pupils and university students whose parents live off of income acquired without work, 16 October 1940.

[70]   Some wage levels and prices of foodstuffs are provided here to give an idea of the relative size of tuition fees under the conditions of that time. For instance, the net salary of the Estonian Leninist Communist Youth Society (hereinafter ELKNÜ) Tallinn Municipal Committee accountant for two weeks was 236 roubles and 47 kopeks in January of 1946. A janitor's net wages for two weeks was 75 roubles. [RA, ERAF.176.4.33, wages of ELKNÜ Tallinn Municipal Committee technical manpower, 15–30 January 1946]. The salaries of employees in responsible positions were naturally higher. The net salary for the 1st Secretary of the ELKNÜ Tallinn Municipal Committee for half a month was 418 roubles, and 450 roubles for the propaganda secretary [RA, ERAF.176.4.33, salaries of ELKNÜ Tallinn Municipal Committee employees in responsible positions, 1–15 March 1946]. At the same time in 1945, the free market price per kilogram of potatoes was 7–8 roubles and the price per kilogram of pork was 120 roubles. The same price had to be paid for one egg as for a kilo of potatoes. Conditions in the

exempted from tuition fees if the pension was their only source of income. Veterans of the so-called Great Patriotic War, disabled persons, the children of soldiers killed in the war, and active military personnel were also exempted. Children from orphanages could study free of charge in secondary schools and technical schools, but not at universities.[71] Working intellectuals could apply for exemption from tuition fees, but 'keepers of so-called spiritual occupations (pastors, etc.)' and persons who had previously been part of the senior staff of the police and the Kaitseliit were not included.[72] Tuition fees were not completely done away with in secondary schools until 1 September 1956.[73]

Summary

In Soviet ideology, class struggle envisaged the destruction of the so-called class of exploiters and the achievement of a classless society through the dictatorship of the proletariat. Social groups that had owned property or

---

countryside were not at all better. Farms were required to give the state tribute in kind at prices that essentially meant giving them as gifts. The state 'purchased' potatoes at the price 5.5 kopeks/kg, pork at 0.83–1.18 roubles/kg, and eggs at 24 kopeks/egg. While the situation until the monetary reform of 1947 was complicated but nevertheless still tolerable, market prices admittedly dropped after monetary reform, but incomes also decreased and people started accumulating debts. This in turn meant fines that were beyond people's means or imprisonment for up to two years. Starting in 1948, the penalty was already banishment into exile and in just the summer of that same year, 12,000 peasants from the Russian SFSR were sent into exile for not fulfilling their obligations. (See further in this volume: Indrek Paavle, Grain and Eggs in the Service of the Regime: Coercive Procurement in Estonian Villages in the 1940s).

[71] *ENSV Teataja* 1946, 26, 214, Estonian SSR Council of Ministers ordinance concerning the collection of tuition fees from the students of institutions of higher education, technical schools and other special curriculum schools, and pupils in the 8th, 9th, 10th and 11th grades of general education secondary schools, 25 April 1946.

[72] *ENSV Teataja* 1940, 27, 315, Instructions for doing away with tuition fees for the children of workers, working peasants and working intellectuals and for assigning tuition fees for those pupils and university students whose parents live off of income acquired without work, 16 October 1940.

[73] Directives issued by the Soviet Union's Minister of Higher Education, 5 January–19 October 1956, RA, ERA.R-14.1.1.

belonged to the class of intellectuals before the revolution were counted as exploiters: farmers, teachers, clergymen, entrepreneurs, politicians, and others – in principle, everyone who was not a poor peasant or a worker. According to contrived theory of communism, which claimed to be implementing Marxism, the bourgeoisie and the workers formed classes that were opposed to each other. Their peaceful coexistence could not be possible. In the new society that was to be created, the bourgeoisie were not supposed to have any place whatsoever. They were to be liquidated. During the initial years of the Red Terror, executions by firing squad and deportation were spoken of openly. Later this became vague rhetoric concerning the destruction of class society. The rules for carrying this out were admittedly not phrased very precisely, but the Soviet Union never started honouring the first article of the Universal Declaration of Human Rights passed in 1948, according to which all people are equal in terms of their rights.

After Stalin's death, repression under the label of class struggle admittedly became more concealed but did not completely disappear until the collapse of the Soviet Union. Social origin quite often became a hindering circumstance in acquiring an education, in working, participating in public life, and other such fields. The milder form of class struggle generally was not reflected in the documentation or was represented there in a form that distorted reality. For instance, candidates that were unsuitable in terms of their social origin were eliminated from among university applicants even before the entrance examinations, imparting the decision to them verbally. In cases of dismissal from work due to social origin, the reason for this was often presented in the decision as not coming to grips with the requirements of the job. Thereat it should be recalled that the making of the decisions described above frequently was reduced to the capacity for empathy of the persons making the decisions and their skill in steering a middle course. A person expelled from one kolkhoz as a member of the household of an enemy of the people could find work in another kolkhoz. It depended on the chairman. Similarly, a young person left behind the closed door of one institution of higher education due to unsuitable social origin could enrol in another if someone with a heart could be found there whose word counted.

Publishing Activities by the Secret Services of a Totalitarian Regime: The Case of the Estonian SSR's KGB

*Ivo Juurvee**

The USSR State Security Committee (KGB) had a number of facets. In published works in the English-language, the KGB is known as primarily an espionage organisation. In Eastern Europe and Russia there is more emphasis on the KGB also being an agency for repression. The attempts by the KGB to influence public opinion or specific target groups in the West are known as 'active measures' but similar activities inside the Soviet Union have received much less attention. However, in attempting to examine this topic in more detail, problems of limited sources and complicated methodology inevitably arise. This article attempts to clarify the extent of KGB activity in the publication of books in its operational interests using the Estonian SSR KGB as an example.

As an introduction, here are two well-known examples of how the KGB Second Directorate (counter-intelligence) determined the content of books in the USSR. Both examples have been taken from the memoirs of high-level counter-intelligence officers, although the genre and target group of these books is quite different.

KGB counter-intelligence officer Viktor Cherkashin has described in his memoirs, which were published in 2005, the measures implemented by the KGB following the news reaching the Western media of the unsuc-

* First published: Ivo Juurvee, 'Totalitaarse režiimi eriteenistuse kirjastustege-vusest Eesti NSV KGB näitel', – *Nõukogude Eesti külma sõja ajal*, ed. Tõnu Tann-berg, Eesti Ajalooarhiivi toimetised = Acta et commentationes Archivi Historici Estoniae, 23(30)) (Tartu: Eesti Ajalooarhiiv, 2015), 243–261.

cessful attempt to recruit the Ukrainian-American diplomat Constantine Warwariv:

We shot back, publishing a book, detailing episodes of Nazi collabora-tion that was translated and published in the West. [...] Needless to say, we weren't interested in punishing Nazi collaborators. The entire incident con-cerned the KGB's operational interests – and at that it was a great success. [1]

The book mentioned by Cherkashin, 'White paper: evidence, facts, comments' was published in 1979. This 280-page collection is comprised of two parts: 'In an unfair world' and 'Espionage and sabotage under the banner of "human rights"', where the Warwariv case is covered in the 11-page chapter headed 'Patronising of criminals'.[2] Although the content of the book supports Cherkashin's claim that it was published in the op-erational interests of the KGB, there are no direct references to the Soviet secret services.

The most renowned author of spy stories in the Soviet Union was Yulian Semyonov (1931–1993), whose fame was increased by the films and television series that were based on his books. In the book 'TASS is authorised to announce...' (1979[3], in Estonian 1981[4], in English 1988[5]), the author depicts all KGB workers and Soviet politics as being blemish-free, and the opposition as completely immoral – which is usual in Soviet literature. The attentive reader, however, could also note that the author is well aware of different tactics used by secret services at that time. Would it be paranoid, in this situation, to suspect the guiding hand of the KGB? It is possible to check since Vyacheslav Kevorkov, friend of the author and Major General in the Second Directorate of the KGB, has written thus about the origins of the book:

---

[1]   Victor Cherkashin, Gregory Feifer, *Spy handler: Memoir of a KGB officer. The true story of the man who recruited Robert Hansen and Aldrich Ames* (New York: Basic Books, 2005), 128–129.

[2]   *Belaia kniga: svidetel'stva, fakty, dokumenty: sbornik* (Moscow: Iuridicheskaia literatura 1979), 122–132.

[3]   Iulian Semenov, *TASS upolnomochen zaiavit'* (Moscow: Sovetskaia Rossiia 1979).

[4]   Julian Semjonov, *TASS on volitatud teatama... : jutustus* [TASS is authorised to announce] (Tallinn: Eesti Raamat, 1981.

[5]   Julian Semyonov, *TASS is authorised to announce...* (London: Avon Books, 1988).

The moment arrived when our counter-intelligence exposed the spy Alek-sandr Ogorodnik.[6] *He had been under observation for some time but when our suspicions had been confirmed, I phoned Yulian on my own initiative. We met at the 'Uzbekistan' restaurant, which is close to the Lubyanka*[7]*, and I told him the whole story. Yulian immediately got very excited – he wanted to write about it. Andropov*[8]*, who liked him a lot, agreed immediately. A few days later Yulian came to me in the [state security] office. I had prepared three folders for him, and said: 'OK, have a look, I'm off to have something to eat.' I came back in forty minutes. No sign of him. I asked the secretary: 'Zina, where's Semyonov?' [Zinaida answered:] 'He said he's read it, and he's off.' I was confused: it took us three years to write it up, but he's read it all in forty minutes?! At our next meeting, Yulian explained: 'I did look at the documents but it's much easier for me to make it up rather than examine all those interrogations and observations. The author is the master of the situation.'*[9]

Any memoir, especially one written by a KGB general, cannot be taken at face value, which means we will probably never find out whether Kevorkov first spoke to Semyonov, and only then asked for Andropov's approval (which would have meant revealing a state secret, and could have resulted in severe punishment) or was it the other way around (which would not have been nearly as heroic, but much more logical). The fact remains that a novel was indeed written, based to a degree on actual events – and classified documents.

In 1972, or 5–7 years before these events, a comprehensive top secret lexicon was published that defined the terms used by KGB counterintelligence.[10] This was the first book of its kind to present not only the relevant

---

[6] Aleksandr Ogorodnik was a Soviet diplomat who was arrested in 1977, suspected of spying for America. It is claimed he committed suicide immediately after his arrest.

[7] Lubyanka Square, location of KGB headquarters in Moscow.

[8] Yuri Andropov, Chairman of USSR KGB 1967–1982.

[9] Ol'ga Semenova, *Iulian Semenov* (Moscow: Molodaia gvardiia 2011), 320. The author of the book, Olga Semyonova is Yulian Semyonov's daughter.

[10] *Kontrrazvedyvatel'nyi slovar'* (Moscow: Vysshaia krasnoznamennaia shkola Komiteta Gosudarstvennoi Bezopasnosti pri Sovete Ministrov SSSR im. F. E. Dzerzhinskogo 1972). See the publication in the Estonian National Archives library. Abbreviated English-language version, where a number of keywords referring to the Estonian exile community (i.e. basically those persons who in 1944 fled to the

vocabulary and current operational methods but also a compilation of the accumulated knowledge and traditions of decades. The lexicon contains two keywords that explain the possibility for the public use of secret information:

- *Transparency (glasnost) in the work of KGB agencies* [Glasnost' v rabote organov KGB] – *overt use of KGB material to resolve certain problems which fall within the agencies' remit (combating acts of ideological sabotage[11], tracking down perpetrators of crimes against the state, etc.). Transparency in the work of the KGB is based on drawing on a broad spectrum of society, active members of the Party, Soviet and public organisations and individual citizens as well as the press. Creating transparency in the work of the KGB must not lead to any disclosure of operational methods. Transparency is one of the manifestations of the Leninist principle in the participation of the masses in the work of the KGB.*[12]

West due to the Soviet re-occupation, and their organisations) are also missing, see: Vasili Mitrokhin, *KGB Lexicon: The Soviet Intelligence Officers Handbook* (London: Routledge, 2002).

[11] 'Ideological sabotage [*Diversiia ideologicheskaia*] – one of the basic forms of subversive activity carried out by the intelligence and other special services of imperialist states and their ideological and propaganda centres. It takes the form of measures and operations involving agitation and propaganda or intelligence gathering and organisation, carried out by special forces and special facilities with the aim of inspiring, stimulating and exploiting anti-socialist tendencies, processes and forces in order to undermine or weaken the state and public order in each individual socialist country as well as the unity and harmony of the socialist countries as a whole. Ideological sabotage is targeted most strongly against the Soviet Union as the main, key force standing in the way of the plundering aspirations of imperialism. As practised by the anti-Communist centres and intelligence agencies of the imperialist states, it may take the form of using subversive propaganda to exert a hostile ideological and political influence on the citizens of socialist countries (subversive propaganda). It may also involve establishing illegal opposition groups and organisations within a socialist society [...]. Acts of ideological sabotage and ideological sabotage operations are carried out in close cooperation with political intelligence work (espionage) and are built on material which has been acquired and inspired by political intelligence. The political intelligence service provides the intelligence and information required for ideological sabotage. (*Kontrrazvedyvatel'nyi slovar'*, 90–91; Mitrokhin, *KGB Lexicon*, 202–203).

[333] *Kontrrazvedyvatel'nyi slovar'*, 72–73; Mitrokhin, *KGB Lexicon*, 188–189.

- *Compromising [komprometatsiia] – method of operational disruption of subversive enemy activity. It consists of using overt and covert facilities to bring to the attention of the superiors of the person one is seeking to compromise reliable or fabricated information indicating that the person has been behaving in an unseemly manner. The method is used by intelligence or counter-intelligence agencies against:*
  - *state, political and other bourgeois personalities who are actively engaged in subversion against the USSR; the heads of anti-Soviet nationalist and religious centres and organisations abroad;*
  - *nationalist and religious authorities conducting hostile activities on Soviet soil;*
  - *intelligence officers and agents of bourgeois states operating under official cover in the Soviet Union, and certain other individuals.*

The consequence is that the people or organisations which have been compromised wholly or partly cease their subversive activity against the USSR.[13]

Regarding these definitions, it is important to realise that this could be done only in the interests of the KGB, and only in carrying out KGB tasks. It is certain that the use of this information could not only be due to the vanity of some KGB officer who was not happy in his work, although something like that could be inferred from Kevorkov's reminiscences cited above.

It should also be noted that 'White paper' and 'TASS is authorised to announce...' are very different books as regards content and genre, and that the KGB connection and aims of publication are also different.

Methodology

The participation of the Estonian SSR KGB in publishing activities has been briefly mentioned in literature,[14] however, the question remains: what is the scope of books that should be used for in-depth analysis? Since the

---

[13] *Kontrrazvedyvatel'nyi slovar'*, 135–136; Mitrokhin, *KGB Lexicon*, 230.

[14] Aile Möldre, *Eesti raamatu 100 aastat* [100 Years of the Estonian-Language Book] (Tallinn: PostFactum, 2018), 104–105; Ivo Juurvee, *100 aastat luuret ja vastuluuret Eestis* [100 Years of Intelligence and Counter-Intelligence in Estonia] (Tallinn: Post Factum, 2018), 116–119.

Soviet Union did not have a capitalist market economy, we must discount the obvious and simplest way of researching the issue: to examine the books where the cost of publication was covered by the KGB. All publishing houses in the Soviet Union, as in the Estonian SSR, belonged to the state, and commercial gain from book publishing was often not of primary importance. (For the same reason, this article deals with copies printed not copies sold.)

The problem becomes even more complicated because Soviet society was inundated with propaganda, and the books directed for publication by the Estonian Communist Party (ECP) could by chance also fall in line with the operational interests of the Estonian SSR KGB. This is why the following methodology is used: to examine three characteristics in the books, and only analyse those that correspond to at least two of them. These characteristics are as follows:

- The aim of the book is in accordance with the operational interests of the KGB, or is in the interests of the KGB's public image.
- Classified documents, either produced by or held by the KGB, have been used in the writing / compilation of the book.
- The author of the book, or the consultant, is known to be a KGB officer, or a collaborator.

I will only be analysing books that have been published in the Estonian SSR, although there is reason to believe that the Estonian SSR KGB also had a role in at least two works that were published elsewhere in the Soviet Union.[15] At some stage a distinction has to be drawn between a book and a booklet. Here a publication is defined as a book if it has at least 50 pages, and at least 1,000 copies were printed. This means that publications comprising only a few pages that were printed on newsprint (e.g. some of the newspaper *Kodumaa* (Homeland) supplements), or publications purporting to promote research that had small print runs (e.g. publications by the Estonian SSR Academy of Sciences that discuss Estonian diaspora – KGB connections existed in the case of such booklets as well) are not analysed.

In addition, some other restrictions should be made, where the reasons can be explained by using the example of the previously mentioned novel

---

[15]   For example: *V poedinke s abverom: Dokumental'nyi ocherk o chekistakh Leningradskogo fronta 1941–1945*, (Moscow: Voenizdat, 1968); *V poedinke s abverom: Dokumental'nyi ocherk o chekistakh Leningradskogo fronta 1941–1945. Izd. 2-e, ispr. i dop.* (Leningrad: Lenizdat, 1974).

by Yulian Semyonov, 'TASS is authorised to announce...', which was translated into Estonian and published in the popular series of crime fiction
'Mirabilia'. The translations of books that were published elsewhere have
been excluded from observation for two reasons. Firstly, in these cases it
is not always possible to research in detail whether and to what extent the
secret service was involved in the writing of the original. (Incidentally,
if it was ideologically convenient, works by authors with a background
in Western secret services were also published in the Estonian SSR. For
example, the same 'Mirabilia' series also includes a book by John le Carré[16] and a number of spy and crime novels by Graham Greene were also
published.) Secondly, in the case of USSR authors, it is not possible to
clarify whether the KGB actually had to do anything to get these books
published: there was no doubt that with an author as popular as Semyonov, the publishing house also had a financial interest in publishing his
writings. In addition to literature, this also applies to books that could
perhaps be called 'popular science literature'.[17]

For the same reasons, this analysis does not cover feature films, although
they could have had an even greater impact than books (e.g. in 1984, a TV
serial of the same name was produced based on the novel *TASS is authorised
to announce...*). There is documentary proof that three full-length feature
films were produced, following KGB instructions, in the Estonian SSR: *Kutsumata külalised* (Unwelcome guests) (Tallinna Kinostuudio, 1959), *Valge
laev* (The White ship) (Tallinnfilm, 1970) and *Metskannikesed* (Wild violets)
(Tallinnfilm, 1980), but these are discussed in detail elsewhere.[18]

Many of the examined books were not included in the list since they fulfilled only one condition and fulfilling a second was doubtful. In some cases,

---

[16]   John le Carré, *Väikeses saksa linnas* [A Small Town in Germany] (Tallinn:
Eesti Raamat, 1973).

[17]   For example: Nikolai Jakovlev, *LKA NSV Liidu vastu* [CIA Target the USSR]
(Tallinn: Eesti Raamat, 1983).

[18]   These films have been screened in two film programs (the 'Riiulilt alla' [Off
the shelf] program by the Estonian History Museum at Maarjamäe, curators
Olev Liivik and Hiljar Tammela, and in the Helsinki cinema Orion program
'Propaganda in Soviet Estonian Cinema', curators Ivo Juurvee and Olev Liivik),
where extensive comment was provided by historians: *Kutsumata külalised* (10
December 2011, commented by Pearu Kuusk), *Valge laev* (22 October 2011 and 8
September 2012, commented by Ivo Juurvee), *Metskannikesed* (8 September 2012,
commented by Pearu Kuusk).

such exclusion is rather borderline. For example, the book by the journalist Sergei Kuznetsov, *Paid with a life* (1964),[19] was not considered research material. In this book, the 'forest brothers' are blamed for imaginary crimes. Kuznetsov was later one of the authors of collections published openly by the KGB, but the book does not seem to be based on KGB documents, and the nature of the author's possible relations with the KGB at the time of publication is not known. Should information indicating the involvement of the KGB with the publication of the book come to light in the course of further research, this work could be added to the list. Estonian diaspora author and publisher Bernard Kangro's collection of poetry *Evening in a foreign land* (1966),[20] which was compiled by Jaan Kross and published in 1966 as a supplement of the Tallinn newspaper *Homeland* (Kodumaa), has also been excluded. This newspaper was edited by Andrus Roolaht, who has himself admitted to cooperating with the KGB.[21] Although the distribution – 10,000 copies – to the Estonian diaspora of melancholy poems by a respected poet was apparently meant to lessen their fighting spirit in the political struggle, and these poems were not freely available in the Estonian SSR, they are not based on KGB documents, and so this book will not be examined further. The many books that were meant to encourage the Estonian diaspora to repatriate to the Soviet Union are also seen as borderline cases and will not be analysed in this article.[22]

The researchers do not have access to the Estonian SSR KGB's own materials on its publishing activity for academic study. Taking into account the above-mentioned characteristics and restrictions, 44 books have been found that could be the subjects of research (see table). The list cannot be considered final since the presence of some of the books there could also be disputed.

---

[19] Sergei Kuznetsov, *Elu hinnaga* (Tallinn: Eesti Riiklik Kirjastus, 1964).

[20] Bernard Kangro, *Võõramaa õhtu* (Tallinn: [supplement to the newspaper *Kodumaa*], 1966).

[21] Pekka Erelt, 'Kahe võimu hääletoru' [Bullhorn for two powers], *Eesti Ekspress*, 2 May 2002.

[22] *Meie kodumaa* [Our Homeland], (Tallinn: Komitee 'Kodumaale tagasipöördumise eest', 1959); Viktor Seppel, *Sünnimaale tagasisaabunud jutustavad: ajakirjaniku märkmeid* [Returnees to the homeland speak out] (Tallinn: Väliseestlastega Sidemete Arendamise Komitee, 1960); *Omas kodus: artiklite kogumik* [In one's own home: Collection of the Articles] (Tallinn: Kommunist, 1963).

Table: Books published in Estonian SSR KGB interests 1960–1990.*

	Author(s) or editor(s)	Original title	Language	Title in English	Year	Publishing house	Pages	Copies print-ed	Target audience
1	Gaspl, Igor	Tõestisündinud lood	Estonian	True stories	1960	Eesti Riiklik Kirjastus	120	8,000	Estonian SSR
2	Raudsepp, Vladimir (ed.)	Inimesed, olge valvsad!: Materjale kohtuprotsessist A. Mere, R. Gerretsi ja J. Viigi kriminaalasjas	Estonian	People, be watchful!: Documents from the criminal court case against A. Meri, R. Gerrets and J. Viik	1961	Eesti Riiklik Kirjastus	280	7,000	Estonian SSR
3	Raudsepp, Vladimir (ed.)	Liudi, bud'te bditel'ny! Sudebnyi protsess nad fashistskimi ubiitsami A. Mere, R. Gerretsom i Ia. Viikom: 6–18 marta 1961	Russian	People, be watchful!: Documents from the criminal court case against A. Meri, R. Gerrets and J. Viik	1961	Estgosizdat	304	3,000	USSR
4	N/A	Kaelani soos	Estonian	Up to the neck in the swamp	1962	N/A	96	N/A	Estonian Diaspora
5	Martinson, Ervin	Haakristi teenrid	Estonian	Servants of the swastika	1962	Eesti Riiklik Kirjastus	280	20,000	Estonian SSR

6	Compendium	12000: Tartus 16.–20. jaanuaril 1962 massi-mõrvarite Juhan Jüriste, Karl Linnase ja Ervin Viksi üle peetud kohtuprotsessi mater-jale	Estonian	12,000: Materials from the trial of the mass murderers Juhan Jüriste, Karl Linnas and Ervin Viks, held at Tartu on 16-20 January 1962	1962	Eesti Riiklik Kirjastus	224	10,000	Estonian SSR
7	Dõmov, V. (Dymov, Vasil-ii Andreevich)	Vaenlane ei maga	Estonian	The enemy never sleeps	1962	Eesti Riiklik Kirjastus	80	10,000	Estonian SSR
8	Kruus, Raul (ed.)	People, be watchful!	English	People, be watchful!	1962	Estonian State Publishing House	276	3,000	English speakers abroad
9	Compendium	12000: materialy sudebnogo protsessa nad fashistskimi ubiit-sami Iukhanom Iuriste, Karlom Linnasom i Ervinom Viksom v Tartu 16–20 ianvaria 1962 god	Russian	12,000: Materials from the trial of the mass murderers Juhan Jüriste, Karl Linnas and Ervin Viks, held at Tartu on 16-20 January 1962	1962	Eesti Riiklik Kirjastus	244	5,000	USSR
10	Compendium	Piinlikd lood: Kogu-mik satiire väliseest-lastest	Estonian	Embarasing stories: Collection of satires on exile Estonians	1963	Kodumaa	80	10,000	Estonian Diaspora

	Author	Estonian title	Language	English title	Year	Publisher	No.	Copies	Audience
11	Compendium	12000: Materials from the trial of the mass murderers Juhan Jüriste, Karl Linnas and Ervin Viks, held at Tartu on January 16–20 1962	English	12,000: Materials from the trial of the mass murderers Juhan Jüriste, Karl Linnas and Ervin Viks, held at Tartu on 16-20 January 1962	1963	Eesti Riiklik Kirjastus	120	1,000	English speakers abroad
12	N/A	Eesti riik ja rahvas II maailmasõjas XI	Estonian	The Estonian state and its people in the Second World War, XI	1964	Kodumaa	136	N/A (est. 6,500)	Estonian Diaspora
13	Valge, V (Beliaev, Vasilii Nikitich)	Metsa hämaruses	Estonian	In the dimness of the woods	1965	Eesti Raamat	68	10,000	Estonian SSR
14	N/A	Eesti riik ja rahvas II maailmasõjas	Estonian	The Estonian state and its people in the Second World War, XI	1966	Kodumaa	111	N/A (est. 6,500)	Estonian Diaspora
15	Barkov, Leonid	Mõrvarid ei pääse karistusest: Eesti kodanlike natsionalistide sidemeist hitlerlastega	Estonian	Murderers will not escape punishment: Estonian bourgeois nationalists' contacts with Hitlerites	1966	Eesti Raamat	240	12,000	Estonian SSR
16	Haman, Arthur	Sõbrad ja vaenlased: Mälestuskilde (Faktid ja kommentaarid)	Estonian	Friends and enemies: Fragments of memory	1967	Kodumaa	72	N/A (est. 6,500)	Estonian Diaspora
17	N/A	Eesti riik ja rahvas II maailmasõjas XIII	Estonian	The Estonian state and its people in the Second World War, XIII	1968	Kodumaa	144	N/A (est. 6,500)	Estonian Diaspora

No.	Author	Original title	Language	English title	Year	Publisher	Pages	Print run	Place / notes
18	Kivimaa, Enn	Vähid nailonis ehk, Toimik "Don J..." (Faktid ja kommentaarid)	Estonian	Crayfish in nylon, or the file 'Don J...'	1968	Kodumaa	120	N/A (est. 6,500)	Estonian Diaspora
19	Saar, Ants	Ebatavalised kohtumised: Reportaažid kommentaaridega	Estonian	Unconventional encounters: Reports, including commentary	1968	Eesti Raamat	104	10,000	Estonian SSR
20	Mikenberg, Ralf	Ees on välisreis	Estonian	A foreign trip awaits	1968	Eesti Raamat	80	8,000	Estonian SSR, handbook for people travelling abroad
21	Hanschmidt, Alfred	Nähtamatu duell	Estonian	Invisible duel	1969	Eesti Raamat	184	15,000	Estonian SSR
22	Martinson, Ervin	Elukutse - reetmine	Estonian	Profession - betrayal	1970	Eesti Raamat	336	5,000	Estonian SSR
23	N/A	Eesti riik ja rahvas II maailmasõjas XIV	Estonian	The Estonian state and its people in the Second World War, XIV	1971	Kodumaa	160	6,500	Estonian Diaspora
24	Barkov, Leonid	Beliaev, Vasilii Nikitich	Russian	In the maze of the Abwehr	1971	Eesti Raamat	140	30,000	USSR (icluding Russian language readers in ESSR)

25	N/A	Eesti riik ja rahvas II maailmasõjas XV	Estonian	The Estonian state and its people in the Second World War, XV	1972	Kodumaa	136	6,500	Estonian Diaspora
26	Kordes, Rein	Eesti emigrantide saatusaastad: Esimene osa	Estonian	Estonian emigres' years of destiny: Part one	1974	Perioodika	184	5,500	Estonian Diaspora
27	Barkov, Leonid	Abwehr Eestis	Estonian	The Abwehr in Estonia	1974	Eesti Raamat	128	15,000	Estonian SSR
28	Mikenberg, Ralf	Ees on välisreis (2. täiendatud trükk)	Estonian	A foreign trip awaits (2nd edition for updates)	1975	Eesti Raamat	120	18,000	Estonian SSR, handbook for people travelling abroad
29	Kordes, Rein	Mineviku teed ja rajad: Reportaaž	Estonian	Paths and tracks from the past: Report	1976	Perioodika	316	6,000	Estonian Diaspora
30	Kordes, Rein	Eesti emigrantide saatusaastad: Teine osa	Estonian	Estonian emigres' years of destiny: Part two	1978	Perioodika	168	6,000	Estonian Diaspora
31	Mikenberg, Ralf	Kultuurisidemetest ja turismist	Estonian	On cultural ties and tourism	1978	Eesti Raamat	128	4,000	Estonian SSR, handbook for people interested in tourism

No.	Author	Title	Language	Title (English)	Year	Publisher	Pages	Print run	Audience
32	Taevere, D. Mihhailov, R.	Agoonia	Estonian	Agony	1979	Eesti Raamat	248	36,000	Estonian SSR
33	Kordes, Rein	Eesti emigrantide saatusaastad: Kolmas osa	Estonian	Estonian emigres' years of destiny: Part three	1980	Perioodika	160	6,000	Estonian Diaspora
34	Tiheda, T.	Blood-Soaked Traces of Bourgeois Nationalism	English	Blood-Soaked Traces of Bourgeois Nationalism	1980	Perioodika	64	6,000	English speakers abroad
35	Salu, H. (ed.)	Piinlikd lood: Eesti emigrantliku ladviku poliitilisest palgest	Estonian	Embrassing stories: the true face of the Estonian emigrant elite	1982	Perioodika	96	5,300	Estonian Diaspora
36	Papulovskii, I. Nikishin, V. (eds.)	Kompromissy iskliuchaiutsia: Rasskazy o chekistakh Estonii	Russian	There are no compromises: stories about Estonian Chekists	1982	Eesti Raamat	296	40,000	USSR (icluding Russian language readers in ESSR)
37	Salu, H. (ed.)	Piinlikd lood II: Eesti emigrantliku ladviku poliitilisest palgest	Estonian	Embrassing stories II: the true face of the Estonian emigrant elite	1983	Perioodika	56	6,500	Estonian Diaspora
38	Papulovski, I., Nikišin, V. (eds.)	Kompromiss on välistatud: Lugusid Eesti tšekistidest	Estonian	There is no compromise: stories about Estonian Chekists	1984	Eesti Raamat	272	30,000	Estonian SSR
39	Mikenberg, Ralf	Ideoloogiline võitlus ja psühholoogiline sõda	Estonian	Ideological struggle and psychological war	1985	Eesti Raamat	120	3,500	Estonian SSR
40	Koit, Ülo (ed.)	Mineviku varjud	Estonian	Shadows of the past	1986	Perioodika	144	10,000	Estonian SSR

41	Mihhailov, Rafael	Kutsumata külaline	Estonian	Uninvited guest	1986	Eesti Raamat	224	36,000	Estonian SSR
42	Papulovskii, Ivan; Miurk, Val'ter	Operatsiia "Sinii treugol'nik": Rasskazy o chekistakh Estonii	Russian	Operation 'Blue Triangle': stories about Estonian Chekists	1988	Eesti Raamat	464	35,000	USSR (icluding Russian language readers in ESSR)
43	Roolaht, Andrus	Nii see oli...: Kroonika ühest unustuseliva maetud ajastust	Estonian	And so it was...: Chronicle of an era shrouded in oblivion	1990	Perioodika	384	30,000	Estonian SSR
44	Papulovski, Ivan	Öised külalised	Estonian	Night guests	1990	Olion	64	25,000	Estonian SSR

★ Books published in Estonian SSR 1960–1990 that have at least two of the three following characteristics: the aim of the book is in accordance with the operational interests of the KGB, or is in the interests of the KGB's public image; classified documents, either produced by or held by the KGB, have been used in the writing / compiling the book; the author of the book, or the consultant, is known to be a KGB officer, or a collaborator.

Results

The material listed in the table is varied in content and also voluminous: 44 titles from the period 1960–1990, 7,755 pages in total. These books had a combined print run of over half a million copies. The exact number cannot be determined, however. Although Soviet publishing rules stipulated that the print run be recorded in all books, this requirement was ignored for some of the books meant for the Estonian diaspora. In the interest of graphs and statistical overviews, an average print run (of those books targeted at expatriates where the print run is recorded) of 6,500 copies is used for those books targeted at expatriates where the print run is not recorded, but the word 'estimated' is added.

Regarding genre, the most important were documentary stories and reports, and in books meant for the diaspora, the 'collage technique' was also used (i.e. a mix of exile publications, archive materials and the author's fantasy). There is also 'suggestion' literature and handbooks.

Books meant for domestic consumption (and at the start of the 1960s, also two English-language books) were published by the 'Eesti Riiklik Kirjastus' (Estonian State Publishing House) (as of 1964, 'Eesti Raamat' (Estonian Book)).

At the end of 1989, 'Eesti Raamat' became 'Olion', which managed to publish one book at the beginning of 1990. The newspaper *Kodumaa* (Homeland), established on recommendation from the KGB, published books meant for foreign consumption, and as of the mid-1970s this was done by the 'Perioodika' publishing group.

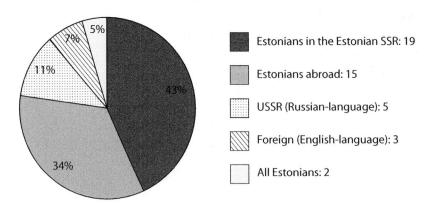

Figure 1. Target group, by number of titles.

The authors are also very different regarding their backgrounds, literary content and experiences. They often conceal their identities by using pseudonyms – e.g. Vassili Dymov, Rein Kordes, Raul Kruus, Rafael Mikhailov, T. Tiheda, Vassili Valge[23] – sometimes it is quite easy to identify the actual author, but in other cases it is impossible. Those using their actual names include active KGB officers (Leonid Barkov, Ralf Mikenberg), former Chekists (Ervin Martinson, Dmitri Taevere), journalists (Igor Gaspl, Ivan Papulovski), persons coopted as KGB collaborators (Juhan Tuldava (alias Arthur Haman), Andrus Roolaht) and even the chairman of the Association for Developing Cultural Ties with Estonians Abroad (VEKSA), Ülo Koit. This is why the background story for the appearance of these books is also probably different.

As the task of this article is not to carry out a detailed analysis of the content of the books, some statistics will be provided. Primarily: who was the target group for these books? In order to determine this, the language of the books is examined, together with the publishing house and also the content. There are two possibilities for presenting the data, which provide very different results: the number of titles of published books (Figure 1) and the print run (Figure 2).

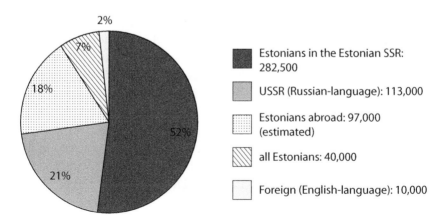

Figure 2. Target groups, by book print run.

---

[23]   In the Russian-language masthead of the same book, we find Vassili Nikitich Belyayev instead of V. Valge.

These statistics demonstrate to some degree the preferences of the KGB's publishing activities. The book titles targeting only the Estonian diaspora constitute almost one-third, and together with the English-language books, two-fifths. Their print runs, however, were smaller than for the books meant for the Soviet Union: the print runs of the one-third of the books targeting the diaspora account for only 18% of the total print runs, and in the case of English-language books the difference is even greater: 5% of the book titles used only 2% of the total print run.

Of the book titles, 43% were meant for domestic consumption in the Estonian SSR, and this accounted for 52% of the total print run. It is therefore possible to say that, generally speaking, half the operation related to book publishing by the Estonian SSR KGB was directed at Estonians living in the Estonian SSR, and the other half was divided between the target groups of diaspora Estonians and Russian-speakers.

The average book print run, by target group (Figure 3), was the largest for the Soviet domestic market, including books meant for the Russian-speaking population in the Estonian SSR, which had print runs averaging 22,600 copies. The average print run for English-language books, however, was the smallest with only 3,333 copies. The large print runs of the Russian-language books are not surprising, considering the size of the Soviet Union. The possibilities for distributing English-language books, however, as well its aims, were much more restricted: only persons visiting the Estonian SSR, or foreigners visiting Soviet embassies, perhaps also some members of foreign communist parties who supported the Soviet Union, could be easily reached. The average print run for books meant for the Estonian SSR is just under 15,000 copies, but the size of the print runs also varies more than ten times within this target group. Ralf Mikenberg's book *Ideological struggle and psychological war* (1985) had a print run of 3,500 copies, but the short story *Uninvited guest* (1986), published under the pseudonym Rafael Mikhailov,[24] had a print run of even 36,000. Seven books that targeted Estonians living abroad had their print run recorded, and their average is 6,485 copies.

---

[24]   According to Kadi Mikk, the pseudonym Rafael Mikhailov belongs to Himmel Sarv, see: Kadi Mikk, 'Metsavendade kujutamine nõukogude propagandakirjanduses' [Image of 'Forest Brothers' in Soviet written propaganda] (Master's thesis, University of Tartu, 2013), 68.

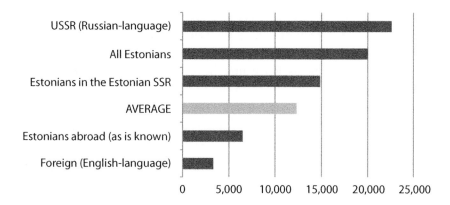

Figure 3. Average book print run, by target group.

Changes over the years in the operations associated with the publishing activities of the Estonian SSR KGB are also reflected in the statistics (Figure 4 and 5).

But here again, the graphs indicating print runs and titles do not correspond. Generally, one could draw the conclusion that the number of titles was large at the beginning of the 1960s, but that print runs increased later, especially in the 1980s. The fact that greater activity and print run increases can be noted in the second half of the 1980s, but at the same time no books could be added to this list from 1987 and 1989 (the methodology used does not suit finding books that diverge from the cliché), could be due to the Estonian SSR KGB having to adapt to the new circumstances of Gorbachev's perestroika and glasnost era.

All the books under discussion have been published during the period 1960–1990, and one might ask: were there none before or after? The subsequent period is indeed brief since the Estonian SSR KGB was disbanded in 1991, and the author has not succeeded in finding relevant books that were published during this period. Either the KGB had given up the fight for public opinion or it was using more refined methods. The latter possibility is more feasible since during the period 1990–1991, there was a position in the KGB titled 'Assistant to the Chairman of the ESSR KGB in the field of public relations', which was held by Lemmik Lehtmets, who had earlier worked in the Fifth Department of the Estonian SSR KGB.[25]

In the analysis of activities before 1960, one can rely, to some degree, on the KGB's own documents. Regarding the period 1954 – when the KGB was established – to 1958, reports from the Second and Fourth Departments have survived in Estonia. These describe the publication of newspapers, and publishing articles in existing newspapers[26] in the interests of KGB operations, and also even the distribution of leaflets abroad.[27] It is apparent that over the years, the extent of such activities increased, and the KGB itself

---

[25]   Kaitsepolitseiameti 19 February 2004. a teadaanne nr. 525 (Announcement of the Internal Security Service) – *Riigi Teataja Lisa 2004*, 79, 0: https://www. riigiteataja.ee/akt/770027, 1 July 2018.

[26]   *Aruanne ENSV Ministrite Nõukogu juures asuva Riikliku Julgeoleku Komitee 2. vastuluureosakonna tööst ajavahemikul 1. IV 1954 – 1. IV 1955* [Report on the work of the State Security Committee's 2nd Counter-Espionage Department, during the period 1 April 1954 – 1 April 1955], eds. Jüri Ojamaa and Jaak Hion (Tallinn: UMARA, 1997), 10; *Aruanne Eesti NSV MN juures asuva RJK 2. osakonna agentuur- ja operatiivtöö kohta 1956. aastal. Aruanne Eesti NSV MN juures asuva RJK 4. osakonna agentuur- ja operatiivtöö kohta 1956. aastal* [Reports on the work of the State Security Committee's 2nd and 4th departments in 1956], eds. Jüri Ojamaa and Jaak Hion (Tallinn: Umara, 2000) –, 59–61; *Aruanne Eesti NSV MN juures asuva RJK 2. osakonna agentuur- ja operatiivtöö kohta 1957. aastal. Aruanne Eesti NSV MN juures asuva RJK 4. osakonna agentuur- ja operatiivtöö kohta 1957. aastal* [Reports on the work of the State Security Committee's 2nd and 4th departments in 1957], eds. Jüri Ojamaa and Jaak Hion (Tallinn: Eesti Rahvusarhiiv, 2002), 79, 223–224; *Aruanne Eesti NSV Ministrite Nõukogu juures asuva Riikliku Julgeoleku Komitee 2. osakonna agentuur- ja operatiivtöö tulemuste kohta 1958. aastal; Aruanne Eesti NSV Ministrite Nõukogu juures asuva Riikliku Julgeoleku Komitee 4. osakonna agentuur- ja operatiivtöö tulemuste kohta 1958. aastal* [Reports on the work of the State Security Committee's 2nd and 4th departments in 1958], eds. Jüri Ojamaa and Jaak Hion (Tallinn: Rahvusarhiiv, 2005), 138–139, 150, 152, 173, 189, 200.

[27]   *Aruanne ENSV Ministrite Nõukogu juures asuva Riikliku Julgeoleku Komitee 2. vastuluureosakonna tööst ajavahemikul 1.IV 1954 – 1.IV 1955* [Report on the work of the State Security Committee's 2nd Counter-Intelligence Department during the period 1 April 1954 – 1 April 1955], eds. Jüri Ojamaa and Jaak Hion (Tallinn: UMARA, 1997), 54.

considered the impact of such measures to be positive. In the reports referring to the period 1954–1958, there is not a word about book publishing.[28]
Articles published in 1957 and the beginning of 1958 in the newspapers
Sovetskaya Estoniya (Soviet Estonia, in Russian) and *Rahva Hääl* (People's
Voice, in Estonian) that were based on KGB documents were later repub-
lished in books, up to 1990. In its 1957 report, the Fourth Department of
the Estonian SSR KGB assessed the impact of these articles as follows: 'The
information received testifies to the fact that the published material played
a positive role, and that the local populations react approvingly.'[29] The
conclusion, therefore, may be drawn that the methods tested during the
late 1950s in newspapers were utilised only as of 1960 in book publishing,
when the book *True stories* by the journalist Igor Gaspli of the newspaper
'*Sovetskaya Estoniya*' was published.

Further Research Opportunities

The above list and statistics demonstrate, on the basis of limited characteristics, how the Estonian SSR KGB and its workers published books in
the operational interests of the KGB, or to develop its image, and what
the results of this were, in figures. This, however, does not provide the
answer even to the question: are the 44 titles in half a million copies over
31 years a lot or a few? Answering this question is not simple since the
answer depends on comparison, but there is not much that can be used
for comparison. The number of books is not large compared to the overall number of books and booklets published in the Estonian SSR that
remained in the range of between 1,400 and 2,400 items per year in the
1960s to the 1980s.[30]

---

[28] Repatriation propaganda, which later was the responsibility of the KGB, had
already been carried out among the Estonian diaspora via printed material since
1945, but there is no information as to whether anything was also published in
this field during the period 1954–1958 that could be classified as a book, in the
context of this article.

[29] *Aruanne Eesti NSV MN juures asuva RJK 2. osakonna agentuur- ja operatiivtöö kohta 1957*, 79, 224.

[30] Möldre, *Eesti raamatu 100*, 109–110.

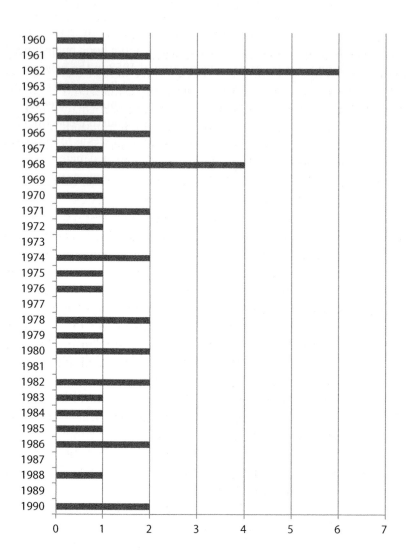

Figure 4. Number of books published, by year.

Figure 5. Total print run of published books, by year (* indicates that the print run of at least one book in that year is an estimate).

In order to achieve results that are more broadly useful to historical research, and which also have interdisciplinary value, one should concentrate on five connected problem areas:

- publishing activity and its aims;
- the books' authors, their backgrounds, motives and their creative processes;
- the books' content, the KGB's basic narratives and their development;
- the books' impact;
- similar activity by the KGB using different channels (journalism and film), and the same processes elsewhere in the Soviet Union and in Eastern Europe.

The research does not need to start from nothing: there has already been research on publishing activity in the Estonian SSR,[31] and some of the books included in the list have been analysed based on their content[32] or author.[33] Publishing has been examined in recently published memoirs[34] and interesting additional information on this topic can be gained from interviews with participants.[35]

Although it is known when the books were published, who directed this activity and how initially remains an open question. What was the role of the Central Committee of the Estonian Communist Party, or the Estonian SSR KGB, or the Estonian SSR Literature Committee, and to what extent did their central organisations in Moscow interfere? Was the same model followed for all the books or not? Which KGB structural

---

[31] Ilona Kään, 'Kirjastus "Eesti Raamat" 1964–2002' [Publishing house 'Eesti Raamat' 1964–2002] (Diploma thesis, Tallinn Pedagogical University, 2003).

[32] Mikk, 'Metsavendade kujutamine'.

[33] Ivo Juurvee, 'Idabloki eriteenistuste võitlustest Külma sõja ajaloorindel Andrus Roolahe ja Julius Maderi näitel' [Eastern bloc secret services' fight on the history front of the Cold War, based on the examples of Andrus Roolaht and Julius Mader], *Ajalooline Ajakiri*, no. 1–2 (2009): 47–76.

[34] Eenok Kornel. *Kuldset keskteed ei ole: Mälestusi, äratundmisi, pealtnägemisi* [There is no middle way: Memories, realisations, observations] (Tallinn: Olion, 2011); Aare Laanemäe, *Kümme aastat valges majas: Ausalt ja avameelselt* [Ten years in the white house: Honestly and openly] (Tallinn: Argo, 2013).

[35] Telephone interview by the author with Heino Kään, senior employee of the Eesti Raamat publishing house, 26 April 2013 and corrections made by the interviewee to the interview transcript.

units were involved with the publishing and what was the impact on this activity of the structural changes in the KGB? What were the precise target groups for the books and what was the expected impact? To what extent, if at all, did the books come about as a result of the author's own initiative – this can be presumed in the case of one or two of the books – and did the publishing house have room to manoeuvre?

And here we arrive at the authors, most of whom led adventurous lives where writing the books analysed here is just one episode in their lives. It is perhaps somewhat surprising that at first glance, the motives also seem to be varied: carrying out an order (in the case of journalists, perhaps a work task) or being paid well for it are not at all the only ones. Other motives seem to be vanity, careerism and perhaps also abstract revenge.

Indications of how the books were written can also be found in the books themselves, although they do occasionally seem insincere. It is difficult to believe Ants Saar, who credits the loquaciousness of KGB officers for the backstory to the book *Unconventional encounters* ('During the court recess, however, I sought out the men who had carried out the preliminary investigation. The recess dragged on, and we stayed seated on the bench under the window'[36]) and emphasises chance ('Having reached liberated Tallinn, this book's author happened, quite accidentally, upon one of the files of the time'[37]). On the other hand, the description given by Igor Gaspl regarding his cooperation with retired Lieutenant-Colonel Nikolai Polyakov, probably at his Estonian SSR KGB headquarters on Pagari Street in Tallinn, seems quite feasible: 'The office provided for my and Polyakov's use was an ordinary, simple office. It was furnished only with a large office desk, a few chairs and a safe that had been squeezed into the corner right next to the door. On the desk, where the boss generally had no unnecessary papers, there was a large pile of folders. Our task was to sort through them, and put down on paper, in approximately the right order, a story that was of interest to us.'[38]

In the case of such writings, the aspect of the so-called creative process is of even greater interest since there is so little information on it in

---

[36] Ants Saar, *Ebatavalised kohtumised* [Unconventional encounters] (Tallinn: Eesti Raamat, 1968), 29.

[37] *Ibid.*, p. 32.

[38] Igor Gaspl, 'Lõks "penidele"' [A trap set for 'curs'], – *Kompromiss on välistatud: Lugusid Eesti tšekistidest* [No compromise: stories about Estonian Chekists] (Tallinn: Eesti Raamat, 1984), 187.

research literature and memoirs. A rare known example from the West is from the early years of the Cold War, and from a faraway country. In 1954, Vladimir Petrov and Evdokia Petrova, a married couple who were Soviet espionage officers, defected in Australia. Two years later, a book of memoirs titled *Empire of Fear* was published, with the Petrovs as authors, which in addition to containing comprehensive information was also well written.[39] The fact that the Australian counter-intelligence service ASIO (Australian Security Intelligence Organisation) was behind the book was soon made public due to the opposition's skilled questions to the Prime Minister in Australia's parliament.[40] In 1980, the memoirs of the book's actual ghost author, Michael Thwaites, were published, in which he also described the backstory to the book, including the related contracts and the emotions during the writing process.[41] At the time of the Petrovs' defection, Thwaites was number two in ASIO, but his talent for poetry had already stood out during his studies at Oxford, which explains the accomplished style of *Empire of Fear*. As far as the books analysed in this article are concerned, perhaps *Friends and enemies* (1967), written as a memoir, and the pedagogically pedantic *Crayfish in nylon* (1968) are outstanding in their style.

Analysis of the books' narratives, and their development, is the least demanding activity regarding the source material – the books themselves are sufficient. Already during the initial observation, one notices ample repetitions across the decades, and the constancy of the basic narratives in the documentary stories. The 'anti-fascist struggle' of the Chekists occupies a central place, and in the case of anti-Soviet persons, there is usually a revelation in the development of the story that they cooperated with the Germans during World War II. During the 1960s and 1970s, however, a major difference can be seen in the content of the books between those targeting the USSR and those meant for the foreign market. Regarding the source material, it would be more complicated and time-consuming to

---

[39]   Vladimir Petrov and Evdokia Petrova, *Empire of Fear* (London: Andre Deutsch, 1956).

[40]   As it turned out years later, the opposition was able to ask such precise questions because it already knew many of the answers – information had leaked from ASIO. See Robert Manne, *The Petrov Affair: Politics and espionage* (Sydney: Pergamon, 1987), 103, 250, 256.

[41]   Michael Thwaites, *Truth Will Out: ASIO and the Petrovs* (Sydney: Collins, 1980).

discover the real-life, existing (or non-existent) prototypes for the activities described in the books.

Assessing the impact of the works is perhaps the most important task, but also the most complex. Initially it seemed that the desired results had not been clearly stated by the KGB, or that there had even been no aim at all, which means that it is not possible to scientifically assess the extent to which the KGB achieved its aims. There are also other methodological problems – even if the KGB achieved its desired effect, it could be impossible to scientifically prove its causal relationship with the published books. The textbook *The fundamentals of Communist propaganda*, published in the Estonian SSR in 1981, says: 'The current system for Communist propaganda stands out with its reach, the network of channels for influencing ideas, the constant increase in their numbers, and qualitative improvements.'[42] The choice of channels for the KGB was also much broader than just books. In this article, there is also mention of the association of the Estonian SSR KGB with the publishing of newspaper articles with fabricated and compromising content, and its consulting role for feature film scripts. Considering the way that the various forms of media were synchronised during these decades, and that journalists moved between written and spoken media, it is clear that the KGB was also involved in radio and television. This topic also still needs to be analysed in more detail.

In examining the activities of the Estonian SSR KGB, it is important to also take into account the materials and experiences of its central bodies and of its branches in other regions. The operations of the KGB were managed from one centre and this is why its behavioural patterns were mostly the same everywhere, but the archival material that has been preserved in Estonia might perhaps not suffice for a thorough understanding of this. Perhaps it is possible to get valuable information on this from outside Estonia. And also conversely: perhaps one of the major opportunities for this area of research lies herein – processes in the Estonian SSR will help in understanding what happened elsewhere in the USSR and Eastern Europe.[43]

---

[42] *Kommunistliku propaganda alused: Õppevahend marksismi-leninismi ülikoolidele, parteiaktiivi koolidele ja seminaridele* [The fundamentals of Communist propaganda: teaching material for Marxist-Leninist universities, schools and seminars for Party activists] (Tallinn: Eesti Raamat, 1981), 43.

[43] In September of 2013, the conference 'Need to Know III. Them vs Us: Image of the Enemy' was held in Visby, with participation by secret services history

Summary

Although the intrusion by the secret services of totalitarian states in all aspects of life is occasionally mentioned, there certainly has not been research in all these aspects. This article, using the example of the Estonian SSR KGB, has examined the interference of this service in the formation of public opinion through book publishing, and the extent of this activity has been ascertained.

The books that have been chosen as the subject of the research are those where the aim was in accordance with the operational interests of the KGB or with forming the reputation of the KGB. The writing/compiling of these books involved documents that belonged to the KGB itself or were in the hands of the KGB. These documents were classified and/or the author was a KGB officer or coopted person. There were 44 such books from the period 1960–1990, taking into account the set restrictions, but this number could vary to some degree as a result of further research. It is most probable, however, that no books matching the same criteria were published in the Estonian SSR before 1960.

The 44 books that were discovered differed greatly both in content and in the authors, but there are also many similarities and repetitions. An estimated total of half a million copies of such books were printed in Estonian, Russian and English. Around half the total output targeted the Estonian-speaking reader in the Estonian SSR, and the other half aimed at other target groups: Russian-speaking readers in the Estonian SSR and elsewhere in the Soviet Union, exile Estonians and English-speaking foreigners.

Nevertheless, there is still not much known about the publishing process from the initial idea to distribution. Further research is needed on both the publishing process and its goals; the books' authors and their backgrounds and motives; content, the KGB's basic narratives and their development. The impact of such books is particularly important but the relevant research creates various methodological problems. One promising research field is the KGB's similar activity in influencing public opin-

---

researchers from 14 countries. This author presented 'Permanent Struggle against Fascism: Self-representation of the Estonian SSR KGB in Literature and Cinema'. The following discussion brought out the understanding that this is not just an Estonian SSR-specific phenomenon, and that it deserves to be further studied, also elsewhere in Eastern Europe.

ion by using other channels (press and cinema) in both the Estonian SSR and elsewhere in the Soviet Union and in Eastern Europe.

Information on the use of the printed word in the interests of totalitarian secret services in the Estonian SSR could also assist in the better understanding of what took place in the rest of Eastern Europe, and vice versa. Considering that the Estonian SSR KGB was just one small regional sub-unit of the USSR KGB, the total volume of such books could be very large indeed.

One of the Possibilities for Systematising Soviet Repressions

Aivar Niglas[*]

Introduction

State coercion was one of the Soviet Union's most important means of governance. It was used most intensively during Joseph Stalin's reign, yet it was important before that and after his death as well.

The use of coercive measures that have restricted people's rights and freedoms to the greatest degree earn the primary attention of historians: sentencing to death, imprisonment and deportation into exile. The use of such harsh measures is traditionally regulated by penal law.[1] Coercive measures were also used outside of the law in the Soviet Union contrary to its own laws, concealing them behind formulations of 'non-punitive measures'. Evidently for this reason, terms that emphasise punishment a little less and that attempt to define the use of coercive measures a little more comprehensively have been adopted in both historical literature and the drafting of legislation: political, extrajudicial and unlawful repressions, mass repressions, terror, etc.

Upon closer examination, however, these terms prove to be indefinite and difficult to delineate. They are either evaluative and not sufficiently perspicuous to account for all important spheres of ensuring coercion,

---

[*] First published: Aivar Niglas, 'Üks NSV Liidu repressioonide süstematiseerimise võimalusi', *Tuna: ajalookultuuri ajakiri*, no. 4 (2011): 61–78.

[1] The term 'penal law' is used in Estonia's current legal system. This field was referred to as 'criminal law' in the Soviet Union. These terms are used as synonyms in this article.

or they leave out some groups of individuals. Many terms do little more than to split the object in two and do not offer any sort of comprehensive framework for systematising repressions. It is not possible to systematise repressions by using these terms, nor can different groups of repressed persons be differentiated sufficiently clearly.

This is the case even if the aim is to identify the size of groups, for instance. What are the criteria for determining the number of persons who have been repressed for political reasons? Where does the boundary lay separating mass repression from non-mass repression? If judicial repressions can be defined by way of institutions referred to as courts, then where did extrajudicial repression begin and end? Were repressions that were not unlawful lawful, etc.? It is difficult, or sometimes even impossible, to answer these questions.

This article offers one possibility for systematisation deriving from a legal basis. By *law* I mean *law* in the sense of a democratic state based on the rule of law. *Law* is necessary because by the formal recognition of *law*, Soviet law was used as a fig leaf to justify and conceal violence that had taken place in the Soviet Union. The article focuses on the most repressive measures of a punitive nature for enforcing coercion.

State Coercive Measures

Soviet legal theory distinguished between three types of state coercive measures: liability measures, preventive measures and obstructive measures.

What differentiated liability measures from the other types of measures was primarily the fact that they were applied post-factum after the offence had been committed. Liability measures were categorised as proprietary (compensation of damages) and punitive. The latter, in turn, were divided up into criminal, administrative, disciplinary and procedural penalties. The harshness of the penalty was manifested in the **losses and restrictions** inflicted upon the offender, in other words what the penalty actually meant for the offender: loss of life (death penalty), loss of personal freedom (loss of liberty), restriction of freedom to choose one's place of residence (residential penalties), restrictions in the sphere of property (monetary fines and the confiscation of property), etc. The losses and restrictions suffered by the individual from criminal penalties were greater compared to the other penalties.

Preventive measures were applied in the event of the actual and concrete threat of an attack that would endanger society in order to prevent this threat from becoming reality. For instance, procedural preventive measures to ensure that an offender would turn up at the investigating organ and in court, assigning the offender to compulsory treatment for contagious diseases, etc. belonged to the category of preventive measures.

Obstructive measures were applied when the threat to society was becoming reality and an attack took place. The aim of obstructive measures was to prevent the attack from being brought to completion.[2]

Regarding this topic, attention is mainly on criminally punitive liability measures, in connection with which the concepts of **punishment** (penalties) and **repression** need to be clarified. In the sense of a state based on the rule of law, the concept of punishment can be analysed in various ways. According to one definition, it consists of a formally judicial aspect, in other words legal consequences prescribed in provisions as punishments, and a substantive aspect, in other words forfeiture applied to the convicted offender for an offence, by which the state damages the individual's constitutional standing, expresses social-ethical condemnation as a public decision based on values, and forces the individual to bear responsibility for his deed (obliges him to bear the negative consequences or sanctions that accompany his deed).[3] According to Soviet theory of criminal law, punishment was a 'means of state coercion that is one of the measures of legal liability applicable to a convicted offender for committing a criminal offence on the basis of a court verdict. It causes certain losses or restrictions for the convicted offender and in this manner expresses a negative assessment of the criminal offence and the judicial, and thus also the political-moral, condemnation of the convicted offender compatible to the social hazard of the criminal offence committed and the guilt of the offender who committed it. The aim of punishment is repression for a committed criminal offence, and also the correction and re-education of the convicted offender, and the prevention of the commission of new criminal offences by that same criminal offender and other individuals.[4]

---

2   Ilmar Rebane, *Nõukogude kriminaalõigus, 2, Õpetus karistusest: üldosa* [Soviet Criminal Law. General Part. Doctrine of Punishment] (Tartu: Tartu Riiklik Ülikool, 1974), 17–21, 26.

3   Jaan Sootak, *Sanktsiooniõigus: karistusõiguslikud sanktsioonid ja nende kohaldamine* [Penal Law] (Tallinn: Juura, 2007), 74.

4   Rebane, *Nõukogude kriminaalõigus*, 3.

Thus there is not much difference between the concept of punishment in the law of a state based on the rule of law and in Soviet law in the sense that both divide the concept of punishment into several parts in terms of legal philosophy: as 'social-ethical' or 'political-moral' condemnation in terms of aims, along with the prevention of new criminal offences, and 'restrictions and losses' or 'forfeiture' demonstrating the actual consequences of punishment. The concept of repression refers to the content of punishment, that which was referred to as losses and restrictions in Soviet penal law and which has been replaced by the term **forfeitures** in current Estonian penal law. The greater the forfeitures and the longer they last, the more repressive they are. Thus punishment and repression are not synonyms.[5]

In a state based on the rule of law, the concept of repression is a part of the concept of punishment. One can be repressed only for deeds defined as criminal offences in legal provisions using legal liability measures and by court proceeding (leaving aside less repressive disciplinary and other punishments that can be applied extrajudicially). On the contrary, repression in the Soviet Union went beyond the framework of the concept of punishment and also beyond the law in its meaning in a state based on the rule of law. Forfeitures inherent to punishments also started being applied extrajudicially to individuals who had not committed a punishable deed, to say nothing of shortcomings in defining the deed as a criminal offence. Soviet legal provisions also allowed repression of persons who had not committed any punishable deeds (until 1958), although this was limited to socially hazardous (*sotsialno opasnye*) individuals.[6] Other groups

---

[5]   *Ibid.*, 26–27.

[6]   Mostly representatives of the 'exploitative classes' belonged to the category of 'socially hazardous' persons: bankers, politicians, nobles, prison guards, policemen, the owners of enterprises in the era of the Russian Empire, etc., after the end of the New Economic Policy (NEP) entrepreneurs from the NEP era as well. This coincided partially with the group of persons deprived of voting rights by the constitution in the 1920s (the so-called *lishentsy*, the deprived, who can be included among those who were repressed normatively but without having committed any punishable deed. When new territories were captured, representatives of the 'exploitative classes' in those areas also became potential objects of repression. 'Socially hazardous element' (*sotsial'no-opasnyi element*) was the most widely used term alongside which 'element hazardous to society' (*obshchestvenno opasnyi element*) was also used, primarily in legal provisions. The criteria of hazardousness to society were not set out in these provisions. There is also no

that had committed no punishable deeds were actually also repressed and alongside general group attributes, the reason for repression became the prevention of anti-state activity or activity that did not suit the regime. Thus in the case of the Soviet Union, we can speak of the disappearance of boundaries separating liability measures from the remainder of state coercive measures, punitive from non-punitive measures, and the criminal offence from the sphere outside of it.

The meaning of the concept of repression emphasising the content of punishment helps to eliminate formal barriers deriving from the concept of punishment that considers only measures defined as punishment in legal provisions to be punishment. Thus the concept of repression applicable to the Soviet Union includes all measures by which forfeitures were caused that corresponded to criminal punishment. In order to distinguish between punishment and repression, which is also important, let us refer to as punishment only measures defined as punishments in the provisions of Soviet criminal law, and to the act of punishment as the implementation of these measures. Thus while repression should theoretically be part of the concept of punishment, in the case of the Soviet Union, the situation is the opposite – repression is the general concept and punishment is a partitive concept. The suitability of the word 'repression' is also indicated by the fact that it can denote extrajudicial punishment and the application of measures of a punishing nature, since only the activity of institutions defined in legal provisions as courts is categorised as the administration of justice by court trial.

Evidently, it is precisely for these reasons that the word 'repression' was adopted more broadly at the end of the 1980s. Nowadays as well, the concept of repression is appropriate in every respect for use in reference to the Soviet Union and it is one of the most important concepts of this article.

The clarification of the concept of repression alone is not enough for systematisation.

---

evidence that they were prescribed in some other source. No criminal offence had to be committed previously in order to be declared hazardous to society. The court had the right to declare persons hazardous to society and to send them into exile even in the event of a court verdict of acquittal.

The Law of States Based on the Rule of Law versus Soviet Law

One further fundamental question needs to be answered. To what extent is *law* compatible with Soviet law at all? The Soviet Union was not a state based on the rule of law, which was demonstrated even just by the absence of the separation of powers. Power was concentrated in the hands of a small group of individuals. Those in power had legal provisions drawn up that suited themselves and had them suitably justified in literature on legal theory. These provisions could be adhered to but this was abandoned if it started hampering governance. Under such conditions, legal concepts also lost their actual meaning. Courts and judges were not independent and did not administer justice, but rather followed the orders from those in power as part of the power apparatus. Law did not have the force of law in the sense of a state based on the rule of law, etc. The distortion of the meaning of the concepts of punishment and criminal offences has already been discussed above.[7] Here no particular 'socialist law' or Soviet law can be spoken of at all.

The field referred to as law in the Soviet Union was founded on the European legal tradition based on Roman law, distorting it and leaving out certain important elements. The positivist, sociological school of criminal law that emerged in Europe in the 18th–19th centuries was the direct model for the Soviet Union's criminal law.[8] The Russian Empire's criminal law was also founded on European legal tradition, as was that part of the Russian Empire's criminal law that the Bolsheviks adopted. The singularity of Soviet law was stressed for ideological reasons only in the Soviet Union itself as part of the contrasting of the capitalist and communist forms of government as opposites. In analysing and describing the Soviet legal order from the position of a state based on the rule of law, and using concepts of a state based on the rule of law, the danger arises of identifying Soviet law with the law of a state based on the rule of law. This can

---

[7]   The concepts of punishment and criminal offence already started approaching their classical meanings in Soviet legal theory during Stalin's rule and acquired them after new fundamental laws (statutes) of criminal law went into effect in 1958. This nevertheless does not change the nature of the problem.

[8]   Jaan Sootak, *Veritasust kriminaalteraapiani: käsitlusi kriminaalõiguse ajaloost* [From Blood Feud to Criminal Therapy: Considerations from the History of Criminal Law], (Tallinn: Juura, 1998), 254–255.

be avoided by emphasising the fact that they have been matched up artificially. In order to better illustrate this, I call it the **method of equating meanings**. This is not a method in the sense of practical usability since it is not a body of specific means for analysis and comparison. It denotes the fundamental difference between *law* and Soviet law. The method indicates that the identification of Soviet law with *law* is not done naturally on the grounds of essential similarity, but rather that this is an artificial construct. Identification takes place through formal attributes. *Law* as a complete and freely developing system provides us with a systematic point of departure and also a system of concepts to cover fields that have been distorted or left out of Soviet law. Due to the distortion of *law*, the law of the Soviet Union itself cannot be taken as the point of departure for this. This would mean the approval of distortions. We do not use *law*, including concepts of *law*, so much for explaining the functioning of the field referred to as law in the Soviet Union, but for explaining how this non-law functioned at the state level.

One of the most widespread modes for categorising repressions requires a more comprehensive analysis.

Political and Non-Political Repression?

Let us state right from the outset that politicalness is not a particularly good definition as a basis for systematising the Soviet Union's repressions. It is an ambiguous term without any clear content and with a vague meaning, which is often used regardless of this. There is no generally recognised definition of political repression and it is also unclear why repressions have to be categorised in such a way at all.

The categorisation of criminal offences as political and non-political by employing the word 'political' was not used all that often in the Soviet Union's official bureaucratic usage. Normative usage in criminal law did not recognise this term at all, and it was rarely found in the documents of the system of repression. Abbreviated terms for the description of criminal offences were preferred.

The reason why the concept of political repression is often used in current historical literature has to be sought elsewhere. The reason for this is quite likely the Soviet Union's legislation of general application issued at the end of the 1980s and the early 1990s, first and foremost the Russian

SFSR law of 1991 'Concerning the rehabilitation of victims of political repressions'. This law remains in effect in Russia in amended form to this day.

There is nevertheless no point in seeking a more precise explanation from this law. A passage resembling an explanation is in §1: 'State means of coercion applied for **political motives** are recognised as **political repressions** [...].' That is all. The list that follows includes the harshest types of Soviet punishment and all institutions that have conducted court trials, and is thus too all-inclusive to be considered an explanation of the concept of political repression. The explanation that political repression is a means of coercion of a political nature does not add any further insight into the concept. This legislation leaves the interpretation of political motivation to the courts and the prosecutor's office. What is and what is not political in the sense of this legislation could only be demonstrated by the practice of applying this legislation.[9]

If we attempt to somehow interpret political repression, it should definitely include the idea of opposition to the powers that be, but not the idea of acts in opposition to the powers that be, since people in the Soviet Union were also repressed without committing any punishable acts. This alone already limits the possibilities for clear wording. The fact that it is not easy to distinguish opposition to the powers that be from other opposition in the case of the Soviet Union is an even greater obstacle, since the regime recognised only one ideology and totally controlled society.

---

[9]   This legislation has two further important shortcomings: 1) it rules out the rehabilitation of persons punished for certain criminal offences 'on the grounds of sufficient evidence' even if these persons were repressed extrajudicially (§4). Such instances of repression would be null and void from the standpoint of *law* and would not even require a separate rehabilitation decision; 2) among others, persons punished for 'war crimes, crimes against peace, crimes against humanity, and crimes against the administration of justice' are not subject to rehabilitation. This seemingly is a just provision, but in today's Russia, where the prosecution of persons who have committed the listed crimes in the Soviet Union is avoided, this legislation contributes to avoiding responsibility. The proper assessment of the Soviet Union's repressions inherent to a state based on the rule of law would require the nullification of all *unlawful* repression verdicts, regardless of the content of the charges, and the initiation of new criminal cases. The nullification of the verdicts of persons punished for the above-mentioned crimes, however, and the initiation of new criminal cases would place on the agenda the need to launch investigations regarding persons suspected of committing similar crimes that were not punished during the existence of the Soviet Union.

Thus, for the regime, every act or omission of action was in opposition to the powers that be.

The concept of political repression has two concealed and hitherto undifferentiated meanings that people are not aware of.

1) The meaning of groundless, unfounded, unjustified, wrong, etc. actions, which I henceforth refer to in general as **unjustified repression** or **unjustified action**. I use this as a temporary, neutral and very general term for explaining other terms in order to avoid using political repression and words with a shade of law.

The Russian Federation's so-called rehabilitation law expresses this most clearly. It prescribes the nullification of the repression verdicts for some repressed persons in the Soviet Union, in other words their rehabilitation, and in some cases also the compensation of sufferings. People who are not rehabilitated consequently remain rightly repressed. The concept of political repression is not used in rehabilitation legislation in all of the Soviet Union's successor states and former dependent states,[10] but since they prescribe the nullification of only some repression verdicts or the ascertainment of groups of persons who have suffered due to the Soviet Union's repressions, the categorisation of repressions as justified and unjustified exists in this legislation as well.[11]

---

[10]   By rehabilitation legislation, I mean legislation in a very general sense that has been adopted to nullify 'Soviet era' repression verdicts so that I can avoid writing out the full titles of these acts of legislation. The word 'rehabilitation' started being used in the Soviet Union in the meaning of nullifying repression verdicts and is used in this way to this day in the former Soviet Union's successor states and dependent states. The influentiality of 'Soviet law' nevertheless differs. Rehabilitation is used in Estonia and, due to the effect of the German Democratic Republic (GDR), in present day Germany as well, primarily in reference to the nullification of repression verdicts from the time of the Soviet Union and the GDR. The term is used to a small extent in Estonian law in the criminal procedure code (§199 and 274). Present day Russian law, however, has fully adopted this term and treats rehabilitation as an institute of criminal trial law.

[11]   This is nevertheless not an all-encompassing generalisation because it was not possible for me to peruse the content of the laws in the Soviet Union's former dependent states (with the exception of the German Federal Republic legislation concerning the German Democratic Republic) due to the language barrier. For Estonia's legislation (Persons Repressed by Occupying Powers Act, Riigi Teataja

German legislation is an exception, which places the verdict's legality at the forefront instead of politicalness: 'Penal law verdicts handed down in the period from 8 May 1945 to 2 October 1990 in the region mentioned by the German Supreme Court in Article 3 (the region joining the federation) of the unification agreement [of West and East Germany. *Author's remark*] are to be declared in violation of the principles of a state based on the rule of law on the basis of the corresponding application and nullified if the verdicts do not conform to the more important principles of freedom of a state based on the rule of law, especially if said verdicts served political objectives. As a rule, this affects punishments in accordance with the following acts of law: [...].'[12]

[State Gazette], henceforth RT I 2003, 88, 589). As a matter of fact, these are not actually rehabilitation laws since their aim is not to nullify the Soviet Union's repression verdicts. This legislation ascertains (as one objective) groups of persons who have suffered at the hands of the Communist and National Socialist regimes. The Latvian and Lithuanian laws define the concept of repression for political reasons by way of listing the groups of persons with this status. The concept itself is not defined. The Estonian law does not use the concept of political repression. At the same time, the 'Extrajudicially repressed and groundlessly convicted persons act' adopted on 19 February 1992 and its amendment legislation adopted on 23 November 1993 remain in effect in Estonia (RT 1992, 7, 103; 1993, 76, 1128). This legislation also does not use the concept of political repression but sets the nullification of the Soviet Union's repression verdicts as its objective. The legislation also lists the sections of the Russian SFSR and the Estonian SSR criminal codes that are subject to nullification. Compared to the law adopted in 2004, the legislation from 1992 and 1993 is farther from the idea of the state based on the rule of law because the Republic of Estonia as a state based on the rule of law, which considers its incorporation into the Soviet Union to be null and void, need not take the obligation upon itself of nullifying the repression verdicts of the Soviet Union as a state that was not based on the rule of law. The laws of other former Soviet republics are strongly influenced by the Russian Federation's rehabilitation legislation (which is essentially the Russian SFSR rehabilitation law of 1991) and hence they set as their aim the nullification of the Soviet Union's repression verdicts based on the political reasons for those repressions. The texts of these laws are published in the collection: *Sbornik zakonodatel'nykh i normativnykh aktov o reabilitatsii zhertv politicheskikh repressii. Tom II* (Kursk: General'naia Prokuratura RF, 1999), 108–122.

[12]   Gesetz über die Rehabilitierung und Entschädigung von Opfern rechtsstaatswidriger Strafverfolgungsmaßnahmen im Beitrittsgebiet (Strafrechtliches Rehabilitierungsgesetz – StrRehaG), 29 October 1992, http://www.gesetze-im-internet.de/strrehag/BJNR118140992.html, 1 June 2018.

Thus the objects of the German legislation are all court verdicts during the period and in the territory prescribed in the legislation.

Such clear boundaries are not drawn in historical literature. Consideration of repressions as justified / not justified exists implicitly, primarily through paying greater attention to certain groups (mass executions, counterrevolutionary crimes, deportations into exile by extrajudicial institutions, etc.) and by dividing repressed persons into 'criminals' and 'politicals'.

John Arch Getty, Gabor Tamas Rittersporn and Viktor Zemskov have written that: 'From this point of view, the regime's distinction between "political" and "non-political" offenders is of doubtful relevance. Unless we are prepared to accept broad Stalinist definitions of "counterrevolutionary" offences or the equally tendentious Western categorisation of *all* arrests during Stalin's time (even those for crimes punishable in any society) as political, we should devise ways to separate ordinary criminality from genuine opposition to the system as well as from other reasons for which people were subjected to penal repression.'[13]

Anne Appelbaum argues: 'If the politicals were not necessarily political, the vast majority of criminal prisoners were not necessarily criminals either. While there were some professional criminals and, during the war years, some genuine war criminals and Nazi collaborators in the camps, most of the others had been convicted of so-called "ordinary" or non-political crimes that in the other societies would not be considered crimes at all.'[14]

2) The simplest approach is to categorise repressions according to the descriptions of criminal offences and general group attributes (of that type). The group of descriptions of criminal offences referred to as counterrevolutionary crimes in Soviet criminal law are always categorised under the term of political repression. The legal institute of the description of a criminal offence is part of the sphere of substantive law. Leaving aside other definitions and focusing on the counterrevolutionary as the most

---

[13]   J. Arch Getty, Gabor T. Rittersporn, Viktor Zemskov, 'Victims of the Soviet Penal System in the Pre-war Years: a First Approach on the Basis of Archival Evidence', – *American Historical Review*, October (1993): 1033.

[14]   Anne Applebaum, Gulag: a history of the Soviet camps (London: Lane, 2003), 272.

political of descriptions of criminal offences, it can be asserted that political repression is also a term primarily from the sphere of substantive law.

These two connotations of political repression highlight two important shortcomings. **First,** if we recognise the two attributes mentioned at the beginning of this subchapter together (unjustified activity and being part of substantive law) as part of the concept of political repression, all acts that are treated as universal criminal offences, meaning deeds that are considered crimes in all countries, for which a substantive equivalent can be found among counterrevolutionary crimes, should be considered political and thus unjustified. § 232 of the Penal Code of the Republic of Estonia (KarS) (treason) corresponds to the meaning of § 58^{1a} and 58^{1b} of the 1926 Russian SFSR Criminal Code (betrayal of the homeland), KarS § 231 (violent action directed against the independence and sovereignty of the Republic of Estonia) could correspond to § 58^2 (armed rebellion), KarS § 233, 234, 242–243 correspond to the content of § 58^6 (espionage), KarS § 237 (terrorism) corresponds to § 58^8 (terrorism), KarS § 405, 406 (causing explosions and the disturbance and damage of vital systems) partially correspond to § 58^9 (damaging and destruction of objects of infrastructure), KarS § 255, 256 (criminal association and its organisation) partially reflect the idea of § 58^{11} (counterrevolutionary crimes in the form of an organisation).

The absurdity of such an approach is obvious and demonstrates that the concept of political repression cannot consist simultaneously of a point of departure in substantive law and the additional meaning of unjustified activity. **Secondly,** taking only the political motive into consideration discounts other motives. Yet should repression carried out under other motives be considered justified just because it is not political? Although the political nature of the motive is difficult to explicate, nobody would probably argue too strenuously against the USSR Supreme Soviet enactment of 26 June 1940 'Concerning the transition to an eight-hour workday, seven-day work week and prohibition of workers and employees from leaving enterprises and institutions of their own accord' as an example of non-political repression. This enactment allowed leaving work of one's own accord to be punished by imprisonment for two to four months. Leaving work of one's own accord in and of itself cannot be hazardous to society, and the seriousness of the deed does not fit the harshness of the punishment at all. It is difficult to characterise punishment by way of this enactment as justified action. The need to define this disappears altogether if it is assessed from the position of a state based on the rule of law.

The fact that the simultaneous existence of several attributes allowing categorisation as being unjustified was inherent to a large number of Stalin-era repressions may contribute to the search for repressions carried out unjustifiably from among repressions as a whole: extrajudiciality; the absence of a crime; contradiction of Soviet laws; crimes against humanity and war crimes; etc. Unjustifiability is obvious in such cases and its identification does not require any particular effort. For this reason, it is natural that historians pay greater attention to them and relegate to the background repressions that do not manifest attributes of unjustified repression as clearly (for instance, the assemblages of crimes in the special section of the 1926 RSFSR Criminal Code, which were not categorised under § 58, 59, 122–137 and 193).

It would be easy to categorise persons among them who had been punished for so-called classical crimes such as theft, murder, rape, etc. as 'criminals' according to the formal descriptions of criminal offences. These crimes were no doubt actually committed as well, yet in a *legal* sense, a person cannot be referred to as a criminal offender before his guilt has been proven and the court has handed down a verdict of conviction. Yet this was the weakest point of the Soviet Union's legal system.

The institutional part of state government referred to as the Soviet Union's law enforcement authorities was incapable of guaranteeing honest and impartial administration of justice. This did not apply to only certain groups of crimes, it applied in general to all crimes. For this reason, we can never be certain that the guilt of persons convicted in the Soviet Union had actually been proven, and the search for the unjustified part of the Soviet Union's repressions is a dead end. In a *legal* sense, not a single case of repression was justified. The Soviet Union's legal system can only be analysed and described as not being based on the rule of law, and if we wish to provide an orderly, systematic overview of the Soviet Union's repressions, criteria must be used for this according to which all repressions could be described, not only a certain part of them.

Present day rehabilitation laws should also be regarded as decisions by which only a certain part of repression verdicts that did not measure up to the principles of a state based on the rule of law are nullified and partial compensation for sufferings is determined. These laws cannot be taken into consideration as models for categorising repressions as justified and unjustified.

Politicalness can admittedly be used to define repressions, but under the condition that it does not have the additional meaning of unjustified action and that the grounds for the definition are explained. In identifying politicalness with opposition to the state, it is better to limit this identification to individual cases with clear attributes of opposition to the state. Such examples would be repressions of representatives of political forces that lost in the power struggle against the Bolsheviks (the socialist-revolutionaries, the Mensheviks, etc.) or repressions motivated by the power struggle among the Bolsheviks themselves (Lev Kamenev, Grigori Zinovev, Lavrentiy Beria). Punishments imposed according to counterrevolutionary categories of crime can be referred to as political repressions, but it is difficult to understand the advantages of using this classification. It is inferior to the concept of counterrevolutionary crime in terms of its capacity to delineate.

Thus the mode of systematising that categorises repressions as political and non-political, and also as justified and unjustified, falls by the wayside. The next chapter offers a different possibility for systematisation.

The Soviet Union's System of Repression

As is inherent for a state that is not based on the rule of law, the Soviet Union was to a great extent run by way of secret *ad hoc* decisions that did not even always have to be in writing or in harmony with the Soviet Union's legal provisions, nor did they have to form a logical whole together with other decisions in their particular field (for instance special banishment[15]). It was not necessary to pay attention to contradictions

---

[15]   I use the word 'banishment' as a general term for all categories of exile. There were four categories of exile and their designations are translated as follows: *vysylka* – deportation, *ssylka* – forced banishment, *ssylka na poselenie* – special forced banishment, *spetsposelenie* – special banishment. I also include in the latter category groups in reference to which the following designations were used: *trudposelenie* – labour banishment, *trudpereselenie* – labour resettlement, and *spetspereselenie* – special resettlement. See further: Aivar Niglas, 'Release ahead of time of Estonian citizens and residents repressed for political reasons by the Soviet authorities and their rehabilitation from 1953 to the 1960s', – *Estonia since 1944: reports of the Estonian International Commission for the Investigation of*

between acts of legislation, terminological imprecision, or the absence of regulation in some fields of activity, since this did not directly interfere with the governance of the state. When rigid, centralised administration is added to this, it is no wonder that the result was a rather complicated system with abundant exceptions that was manifested even in all manner of official designations preceded by the qualificatory adjective 'special'. It is even difficult to assess which was the rule in the Soviet Union, regularity or exceptionality.

Any description of the Soviet Union's system of repression that aspires to comprehensiveness has to take these circumstances into consideration. The description of the system needs more attributes in order to establish the categories judicial / non-judicial, mass / non-mass, or even political / non-political. First and foremost, such attributes are required that most clearly set apart the similarities and differences between repressions.

The centre of gravity in explaining the system of repression is indicated in the diagram (see the adjacent diagram). The following portion of the article explains the diagram and for this reason is in some places in a laconic style dominated by keywords. The diagram shows in a simplified way how the system functioned. The detailed listing of all the full-tones and grey tones of repressions can make it difficult to comprehend the description of the system. For this reason, the description touches on only the most important attributes.

The most important attributes of repressions are divided into four levels. The most important of them, the normativity level, is the last since understanding it requires familiarity with the first three levels.

The first level can conditionally be designated as the **stage of preparation for repression**. Naturally, treating this as a separate stage is also conditional. The preparation of repressions was not an independent, clearly defined field, rather it derived from the secretive and to a great extent informal administration of the Soviet Union. At the same time, this stage occupied an important place in the chain of individual stages of repression. At this stage, the groups of people subject to repression, the duration of repression, etc. were determined, card files and lists were drawn up

Crimes Against Humanity, compiled by Peeter Kaasik et al., eds. Toomas Hiio, Meelis Maripuu and Indrek Paavle (Tallinn, Estonian Foundation for the Investigation of Crimes Against Humanity, 2009), 462–467.

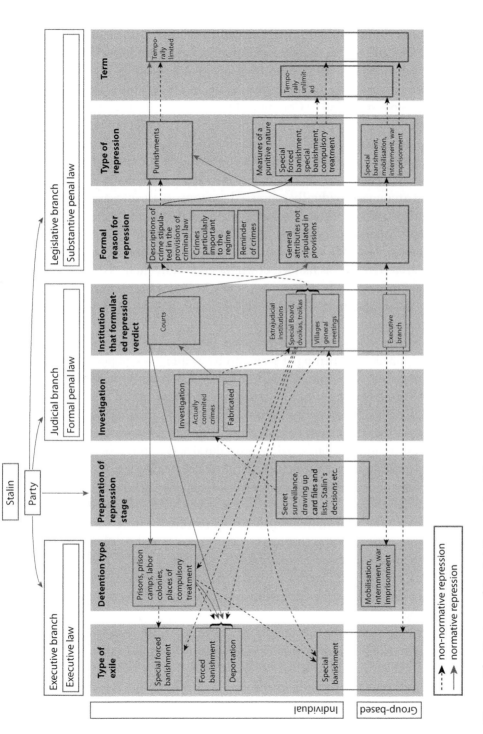

Figure: The System of Soviet Repressive Measures.

to the point where Stalin himself decided on the life or death of specific people. Everything that followed was more or less a formality. This stage can certainly also be divided up into separate parts: operational work of investigative organs, the decision-making mechanism that originated from decisions made by the Communist Party in the overall chain of command, Stalin's direct orders, the informal part that was not put in writing, etc. The detailed analysis of this level is not the topic of this article.

The second level indicates repression on an individual and group basis.

Persons to whom four attributes generally applied simultaneously were counted among **individually repressed persons**: 1) an act was committed, 2) investigation proceedings were formulated in accordance with the provisions for criminal proceedings, 3) the descriptions of the criminal offence prescribed in the provisions were used to formulate the repression, 4) a separate verdict was handed down for each individual. As an exception, the first point did not apply to socially hazardous persons repressed without having committed a punishable act, who could be repressed without committing a punishable act.

In the case of **group-based repression**, the opposite of these four conditions applied. The opening of account-observation files on persons sent into banishment, who comprised the majority of persons repressed on the basis of belonging to a group, and group-based repression can additionally be qualified as repression carried out according to simplified procedure or as expedited repression because unlike individual repression, it was not necessary to carry out separate procedural acts in the case of group-based repression in order to achieve its ultimate objective, in other words the transfer of people to their destinations (primarily into banishment).

I use the categorisation 'group-based' in place of the rather widespread term 'mass'. The topic of this article would require the differentiation of mass from non-mass and the numerical expression of the difference between them. This, however, would not be possible because 'mass' (in the meaning of large numbers) is a word with a vague meaning. In group-based systematisation, the determination of the size of the group is unnecessary.

Seven attributes of penal law are placed on the third level and are, in turn, distributed among formal law, substantive law and executive law based on the three-pillar theory of penal law: 1) pre-trial investigation (*investigation*), 2) judicial investigation (*the institution that formulated the repression verdict*), 3) description of the criminal offence (*the formal reason for repression*), 4) category of punishment (*category of repression*), 5) term of punishment (*term*), 6) type of penal institution (*type of detention involving deprivation of liberty*), 7) category of banishment. This list of attributes can naturally be extended. Restriction of freedom that does not involve imprisonment can be added (loss of rights, forced labour without imprisonment, etc.), deprivation of liberty in penal institutions can be divided up into different parts according to regimen, etc. The designations of attributes used in the diagram are in parentheses.

The fourth level categorises repressions as normative and non-normative. In states based on the rule of law, legal provision is one of the most important and utilised general terms in drafting legislation. In other words, it is the written behavioural guideline or rule of any particular piece of legislation. Still, all legislation does not contain provisions and thus is not legislation of general application. From the standpoint of this article, four attributes of legal provisions need to be highlighted.

1) 'Legislation of general application, or general legislation, is aimed at establishing objective law. It contains generally binding behavioural rules, or legal provisions. The inclusion of legal provisions in legislation is the first criterion for differentiating legislation of general application from legislation that is not of general application. The existence of legal provisions gives legislation of general application general meaning: it applies to an undefined circle of individuals and is subject to implementation an undefined number of times, for which reason it is also known as general legal legislation. [...]

Legislation that is not of general application, in other words an individual act, is the kind of legislation that provides subjective rights (that belong to the given subject) and places obligations on a specific subject or a precisely defined circle of subjects. For this reason, this is also known as legislation of specific application. Such legislation does not contain legal provisions, rather it applies legal provisions, obliging a specific individual to behave in a specific way, for which reason they are by their nature acts for applying law. For instance, court verdicts, directives, decisions for honouring or pardoning a person, and other such acts pertaining to an individual subject are legislation that is not of general application, in other words individual acts.

Different state organs establish legislation. Each state organ has its jurisdiction depending on its functions, its place in the state apparatus, and the extent of its jurisdiction. By virtue of this, legislation of different state organs has different legal force. [...]

Legislation of general application forms a hierarchical system in every country, the highest-ranking act of which is law. Law is legislation of general application that the highest-ranking representative body (parliament) of state authority has adopted or which is the direct expression of the will of the people (by way of referendum). The highest-ranking legal force of law derives from the position of parliament, the state organ that passes legislation, in the system of state organs. Parliament, which bears different designations in different countries [...], is the state's highest-ranking organ of legislative power and the representative organ of the people. For this reason, legislation of general application established by parliament – laws – has the highest-ranking legal force in relation to the legislation of other state organs. All other legislation has to conform to the law. By fulfilling this requirement, the primacy of law is safeguarded.'[16]

2) Considering the distinctiveness of the regime that ruled the Soviet Union, the principle of notification, or disclosure, rises to second place in importance after the criterion of comparing the general and the individual in assessing normativity:

'What is not disclosed is not law. [...] This applies to all material laws, that is to legislation that contains legal provisions. Thus notification (disclosure) is the prerequisite and condition not only of the legality of a law, but also of legal existence. Official and unofficial disclosure has to be differentiated. Unofficial disclosure has quite a significant role in the explanation of laws, information of citizens and shaping their legal awareness. Here the following possibilities can be named:

- publications of laws and their collections;
- brochures, books, periodicals [...], radio and television prepared by ministries and other institutions;
- explanations and advice of lawyers.

Official notification takes place in a publication prescribed by law and only the texts of laws published in such a publication have legal meaning.'[17]

---

[16]   Advig Kiris et al., *Õigusõpetus: õpik* [The Teaching of Law: a Textbook] (Tallinn: Külim, 2009), 66–67.

[17]   Kalle Merusk et al., *Õigusriigi printsiip ja normitehnika* [The Principle of a State Based on Law and Norm Technique] (Tartu: Eesti Üiguskeskus, 1999), 18.

3) The state of being written.
4) Internal orderliness and clarity of wording.

The requirement of disclosing legal provisions applied in the Soviet Union as well.[18] Laws as the most important provisions were public, but they could be amended by secret decisions, or secret acts could be issued that were not referred to as laws but had the force of law.[19] Considering the fact that the greater portion of the governance of the Soviet Union was secret, the condition of publicness provides an opportunity for systematisation.

I call those repressions normative that **broadly speaking were formalised** in conformity to provisions.

There is no point in interpreting the normativity of repressions as the fulfilment of legal provisions, meaning their substantive, actual observance because this was not expected of the Soviet Union's legal system. The legal system had to formulate a certain portion of repressions more

---

[18]   See the 1936 Constitution of the Soviet Union, § 40 and the 1977 Constitution of the Soviet Union, § 116.

[19]   The USSR Supreme Soviet Presidium directive issued on 25 February 1961, which was not published in the official publication *Vedomosti Verkhovnogo Soveta SSSR*, gave the Estonian SSR Supreme Court permission by way of exception to not apply § 6 (The laws in effect at the time when the deed was committed determine the criminality and punishability of the deed, laws eliminating punishability or reducing the penalty have retroactive effect, laws establishing punishability or increasing the penalty do not have retroactive effect.) and § 41 (Regulated expiration deadlines for criminal prosecution. The maximum period for bringing criminal charges was ten years. After that the crime expired. The expiration deadline was extended if the person committed a new crime or concealed himself from investigation or the court. The court decided on the application of expiration in cases of crimes for which the death penalty was prescribed. If the court did not consider it possible to apply expiration and proceeded to deliberate the case, the death penalty could not be applied and it had to be replaced by imprisonment.) of the law stating the foundations for criminal legislation in the Soviet Union and its union republics in the case against Ain-Ervin Meri, Ralf Gerrets and Jaan Viik. This made it possible to sentence them to death (Investigation file of Ain-Ervin Mere, Ralf Gerrets and Jaan Viik, RA, ERAF.129SM.1.28653, vol. 19., 503, 517–525). The same kind of legal practice was also used to sentence convicted 'war criminals' to death in the Estonian SSR in the early 1960s. The Soviet Union enacted this legal practice at the legal provision level on 4 March 1965 with the USSR Supreme Soviet Presidium enactment 'Concerning the punishment of persons guilty of crimes against peace and humankind, and war crimes regardless of the time when the crime was committed'.

or less in conformity to provisions, and even that much was not required regarding other repressions. Since substantively speaking, it was not necessary to observe laws, ignoring formulation requirements also could not in any way affect the end result of repression. For instance, while the absence of some particular piece of evidence in a criminal case can lead to the acquittal of the accused in a state based on the rule of law, then the absence of such 'details' did not become an obstacle to the imposition of penalties in the Soviet Union. Even a properly formulated criminal case could actually have been fabricated. Regarding the Soviet Union, proper formulation is an indication more of the diligence of the person who drew up the documents and of the supervisors who checked his work. This does not prove the guilt of the penalised person. For this reason, it was sufficient if repressions **broadly** conformed to the provisions, which means that repressions can be categorised as normative primarily if five conditions are fulfilled:

1) Repression contained the stage of investigation, and provisions of criminal procedure were used to formulate this in writing: laws from 1924 and 1958 that formed the foundation for criminal procedure in the Soviet Union and its union republics (*Osnovy sudoproizvodstva Soiuza SSR i soiuznykh respublik*)[20], codes for criminal proceedings);

2) institutions (courts, tribunals) that had the right to apply repression as prescribed by legal provisions formally handed down repression verdicts: in constitutions, in fundamental laws from 1924 on the court administration of the Soviet Union and its union republics (*Osnovy sudoustroistva Soiuza SSR i soiuznykh respublik*), from 1938 on the court administration of the Soviet Union, its union republics and autonomous republics (*Osnovy sudoustroistva Soiuza SSR i soiuznykh respublik*) and from 1958 on court administration legislation applying to the Soviet Union, its union republics and autonomous republics (*Osnovy zakonodatelstva o sudoustroistve Soiuza SSR, soiuznykh i avtonomnykh respublik*)[21];

---

[20]   *Sobranie zakonov i rasporiazhenii Raboche-Krestianskogo Pravitel'stva SSSR,* 1924, 24, 206; *Vedomosti Verkhovnogo Soveta SSSR,* 1959, 1.

[21]   *Sobranie zakonov* 1924, 23, 203; *Vedomosti Verhovnogo Soveta* 1938, 11; *Vedomosti Verkhovnogo Soveta* 1959, 1.

3) the justification for repression (description of the crime, social hazard) was drawn from the provisions of the material part of criminal law: the fundamental laws from 1924 and 1958 on criminal legislation of the Soviet Union and its union republics (respectively *Osnovnye nachala ugolovnogo zakonodatelstva Soiuza SSR i soiuznykh respublik and Osnovy ugolovnogo zakonodatel'stva Soiuza SSR i soiuznyh respublik*)[22], criminal codes, public individual acts of criminal law;

4) the category of repression (punishment) was stated in writing in the provisions of the material part of criminal law;

5) the extent of repression did not exceed the limits set by the provisions of the material part of criminal law.

These correspond to what was known in the Soviet Union as punishment pursuant to criminal procedure, or repression. Normative repression nevertheless cannot be defined as only repression pursuant to criminal procedure. Repression pursuant to criminal procedure admittedly occupies the most important place regarding normative repression, but the meaning of normative repression is broader. Repressions applied on the basis of non-criminal legal provisions, yet listed in the provisions of criminal law as punishments are also categorised as normative repression. The deprivation of certain population groups of voting rights (*lishentsy*) on the basis of § 65 of the Russian SFSR Constitution of 1918 can be considered as such. Deprivation of voting rights was also a criminal punishment (§ 40 of the RSFSR Criminal Code of 1922).[23] Deprivation of voting rights by way of the constitution was the application of repression based on provisions, but not repression pursuant to criminal procedure. Both can be considered as repression due to the same designations.

Thus non-normative repressions are those based on acts that did not conform to the criteria of the concept of legal provision, primarily the principle of publicness.

Normativity and non-normativity could also be referred to as public and non-public repressions, but in such a case the connection to the Soviet

---

[22]   *Sobranie zakonov* 1924, 24, 205; *Vedomosti Verkhovnogo Soveta* 1959, 1.

[23]   *Sobranie uzakonenii i rasporiazhenii Rabochego i Krestianskogo Pravitel'stva.* 1918, 51, 582; 1922, 15, 153.

Union's legislation is not so clear. This would also not be quite correct since even in the case of normative repression, most of the procedure of repression remained hidden from society. Only the provisions were public.

The poor normative technique, in other words terminological imprecision and poor wording, of the Soviet Union's legal provisions and more broadly of the acts that formed the basis for repression merits attention. This is more noticeable in the non-normative acts regarding repression and in the provisions of criminal law that were in effect until the end of the 1950s. Examples that can be pointed out are the vague definition of counterrevolutionary crime; social hazardousness, which was not defined and the meaning of which is quite difficult to ascertain even in retrospect; the concept of rehabilitation, which was never given an adequate explanation; the numerous corrections that were made in the 1920s and 1930s in the statute regulating war tribunals, as a result of which differentiating provisions that were in effect from those that were not in effect became quite difficult at times, etc.[24]

Returning to the categorisation of repressions as being normative and non-normative – this appears to have been as follows.

I) **Normative** repression could be preceded by a **preparatory stage**, but not in all cases. Investigative agencies could launch **investigations** (see the arrows pointing to the right on the diagram) without any lengthy preparation as well, for instance activated by some particular event. As a general rule, efforts were made to formulate investigation, meaning arrest, interrogation and putting the accused on trial, in accordance with the rules of criminal procedure, which, however, does not indicate a person's actual guilt because guilt could always be **fabricated**. This was used extensively in the Soviet Union. The court was always stipulated in provisions as the **institution that formulated repression verdicts**: the Supreme Court of the Soviet Union, the courts of the Soviet republics, various tribunals, etc. The **formal** reason for **repression** was formulated according to the descriptions of crime stipulated in the provisions of criminal law. Most of these were contained in codified form in criminal codes, while a small portion of them were established as acts separate from criminal codes. **Punishment by court verdict** on the basis of **general attributes not stipu-**

---

[24]   *Istoriia zakonodatel'stva SSSR i RSFSR po ugolovnomu protsessu i organizatsii suda i prokuratury. Sbornik dokumentov* (Moscow: Gosiurizdat, 1955), 377–382.

lated in provisions denotes repression on the basis of social hazardousness in the diagram. This was an exception. Repression according to attributes not stipulated in provisions was inherent to primarily non-normative repression. Instead of categorising descriptions of crimes as 'political' and 'criminal', I have categorised them as **particularly important to the regime** and **remainder of crimes**. This does not aspire to precise delineation. I denote descriptions of crimes to which the regime paid greater attention as belonging to the first category. These were primarily crimes against the state, including counterrevolutionary crimes, but I retain the option of also including trials held as part of some particular campaign, which meant paying greater attention to certain descriptions of crimes from time to time. Campaigns were ordinarily associated with fulfilling some sort of other objectives beyond criminal law, like collectivisation or industrialisation, for instance.[25] It should not be forgotten that the legal system was one of the levers used for governing the state in the Soviet Union. Only punishments were used as a **type of repression** in normative repression. The **term** of punishment was limited, but only within the framework of one criminal case. A person who had become an enemy of the regime could be repressed again for essentially the same reason, even though the stated reason was formally different. Towards the end of Stalin's life, the term of lifelong repression started being shaped by automatically sending persons who belonged to certain categories into banishment after their release from penal institutions. Types of penal institutions and their regimens and banishment penalties were stipulated in the provisions. **Deportation** and **forced banishment** (see the arrows pointing to the left on the diagram) were treated as independent punishments and as additional punishments to be applied after the punishment of imprisonment (imprisonment was also imposed as a separate punishment; this is not indicated separately on the diagram). Extrajudicial institutions also had the right to apply deportation and forced banishment. Such cases are designated as non-normative repression.

II) **Non-normative repression** was divided into two categories, a) individual and b) group-based repression.

a) The attributes of individual non-normative repression overlap to a great extent with individual normative repression. The differences emerge

---

[25]   Piter Solomon, *Sovetskaia iustitsiia pri Staline* [Soviet Criminal Justice Under Stalin] (Moscow: ROSSPEN, 2008), 78–102, 127--137.

most clearly in the **institution that formulated the repression verdict**. In the case of non-normative repression, some **extrajudicial institution** handed down the verdict: the Special Board (*Osoboe Soveshchanie*), which operated permanently, **dvoikas** (*dvoika*) and **troikas** (*troika*) formed on an *ad hoc* basis, **general meetings** of **villages** or of collective farmers, or other such bodies. General meetings were given the right to deport (actually to send people into special banishment) in 1948 with the aim of combating shirkers (this did not extend to Estonia, Latvia and Lithuania). As for individual normative repression, formulation in accordance with the provisions for the **formal reason, type** and **term of repression** was also inherent to individual non-normative repression. This meant a temporally limited term of punishment.

A change took place after the Second World War (in 1948) when **temporally unlimited measures of a punitive nature** started being applied to certain groups of penalised persons. These groups were especially hazardous anti-state criminals (punished for more serious crimes including counterrevolutionary crimes) who had been sent into **special forced banishment** after serving their sentences, and persons who were sent into **special banishment** after serving their sentences to join their families who had previously been sent into special banishment. The former of these two modes of repression was adopted in 1948, and the other was adopted in 1952.

Persons sent into special banishment for up to 8 years by a **village general meeting** or a general meeting of collective farmers were individually non-normatively repressed **special settlers with temporal limitations**.[26]

People could also be repressed under the guise of measures that were seemingly non-repressive. This was done as individual non-normative repression in the form of sending the person who was subject to repression to a psycho-neurological hospital for compulsory treatment (for instance, §26 of the Russian SFSR Criminal Code of 1926). Compulsory treatment was a means of treatment, prevention or obstruction. In the Soviet Union, however, it was used as a liability measure of a punitive nature. It was used, for instance, in the Soviet Union after Stalin's death (evidently also earlier but there is less information about this) on so-called dissidents and

---

[26]   *Istoriia stalinskogo GULAGa: konets 1920-kh–pervaia polovina 1950-kh godov: sobranie dokumentov v 7 t., Tom 1, Massovye repressii v SSSR*, comp. I. A. Ziuzina, eds. N. Vert, S. V. Mironenko (Moscow: ROSSPEN, 2004), 572–574.

persons who had tried to escape abroad. Compared to persons similarly repressed non-normatively on a group basis (mobilised or interned persons, etc.), repression in the form of compulsory treatment was more like a punishment because a deed formed the basis for applying repression. The term of compulsory treatment could be limited or unlimited (to recall the fate of the President of the Republic of Estonia Konstantin Päts).

Forcibly sending people for treatment was permitted by provisions and thus was not contrary to provisions in and of itself. It became non-normative due to its use for punitive purposes contrary to its stated purpose. Repression in the form of compulsory treatment could be accompanied by a forfeiture that was inherent only to this form of repression, namely the deliberate damaging of a person's health by forcing them to take unnecessary medications.

All repressions do not conform to a clear division between individual and group-based repression. Special forced settlers, sent into special banishment after imprisonment on the basis of the USSR Supreme Soviet Presidium enactment of 11 March 1952, and the shooting of 210 prisoners imprisoned in the course of the 'Great Terror' of 1937 in a special prison in the Solovets Islands on the basis of one decision (in the form of a list) handed down by a Special Troika of the NKVD Leningrad oblast, have in common the distinction of having been punished a second time for the same thing.[27] If we leave out those special forced settlers who were released before 1948 and concerning whom the Special Board handed down a verdict to send them into special forced banishment, almost all of the attributes of individual repression were missing from the second repression of the remainder of repressed persons, for which reason they would be categorised as group-based repressed persons. In the diagram, however, they are nevertheless categorised under individual repression since the first repression provided the reason for the second repression and was individual. This circumstance set them apart from group-based repressed persons, the vast majority of whom had been sent directly into banishment in the course of mass operations, and this banishment did not depend on any previous punishment. It is possible that there were even

---

[27]   *Leningradskii martirolog 1937–1938: kniga pamiati zhertv politicheskikh repressii, Vol. I*, ed. A. Ia. Razumov (Sankt-Peterburg: Izdatel'stvo Rossiiskoi natsional'noi biblioteki, 1996), illustration 82.

more groups that did not fit neatly into the categorisation of individual and group-based repression.

b) Group-based repression was the field of repressions that conformed the least to provisions. It did not have an **investigation stage**; generally speaking, a **court** or an **organ resembling a court** (the Special Board, a troika, etc.) did not hand down a verdict which had at least some sort of individual nature due to the necessary elements of the offence contained in it (excluding exceptions, for instance the shootings according to lists from the time of the Great Terror); the grounds for the repression were not so much a particular deed as the attributes of a group. The circle of persons subject to group-based repression was determined **during the preparation stage of repression**. The substantive repression verdict was handed down at that same stage. **The institutions that formulated the repression verdict** were predominantly organs of executive power, the USSR Council of Ministers and its predecessor, and during the war the State Defence Committee.[28] At least four group-based measures of a punitive nature can be discerned in total: **special banishment, mobilisation, internment** and **imprisonment of POWs**. Special banishment was a completely repressive measure. It had no non-repressive aspect, unlike mobilisation and internment, which were used for their stated purpose, although people were also repressed under the guise of these measures. The term of repression was unlimited for the greater portion of special settlers who belonged to the category of group-based non-normatively repressed persons. The so-called Vlassovites, Soviet citizens who had belonged to the ranks of the Germany Army and who were sent into special banishment for 6 years in 1945, were an example of special settlers with a temporally limited term.

The deportation of Soviet citizens of German nationality within the Soviet Union during the Second World War, and the deportation of Germans who were citizens of foreign countries to the Soviet Union at the end of the war and after the war are the clearest examples of repression under the aegis of **mobilisation** and **internment**. The forfeitures resembling punishments caused to those persons are indicative of repression: forced departure from their permanent place of residence and being forced to live in a new place of residence, labour obligations, restriction of freedom of

---

[28]   Hilda Sabbo, *Võimatu vaikida* [Impossible to Remain Silent], vol. II (Tallinn: Hilda Sabbo, 1996), 1226–1248; *Reabilitatsiia: kak eto bylo: dokumenty Prezidiuma TsK KPSS i drugie materialy, Tom I, Mart 1953 – fevral' 1956*, comp. A. N. Artizov et al. (Moscow: Mezhdunarodnyi fond Demokratiia, 2000), 99–102.

movement, the establishment of the internal rules of Soviet prison camps, including making feeding dependent on the productivity of work, etc.[29] Leaving aside the coercion to leave one's permanent place of residence, the remaining forfeitures were also inherent to prisoners of war taken by the Soviet Union in the course of the Second World War. The factor of time is important in their case. While considering imprisonment during the war as repression could still be debatable because taking prisoners was a step that was forced on the Soviet Union, and only living conditions and labour obligations compared to the Soviet Union's so-called ordinary imprisonment could be taken into consideration as a gauge of repression, then the continuation of imprisonment lasting for years after the end of the war as the reason for keeping people in prison is a clear attribute of repression.

Like compulsory treatment, mobilisation, internment and imprisonment of POWs are categorised as non-normative repressions due to their use for purposes other than their stated original purposes. Special banishment, however, is not even possible to define as being normative since it was an utterly secret measure.

The Problem of Differentiating Repression from Non-Repression

The problem of differentiating between repression and non-repression could not arise in a state based on the rule of law since state compulsion is not the primary means for administering society, punishments and the procedures for their application are set in writing in legal provisions, and these procedures are also followed. Thus, it is possible to delineate repression on the basis of formal attributes.

This problem, however, arises in the case of the Soviet Union because coercion was of great importance in the administration of the state. It was perhaps greater under Stalin's rule, but it continued to occupy an important place after his death as well, which makes the determination of varying severities of coercion topical. Since repression was not limited

---

[29] *Nakazannyi narod: repressii protiv rossiiskikh nemtsev*, ed. I. L. Shcherbakova (Moscow: Zven'ia, 1999), 133–136; Pavel Polian, *Ne po svoei vole...: istoriia i geografiia prinuditel'nykh migratsii v SSSR* (Moscow: O.G.I - Memorial, 2001), 191–194, 221–223, 234.

to punishments that were set in writing in legal provisions, and since repression was also concealed behind non-repressive measures as well, there were no clear formal attributes for defining repression, and it is quite difficult to draw the boundary between repressive coercion and the remainder of state coercion. This is also the case if forfeitures are taken as the point of departure.

If the ban on leaving the Soviet Union without permission is interpreted as coercion to live in the Soviet Union, then this would be classified as an obstructive measure and could thus be considered a non-repressive means of coercion. Alongside this there is also coercion that cannot be delineated so easily. The passport system established in 1933 made registration in one's permanent place of residence mandatory, which essentially meant the obligation to live in that place. Getting a job and enrolling in an educational institution, along with changing jobs and schools, were also connected to registration of permanent residence. Violation of the passport regimen, meaning living without registering in places (primarily cities) where registration was required, was a punishable offence. All Soviet citizens were not issued with passports, yet it was not possible to change one's place of residence without a passport. In this way, part of the Soviet Union's population was tied to its current place of residence. Owning a passport did not yet automatically mean permission to change one's place of residence, but a passport at least provided the legal opportunity to do so. Persons without passports had the right to leave their place of residence only temporarily. The forfeitures caused by not issuing passports corresponded to the forfeitures of the criminal penalty known as forced banishment, which in the same way meant the obligation to live in one particular place.[30] If the criterion of the act committed had been taken into consideration in the Soviet Union, the forfeitures of forced banishment could be treated as forfeitures caused by a crime and thus they could be differentiated from the forfeitures of the passport regimen. Yet since deportation could be applied without the commission of a punishable deed (on the basis of hazardousness to society) and even without a court verdict (by decision of the Special Board), the existence of a crime or a court verdict cannot be used as a criterion of delineation.

---

[30]   Indrek Paavle, 'Ebaühtlane ühtne süsteem. Sovetliku passisüsteemi kujunemine, regulatsioon ja rakendamine Eesti NSV-s' [A Non-uniform Uniform System. The Development, Regulation and Implementation of the Soviet Passport System in the Estonian SSR], *Tuna*, no. 4 (2010): 46–47, 52.

There admittedly are possibilities for differentiating between forced banishment and persons who were not issued passports. Forced settlers had to register regularly at the local militia (Soviet police force) precinct and they were forced to leave their permanent place of residence. Such circumstances can be considered as supplementary forfeitures, but is that enough to consider persons who were not issued passports as not having been repressed? The existence of forfeitures inherent only to forced banishment does not alter the fact that they also shared in common forfeitures that corresponded to punishment.

I leave the question unanswered of whether it is possible in the case of the Soviet Union to draw a precise boundary between repressive coercion and other coercion by the state. This would require working through a larger amount of factual material and more thorough analysis than is possible within the framework of this article. I will limit myself to making note of the problem and the recognition that drawing a clear boundary could prove to be impossible. It may only be possible to present the Soviet Union's state coercion as a series of measures proceeding from harsher to milder where there is no clear point of transition.

Changes in the System of Repression brought by De-Stalinisation

The greater portion of the non-normative part of the system of repression was liquidated in the course of de-Stalinisation. The Special Board was done away with, along with the special banishment and special forced banishment categories of exile. Group-based repression was stopped completely.

As a result of this, the total number of repressed persons and the relative proportion of extrajudicial repression dropped significantly; new fundamental legislation went into effect in criminal law; the importance of state coercion in state governance decreased; the likelihood of falling victim to repression for trivial reasons decreased, which helped to reduce the atmosphere of fear, etc., but the fundamental principles of state governance remained the same and the justice system did not become *more lawful.* It was more a transformation of the system that took place through de-Stalinisation. The tunic was exchanged for the suit jacket. Greater attention started being paid to the formulation of repressions. Repressions with so obvious non-normative attributes such as Stalin-era repressions by decision of the Special Board or mass deportations were avoided. Repression became more normative, in other words it conformed more to existing provisions. Substantively unlawful repressions were adapted with better provisions than before. The most vivid example of this was the application of compulsory treatment with punitive aims. In order to schematically depict the system of repression that emerged after de-Stalinisation, the box denoting Stalin, the part representing group-based repression, and the arrows indicating non-normative punishment (excluding compulsory treatment) have to be removed from the diagram.

The quality of legal provisions was improved. The outmoded analogy of law and the permission of repression without a punishable deed having been committed (on the basis of hazardousness to society) disappeared from the Soviet Union's legal theory and legal provisions. The standard language of legal provisions improved, which was manifested, for instance, by the replacement of the vaguely worded Stalin-era concept of counterrevolutionary crimes with the concept of especially hazardous state crimes, and by improvement in the wording of the descriptions of crimes that belonged to this category.

The qualification of the employees of law enforcement organs improved, which is indicated by improvement in the quality of language usage and formulation of investigation files and documents in general associated with repression (changes can be noticed earlier already, but this was not characteristic of Stalin's reign as a whole).[31] The fact that the Soviet Union became slightly more open to the rest of the world, and that the theme of human rights, which became topical after the Second World War, made its way into the provisions of international law may have had its effect on improving lawfulness in the Soviet Union. The domestic legal system had to at least externally conform to those provisions of international law in order to ward off international pressure.

While it is relatively easy to define groups among Stalin-era repressions with clear attributes of unjustified repression, and the number of persons in those groups was relatively large, then those attributes and also the

---

[31]   See for instance the reports of state security organs provided by Oleg Mozokhin, which became more orderly starting from the end of the 1940s and the comparability of data from different years improved, see: Oleg Mozokhin, *Pravo na repressii: vnesudebnye polnomochiia organov gosudarstvennoi bezopasnosti (1918–1953)* (Moscow; Zhukovski: Kuchkovo pole, 2006), 246–465.

number of people who belonged to those groups decreased significantly after de-Stalinisation. As a matter of fact, only two descriptions of crimes with clear attributes of unjustified repression can be named: anti-Soviet agitation and propaganda (§68 of the Estonian SSR Criminal Code), dissemination of knowingly false fabrications denigrating the Soviet political system or social order (§194[1] of the Estonian SSR Criminal Code), and perhaps as a third, violation of the law separating church from state and schools from church (§137 of the ESSR Criminal Code). Primarily the two former categorisations of crime were used to punish dissidents, or they were convicted of hooliganism instead (§195 of the ESSR Criminal Code). Punishment could be masked by sending the individuals in question for compulsory treatment. Since compulsory treatment was also used for its originally stated purpose, punishment by way of compulsory treatment can be identified only by examining individual cases. The problem emerges here that it is not necessarily always possible to differentiate between punishment and an actual need for treatment.

Research of the Soviet Union's repressions after de-Stalinisation has to rely more on individual cases and on drawing conclusions and making generalisations based on them due to the increase in normativity and the decrease in repressions with clear attributes of unjustified repression.

Summary

The clarification of concepts is important in systematising Soviet repressions. One of the most important is the concept of repression. This is a legal concept that refers to the content of a punishment, what punishment actually entails for a person. In the case of the Soviet Union, it is important to focus on the substantive meaning of punishment since measures resembling punishments were also applied in the Soviet Union without formally referring to them as punishments. The concept of repression helps to tie measures resembling punishments to actual punishments due to their substantive similarity. Thus all measures that substantively corresponded to Soviet criminal punishments can be considered as repression. No clear distinction can be drawn between repressive and non-repressive measures due to the large proportion of state coercion in the governance of the Soviet Union because the weight of means backing up coercion differed and the repressive nature of all means cannot be clearly defined.

The inclusion of law and legal concepts in the discussion is inevitably accompanied by the need to answer the question: to what extent can law be relied on at all in researching Soviet repressions or the history of the Soviet Union? Regardless of the existence of a field called law, the Soviet Union was not a state based on the rule of law and when using legal terminology in reference to the Soviet Union, they should be placed in quotation marks. This article suggests the method of equating meanings as a solution. According to this approach, the analysis of the Soviet Union and its legal system is admittedly carried out from the standpoint of a state based on the rule of law, but this does not mean the identification of Soviet law with the law of a state based on the rule of law. Law deriving from a state based on the rule of law has an ancillary role. This helps to explain the functioning of the Soviet Union as a state not based on the rule of law. This method also stresses the difference between these two legal systems and their artificial and formal correlation. Figuratively speaking, the method helps to justify using these legal terms without quotation marks.

The concept of legal provisions and the theory of the three pillars of penal law form the basis for systematising the Soviet Union's repressions. Repressions carried out according to Soviet legal provisions were normative and those carried out according to other acts of legislation were non-normative. The most important criterion for differentiating a normative act from a non-normative act is the public accessibility of the act. When the preparation stage of repressions is added to the three pillars of penal law, material penal law, procedural law and executive law, a four-level background system, so to speak, is formed, by way of which one type of repression can be divided into different stages. This categorisation provides a uniform basis for comparing different types of repression and also makes it possible to show those attributes that were differentiated from one another.

This mode of systematisation applies primarily to the Stalin-era Soviet Union. Although it can also be extended to the Soviet Union after Stalin's death, this is nevertheless not as representative because as a result of de-Stalinisation, the Soviet Union's legal system started externally becoming more like a state based on the rule of law, and it is more difficult to retrospectively identify repressions that did not measure up to legal provisions.

Separate attention was directed in the article to the concept of political repression that has been used relatively abundantly in historical literature, and to the categorisation tied to this concept of repressions as being justified and not justified. It is complicated to define the concept of political repression. One of the reasons for this may be that the concept is given the additional meaning of unjustified activity. The concept of repression derives from law and thus the justification of repressions should also be assessed from this basis. From the standpoint of legality in its meaning as understood in states based on the rule of law, however, the categorisation of Soviet repressions as justified and unjustified is pointless because the Soviet Union was not a state based on the rule of law. In the legal sense, all of the Soviet Union's repressions were unjustified.

All modes of repression admittedly cannot be clearly categorised using the means suggested in the article for systematising Soviet repressions, yet this approach at least provides some kind of framework for obtaining an overview of repressions. It should be regarded as one means for describing the system, not as an exact reflection of the system. The Soviet Union's system of repression was not planned from the very beginning to take this form, rather it evolved over a long period of time under the conditions of a state not based on the rule of law, often also caused by political interests of the moment, with its many exceptions that deviated from its general scheme. It is most likely impossible to provide a simple, clear-cut overview of the Soviet Union's system of repression that at the same time includes all exceptions.

'Spetskadry': Nomenklatura and State Security in the Estonian SSR in 1940–1953

Meelis Saueauk[*]

Introduction

The Russian term nomenklatura denotes the secret list, established by the CPSU leadership, of the most important positions in agencies and organisations where appointments and dismissals required the approval of the Party's Committees. This provided Party organs with the power to appoint officials to key positions, and thereby to lead society. Understandably, the top-ranking officers of the Soviet Union's espionage and security services, or the 'State Security organs', also belonged to the nomenklatura. State Security officers formed the central part of the so-called 'special cadre' (Russian: *spetskadry* – a shortened form of the term *spetsial'nye kadry*), which included personnel from military and secret authorities – security, internal and defence ministries, but also justice authorities, etc. The majority of personnel in the Stalinist system of repression, therefore, belonged to the 'special cadre'. The security organs were one of the more important pillars of support for the Soviet regime and partocracy since they were the principal actors in uncovering enemies of the regime, and 'politically untrustworthy' persons. During the period when Joseph Stalin was in power, when the most violent stage of the Sovietisation of Estonia was being carried out, the nomenklatura system formed one notable connection between the Party and security organs, whereby it is possible to

[*]   First published: Meelis Saueauk, '"Erikaader": nomenklatuur ja julgeole-kuorganid Eesti NSV-s 1940–1953', *Ajalooline ajakiri = The Estonian Historical Journal*: Nomenklatuurisüsteem Eesti NSV-s = The nomenklatura system in the Estonian SSR, no. 4 (2015): 407–440.

not only follow the personnel policies of the Party but also the power relations and the process of Sovietisation in general. The aim of this article is to review the security organs and the nomenklatura system as both object and subject, using the Stalin-era Estonian SSR as an example.

The special role of Soviet State Security in the nomenklatura system has already been noted by several authors. Mikhail Voslenski has written that although the KGB system was part of the Party nomenklatura, and therefore belonged to the 'ruling class', it still had a somewhat special role in the nomenklatura, together with the armed forces, because it was the support structure for this class.[1] Oleg Khlevnyuk has noted, as one characteristic of the Stalin era, that Stalin in particular used regular cadre purges (selecting and relocating persons belonging to the nomenklatura was the 'centre of gravity' of personnel work) and structural changes to maintain his dictatorial power over the security organs.[2] These standpoints can also be accepted as preconditions when analysing the Estonian SSR case. A separate issue, however, is defining the State Security organs and the cadre. Valdur Ohmann, one of the first to research the Estonian SSR's 'Chekists', has analysed their cadre as well as officials in the Ministry of Internal Affairs.[3] This author has separately examined the State Security organs and their nomenklatura, primarily within the framework of the relationship between security and Party organs in the period 1944–53. He has come to the conclusion that, regarding the nomenklatura, the role of the Estonian Communist Party (ECP) tended to be a formality, and the

---

[1]   Mikhail Sergeevich Voslenskii, *Nomenklatura: gospodstvuiushchii klass Sovetskogo Soiuza* (Moscow: Sovetskaia Rossiia, 1991), 395–397.

[2]   Oleg Khlevnjuk, 'Stalin i organy gosudarstvennoi bezopasnosti v poslevoennyi period', *Cahiers du monde russe*, no. 42/2–3–4 (2001): 535–548, here 537.

[3]   See also: Valdur Ohmann, 'Eesti NSV Siseministeeriumi institutsionaalne areng ja arhivaalid (1940–1954)' [Institutional development and archives of the Estonian SSR's Ministry of Internal Affairs] (Master's thesis, supervisor Tõnu Tannberg, University of Tartu, 2000) and Valdur Ohmann, 'Eesti NSV siseministeeriumi struktuur 1940.–1954. aastal' [Structure of the Estonian SSR's Ministry of Internal Affairs], *Eesti NSV aastatel 1940–1953: sovetiseerimise mehhanismid ja tagajärjed Nõukogude Liidu ja Ida-Euroopa arengute kontekstis* [Soviet Estonia 1944–1953: Mechanisms and consequences of sovietization in Estonia in the context of the Soviet Union and Eastern Europe], ed. Tõnu Tannberg (Tartu: Eesti Ajalooarhiiv, 2007), 297–320.

fact that the security organs carried out background checks on the entire nomenklatura gave them a special role.[4]

In regard to this same period, Mariliis Hämäläinen has systematically analysed the State Security's nomenklatura within the ECP nomenklatura.[5] She has grouped the State Security's organs' nomenklatura as part of the 'power structures' (so-called *siloviki*) sector, which also includes authorities from the Ministry of Internal Affairs, the Ministry of Defence, military preparedness, etc. However, it should be noted that the nomenklatura was occasionally regrouped, and this therefore casts doubt on the usefulness of such categorisation, especially from the aspect of analysis. Hämäläinen has also described in more detail both the CPSU CC and the ECP CC nomenklatura in the period 1947–1953. However, the entire Stalinist period would need to be analysed from the aspect of the security organs' nomenklatura in particular, including the forms and changes in categorisation at the time. More detailed explanations are also required for the reasons for the changes to the composition of the nomenklatura, and also for the question of whether and how the nomenklatura system (in this case, regarding the State Security) actually worked. The fundamental issues for this article are therefore: did the ECP leadership, as a result of the nomenklatura system, also have the right to appoint the leaders of the State Security, and did so-called patron-client relationships develop, which are considered to be a characteristic part of the nomenklatura system?[6] In addition, we seek to answer the questions: what proportion of the State Security personnel belonged to the nomenklatura and what was the ethnic background of the persons appointed to nomenklatura positions during various periods? Also, considering that the top leadership of the security organs was simultaneously part of both the ECP and the CPSU nomenklatura, what were their management relationships? And finally: did the

---

[4]   Meelis Saueauk, *Propaganda ja terror: Nõukogude julgeolekuorganid ja Eestimaa Kommunistlik Partei Eesti sovetiseerimisel 1944–1953* [Propaganda and Terror: Soviet security organs and the Estonian Communist Party during the Sovietisation of Estonia 1944–1953] (Tallinn: SE&JS, 2015).

[5]   Mariliis Hämäläinen, *Eestimaa Kommunistliku Partei Keskkomitee nomenklatuur 1945–1953* [Nomenklatura of the Estonian Communist Party's Central Committee 1944–1953] (Tartu: University of Tartu Press, 2011).

[6]   See for instance: John P. Willerton, *Patronage and politics in the USSR* (Cambridge: Cambridge University Press, 1992).

security organs have a role in the implementation of the nomenklatura system, and if so, what was it?

The CPSU CC[7] and ECP CC[8] nomenklaturas from the ECP CC collection in the Estonian National Archives are used in this article. When possible, these are compared to the structures and personnel of the State Security. As regards the appointment of nomenklatura officials, the sources have mostly been the published agendas of the ECP CC Bureau[9] and personnel records. For the operation of the nomenklatura system, materials from the ECP Central Committee archival collection have mostly been used. As a rule, the analysis has been restricted to the union republic level, leaving aside the lower Party levels, which also had their own nomenklatura.

Role of State Security in the Soviet Union's Nomenklatura System

It was already claimed in the classified KGB history textbook that as of the establishment of the State Security organs in 1917, the government and Party leadership, including Vladimir Ulyanov-Lenin personally, paid particular attention to ensuring that the State Security apparatus – starting with the leadership – was under the management and control of Bolshevik-Communists.[10] There is clearly no reason to doubt this claim since the security service operated in the interests of the Bolshevik government and long-serving Party members were placed at its head.

---

[7]   AUCP(B) CC nomenklatura for 1942, RA, ERAF.1.1.328, 6–7; nomenklaturas for 1944, 1945, 1946, 1947, 1949, 1950 and 1952: all in RA, ERAF.1.307.109.

[8]   ECP(B) CC nomenklatura for 1941: RA, ERAF.1.4. 71, 19–20; for 1945: RA, ERAF.1.4.188, 168–169; 1946: RA, ERAF.1.4.324, 18–58; 1947: RA, ERAF.1.4.404, 102–104; 1949: RA, ERAF.1.4.719, 143; 1950: RA, ERAF.1.4.1975, 170 and 1952: RA, ERAF.1.4.1374, 74.

[9]   *EKP KK büroo istungite regestid I: 1940–1954* [ECP CC bureau session records], comp. Tõnu Tannberg, ed. Velly Roots (Tartu: Estonian History Archive, 2006).

[10]   *Istoriia sovetskikh organov gosudarstvennoi bezopasnosti: Uchebnik*, editor-in chief V. M. Chebrikov (Moscow: Vyshaia Krasnoznamennaia Shkola KGB SSSR imeni F. E. Dzerzhinskogo, 1977).

We do not have a good overview of how the nomenklatura system developed in the 1920s to 1930s but we do know, for example, that in 1925, 38 of the 39 top officers in the OGPU were Party members. Already in October of 1924, the procedure was established where candidates for the positions of provincial prosecutor and head of the GPU had to be approved by the AUCP(B) Central Committee and the provincial Party committees, which also approved the GPU's top officers in the municipal and regional departments. The social background of the candidate for the position was considered very important (the preference was for workers or peasants).[11] But there is data from 1925 on top OGPU officers belonging to the 'AUCP(B) CC nomenklatura'. According to the instruction of 25 May 1926, such officers could be transferred from one position to another only by a decision from the Central Committee.[12] Heads of State Security, together with Party secretaries, became the most important nomenklatura officials in the regions, forming 'clans', which began to irritate even Stalin himself.[13]

In 1934, the State Security organs, together with other public order sectors and other such authorities, were reorganised as the USSR People's Commissariat for Internal Affairs (USSR NKVD). During the Party purges that began in 1936, and during the mass repressions or 'Great Terror' that accompanied them, the leaderships of the Party and NKVD responsible for the districts and other territorial units, were replaced. To a large degree, this meant the physical destruction of former Party leaders and NKVD chiefs. In 1936, however, Genrikh Yagoda, the USSR People's Commissar for Internal Affairs, set up a procedure whereby the security service would hire staff without prior checking and approval by Party organs.[14]

---

[11] B. Pavlov, 'Stanovlenie kontrolia partiinoi nomenklatury nad pravo-okhranitel'noi sistemoi 1921–1925 godakh', *Voprosy istorii*, no. 1 (2004): 32–50, here 36.

[12] *Istoriia sovetskikh organov*, 197.

[13] See also: James Harris, 'Dual subordination? The political police and the Party in the Urals region 1918–1953', *Cahiers du monde russe*, no. 42/2–4 (2001): 423–445.

[14] Aleksei Georgievich Tepliakov, *Mashina terrora: OGPU-NKVD Sibiri v 1929–1941 gg.* (Moscow: Novyi khronograf, 2008), 454.

When the 'purge' ended, the procedure for checking and approval was reinstated in the security organs and other sectors of national importance. For this, the AUCP(B) CC Politburo decided in September of 1938, during the final stage of the 'Great Terror', to establish a procedure for recording, checking and approving 'responsible workers' (i.e. top officials) by the AUCP(B) Central Committee – in the People's Commissariats for foreign affairs, defence, navy, internal affairs, defence industry, and in the Defence Committee, Party Control Commission and Soviet Control Commission. The people working at the headquarters – ranging from the leadership to deputy heads of departments – had to be part of the nomenklatura.[15] In the local NKVD, the following had to be part of the nomenklatura: people's commissars (of the union republics), their deputies, NKVD department heads of the union republics and the autonomous republics, the heads, deputies and department heads of the NKVD organs in the oblasts, krais ja regions, as well as the heads of the NKVD municipal and raion departments. Recording and checking these officials was the responsibility of the AUCP(B) CC department for leading Party organs, where one of the sectors created was for officials in the NKVD and the courts / Prosecutor's Office. The personnel files of NKVD officers had to be submitted first, and they had to be checked and submitted for approval within one month.[16] Although the term 'nomenklatura' was not used in the decree, this was in essence a determination of the USSR-wide nomenklatura regarding the cadre of the State Security and the military sector.

Thereafter, in December of 1938, a AUCP(B) CC directive was issued to local Party organs, city, oblast and krai Committee Bureaus, and to the Central Committees of 'national Communist parties' (the Communist parties in the union republics), regarding their responsibilities in working with the heads of local NKVD. Since a regulation similar to this could have also been in effect in Estonia after the annexation, this document is analysed in more detail below.

---

[15]   The leadership consisted of the people's commissar and his deputies; in the departments, the larger structural units were the head offices and administrative offices. The heads of the smaller sub-units of the departments (e.g. divisions), therefore, were not included in the nomeklatura.

[16]   *Lubianka: Stalin i Glavnoe upravlenie gosbezopasnosti: arkhiv Stalina: dokumenty vysshikh organov partiinoi i gosudarstvennoi vlasti, 1937–1938*, comp. V. N. Haustov, V. P. Naumov and N. S. Plotnikova (Moscow: Mezhdunarodnyi fond Demokratiia, Materik, 2004), 550–552.

Local Party organs were obliged to record all the top officers of the local NKVD organs listed above, to compile an applicable 'list' (in other words, a nomenclature, although this term is not used in the document) and to set up a record file for all officers. A thorough check had to be carried out on those recorded officers, carefully analysing all the documents referring to them (personnel files, 'special check' materials, etc.[17]). This was done personally without waiting for the head of the NKVD to submit them for approval. This check was meant to purge the NKVD of all hostile persons who had been employed through deceit, and also of all politically unreliable persons. The applicable Party Committee Bureau was to review the candidates for nomenklatura positions presented by the local NKVD heads, and approve the appointments of only the honest, thoroughly checked Bolsheviks who were unconditionally loyal to the Party (this made it clear that only Party members could be appointed to the top leadership of the State Security). The head of the local department for directing Party organs, and Party Committee secretary, had to personally meet each candidate. In order to confirm the appointment of the heads of the NKVD municipal and raion departments, the opinion of the relevant Party Committee's first secretary was mandatory, and it had to be approved by the Party Committee's Bureau. After confirmation by the local Party organ, the NKVD chief had to send the materials, together with the Party Committee's decision, to the USSR NKVD, which in turn had to present the person to the AUCP(B) Central Committee for approval. In addition, the local Party Committee's First Secretary had to report to the AUCP(B) Central Committee regarding the whole process and note any problems that had arisen. The local Party Committees were also obliged to carry out similar checks, in cooperation with NKVD leaders, on lower level NKVD officers. Hiring new officers required a decision by the local Party Committee.[18] Based on the example of the Siberia region, however, it could be said that NKVD leaders were strongly opposed to following these directives and attempted to use various methods to circumvent them.[19] Unfortunately, there is a lack of reliable information on how long these specific rules were in effect, and whether these same rules were also applied to the Estonian SSR and other annexed territories. Nevertheless, it

---

[17]   Background check, or security check, which is discussed in more detail later.

[18]   *Lubianka: Stalin i Glavnoe*, 606–606.

[19]   Tepliakov, Mashina terrora, 454–459.

has been claimed that it was specifically in the late 1930s that the nomen-klatura principle was finally set in place, and that later on it was only modernised.[20] There definitely would have been some organisational changes in the way the State Security nomenklatura was managed when, in March of 1939, the Cadre Administration – and within it the NKVD cadre department – was formed on the basis of the AUCP(B) CC department for directing Party organs. The AUCP(B) CC Secretary Georgy Malenkov, who had quickly risen to power with Stalin's support, became the chief of the Cadre Administration.

Although there was an attempt to bind together the overlapping part of the nomenklatura system – that is, between the Party's top management organ, the AUCP(B) Central Committee, and its subordinate level of local Party organisations (also including the Party central committees of the union republics), there was already an inherent conflict. The union republic leadership and the other local Party organs had to simultaneously work mostly with the same nomenklatura as the AUCP(B) Central Committee. Taking into account, however, the attempts by Stalin and the central powers in the Kremlin to centralise the management of the State Security, conflicts could occur if the Party leadership of the union republic tried to take too much control over the work regarding the security nomenklatura.

It cannot be ruled out that the AUCP(B) CC needed control of the NKVD of the lower-ranking Party organs merely to keep security under tighter control with the help of locally sourced information. However, an independent cadre policy regarding security officers was not expected at the local level. Naturally, this did not spare local Party leaderships, in particular, from blame when personnel mistakes were made. Similar conflicts could also occur between the Party organs at the union republic level and its subordinate local Party organs.

Changes in the Nomenklatura of the Soviet State Security in the Estonian SSR, 1940–1953

The first steps in dismantling the system of government of the Republic of Estonia began immediately in June of 1940, after additional Red Army

---

[20]   T. Korzhikhina, Ju. Figatner, 'Sovetskaia nomenklatura: stanovlenie, mekha-nizmy deistviia', *Voprosy istorii*, no. 7 (1993): 25–34, here 29.

units marched in. Establishing the Soviet system of government, however, could begin only after the formation of the Estonian SSR, and its incorporation as part of the Soviet Union in August of 1940. An important part of Sovietisation was the formation of the Party apparatus and the NKVD. The right of appointing positions in the Party apparatus, which was the foundation for the nomenklatura system, was also introduced immediately in the territories annexed by the Soviet Union, but the implementation of this bureaucratic procedure, and the approval of the nomenklatura list, was time-consuming and could not take place overnight. For example, setting up the nomenklatura system was already on the agenda for the first session of the Lithuanian CP CC Secretariat on 11 September 1940, where the Central Committee's Cadre Department was directed to compile the nomenklatura list for the leading cadre of the people's commissariats, who would then be appointed by the Central Committee. The people's commissariats were directed to present all top officials for approval. The reassignment of already approved officials or their dismissal could take place only with the permission of the Central Committee.[21]

As a rule, the Party Committee followed a hierarchical scheme for appointments in the authorities, and in the approval process, whereby top officials were appointed first, followed by the lower ranks. Thus the local communist Boris Kumm was appointed the Estonian SSR People's Commissar for Internal Affairs (i.e. the head of a union republic's NKVD), and was already appointed as a member of the government on 25 August 1940 (it has been claimed that the USSR NKVD order regarding his appointment arrived on 11 September 1940[22]), even though the Estonian SSR People's Commissariat for Internal Affairs (ESSR NKVD) was formed by a written order issued by the USSR NKVD on 29 August 1940. Yet considering that the sessions of the ECP Central Committee Bureau were documented only as of 9 September 1940, no written record of the ECP's approval of Kumm can be found. In his memoirs, Boris Kumm has himself described how he became People's Commissar: 'How members of the Council of the People's Commissars were decided, I don't know. I was

---

[21]   Nijolė Maslauskienė, Inga Petravičiūtė, *Okupantai ir kolaborantai: pirmoji sovietinė okupacija (1940–1941) = Occupants and collaborators: the first Soviet occupation 1940–1941* (Vilnius: Margi raštai, 2007), 181.

[22]   Nikita Petrov and Konstantin Skorkin, *Kto rukovodil NKVD 1934–1941: spravochnik* (Moscow: Zven'ia, 1999), 258.

nominated as People's Commissar but I only found out about it from [Johannes] Lauristin at the Riigivolikogu [the lower chamber of Estonian Parliament] session and at the last moment, before his speech on the membership of the Council of People's Commissars.'[23]

It can be seen from the minutes of the sessions of the ECP (as of October 1940, the ECP(B)) Central Committee Bureau that NKVD officers were indeed among the first to be appointed (after the members of the Central Committee itself, and the Party secretaries of the cities/counties). Thus the NKVD Special Department officials of the Red Army's Estonian Territorial Military Unit (22nd Rifle Corps), including the lower ranks, were already appointed at the CC Bureau's third session on 14 September, and many top officials of the Estonian SSR NKVD Central Administration (from the deputy people's commissar to divisional heads, a total of 29 officials) were appointed at the fourth session of the CC Bureau on 20 September 1940.[24] It is probable that decisions made here and later on were guided by the AUCP(B) CC nomenklatura list and instructions, as well as by their own assessments. The approval of top NKVD officers also continued later – for example, a number of local department heads were approved in February of 1941.[25]

The leadership of the ESSR NKVD included People's Commissar Boris Kumm, Deputy People's Commissars Aleksei Shkurin (from the USSR NKVD) and Andres (Andrei) Murro (a local Communist with a background similar to Kumm's), and the Deputy People's Commissar for cadre issues, Karl Hansson (Hanson, an Estonian communist who like Kumm and Murro had been imprisoned in the Republic of Estonia but, unlike the others, had gone to the Soviet Union in 1936). As with Kumm, the ECP(B) Central Committee did not implement an approval process for Shkurin. This refers to Shkurin's special status as the actual head of the management of the operational work of the security organs. Murro and Hansson were among the first to be appointed on 20 September 1940.

It is not clear how well the ECP(B) Central Committee understood the structure of the ESSR NKVD, which should have been the basis for systematic nomenklatura work. Its structure followed the USSR NKVD's structure, in reduced form, and had almost nothing in common with the

23   Boris Kumm, memoirs, 3 July 1951, RA, ERAF.247.51.187, 6.

24   *EKP KK büroo*, 11–12.

25   *Ibid.*, 24.

previous Ministry of Internal Affairs of the Republic of Estonia, which Kumm took over on 31 August 1940 from the 'red' interior minister of the time, Maksim Unt. The people's commissar and his deputies formed the leadership of the Commissariat (including the deputy for cadre issues, who was also the head of the Cadre Department), under the jurisdiction of which was the central administration in Tallinn and the local ('peripheral') sub-units (departments or divisions) in the cities and counties. The departments of the State Security Administration formed the main part of the central system, which mostly consisted of two or more divisions and was managed by a department head and a deputy (or deputies). A division was an even smaller sub-unit, consisting of the head of the division, his deputy and generally 5–9 officials. The central administration also contained divisions that reported directly, and other sub-units (e.g. secretariat). The title of a rank and file operational agent in the State Security was 'operational commissioner'. Operational commissioners, together with the top officials and officers with special military rank (who were later in military service) who directly administered operational work, belonged to the group of so-called operational personnel. Agents who carried out pre-trial investigations of arrested individuals held the title 'investigator'. Non-operational personnel consisted of technical and administrative personnel.[26]

The decree issued by the USSR Supreme Soviet Presidium on 3 February 1941 detached the sub-units dealing with state security from the NKVD and reorganised them to establish the People's Commissariat for State Security (NKGB) – and in Estonia, the ESSR NKGB. Although most operational personnel continued to fulfil their previous tasks, the structural units were renamed. The new structure also required a new nomenklatura and appointments. Thus Boris Kumm was confirmed as the People's Commissar for State Security at the CC Bureau session on 14 March 1941. This was followed by the appointment of the lower ranks of the top NKGB officers.

---

[26]   For details on the structures of the ESSR NKVD formed in 1940 and the ESSR NKGB formed in 1941, see Ohmann, 'Eesti NSV siseministeeriumi struktuur' and *Sõja ja rahu vahel. II köide, Esimene punane aasta: okupeeritud Eesti julgeolekupoliitiline olukord sõja alguseni* [Between War and Peace, II: The first 'red' year: the security-political situation in occupied Estonia up to the beginning of the war], editor-in-chief Enn Tarvel, ed. Meelis Maripuu (Tallinn: S-Keskus, 2010), 416–421.

The first complete nomenklatura for the ECP(B) Central Committee (and also the municipal and county committees) was decided at the ECP(B) CC Bureau's session on 8 May 1941: officials holding nomenklatura positions were to be appointed and reassigned only by decision of the Party Committee. In the ESSR NKGB, not only the top officials (starting with the People's Commissar) but also all operational personnel down to the deputy operational commissioner (the lowest position in the operational section) were members of the ECP(B) CC nomenklatura. This was a notable difference compared to other people's commissariats and even to the ESSR NKVD, where only the top officers belonged to the nomenklatura. It should be noted that the top positions in the local NKGB organs (up to the divisional heads of municipal departments) which were included in the nomenklatura of the ECP(B) municipal and county committees were also part of the Central Committee's nomenklatura. The Secretaries of the Party organisations of the people's commissariats were also part of the Central Committee's nomenklatura, i.e. including the Secretary of the NKGB Party Committee.[27] However, the heads and deputies, the head of the secretariat, and also the investigators, etc. of the NKGB Central Administration's divisions were not included in the Central Committee's nomenklatura. Considering that the nomenklatura also included assistant operatives, it could be presumed that the aim was to subordinate the entire operational group of the ESSR NKGB to ECP(B) CC control, and that the omission of some positions (including divisional heads) was due to an error, or to an incomplete understanding of the NKGB's structure on the part of the ECP(B) CC Cadre Department, who compiled the list.

Due to the imminent start of the German-Soviet war, changes were made in the structure of the State Security: the decree issued by the USSR Supreme Soviet Presidium on 20 July 1941 merged the NKVD and NKGB to again form the People's Commissariat for Internal Affairs (NKVD). The new structure and organisation of personnel, which was similar to that in effect in 1940, were also decided in August for the ESSR NKVD, although they were not fully implemented. There is no information that the personnel in the CC Bureau had been appointed to new positions. In November of 1941, the ESSR NKVD was disbanded and those officials who arrived in the Soviet rear area were appointed to new positions in the

---

27   RA, ERAF.1.4.71, 19–20.

various sub-units of the USSR NKVD. Naturally, the ECP(B) CC Bureau no longer confirmed their appointment.

At the end of 1942, when the AUCP(B) CC Cadre Administration wanted information on persons from the Estonian SSR holding USSR-wide nomenklatura positions, the ECP(B) CC took the list of top ESSR NKVD officials as of August 1941 as its basis. In the AUCP(B) CC nomenklatura of the time, the NKVD and the People's Commissariat for Defence formed one of the six sub-groups. The nomenklatura list for the NKVD included the People's Commissar and his deputies (also the deputy for non-operational issues), the Central Administration's department heads and the heads of the local (municipal and raion) departments, and also top officials from the Militia (the Soviet police force), labour camps and the highways administration, a total of 14 categories of positions.[28] The security personnel categories therefore matched the nomenklatura categories established in 1938, leading to the conclusion that the AUCP(B) CC nomenklatura could have remained unchanged since at least this time in terms of the top officials in a union republic's NKVD.[29] From here on, there is a system that can be monitored, and for the AUCP(B) CC nomenklatura, the security organs and military sector were grouped into one sub-category – at least in part (union republic). This also included the theoretically voluntary organisations associated with the military sector at the time, such as OSOAVIAKhIM[30].

In April of 1943, the NKVD and NKGB were again split into two separate people's commissariats, where the new NKGB structure was markedly different from its 1941 structure, primarily due to the names of its sub-units. This presumed new appointments. However, the ESSR NKGB was not formed at that point, and therefore ECP(B) CC personnel could not have known in October of 1943 which ESSR NKGB positions should be included in the future ECP(B) CC nomenklatura.[31] The Estonian, Latvian

---

[28] List of positions, included in the AUCP(B) CC nomenklatura, 24 November 1942, RA, ERAF.1.1.328, 6–7.

[29] See the Appendix 1: ESSR NKGB/MGB positions in the (basic) nomenklatura of the AUCP(B) Central Committee and ECP(B) Central Committee, 1941–1953.

[30] Association to Assist State Defence and Work in Aviation and Chemistry, which operated in the Soviet Union during the period 1927–1948.

[31] See: Draft of the list of positions included in the ECP(B) CC nomenklatura, with an accompanying letter from the ECP(B) CC Cadre Department, and ad-

and Lithuanian NKGB operational groups that were formed, based on the written order issued by the USSR NKGB on 30 November 1943, began with the re-formation of the NKGB organs in preparation for taking these territories over again from the Germans. In March of 1944, when the Red Army had already reached the territory of the Republic of Estonia, the Estonian SSR NKGB was again formed in the municipalities beyond the Narva River, but now with a new structure and mostly new personnel. The Politburo appointed the new-old People's Commissar for the NKGB Boris Kumm on 27 March 1944. His appointment was not confirmed in the ECP(B) CC Bureau, perhaps because it was not considered necessary since he had already been confirmed in 1941, and he had not been relieved of his duties in the interim. A further reason may be that the 'directive organs' had not issued any order to dismiss the ESSR people's commissars. However, the ECP(B) CC Bureau already started appointing other top ESSR NKGB officials on 27 April 1944, but this was done rather unsystematically. The USSR NKGB Cadre Department's statutes were approved in March of 1944, where one of the department's tasks was the preparation of materials referring to the officials belonging to the AUCP(B) CC nomenklatura. One division in the department also began to manage personnel-related work in the ESSR NKGB, thereby duplicating Party organs.

On 7 September 1944, the ESSR Supreme Soviet Presidium, the ESSR CPC and the ECP(B) CC issued a joint decree in the recently captured town of Võru that re-established Estonian SSR laws, decrees and decisions that had been declared null and void during the German occupation in 1941/44. At the end of the same month, the ECP(B) apparatus, the ESSR people's commissars, and the NKVD and NKGB, moved to Tallinn. Thus began the re-Sovietisation of Estonia. The Politburo decision issued on 11 November formed a singular 'shadow government' to manage the administration of Estonia – the AUCP(B) CC Estonian Bureau, the members of which were the current AUCP(B) CC Deputy Chief of Cadre Administration, Nikolai Shatalin (Chairman), Georgy Perov (Deputy Chairman), the USSR NKVD and NKGB Commissioner in Estonia, Nikolai Sazykin, the recently appointed 1st Secretary of the ECP(B) CC, Nikolai Karotamm, and the Chairman of the Estonian SSR Council of People's Commissars,

---

ditions by N. Karotamm and J. Vares, October 1943, RA, ERAF.1.1.399.

Arnold Veimer.[32] This operated until March of 1947, whereby the NKVD and NKGB Commissioner operated as the top official of these respective authorities. Members of the Estonian Bureau were not even included in the AUCP(B) CC Estonian SSR nomenklatura, not to mention the ECP(B) CC nomenklatura.

The first known 'post war' Estonian SSR AUCP(B) CC nomenklatura of top positions is from November of 1944, where in one part there is a list of positions in the NKVD, NKGB and the People's Commissariat for Defence:

1.   ESSR NKVD People's Commissar;
2.   ESSR NKVD Deputy People's Commissar for non-operational issues;
3.   ESSR NKVD Deputy People's Commissar;
4.   ESSR NKVD Deputy People's Commissar for cadre issues;
5.   ESSR NKVD Deputy People's Commissar for Militia issues;
6.   ESSR NKVD Head of Political Department, Militia Administration;
7.   ESSR NKGB People's Commissar;
8.   ESSR NKGB Deputy People's Commissar;
9.   ESSR NKGB Deputy People's Commissar for cadre issues;
10. ESSR NKGB Head of 2nd Department;
11. ESSR NKGB Head of Investigation Department;
12. ESSR NKGB Head of Department A;
13. ESSR NKGB Head of 5th Department;
14. Estonian Railways NKGB Head of Transport Department;
15. Estonian Basin NKGB Head of Water Transport Department;
16. ESSR War Commissar (area of responsibility of the People's Commissar for Defence);
17. OSOAVIAKhIM Chairman of the Republic's Central Council.[33]

---

[32]   For information on the AUCP(B) CC Estonian Bureau, see: Tõnu Tannberg, "'Selle büroo ülesandeks on...'": ÜK(b)P Keskkomitee Eesti büroo osast Eesti NSV sovetiseerimisel aastail 1944–1947' ['The Task of this Bureau is...': on the Role of the AUCP(B) Central Committee Estonian Bureau in Sovietising the Estonian SSR in 1944–1947], – Nõukogude Eesti külma sõja ajal, ed. Tõnu Tannberg, Eesti Ajalooarhiivi toimetised = Acta et commentationes Archivi Historici Estoniae 23(30) (Tartu: Eesti Ajalooarhiiv, 2015), 11–30.

[33]   List of positions, included in the AUCP(B) CC nomenklatura, 14 November 1944, RA, ERAF.1.307.109, 2v–3.

As we can see, compared to the 1942 nomenklatura, the local heads of NKGB departments are not included, and of the department heads of the Central Administration, only the more important are included. The NKGB transport organs did not report to the ESSR NKGB but directly to the USSR NKGB.

The ECP(B) CC established its nomenklatura in March of 1945. It was forbidden to appoint, dismiss or reassign the cadre listed here without the permission of the ECP(B) CC Bureau. As for the ESSR NKGB, its department heads and their deputies, the heads of its Central Administration's independent divisions, and the heads of its municipal and county departments (divisions) were included in the list, in addition to the People's Commissar and his deputies. Officials from the same categories in the ESSR NKVD were also included. The Party Committee Secretary of the NKGB, as one of the largest ESSR Party organisations, was also included in the list.[34] Therefore, the ECP(B) CC nomenklatura matched that of the AUCP(B) CC as regards the leadership of the People's Commissariat and the department heads, but it was also extended to cover lower-level managers. But already in June of 1945, the AUCP(B) CC also included in its nomenklatura the ESSR NKGB local (municipal and county) department heads, thus returning to the model that was in effect from at least 1938.[35] The practice of Moscow informing Tallinn of changes to the AUCP(B) CC nomenklatura continued. In December of 1945, a new AUCP(B) CC nomenklatura was presented where all the changes had already been taken into account. The number of heads of NKGB central departments included in the nomenklatura had been doubled and, together with the heads of the local departments, the number of officials under Moscow's direct control was now 23, i.e. the largest during the whole Stalinist period.[36] This seems to reflect the tendency – at that particular time, when mass repressions had hit one of their peaks – to concentrate the power to appoint security chiefs even more in Moscow's hands.

In March of 1946, USSR governmental bodies were reorganised, including renaming the people's commissariats as ministries. Changes in

---

[34] List of positions, included in the ECP(B) CC nomenklatura, 13, 16 and 20 June 1945, RA, ERAF.1.4.188, 168–169.

[35] Changes no. 5 to the List of positions, included in the AUCP(B) CC nomenklatura, 20 June 1945, RA, ERAF.1.307.109, 8–9.

[36] RA, ERAF.1.307.109, 22.

structures and personnel followed. Major Viktor Abakumov, the chief of 'Smersh', the Military Counterintelligence Agency, became Minister for State Security (MGB). Under the powerful Abakumov, the MGB and the MVD (Ministry of Internal Affairs, formerly NKVD) now began to distance themselves and rival each other.

There was some delay in these changes spreading to the Estonian SSR. The renaming of the people's commissariats as ministries was apparently the reason for confirming the new ECP(B) CC nomenklatura in September of 1946. As far as the security organs were concerned, this adhered to the previous model – the 1945 ECP(B) CC nomenklatura – but the number of positions changed. As with the USSR-wide nomenklatura, this Stalin-era nomenklatura was also the longest of the lists, with the ESSR MGB alone having 69 positions. The same trend applied to the MGB transport organs.[37] Compared to the USSR-wide nomenklatura, the ECP(B) CC nomenklatura was structured somewhat differently: here the security organs were grouped with the 'special cadre', which also included the top officials from the MVD organs, the Estonian SSR Ministry of Justice, the Supreme Court, the Prosecutor's Office, the Ministry of Foreign Affairs, the War Commissariat, the MVD Forces Military Tribunal and Prosecutor's Office, the Estonian Railway Military Tribunal and Prosecutor's Office, the Water Basin Prosecutor's Office, the OSOAVIAKhIM Central Council, the Red Cross Central Committee, the Kalev Sports Association, and the Council of Ministers Committee for Physical Culture and Sports.

After Aleksei Kuznetsov, the First Secretary of the AUCP(B) Committee for Leningrad city and oblast, replaced Malenkov as head of the AUCP(B) CC Cadre Administration in April of 1946, he started increasing and specifying the leading role of the Party organs again in cadre issues. The following year, Kuznetsov also became (essentially only formally, it must be admitted) the manager of the State Security organs in the AUCP(B) Central Committee. The AUCP(B) CC Organisational Bureau's decision issued on 5 October 1946 established that in the future, the appointment and dismissal of AUCP(B) CC nomenklatura positions would be decided exclusively by the AUCP(B) CC. This meant that the AUCP(B) Central Committee did not merely confirm the appointment

---

[37]   List of positions, included in the ECP(B) CC nomenklatura, 7–9 September 1946, RA, ERAF.1.4.324, 18–58. For the ECP nomenklatura positions in the security organs, see: Hämäläinen, *Eestimaa Kommunistliku Partei*, Appendix 6. Nomenklatura positions associated with power structures.

of officials, but actually made the appointment decisions. Regional Party organs, including the ECP(B) CC and its authorities, were required to submit proposals for the appointment of nomenklatura cadre, together with character references. Party organs were obliged to inform the AUCP(B) CC Organisational Bureau of the positive factors and shortcomings of the cadre with USSR-wide subordination that was located in the regions. The new AUCP(B) CC nomenklatura was also confirmed.[38] As far as the security organs located in the Estonian SSR were concerned, this was quite a short list, including only the ESSR Minister of the MGB and his deputies, a total of 4 positions.[39] It can be assumed that since the previous AUCP(B) CC nomenklatura lists were too long, decisions regarding appointments dragged on, and it was then decided to change this situation.

In accordance with the previously described decision, the ECP(B) Central Committee also approved the new nomenclature in January of 1947, where account had already been taken of the structural changes that had taken place in the MGB at the end of 1946. Here too there was a trend towards reduction: the list no longer included the ESSR MGB divisional heads, and deputies of department heads were added to the reserve nomenklatura list. Compared to the previous list, the positions requiring confirmation were more than halved – from 69 to 29. The Central Committee warned that violating the rules for approving nomenklatura positions would be severely punished.[40]

The following year, in 1947, the AUCP(B) CC nomenklatura was reduced even further in the ESSR MGB section: only the Minister and his first deputy (Colonel Pastelnyak) remained on the list. Overall, the following positions were excluded from the special cadre list of the AUCP(B) CC nomenklatura:

1. ESSR Commissar for War;
2. ESSR Minister of Internal Affairs;
3. ESSR First Deputy of the Minister of Internal Affairs;
4. MVD Corrective Labour Camp and Construction No 907 Administration, Head;

---

[38] *TsK VKP(b) i regional'nye partiinye komitety 1945–1953,* comp. V. V. Denisov et al. (Moscow: ROSSPEN, 2004), 54–56.

[39] List of positions, whose employees are appointed by AUCP(B) CC, 1 November 1946, RA, ERAF.1.307.109, 49v.

[40] RA, ERAF.1.4.403, 14–17; ERAF.1.4.404, 102–104.

5. MVD Corrective Labour Camp and Construction No 907 Administration, Deputy Head for Political Activities and Deputy Head of Political Department;
6. Estonian Railways MGB Guard Department, Head;
7. MVD Estonian School, Head;
8. ESSR Minister of State Security;
9. ESSR First Deputy of Minister of State Security;
10. ESSR Council of Ministers Physical Culture and Sports Committee, Chairman;
11. Volunteer Sports Club *Kalev*, Chairman;
12. ESSR OSOAVIAHIM Central Council, Chairman.[41]

A reorganisation of the entire Party system took place in 1948. The AUCP(B) CC Cadre Administration was dismantled, as well as the cadre departments in local Party organs, including the ECP(B) CC Cadre Department. Supervision of the work with cadre and nomenklatura, as well as the inspection of how decisions were implemented, was handed over to the various 'content' departments. The security organs, the entire 'special cadre' and some other bodies were to be supervised by administration departments – in the Estonian SSR, the ECP(B) CC Administration Department. A new nomenklatura was developed according to these supervisory departments, which for the MGB was analogous to the previous ones. The ESSR MGB had only two positions in the new 1949 AUCP(B) CC nomenklatura as well: the Minister and the First Deputy. In addition, it included the head of the Estonian Railway MGB Guard Administration.[42] The ECP(B) CC 1949 nomenklatura list was also similar to the previous year's (1947) list.[43]

Looking at the proportion of security service nomenklatura (basic nomenklatura) at the time of the deportations of March 1949 (we have exact data on personnel in the ESSR MGB apparatus for this year), we can see that the AUCP(B) CC nomenklatura (two positions) formed 0.15% of the Ministry's entire personnel (1,292 positions), and 2.17% of the ECP(B)

---

[41] List of positions, included in the AUCP(B) CC nomenklatura for the Estonian SSR, 22 December 1947, RA, ERAF.1.307.109, 84v–85.

[42] List of positions, included in the AUCP(B) CC nomenklatura for the Estonian SSR, 16 February 1949, RA, ERAF.1.307.109, 115v.

[43] RA, ERAF.1.4.719, 143.

CC nomenklatura (28). Of the entire AUCP(B) CC Estonian SSR nomen-klatura (245 positions), the ESSR MGB part accounted for 0.82%, and 1.55% of the entire ECP(B) CC nomenklatura (1,803). In 1949, the MGB nomenklatura list was the shortest during the Stalin era, with security officers accounting for only a very minor share – just the top officials.

The AUCP(B) CC nomenklatura for the following year, 1950, was slightly longer, including the ESSR MGB Minister and all his deputies (i.e. two deputy security ministers, the deputy for cadre issues and the deputy for Militia issues, as well as the chief of the Militia Administration).[44] The latter had been transferred together with the Militia to the jurisdiction of the MGB in the same year.

In September of 1950, as a continuation of the Sovietisation of the Estonian administrative system, the municipalities were disbanded – through a decree issued by the ESSR Supreme Soviet Presidium – and 39 rural raions were formed, as well as five cities (Tallinn, Tartu, Pärnu, Narva and Kohtla-Järve) subordinated directly to the ESSR. Excluding Tallinn (the location of ESSR MGB headquarters), MGB departments were now also formed in all raions and cities where they had not previously been. Of course, the MGB was not the only agency that went through a change in structure with the creation of the raions, and these changes were subsequently also followed by the creation of a new ECP(B) CC nomenklatura. The heads of the MGB municipal and raion departments (41) expanded this list to 59 names, to which was also added the record-keeping nomenklatura with the deputies of the operational department heads, a total of 13 positions.[45]

The final Stalin-era nomenklatura was created in association with the establishment of the next stage of the Soviet administrative system – the formation of the oblasts in 1952. According to the decree adopted in May of 1952, three oblasts were formed in the Estonian SSR: the Tallinn, Pärnu and Tartu oblasts. For the MGB this meant the formation of MGB oblast administrations, which were links in the chain of command in the ESSR MGB and MGB raion departments. The oblast administrations were managed by three-member management teams, consisting of the head of the oblast administration, the deputy head, and the deputy head for

---

[44]   List of positions, included in the AUCP(B) CC nomenklatura for the Estonian SSR, 18 January 1950, RA, ERAF.1.307.109, 145v.

[45]   ECP(B) CC nomenklatura, 4 December 1950, RA, ERAF.1.4.1975, 170.

cadre issues. The heads of the oblast administrations were appointed to the AUCP(B) CC new nomenklatura according to each oblast. Regarding the Tallinn oblast, the list also included the head of the Estonian Railways MGB Guard Administration.[46] The applicable ECP(B) CC new nomenklatura included the management of the oblast administrations, but the heads of the raion departments were placed in a lower level nomenklatura.[47] This general nomenklatura remained in force until Stalin's death. The MGB oblast administrations in the Estonian SSR were disbanded by June of 1953.

Implementing the Nomenklatura System

As noted above, the top NKVD officials were among the first whose appointments the ECP(B) CC Bureau already confirmed in September of 1940. The ECP(B) CC First Secretary, Karl Säre, took over the NKVD in general, along with its cadre issues. NKVD People's Commissar Boris Kumm also became a member of the ECP(B) CC Bureau that approved the nomenklatura.

The USSR NKVD proposed the appointment of leading ESSR NKVD personnel (from among Chekists with USSR backgrounds), and initially also partially from among the members of the ECP(B) Central Committee (Communists with Estonian backgrounds). The latter, however, did not have the necessary training for this work (although previous underground experience was beneficial) and they often did not speak Russian. In addition, there were cases where upstanding Estonian citizens who were NKVD officers were exposed as 'provocateurs' who had cooperated with the police of the Republic of Estonia. Thus an application was submitted to the CC Bureau in January to dismiss Nikolai Härms, the head of the ESSR NKVD Secretariat, who had already been arrested in October of 1940 as a former agent of the Estonian Political Police.

It becomes apparent from examining the ethnic background of the nomenklatura cadre that already at this time, almost all heads of central

---

[46]   List of positions, included in the AUCP(B) CC nomenklatura for the Estonian SSR, 4 June 1952; List of positions, included in the AUCP(B) CC nomenklatura for the Tallinn oblast, 4 June 1952, RA, ERAF.1.307.109, 178.

[47]   Nomenklatura of the ECP(B) CC, 14–16 June 1952, RA, ERAF.1.4.1374, 74.

departments were cadre security officials from the USSR and not from the local population. In contrast, the heads of the local departments had native backgrounds, and their deputies were again cadre Chekists from outside of Estonia.

After the formation of the ESSR NKGB, the procedure for confirming the appointment of People's Commissar Kumm was initiated in the CC Bureau on 14 March 1941. Since we have a timeline for Kumm's appointment and confirmation, let us observe how this process actually unfolded. The People's Commissariat for State Security (NKGB) was formed by a decree issued by the USSR Supreme Soviet Presidium on 3 February 1941. Three days later, the People's Commissar of the USSR NKVD, Lavrentiy Beria, the Secretary of the AUCP(B) CC Malenkov, and Beria's deputy Vsevolod Merkulov submitted a special notification to Stalin with proposals regarding the appointment of heads for NKGB territorial organs.[48] This document mostly proposed the current NKVD People's Commissars for the positions of People's Commissar in the union republics, but in the case of the Latvian and Lithuanian SSRs it proposed the deputies of the current People's Commissars who had been sent from the USSR. The Politburo decision on the appointment of the heads of both the NKGB and NKVD territorial organs was made on 25 February.[49] The written order issued by the USSR NKVD formalised the appointment on 26 February 1941 of the NKVD People's Commissars (including ESSR NKVD People's Commissar Andres Murro).[50] On the same day, the NKGB People's Commissars, including ESSR NKGB People's Commissar Kumm, were also appointed. The new People's Commissar Kumm signed his first written order on 3

---

[48] *Lubianka: Stalin i NKVD-NKGB-GUKR 'Smersh': 1939–mart 1946: dokumenty*, comp. V. N. Haustov, V. P. Naumov and N. S. Plotnikova (Moscow: Mezhdunarodnyi fond Demokratiia: Materik, 2006), 235–238.

[49] *Politbiuro TsK RKP(b)-VKP(b): povestki dnia zasedanii 1919–1952: katalog, tom 3. 1940–1952*, ed. G. M. Adibekov and K. M. Anderson (Moscow: ROSSPEN, 2001), 155.

[50] A. Kokurin, 'The basic activity directions of the people's Commissariat of Internal Affairs of the Latvian Soviet Socialist Republic in 1940–1941', *Latvijas Vēsturnieku Komisias raksti, 11, Latvija Nacistiskās Vācijas Okupācijas Varā 1941–1945, Starptautiskās konferences referāti 2003. gada 12.–13. jūnijs, Rīga / Latvia under Nazi German occupation 1941–1945, Materials of an international conference 12–13 June 2003* (Riga: Latvijas vēstures institūta apgāds, 2004), 141–153, here 150.

March, thereby forming the ESSR NKGB and establishing its structure and top officials.[51] The ECP(B) CC Bureau confirmed the appointments of Kumm and Murro as People's Commissars on 14 March, and requested that the AUCP(B) Central Committee also in turn 'confirm this decision'.[52] This, however, was just a formality since, as demonstrated previously, the AUCP(B) Central Committee, in the person of Stalin, had already approved the appointment of the security chiefs. The ESSR Supreme Soviet Presidium then issued a decree on 26 March, which divided the ESSR People's Commissariat for Internal Affairs into two people's commissariats, along with decrees on appointing Murro and Kumm as People's Commissars. Both decrees were published in the *ENSV Teataja* [Official Gazette of ESSR] on 29 March 1941.[53] On 23 April, after the session of the Estonian SSR Supreme Soviet had taken place, a law confirming the previous decrees was published in the *ENSV Teataja*.[54] The appointment of security chiefs, therefore, was decided by the USSR leadership, and the ECP(B) leadership merely confirmed the appointments with its own formal decision.

It is noteworthy that the ECP(B) Central Committee still did not confirm Aleksei Shkurin or Veniamin Gulst, who had been appointed deputies of the NKGB People's Commissar. The Deputy People's Commissar for cadre issues, Sergei Kingissepp (a State Security officer from the USSR) was confirmed by the ECP(B) CC Bureau on 17 April 1941.

Säre and others felt that the Chekists, primarily those State Security officers who had come from the USSR, looked down on them and demonstrated ignorance. They were not prepared to give up without a fight. Thus the ECP(B) CC Bureau issued a decision on 22 March 1941 which referred to major deficiencies in the work of the NKGB, as well as meagre 'contacts with the masses' (a slogan that was used often in Soviet jargon) and the low proportion of local personnel, particularly after the People's Commissariats were split. The Bureau decided to assign People's Commissar Kumm the task of paying closer attention to including local personnel,

---

[51]   Order of the ESSR NKGB no. 001, 5 March 1941, Organisation of the ESSR People's Commissariat for State Security, RA, ERAF.17SM.16.7, 1.

[52]   Minutes no. 3 of the meeting of the ECP(B) CC Bureau, 14, 17 and 22 March 1941, RA, ERAF.1.4.62, 102.

[53]   *ENSV Teataja 1941*, 500–502.

[54]   *Ibid.*, 649.

with the assistance of the ECP(B) CC Cadre Department. The situation where deputies of the heads of the NKGB bypassed their superiors in their activities was considered impermissible. The heads were assigned the task of taking all management and full responsibility upon themselves. Officials to be included in the ECP(B) CC nomenklatura had to be submitted for confirmation to the ECP(B) Central Committee.[55] The confirmation of top officials continued at subsequent Bureau sessions in accordance with the nomenklatura developed in May, but the war breaking out in June of 1941 did not permit much progress. The last pre-war appointment confirmations of divisional heads and deputies of department heads in the central apparatus took place as late as 19 June 1941.

After the war had started, the ECP(B) CC Bureau did not confirm any more nomenklatura officials. This meant that the top officials of the ESSR NKVD, which had been reorganised again in July into a single People's Commissariat for Internal Affairs, were not confirmed. As can be seen from information in ECP(B) CC files, 18 of the 21 AUCP(B) CC nomenklatura positions in the ESSR NKVD (excluding the Militia and Highways Administration) were filled. People's Commissar Kumm and his deputies Veniamin Gulst and Karl Hansson (deputy for cadre issues) from the leadership of the People's Commissariat were transferred to other USSR NKVD organs, whereas the deputy for the Militia, Andres Murro, and the deputy for non-operational issues, Elmar Paju, had been killed in the war. The top positions in the Central Department were filled by security officers sent from the USSR, whereas the heads of local departments were Communists with Estonian backgrounds.[56]

In November of 1941, the ESSR NKVD was disbanded and work with the nomenklatura became a background task for quite some time. Nevertheless, Nikolai Karotamm, the new head of the ECP(B), attempted to adopt the role of mentor for former People's Commissar Kumm, nominating him for the position of NKVD special department head for the planned Red Army Estonian forces, and suggesting that his economic situation suffered in comparison to other people's commissars (Kumm no longer received a people's commissar salary but had to manage with the

---

[55] ECP(B) CC decision On the division of cadre between the People's Commissariats for State Security and Internal Affairs, 22 March 1941, RA, ERAF.1.4.68, 173.

[56] Lists of the AUCP(B) CC nomenclature employees, for the Estonian ESSR during the wartime, 15 December 1942, RA, ERAF.1.1.330.

salary of a USSR NKVD divisional head). While in the Soviet rear area, Karotamm made a number of attempts to initiate the restoration of the Estonian SSR State Security organs, apparently hoping that this would permit him to achieve a certain level of control over them.[57] In the formation of the security organs, however, it was not the wishes of Karotamm that were followed, but rather those of Moscow, and Karotamm was left with a limited number of instruments with which to manage the security system, including cadre work and the nomenklatura system. Following Stalin's example, he considered cadre work to be the 'monopoly of the Party'.

After the ESSR NKGB was restored in March of 1944, the ECP(B) CC Bureau already began confirming the appointment of its top officials in the following month. Among the first to be approved was Aleksandr Mikhailov on 27 April 1944, the ESSR NKGB Deputy People's Commissar, formerly a raion department head in the Leningrad oblast NKGB Administration. We can consider the situation as of 19 January 1945 as an example of how security chiefs were appointed and confirmed. The ECP(B) CC nomenklatura list had not yet been adopted by that time, and it is probable that officials were confirmed at the level for which they were nominated. Among these were the divisional heads of the central system, who were included in the 'ESSR NKGB nomenklatura' (the heads of both independent divisions and departmental divisions, as well as the heads of the secretariat and the internal prison).[58] It can be presumed that since all groups included persons confirmed by the Party, the positions listed in the document were considered part of the ECP(B) CC nomenklatura.

As can be seen in Table 1, around half of the top officials had been approved, but there were also a number of positions that were not filled, which was not unusual, considering the ongoing war and the personnel shortage. All officials were Communist Party members. Regarding ethnic background, there were 34 Russians, eight Estonians (there was not a single Estonian among the heads of the central departments) and three others. The heads of the central departments (except for Jakobson, the head of the Investigation Department) had all served in the Soviet Union

---

[57] Saueauk, *Propaganda ja terror*, 111–116; ECP(B) CC Secretary Karotamm to USSR NKVD Beria, 8 December 1942, RA, ERAF.1.6.1422, 8.

[455] List of the nomenclature employees of the ESSR NKGB, 19 January 1945, RA, ERAF.1.3.434, 2–4.

as security officers before 1940. Therefore, the work of the People's Commissariat was led and organised by persons who predominantly had no background in Estonia.

Table 1. ESSR NKGB nomenklatura, January 1945.

Category of positions	Number of positions	Filled positions	Officials approved by the ECP(B) CC
Leadership (people's commissar, deputies for state security and assistant)	5	4	3*
Heads of central departments	7	5	5
Deputy(ies) of departmental heads	12	10	3**
Divisional heads ***	22	15	5†
Heads of local departments/divisions	11	11	8‡
TOTAL	57	45	24

* Including People's Commissar Kumm, who was considered approved as of 27 April 1944.
** An additional three officials had already been nominated for approval, with Alfred Pressmann and Mikhail Shkurenkov in May of 1944. Both had also worked in the ESSR security organs in 1940/41, and had not been viewed positively by the ECP leadership. Nevertheless, they were approved in March of 1945.
*** Including the heads of the secretariat and the internal prison.
† Another two officials had been proposed for approval.
‡ Another two officials had been proposed for approval.

It is interesting that although the ECP(B) CC Bureau soon approved the Deputy People's Commissar for cadre issues, Vladimir Vedeyev, the ECP(B) Central Committee subsequently no longer approved or dismissed the people's commissar/minister and his deputies. An exception was Deputy Minister Mikhailov, who was approved at the ECP(B) CC Bureau session in 1944, but formally dismissed on 25 April 1951, although he had actually already been dismissed in October of 1950. Vedeyev was indeed approved on 21 February 1945, but later (1951) he was not formally dismissed by the ECP(B) CC Bureau. The ECP(B) Central Committee did not approve Deputy Minister Pavel Pastelnyak (took the position in 1945) or dismiss him (dismissed in 1951). Minister Valentin Moskalenko was not approved or dismissed as MGB Minister, but he was approved on 29 April 1953 as ESSR Minister of Internal Affairs (the procedure for handling the nomenklatura changed somewhat after Stalin's death). However, the ECP(B) CC Bureau did confirm Moskalenko as the Chairman of the Dynamo Sports Association on 11 June 1951, probably because this position did not at that time belong to the AUCP(B) CC nomenklatura, but only to that of the ECP(B) CC. The Minister's deputies who were appointed in 1951 – Mikhail Svinelupov, Aleksandr Chernov and Aleksandr Trapeznikov – were not approved or dismissed by the ECP(B) CC Bureau: in their case, the above-mentioned process was followed, where the MGB Minister's deputies, as part of the AUCP(B) CC nomenklatura, were appointed by the AUCP(B) Central Committee.

Until 1948, preparation for the approval of the nomenklatura, and other issues pertaining to the State Security cadre, was the responsibility of the CC Cadre Department that reported to the ECP(B) CC Cadre Secretary (also the head of the CC Cadre Department), who was meant to cooperate with the Cadre Department that reported to the Deputy People's Commissar/Minister for cadre issues. The ECP(B) CC Cadre Department's so-called 'Special Cadre Sector' (Russian: *sektor spetskadrov*) was is direct contact with the security cadre. There is no doubt that the 'Special Cadre' primarily meant Chekists, NKGB/MGB and NKVD/MVD officers. But this sector was also responsible for the personnel of the Estonian SSR War Commissariat, Ministry of Foreign Affairs, Ministry of Justice, Supreme Court, Prosecutor's Office, etc. – i. e. the organs of repression, military personnel, etc. 'Special', both *osobyi* and *spetsialnyi* in Russian, was often used in Soviet official terminology for designations indicating a connection with state or Party secrets (e.g. 'Special Department', 'special file', etc.).

The Special Cadre sector also had to deal with the materials of AUCP(B) CC nomenklatura officials. Thus in January of 1946, the sector was responsible for a total of 52 AUCP(B) CC nomenklatura positions, 13 of which were from the ESSR NKVD, two from NKGB transport organs and 23 from the ESSR NKGB. All positions from the latter had been filled, nine of them in 1945.[59] This was the period when the number of security agents in the USSR-wide nomenklatura was the largest.

Although the work duties of the ECP(B) CC Cadre Department were worded ambitiously – selection of top-ranking cadre, elimination of anti-Soviet elements, promoting trustworthy personnel, etc.[60] – its actual work with at least the security cadre became problematic, and the authority of the Party apparatus was relatively restricted here. As Anatoli Demidov, who worked as an instructor in special cadre issues, complained at a meeting of the CC administration: 'I'm of no use. It's not possible to get to know the [NKGB and NKVD] personnel in their practical work. Officials who deal with Party or factory personnel are in a better situation; they may know how the director is working, but organisations like the NKVD or NKGB don't want to talk about their work, or how they work, with someone who deals with the special cadre. They do not consider it their responsibility to speak to the Bureau – even if it is just about the general functions of their work. I do not feel that I have support.'[61]

The actual work of the sector consisted mainly of bureaucratic preparation of the approval for State Security nomenklatura officials. That the approval of the appointment of security officials had essentially become a formality is demonstrated by the fact that the approval often took place many months after the actual appointment of the official. It is also not known that the ECP(B) CC Bureau ever opposed the approval of any security officer, although this may not have been documented. But there were problems even with such approvals. As described by the instructor Demidov, the NKVD and NKGB could let a person work for one or two years before they considered it necessary to present the person for approval: '[NKVD and NKGB] are two organisations that do not take into account [the obligation for approval].'[62]

The approval of State Security leaders at that time, however, was not a problem just for the Estonian SSR, which indicates a certain attitude in

---

[59] List of positions, included to the AUCP(B) CC nomenklatura, January, 1946, RA, ERAF.1.307.109, 30–31.

[60] Reference about the work of the ECP(B) CC Cadres department, RA, ERAF.1.48.38, 6.

[61] Minutes of the meeting of the ECP(B) CC instructors, 18 April 1946, RA, ERAF.1.4.380, 42.

[62] *Ibid*, 44.

the leadership of the USSR MGB. On 26 July 1946 the AUCP(B) Central Committee, probably at the initiative of Aleksei Kuznetsov, the new head of the Cadre Administration, adopted a decision on deficiencies in the personnel work of the Ukrainian CP, where among other deficiencies, the fact was presented that the Prosecutor's Office, the Ministry of Justice, the MVD and the MGB submit their nomenklatura cadre to Party organs for approval only after considerable time has elapsed since their actual appointment, which made it more difficult for the Party organs to avoid mistakes in the selection and allocation of personnel.[63] Not long after, in October of 1946, the ECP(B) CC Cadre Secretary Dmitri Kuzmin did send the ESSR MGB a letter which informed the Minister that the MGB Cadre Department had not submitted the personnel list for approval or dismissal to the CC Cadre Department in a timely fashion, which obstructed the normal reporting process to the AUCP(B) Central Committee, and was against the principle of knowing the personnel. The letter requested that the relevant instructions be given to the Cadre Department, and that the relevant materials be submitted to the Central Committee within five days.[64] Even in their wording, these demands were in accordance with the above-mentioned decision by the AUCP(B) CC on the Ukrainian SSR.

On 14 August 1946, the Central Committee Bureau discussed the approval of the new ECP(B) CC nomenklatura. The deputy head of the Cadre Department, Heinrich Laura, who also headed the Special Cadre sector, passed on the information that Minister Kumm wished to include in the nomenklatura the Minister's aide for economic issues. Karotamm did not oppose this. Second Secretary Sergei Sazonov explained the nomenklatura approval relationship between the AUCP(B) CC and the ECP(B) CC, and said that the ECP(B) Central Committee had the right to raise the issue of not approving a particular official with the AUCP(B) Central Committee, but generally the AUCP(B) Central Committee also made a phone call whereby agreement was given to the approval. It was a different matter, however, where the AUCP(B) Central Committee had already approved an official, and sent him to the Estonian SSR since then the ECP(B) Central Committee could no longer change the decision.[65] In practice, up to this

---

[63]   *TsK VKP(b) i regional'nye*, 49–54.

[64]   RA, ERAF.1.48a.89, 42.

[65]   Verbatim of the session of the ECP(B) CC Bureau, 14 August 1946, RA, ERAF.1.4.361, 170.

time, officials included in both nomenklaturas were approved at the same time by the ECP(B) Central Committee, and the AUCP(B) Central Committee was asked to approve the decision.

As demonstrated above, it was determined, together with the new AUCP(B) Central Committee nomenklatura established in October of 1946, that the appointment and dismissal of officials listed there would in future take place only with a AUCP(B) Central Committee decision. As we have seen, no further ESSR MGB appointments-dismissals for positions included in the AUCP(B) CC nomenklatura generally took place at ECP(B) Central Committee Bureau sessions. For example, this was the way the dismissal of Minister Kumm and the appointment of Valentin Moskalenko as Minister of Security took place: the AUCP(B) CC Politburo issued a decision on 24 January 1950. Thus until the end of the Stalin-era, the basic responsibility of the ECP(B) CC was merely the approval and dismissal of department heads regarding the ESSR MGB nomenklatura cadre.

The security nomenklatura was now approved with the formulation 'to adopt the proposal by the ESSR Minister of Security'. According to the ESSR MGB control lists, 26 positions in the basic nomenklatura and 15 in the reserve nomenklatura were filled at the start of 1947. Only four Estonians were included in the basic nomenklatura: Minister Boris Kumm, Eduard Neelus (head of Department 2-N), Alfred Pressmann (head of Department A) and Oskar Borell (head of the Viljandi County Department). There were no Estonians in the reserve nomenklatura.[66]

Due to structural changes in the Party apparatus in 1948, an Administration Department was also formed by the end of the year in the ECP(B) CC system, which was to be responsible for a total of 29 ministries and authorities. Regarding the State Security organs, in addition to the ESSR MGB, this also included the Estonian Railways MGB Guard Administration and the Estonian Maritime Basin MGB Guard Administration, the ESSR MVD, the Estonian SSR MVD Forces War Tribunal, the Estonian SSR MVD Forces Military Prosecutor's office, the MVD Reform-labour Camps, the ESSR Council of Ministers Repatriation Administration, court and prosecutor bodies, the Ministry of State Control, the Minis-

---

[66] Control list of the employees of the ESSR MGB, included in the nomenclature of the AUCP(B) CC, RA, ERAF.1.48a.159, 203–209.

try of Health, the Ministry of Justice, etc.[67] The Special Cadre sector was disbanded together with the Cadre Department. The new department's responsibilities were personnel work, checking adherence to issued decisions, and managing the work of Party organisations in the authorities, including work with the nomenklatura cadre. Nomenklatura officials were confirmed in their positions based on a statement compiled by an official in the Administration Department, to which was added the appointment proposal from the head of the Administration Department. This included a brief characterisation, such as: 'N has extensive experience in work as a Chekist, also skills as an organiser, which he skilfully uses in his practical work.' MGB Reserve Colonel Johannes Tipner, Deputy Head of the Administration Department, became the official who basically worked with MGB issues. The period 1948–49 is characterised by the fact that it was then that the ECP(B) CC, led by Nikolai Karotamm, attempted to establish itself as the leader of the ESSR MGB and security organs in the Estonian SSR. But the nomenklatura system was not the main lever for this since it was of lesser importance in comparison to the repression of the resistance movement or increasing pressure in the 'anti-bandit struggle'. But it is also known that the ineffectiveness of the anti-bandit struggle was Karotamm's justification for asking the AUCP(B) Central Committee to dismiss ESSR MGB Deputy Minister Pavel Pastelnyak, who as we know was a member of the AUCP(B) CC nomenklatura.[68] This was quite a major interference in Moscow's cadre policies, and Moscow did not approve – Pastelnyak kept his job even after Karotamm was dismissed.

In the period 1950–52, the so-called Estonian Case – a purge of the Party – was carried out in the ECP(B), during which the top cadre of the Estonian SSR was replaced. At the same time, the repression of the forest brothers and other so-called 'bourgeois nationalists' was intensified. The 1950 ECP(B) CC 'March Plenum' was an important milestone in the Estonian Case. It resulted in the dismissal of Party chief Nikolai Karotamm and a number of leading figures, including four members of the ECP(B) CC Bureau. A similar campaign was also initiated by the new Minister of Security Moskalenko in the ESSR Ministry of State Security, where

---

[67] Verbatim of the session of the ECP(B) CC § 8, 5 and 8 January 1949, RA, ERAF.1.4.702, 2, 6.

[68] Karotamm to the head of the AUCP(B) CC Administrative department, 20 September 1948, RA, ERAF.1.1.11, 42.

almost the entire nomenklatura cadre was replaced. The new leaders who were appointed were often new arrivals: security officers from outside the Estonian SSR. As a rule, the appointment procedure for the ECP(B) CC nomenklatura cadre continued to be followed. For example, of the 14 central department heads who were part of the ECP(B) CC nomenklatura (in 1950–52 there was a total of 14 department heads[69]), 11 officers were appointed during Moskalenko's time. At the ECP(B) CC Bureau session on 5 October 1950, almost 30 new rayon department heads were approved at the same time. In the case of such a large-scale procedure, this approval could only have been a formality. Taking this into account, as well as Moskalenko's haughty attitude towards the Estonian SSR Party leaders, it is clear that the new top officials tended to be loyal to the Minister and Moscow rather than to the local (Party) leadership.[70]

This policy led to the situation where by the end of Moskalenko's 'rule' in May of 1953, there was not one Estonian among the leading cadre of the ESSR MVD – from the Minister to the department heads (i.e. among the ECP Central Committee's nomenklatura of the time). Estonians accounted for 14.3% of the deputies of department heads, 10% of divisional heads, and 27.6% of operational officials. These figures, however, also include Estonians who had arrived from the Soviet Union, which means that conclusions cannot be drawn from them regarding the proportion of local personnel. There were also no Estonians among the leadership of the oblast administrations. In the Municipal and Raion Department, 13.1% of department heads and their deputies were Estonian, as were 43% of operational personnel. There was only one Estonian among the 11 members of the ESSR MVD Party Committee, and only two Estonians among the 19 secretaries of the Ministry's Party organisations.[71]

---

[69]   See Table 4 in the article by Meelis Saueauk, 'Nõukogude julgeolekuorganid Eestis 1944–1953: ülesanded, struktuur, juhtimine' [Soviet State Security apparatus in Estonia, 1994–1953: tasks, structure, management], *Ajalooline Ajakiri*, no. 1–2 (2009): 77–121 (119).

[70]   See also: Saueauk, *Propaganda ja terror*, 339–340.

[71]   Statement on the situation of the ethnic cadre in the Estonian SSR MVD, and the results of the work carried out by the Estonian SSR MVD regarding the nationalistic underground, 4 June 1953, RA, ERAF.1.126.67, 104–107, published: Tynu Tannberg, *Politika Moskvÿ v respublikakh Baltii v poslevoennÿe godÿ (1944–1956): issledovaniya i dokumentÿ* (Tartu: Tartu University Press, 2008), 286–288.

Role of the State Security in Implementing the Nomenklatura System

Since the basic task of the State Security was to identify and eliminate the anti-Soviet contingent, the security organs were the partners and assistants of the ECP(B) Central Committee in its personnel work. The security system informed the Party leadership of problem areas in the state and Party systems, and also of politically 'compromising material' on personnel. Already in 1940 in the course of establishing the Soviet regime in Estonia, the ECP(B) CC introduced the practice whereby the security organs were sent inquiries regarding personnel, including carrying out background checks on the nomenklatura cadre. Thus by 9 September 1940, the ESSR NKVD had already checked the lists of judges and court officials, where they found members of the Estonian Veterans' Association.[72]

Materials regarding the checks have been preserved in the archives but mostly without the results of the inquiries, and there is also no precise information on how the security organs themselves handled such background checks. Considering the fact that the responses to the checks were prepared by various departments in the security organs, it can be assumed that there were various methods for carrying out such checks.

Regarding the personnel of the security system and the Ministry of Internal Affairs itself, a so-called 'special check' (in Russian: *spetsproverka – spetsialnaia proverka*) or 'special check of past activities' was conducted in the Ministry, and this had to be done before any appointment. In the special check process, which became mandatory in the NKVD in 1936, information was collected on the past of the person and his/her relatives, and checked for the existence of 'compromising material'.[73] According to the classified KGB espionage dictionary, published in 1972, the 'special check' was a system of measures for information collection and checking that was carried out by security organs, and was used regarding citizens of the Soviet Union in the access permit procedure for work with classified documents, entering military service or work in 'regime locations', preparing applications for departing from the state, and applications for citizenship, or relinquishing citizenship. The special check included checking

---

[72] ESSR NKVD People's Commissar Kumm to the ECP(B) Central Committee, 9 September 1940, RA, ERAF.1.1.241, 1.

[73] Tepliakov, *Mashina terrora*, 168.

the catalogues of security organs regarding operational record-keeping, collecting information in the workplace and place of residence, and other necessary measures, including authoritative measures, which were decided on a case by case basis. The check also covered the person's closest relatives. The special check was governed by rules and specific instructions.[74]

The special check of personnel in the Ministry of State Security and Ministry of Internal Affairs was carried out by their own Cadre Departments, which initiated a special-check file on the person who was being checked. At the conclusion of a special check, the person carrying out the check compiled a summary of the results of the special check, and made a recommendation regarding the future career of the person being checked. In the final years of the Stalin-era, the summary of the special check of the candidate was added to the application for appointment, and the material was submitted to the ECP(B) Central Committee. The possibilities for Central Committee cadre officials to independently carry out a background check on security officers and also other nomenklatura officials were very limited.

Regarding the checking of the leading cadre in other institutions of authority, the assistance of the security organs was sought here as well. In the Central Committee, the cadre departments, and other departments dealing with personnel issues, submitted requests to the ESSR MGB to carry out checks (or 'thorough' or 'careful' checks (special checks)). The volume of the inquiries was quite large. For example, we know of 11 letters of inquiry (with attached career statements), from January of 1947, on a total of 62 persons (including 21 persons from the ESSR Council of Ministers). The results were announced by ESSR MGB Department A, whose information was also probably used to carry out the check (the function of the department was to maintain operational record-keeping and applicable catalogues, and also the archives). The results of special checks are as a rule not contained in the inquiries files.[75]

'Compromising materials' were primarily of a political nature, including information on the repression of the person being checked or his/her relatives, also on living abroad or in territory occupied by the Germans,

---

[74] *Kontrrazvedyvatel'nyi slovar'*, ed. V. F. Nikichenko (Moscow: Vyshaia Krasnoznamennaia Shkola KGB SSSR imeni F. E. Dzerzhinskogo, 1972), 318–319.

[75] Correspondence with the ESSR NKGB on the special check of the party and state cadres, 1947, RA, ERAF.1.48a.174.

etc.[76] In the case of a thorough check, the veracity of the information on the submitted application was checked, inquiries were made to other NKGB/MGB organs, and even surveillance actions could be used.

The incidental effect of the special check was that the Central Committee no longer delved independently into personnel checking but waited for the 'statement from Comrade Kumm'.[77] This was the expression used by ECP(B) CC Second Secretary Georgy Kedrov, which indicated that the responsibility for the results of the background check was passed to the MGB. The results of the check and other information on the background of persons that was provided by the NKGB/MGB had to be kept strictly secret – neither the source of the information nor the precise content was to be revealed to the subject. However, if this information was revealed, either accidentally or on purpose, and some facts became publicly known, the CC Bureau considered this to be a violation of Party secrecy and a loss of Bolshevik vigilance, and this was followed by precautionary educational activity.[78] Party officials were obliged to sign declarations regarding keeping state and Party secrets, and according to the decree issued by the USSR Supreme Soviet Presidium on 9 June 1947, Party and criminal prosecution was prescribed for its violation.[79] The ECP(B) CC departmental head Boris Shergalin believed that during work meetings, it needed to be made clear to officials working in the Central Committee administration that terms such as 'according to MGB information' and 'according to special checks' should be used less frequently, and that information from the MGB should generally be used less. He felt that CC officials themselves should try to collect and analyse information. Yefim Stepanov, head of the Central Committee department for Party, trade union and Komsomol organs, even thought that the above terms could be thrown out of the vocabulary

---

[76]   For a list of the categories of 'compromising materials', see for example: Aigi Rahi-Tamm, 'Arhiivid Nõukogude repressiivaparaadi teenistuses: "poliitvärvingute" kartoteek Eestis 1940–1956' [Archives in the service of the Soviet system of repression: the 'political hues' catalogue in Estonia 1940–1956], *Ajalooline Ajakiri*, no. 1/2 (127/128) (2009): 123–153.

[77]   Verbatim of the session of the ECP(B) CC Bureau, 18 August 1949, RA, ERAF.1.4.806, 26.

[78]   Decision of the ECP(B) CC Bureau about the violation of the party clandestinity and vigilance at the ECP(B) CC apparatus, RA, ERAF.1.5.29, 1–2.

[79]   Obligation, 18 November 1947, RA, ERAF.1.6.4467, 18.

of administration officials.[80] There is, however, no basis for claiming that the authority or possibilities of the Central Committee to independently carry out checks had subsequently increased to any degree.

Conclusions and Summary

The principle of the nomenklatura system – to establish Party organ control over (the appointment of) top officials – was already introduced in the Estonian SSR in 1940, even before the ECP CC nomenklatura was instituted. This was generally in accordance with the rules for handling the security nomenklatura that had been developed in the USSR in 1938.

In the USSR-wide nomenklatura, the Soviet State Security organs in the Estonian SSR were grouped together with top personnel from other 'epaulet' ministries – the Ministry of Internal Affairs and the Ministry of Defence. After the reform of the Party organs in 1948, the Ministry of State Security was placed under the management of the Central Committee's Administration Department. To these were added the nomenklatura from the fields of justice, state audit, health and some others. Before the Administration Department was formed, the security cadre was included with the military and justice authorities in the so-called 'special cadre' in the ECP nomenklatura. In grouping according to content, should this be necessary, it would be the most functional to place the state security cadre in the same group as the 'Chekists' from the Ministry of Internal Affairs.

The nomenklatura of the State Security changed mostly due to the constant changes in their structure. Even the names of the organs changed five times in the period 1940–52 (NKVD/NKGB/NKVD/NKGB/MGB), and these name changes were accompanied by structural changes, which could also be due to changes in the administrative map of the union republic. The nomenklatura also changed when the structures of the Party apparatus changed (1948). Changes could also have resulted from the wish of Party authorities to establish the nomenklatura system for top officials at increasingly lower levels (i.e. increasing their numbers) (1945), and eventually also the desire to reduce the size of the nomenklatura to a degree where control would be possible (1946). Nevertheless, changes in

---

[80] Verbatim of the session of the ECP(B) CC Bureau, 15 March 1950 RA, ERAF.1.5.29, 3.

the ECP CC nomenklatura generally mirrored the changes in the USSR-wide nomenklatura, and the local nomenklatura was often developed as a follow-up to the USSR-wide nomenklatura. Regarding the extension of the nomenklatura to a lower level, the ECP Central Committee reacted to Moscow's extension of the nomenklatura by adding to the list of the lower level positions. Regarding the relationships between nomenklatura work USSR-wide and in the union republics, it can be stated that although this initially took place in parallel, as of 1946, the role of the ECP CC was appointment-dismissal at the level of departmental heads, while it was Moscow that dealt with issues pertaining to the leadership of the Ministry.

The relatively small proportion of nomenklatura officials, compared to the total number of officials, should not be over-emphasised. Considering the hierarchical military structure of the security organs in particular, this was quite sufficient for Moscow to control the selection of personnel.

Regarding the ethnic background of the Estonian SSR State Security nomenklatura officials, these were – with very few exceptions – non-Estonian cadre officers sent from the Soviet Union. Estonians were most frequently placed in leading positions in local departments. The replacement in January of 1950 of a minister with a local background by one who had been internally nominated was significant since the last remaining Estonians were subsequently removed from the ESSR MGB Central Administration's nomenklatura positions.

The severity with which the ECP Central Committee monitored the nomenklatura system depended upon Moscow's attitudes and instructions at any particular time. When the order came to follow the nomenklatura system more strictly (1946) then this was also done.

The fact that the State Security organs also carried out background checks on officials in other authorities, including officials in the Party apparatus itself, placed them in a special position in the nomenklatura system. The Ministry actually independently carried out the special check of security officials, whereby Party organs were briefly informed of the results at the time of the appointment. Although the Party apparatus wished to change this situation, it did not have the authority to make such decisions.

Examining the materials pertaining to the nomenklatura provides the researcher with a further opportunity in the history of Soviet State Security, making it possible to acquire information on the structure, leading officials, etc. of Chekist. On the other hand, it is difficult, or even impossible, to assess changes in the nomenklatura without understanding the structural changes and peculiarities of the authority being researched.

It does not seem that the nomenklatura system provided the ECP Central Committee and its leadership with any actual authority in appointing security officials. As a rule, approvals of appointments were decisions that were made *post factum*. This becomes particularly apparent when the implementation of the nomenklatura system is placed in the context of the general relationship between the Estonian SSR security organs and the Party apparatus. In addition, the main topic in the period 1948–49, when the ECP Central Committee was exerting particular pressure on the MGB, was the fight against the resistance movement, and the nomenklatura system was of lesser importance as a means of influence.

Proceeding from the hierarchy of the nomenklatura system, it should be noted that the right to decide on higher level (i.e. USSR-wide) nomenklatura appointments from a lower level (by the ECP CC) did not actually exist, and was essentially limited to providing information and – if necessary – to being held responsible. This also means that a so-called patron-client relationship could not have developed between the First Secretary of the Communist Party and the Minister of State Security. Considering the centralisation of the management of the security organs, all the way up to the dictatorial management by Stalin himself, this was probably a deliberate policy on the part of the Kremlin. The development of patron-relationships between the local leaderships of the Party and the state security organs was avoided. Instead, rivalry and informing were encouraged. It also seems that the state security authority did not expect the ECP Central Committee to actually interfere in their personnel work. If things got difficult, it was always possible to appeal to the secret character of the security organs. Moscow's approval of the appointments of security chiefs added to their independence from local Party authority.

Appendix 1. ESSR NKGB/MGB positions in the (basic) nomenklatura of the AUCP(B) Central Committee and ECP(B) Central Committee, 1941–1953.

POSITION	1938 AUCP(B) CC[1]	1941 ECP(B) CC	1942 AUCP(B) CC[2]	1944 AUCP(B) CC	1945 ECP(B) CC	1945 AUCP(B) CC	1946 ECP(B) CC	1946 AUCP(B) CC	1947 ECP(B) CC	1947 AUCP(B) CC	1949 AUCP(B) CC	1949 ECP(B) CC	1950 AUCP(B) CC	1950 ECP(B) CC	1952 AUCP(B) CC	1952 ECP(B) CC
People's Commissar/Minister	X[3]	X	1	1	X[4]	1	1	1	1	1	1	1	1	1	1	1
Deputy	X	X	4[5]	2	X	3	4[6]	3	4	1[7]	1	4	4	5	4	4
Department Head (central department)	X	X	9	4[8]	X	8	9		9			8		9		11
Deputy		X			X		14		1[9]			1		2		1
Divisional Head					X[10]		29									
Head of local sub-unit[11]	X	X	7[12]		X	11	11		13			13		41[13]	3[14]	9[15]
Deputy		X														
Operational Commissioner		X														
Secretary of the Party Committee		X			X		1		1			1		1		1
TOTAL			21	7		23	69	4	29	2	2	28	5	59	8	27

1 The nomenklatura of NKVD positions in a Union Republic.
2 Actually the ESSR NKVD nomenklatura, as of August 1941, not counting positions in the Militsia Administration and Highways Administration.
3 The position category marked with 'X' is part of the nomenklatura but the number of positions is not known.
4 The People's Commissar and his deputies were listed in the People's Commissars' Council section, not in the NKGB section.
5 Together with the People's Commissar's aide on non-operational issues.
6 1946–50: in the ECP(B) CC nomenklatura, together with the Minister's aide on economic issues.
7 1947–49: only First Deputy.
8 Only the heads of the 2nd, Investigational, A and V Departments.
9 1947–52: in this category, the Deputy Head of the Cadre Department (also the head of the Special Inspectorate).
10 Heads of the independent central divisions.
11 1940–49: Heads of the city and county departments/divisions.
12 This is the number of positions reflected in a report to the AUCP(B) Central Committee.
13 Department heads in the city (Narva and Kohtla-Järve) and raions that were formed in 1950.
14 Heads of the oblast governments.
15 Heads and deputies of oblast governments.

Grain and Eggs in the Service of the Regime: Coercive Procurement in Estonian Villages in the 1940s

Indrek Paavle[*]

Introduction

The aim of the relaunched Sovietisation in the autumn of 1944 was to harmonise Estonian society with the Soviet system. Sovietisation had to ensure the repression of popular resistance and was necessary for ideological purposes because a totalitarian system requires the enforcement of consistent models and a policy of no exceptions. Estonia was an agrarian society with the majority of its population living in the countryside. Hence the key issue of Sovietisation was the securing of the regime in rural areas. However, due to scattered settlements, individual farming, traditional community ties and active resistance it was far more complex to accomplish than in the towns.[1] As a counterbalance, the Soviet regime drew on their experience of subjugating the country from the 1920s–1930s and it could implement its well-tested methods from a redistribution of property, a punitive tax policy and forced collectivisation to terrorise the Baltic countries.

---

[*] First published: Indrek Paavle, 'Vili ja munad režiimi teenistuses: sundandam 1940. aastate Eesti külas', Eesti ajaloost Nõukogude võimu perioodil = Studies in the history of Estonia during the Soviet rule, ed. Tõnu Tannberg, *Ajalooline Ajakiri*, no. 1/2 (2009): 213–229.

[1] David Feest, *Zwangskollektivierung im Baltikum: Die Sowjetisierung des estnischen Dorfes 1944–1953* (Cologne: Böhlau, 2007), 14.

In historical writings on rural society and the agriculture of the Soviet occupation era, the main focus has been on collectivisation. This is well justified because the liquidation of farming and private property brought along the most significant social changes in post-war society. However, the pre-collectivisation period is worthy of note because the methods applied by the authorities were likewise targeted at the subjugation of village society and they were sensed by the people as equally unjust. The main trend of pre-collectivisation agricultural policy, besides the redistribution of property, was an exhausting coercive policy that manifested itself in burdening the population with increasingly large obligations in the pursuance of both economic and political objectives.

The aim of this article is to clarify the aspects of the coercive sale of agricultural produce, one of the major obligations imposed on farmers by Soviet agricultural policy. In comparison with the existing analyses, I aim to give a more detailed review of the sale mechanism and to answer the question regarding the impact of this phenomenon on the other spheres of life and its significance in the context of Sovietisation.

In Soviet Estonian history, tax policy was regarded as preparation for collectivisation, but it was implemented mostly to justify the decisions of the Communist Party.[2] In exile, the history of Soviet agriculture has been studied by Rein Taagepera, who through emphasising the significance of tax policy, divides collectivisation into the taxation phase and the deportation phase.[3] Vassili Popov, Mikhail Beznin and Tatiana Dimoni are the Russian historians who have produced the most thorough studies on farmers' obligations and the tax policy.[4] Elena Zubkova has touched

---

[2]   Ervin Kivimaa, *EKP tegevus vabariigi põllumajanduse kollektiviseerimisel aastail 1944–1950* [Activities of the ECP in the Collectivisation of the Agriculture of the Republic in 1944–1950], (PhD thesis, Tartu State University, 1970); Evald Laasi, *Eesti talumajapidamiste kollektiviseerimise ettevalmistamine ja selle teostamine aastail 1944–1949* [Preparation and Implementation of Collectivisation of Estonian Farming in 1944–1949], (PhD thesis, Tallinn: ESSR Institute of History of Academy of Sciences, 1966).

[3]   Rein Taagepera, *Soviet collectivisation of Estonian agriculture* (Irvine: School of Social Sciences, University of California, 1979).

[4]   Vasilii Popov, 'Khleb kak ob'ekt gosudarstvennoi politiki v SSSR v 1940-e gody', *Otechestvennaia istoriia*, 2 (2000); Vasilij Popov, 'Krest'ianskie nalogi v 40-e gody', *Sotsiologicheskie issledovaniia*, 2 (1997); M. Beznin and T. Dimoni, 'Povinnosti rossiiskikh kolkhoznikov v 1930–1960-e gg', *Otechestvennaia istoriia*, 2 (2002): 96–111.

upon this topic in the context of the Baltic countries, regarding the pre-collective farm era (1944–47) as a special form of Soviet agriculture and considering the difficulties in collecting agricultural produce as one of the main causes of collectivisation.[5] Olaf Mertelsmann has studied Soviet Estonian tax policy in a broader sense in the context of the Sovietisation of the economy and David Feest as a part of the subjugation process of village society.[6]

The Mechanism of the Procurement of Agricultural Produce

Despite the industrialisation process that had started at the end of the 1920s, the post-war Soviet Union continued to be an agrarian society with an employment rate 2.3 times higher in agriculture than in industry and the majority of the state's income coming from agriculture.[8] In order to supply the state with agricultural produce, the Soviet Union operated a state system of procurement where all the most significant decisions were made at a high level – i.e. the Politburo or the Secretariat of the Central Committee of the Communist Party of the Soviet Union, and in the 1940s particularly, the Council of Ministers of the Soviet Union (until 1946 the Council of People's Commissars). In the top brass, this sphere was curated by Georgy Malenkov, a member of the *Politburo*, the Deputy Chairman of the Council of Ministers and the head of the Agricultural Office.[7] Procurement was organised by the Ministry of Procurement of the Soviet Union (until 1946 the People's Commissariat of Procurement) through regional and local agencies that consisted mostly of over 50,000 local agents.[8] Pro-

---

[5]   Elena Zubkova, *Pribaltika i Kreml' 1940–1953* (Moscow: ROSSPEN, 2008).

[6]   Olaf Mertelsmann, *Der stalinistische Umbau in Estland: Von der Markt- zur Kommandowirtschaft* (Hamburg: Dr. Kovač, 2006); Feest, *Zwangskollektivierung*. Olaf Mertelsmann, 'Searching for Reasons for the Forced Collectivisation in the Baltic Republics', 31 October 2008, conference presentation, manuscript.

[7]   See: Yoram Gorlizki, 'Ordinary Stalinism: The Council of Ministers and the Soviet Neo-patrimonial State, 1945–1953', *The Journal of Modern History*, 74:4 (2002): 708.

[8]   Popov, 'Krest'ianskie nalogi', 98.

duce was collected by the Ministry of Procurement's special nationwide associations (*Zagotzerno, Tsentrosoiuz* et al.) through their networks.

Most of the produce was procured through a system of mandatory sale of agricultural produce (dating from 1923) organised on the basis of state plans and quotas. It covered most of the farms and after collectivisation, it became one of the main obligations of collective farms. The establishment of coercive procurement in Estonia began in the spring of 1941 but the outbreak of war made it impossible to collect the produce. Due to the needs of the military industry, farmers had to fulfil the quotas during the German occupation as well.[9]

In the autumn of 1944, the centralised procurement system was swiftly relaunched and as early as September, the first quotas and prices were established, and rural municipality procurement agents were being recruited. By the end of November, the agency was fully staffed but it suffered local human resources problems typical of the new regime – inexperience, lack of discipline, or political incompatibility resulting in high turnover.[10]

The Soviet Estonian authorities wanted to establish the procurement system according to a decentralized state system for buying-up produce that also existed in the Soviet Union, albeit its volumes were tiny in comparison with coercive sale. According to Nikolai Karotamm, this method would have provided an opportunity to use the collected produce for domestic needs in a better way. However, Moscow did not accept the programme drawn up by the ESSR administration – in addition to the whole system being allegedly based on false principles, the planned quotas were considered to be too low and payable sums to producers too high.[11] Henceforth the designation of quotas always followed the same pattern. In Moscow, a nationwide procurement plan was distributed between the Soviet republics (e.g. the grain procurement plan of the Soviet Union in 1945 was 250 million tons, out of which 75,000 tons or 0.03 per cent was Estonia's share). In the category of individual farms, Estonia's share was

---

[9]   Alvin Isberg, *Zu den Bedingungen des Befreiers: Kollaboration und Freiheitsstreben in dem von Deutschland besetzten Estland 1941 bis 1944* (Stockholm: Almqvist & Wiksell, 1992), 60.

[10]   Summary of the work of the ESSR Commissioner's Administration of the USSR People's Commissariat of Procurement, 9 December 1944, RA, ERA.R-1.2.54, 162.

[11]   Correspondence on issues concerning the ESSR procurement plan, RGASPI, f. 17, o. 123, d. 223, 1–15.

just 8%. In a 920,000-ton total plan, Ukraine's share was 295,000 tons, Moldova's share was 205,000 tons, Lithuania's share was 147,000 tons and Latvia's share was 110,000 tons.[12] The ESSR administration distributed the plan among the counties, and the county executive committees, together with state procurement agents, designated average quotas per farm in the rural municipalities. Next, rural municipality procurement agents calculated mandatory quotas for each farm by type of production and delivered the quotas to the farm managers against their signature.[13]

Local authorities were entitled to alter the quotas by up to 30 per cent in their jurisdictions – Soviet authorities within the republic were entitled to alter the county quotas, etc. Rural municipality executive committees were allowed to alter the quotas of farms but they were in no position to alter the total quota of a rural municipality. Therefore, reduced quotas at one place would result in increased quotas at another place, and such differentiation was never widely practised. Some households had a full or partial exemption from fulfilling quotas but the discounts were short-term and too short to help the farms succeed.[14]

Checking on the fulfilment of quotas was the duty of procurement agents and village councils, but rural municipality executive committees did the actual work. Village councils, set up in 1945 as understaffed units without their own budgets and with limited power, failed to cope with their designated tasks and had little say in local life. The administrative reform of 1945 that was supposed to banish 'pre-revolution' units – counties and rural municipalities, was interrupted in 1946 and it was relaunched only in the spring of 1949.[15]

Rates of Quotas

In the autumn of 1944, sale quotas of grain, potatoes, meat and milk were imposed on farms, followed by quotas of eggs, wool and hay in the follow-

---

[12]   RGASPI, f. 17, o. 123, d. 348, 31–32.

[13]   USSR Ministry of Procurement Commissioner's Statutes for Agents of Counties and Rural Municipalities, 13 October 1948, RA, EAA.T-168.2.1148, 117–121.

[14]   Feest, *Zwangskollektivierung*, 192.

[15]   Karotamm to Sepre, October 1945, RA, ERA.R-1.10.13, 45; Karotamm to Veimer, 13 May 1946, RA, ERAF.1.4.71, 116.

ing spring.[16] In the calculation of quotas, the 'consistent principle of the
hectare' was applied according to which the volume of produce to be given
away depended on the total size of a farm, regardless of the actual sowing
area, quality of land or the amount of labour force and machinery. This
method damaged farms in Estonia and Latvia in particular, where large
areas of farmland could be covered by bogs and forests.[17] The guidelines
drawn up in 1946 permitted the deduction of areas covered by buildings
and roads, bogs, bodies of water, sand shoals and limestone surfaces from
the total hectarage in the calculation of quotas. It was considered unac-
ceptable to deduct overgrown fields and pastureland as one could cut the
brushwood. Deductions had to be approved by committees comprising
the chairman of the rural municipality executive committee, the head of
the land department and a procurement agent.[18]

Rates of meat quotas also depended on the hectarage of land, not the
size of livestock. Starting in 1948, hectare-based calculation was imposed
on milk quotas, hence farms without any cows had to start fulfilling milk
quotas as well. The new system was justified by the anti-*kulak* struggle (the
measure was supposed to prevent the hiding of livestock) and the development of livestock breeding, since this particular method was supposed to
encourage the acquisition of livestock – the larger the herd, the easier it
would be to fulfil the quota.[19] The issue of finding the means to buy new
livestock under an enormous load of taxes was neglected. The replacement
system of produce was also in place, i.e. a product that was lacking could
be replaced by another product on the basis of equivalency. For example,
5 kg of grain equalled 1 kg of live weight of meat, 1 kg of grain equalled 4
kg of potatoes, meat and milk could be replaced by eggs, etc.

In 1944, new quotas were established, and it is interesting to observe
the course of publishing the corresponding legal acts. First, quotas similar

---

[16]   ESSR Sovnarkom and ECP(B) CC regulations nos. 142–145, 1 September
1944; no 349–355, 16 June 1945, *ENSV Teataja*, 1944, 2, 12–15; 1945, 23, 349–355.

[17]   Zubkova gives an example of a Latvian farm whose land comprised 20 ha
of bog. According to law, the definition of 'bog' was land 'impassable by horse
or man'. The committee stated that 'no-one had drowned in that bog yet' and
registered the land as arable land that a *kulak*-saboteur had no wish to cultivate,
see: Zubkova, *Pribaltika i Kreml'*, 170.

[18]   ESSR Council of Ministers' regulation no 613, 27 July 1946, *ENSV Teataja*,
1946, 42, 349.

[19]   Information, 21 October 1948, RA, ERAF.1.47.46, 11–13.

to the previous ones were approved, but then a signal must have come from Moscow claiming that they were too low. New higher quotas were approved, and the quotas that were finally published were even higher. Hence three separate decisions were made for each type of product. The increase primarily affected smaller farms – while the grain quota for larger farms was increased by 15% in comparison with 1944, for 10 ha farms the increase was 100%.[20] The average quota in 1946–1950s did not change much apart from the hay quota, which was increased twice in 1949, and the milk quota, which was increased by a third in 1946. From year to year, the system became more complex through regional differentiation, ending up with grain quotas differing by 12 times between large Viljandi County farms and small Saaremaa farms.

The state focused mainly on grain procurement.[21] Estonian farming was traditionally based on livestock and grain had practically never been grown for sale, e.g. in 1938, farms sold only 13% of their grain and kept the rest for personal use.[22] In 1946, the ESSR authorities brought this to Malenkov's attention and suggested decreasing grain quotas by increasing meat quotas. The suggestion was supported by the USSR People's Commissariats of Procurement and Meat and Milk Industry. Consequently, milk quotas were raised without any reduction of other quotas.[23]

Sale quotas were not the only obligation farmers had to fulfil. They also had to give away grain for grinding as barter fees.[24] In 1944–1945, grain was expropriated for the grain fund of the Red Army. In that situation, even the procurement agents did not know whether these quotas were an integral part of the whole quota or if they were to be procured as an extra. Agricultural tax was to be paid in cash and that was regarded as

---

[20]   ECP(B) CC Bureau decisions, 31 March 1945 and 26 April 1945, RA, ERAF.1.4.172, 130; ERAF.1.4.177, 170.

[21]   Procurement of grain was a priority for a number of reasons, e.g. in comparison with other products, it was economically more profitable to produce and store grain. The government collected grain in the state reserve and exported it, even in years of famine.

[22]   Evald Laasi, 'Eesti talurahvas sundkollektiviseerimise eel' [Estonian Farmers on the Eve of Forced Collectivisation], *Sotsialistlik põllumajandus*, 7 (1989), 33.

[23]   RGASPI, f. 17, o. 123, d. 495, 96–97.

[24]   The share of the barter fee was not small, constituting 10% of the ESSR procurement plan, RGASPI, f. 17, o. 123, d. 348, 31–32.

being equally unfair since payable taxes were based on prospective prof-
its, i.e. not the actually cultivated land but the land that could have been
cultivated. In the first post-war years, the agricultural tax was not high (in
1946 the average annual tax in Estonia was 715 roubles) and it remained
in the same range compared to the other regions of the USSR.[25] In addition, people were forced to subscribe to government bonds and make
state insurance payments, the evasion of which could bring about criminal
sanction. On top of everything there was labour conscription, the most
severe of which being winter logging.

Prices

The essence of coercive sale was the requirement to sell quotas of produce at 'consistent procurement prices' that were markedly lower than
cost prices. The difference in price lined the pockets of the government.
In the ESSR, the first prices were established in September of 1944 and in
July of 1945.[26] These procurement prices were valid until the end of 1953
and in the intervening years, prices were differentiated according to the
quality of the produce.

.   There were numerous other rates alongside procurement prices: state
buying-up prices, retail prices and official 'market prices'. Rates of fines for
debtors were calculated on the basis of the 'market prices'. Procurement
prices were ridiculously low. State buying-up prices were higher by a fraction, but only those farmers who had fulfilled their procurement quotas
were allowed to sell at those prices. Retail prices were much higher. In
various memoirs, one can read about cases where the money received for
a cow to fulfil quotas could buy two or three bottles of vodka.[27] The most
significant was the comparison with the free market prices that were many
times higher in the Soviet Union (see Table 1). Market prices kept rising,

---

[25]   Data on Taxing Farms with Agricultural Tax in the ESSR, 1948, RA,
ERAF.1.47.49, 110; Popov, 'Krest'ianskie nalogi', 102.

[26]   ESSR Council of People's Commissars' regulation no. 152-a, 15 September
1944; no. 595, 2 July 1945, *ENSV Teataja*, 1944, 2, 18; 1945, 25, 385.

[27]   Evald Loosaar, *Eesti mehe lugu: mälestused 1939–1971* [The Story of an Estonian Man: Memoirs 1939–1971] (Tallinn: Varrak, 2006), 244; Mertelsmann, *Der
stalinistische Umbau*, 171.

reaching 15 roubles per kilo of potatoes and 150 roubles per kilo of pork in the spring of 1947.[28]

Due to the large price difference, it is irrelevant to use the term 'selling'. It was basically barter procurement. David Feest has regarded it as property tax and Russian history has used the notion *obrok*.[29] The documents often addressed it as coercive procurement and even Party officials had difficulties in using a correct notion. The drafts of resolutions contain corrections where 'to give away' has been replaced by 'to sell'.

Table 1. Prices of Agricultural Produce in 1945.

	Potatoes (kop/kg)	Rye (kop/kg)	Milk (rbl/l)	Eggs (rbl/piece)	Pork (rbl/kg)
Procurement Price	5.5	11.1	0.20	0.24	0.83–1.18
State Buying-up Price	12–15	14.9	0.60	0.25	4.53–7
State Retail Price	40	80	1.20–1.50	0.60–0.75	4–15.50
Official 'market price'	200	600	8	4	20
Free market price (in Tallinn)	700–800	800	15	7.50	120

Compiled by ESSR PCC regulation no. no. 178, 6 October 1944; no. no. 472, 29 May 1945; no. no. 244, 3 November 1944, *ENSV Teataja*, 1944, 3, 32; 1944, 9, 103; 1945, 5, 71; 1945, 22, 332; Harju County EC letter, 30 January 1945, RA, ERA.R-364.1.12, 7. For the sake of comparison, at a market, 1 kg of sugar cost ca 100 roubles, boots cost 1,000-1,300 roubles, a horse cost 10,000–15,000 roubles, etc. The cheapest 40° vodka cost 100 roubles per litre in a shop.

I am going to illustrate the volume of obligations through a fictitious farm in Tartu County with 20 ha of land (incl. 8 ha of fields, 0.25 ha of orchards and vegetable gardens, and 5 ha of hayfields), 2 horses, 4 cows, 3 pigs and 5 sheep. In 1945, a farm like this had to give away 2.5 t of grain, 3.2 t of

---

[28]   Mertelsmann, *Der stalinistische Umbau*, 145.

[29]   Feest, *Zwangskollektivierung*, 193; Beznin, Dimoni, 'Povinnosti', 6.

potatoes, 150 kg of meat, 1,500 litres of milk, 2 kg of wool, 390 kg of hay and 150 eggs to fulfil the quotas. With the 'sale' of these quotas the farm earned (excl. wool and hay) 940 roubles, selling on the market it might have earned 90,000 roubles. In addition, farmers had to give away the skins of all animals slaughtered on the farm and pay an agricultural tax of 1,700 roubles.

Due to the big difference between procurement and free market prices, the state implemented severe measures to prevent the sale of produce on the free market or by a state buying-up system before meeting sale quotas. For this purpose, a regulation was issued every summer prohibiting farmers (later collective farms and collective farmers) from selling grain, flour and home-baked bread until the whole grain procurement plan of the ESSR had been fulfilled, including the farmers who had met all their quotas. It was prohibited to grind grain for farmers who had not met their quotas. The infringement of these bans could bring up to 10 years of imprisonment.[30]

Debts and Punishment Policy

In the initial post-war years, obligations were not yet unattainable, although they made the economic situation of farms more difficult, and the injustice caused by these obligations increased tensions in an anxious atmosphere.

The situation started changing in 1947. A 'new direction' was launched in agriculture in the USSR, bringing with it a new collectivisation campaign. In addition to the non-collectivised Western regions of the USSR, the campaign included the old Soviet republics where the recent massive restoration of individual farms required a renewed collectivisation. A significant reason for relaunching a new agricultural policy was the famine of 1946–1947 in the USSR that killed approximately 2 million people. In historiography it is stated that the famine was organised by the govern-

---

[30]   ESSR Council of Peoples'Commissars regulation no. 311, 23 November 1944, *ENSV Teataja*, 1944, 11, 119; 1945, 32, 506; 1946, 44, 375; 1948, 23, 151; 1949, 22, 135.

ment to enable it to commence the implementation of its economic and political goals.[31]

The 'new direction' became obvious in the tax policy as well. Everyone's obligations increased, but the main innovation was the higher taxation rate imposed on the *kulaks*. In addition to the Baltic countries, this was also practised in the western parts of Ukraine and Belarussia, and in Moldova.[32] First, agricultural taxes on *kulaks* were raised in two consecutive years, resulting in a situation where 2–4 per cent of the farms were paying a fifth of the whole agricultural tax of the entire ESSR. The average tax on an average *kulak* farm in 1947 was 6.7 times higher than the tax on standard farms, and it was 9.8 times higher in 1948. Starting in 1948, doubled sale quotas of milk, grain, potatoes and hay were imposed on *kulaks*.[33] The obligations of 1948 caused dismay in lots of people because the agricultural tax was raised from 3,500 roubles to 10,000 roubles. Its single payment was still possible but it was very clear that prospects had become truly miserable and meeting quotas in the coming years would become impossible.[34] Pessimism developed. Evald Loosaar, an unwealthy farmer from Võru County, reminisced: 'Quotas, taxes and all kinds of obligations oppressed me so severely that I could not sleep at night. I had no idea how to escape from that inhuman, unmanageable situation.'[35] He found a solution in joining a collective farm.

The monetary reform of December 1947, which deprived farmers of their savings, made these hardships even worse.[36] The reform established

---

[31] V. Zima, *Golod v SSSR 1946–1947 godov: Proiskhozhdenie i posledstviia* (Moscow: Institut Rossiiskoi istorii, 1996), 179.

[32] See: David R. Marples, 'Toward a thematic approach to the collectivisation campaign in the Soviet West (1948–1956)', *Canadian Slavonic Papers/ Revue canadienne des slavistes*, no. 3–4 (1991).

[33] ESSR PCC regulation no. 654, 30 August 1947; ESSR PCC regulation no. 743, 9 August 1948; no. 581, 5 August 1949, *ENSV Teataja*, 1947, 25, 218; 1948, 23, 154; 1949, 24, 125; Information about the kulak farms of the ESSR, 19 January 1949, RA, ERAF.1.37a.132, 4; Data on Taxing Farms with Agricultural Tax in the ESSR, 1948, RA, ERAF.1.47.49, 110.

[34] Paul Hinnov, *Kui need talud tapeti* [When these Farms Were Destroyed], (Tartu: Ilmamaa, 1999), 20.

[35] Loosaar, *Eesti mehe lugu*, 274.

[36] With the reform, old roubles were exchanged for new roubles at the exchange rate of 10:1 and deposits up to 3,000 rbl at 1:1. In general, farmers had no deposits

new retail prices and dispensed with ration cards. The normalisation of the economy began throughout the USSR, resulting in falling free market prices and the reduction of farmers' earnings.[37] By 1949, the market prices of agricultural produce had dropped 5–10 times compared to 1945: a kilo of potatoes that had cost 4–8 roubles in January of 1945 had dropped to 40–80 kopecks by April of 1949; the price of a kilo of meat had dropped from 120 roubles to 25–35 roubles and the price of a litre of milk had dropped from 15 roubles to 2–3 roubles.[38]

Due to rising tax burdens and falling incomes, debts were incurred. Debtors were first handled by rural municipal authorities and procurement agents. When the deadlines for fulfilling quotas had passed, lists of debtors were drawn up. Procurement agents went to all farms, distributed written warnings and confiscated the property of debtors. If the debts were not paid within 10 days, the debtors were taken to court. A people's judge imposed a fine that could extend to a fivefold value of the amount owed according to the so-called 'official market prices', and the amount owed had to be paid as well. If the fine remained unpaid, the confiscated property was put up for sale. There was a list of minimum property that should have guaranteed survival for a farmer's family and that could not be expropriated, but there were frequent infringements. The list of minimum property was appreciably shorter for *kulaks*. Repeated failure to fulfil the quotas was considered illegal and it was criminalised. The people's court could pronounce sentences of up to two years imprisonment.

The 'new direction' brought increased pressure to bear on farmers and the toughening of punishment policy. In June of 1948, the USSR Supreme Soviet issued a regulation stipulating deportation (*vysylka*) as the penalty for farmers who did not fulfil their obligations. As early as the summer of that same year, this regulation facilitated the deportation of 12,000 farm-

---

and the majority had no remarkable savings but e.g. a Party organiser in Abja Rural Municipality complained to his colleagues in 1946: 'The *kulaks* of Abja have always been known for their habit of saving piles of cash. Regardless of their lost millions, some men have managed to save at least 50,000 roubles again', Verbatim of the meeting of the Party organisators, 9 August 1946, RA, ERAF.1.4.374, 179.

[37]   Popov, 'Krest'ianskie nalogi', 96.

[38]   Harju County letter, 30 January 1945, RA, ERA.R-364.1.12, 7–9; ESSR Statistics Office data on market prices, 20 May 1949, RA, ERAF.9607.1.396, 2.

ers to the Russian SFSR.[39] The campaign to toughen court practices had begun earlier. In the ESSR, Party and court authorities started requiring that the people's courts stiffen penalties. Thereafter the maximum penalty of two years imprisonment with loss of rights, deportation and confiscation of property was implemented more frequently. Some people's judges were dismissed due to their 'excessive liberalism in procurement matters' and the rest began to implement the harsher penalties.[40]

The number of people convicted for so-called procurement matters is unknown because penalty registers and databases do not normally include such court cases and Ministry of Justice summaries only cover shorter periods. This number was definitely not small. The 1st Department People's Court of Tartu County imposed prison sentences on ca 80 people in 1945–1950 due to failure to meet obligations (incl. labour conscription, sale quotas and monetary taxes).[41] Fines were imposed on a lot more people and we should bear in mind that the total number of people's courts in Estonia was 70.

Another sad aspect needs to be added in the context of punishment policy. A particular pattern was practised after the deportation of 1949 on the people who had been caught not fulfilling the quotas but who had missed the actual deportation. After serving their sentence, the court assigned them to their 'permanent place of residence', i.e. the place where they would have ended up by deportation. A massive deportation of these people never took place and there was a general consensus to leave these people alone, but one could easily end up in court for not fulfilling one's

---

[39] Beznin and Dimoni, 'Povinnosti rossijskikh', 26.

[40] Confidential decree no. 9 issued by the ESSR Ministry of Justice, 13 November 1947, RA, ERA.R-984.3.12, 19; Report, 6 December 1947, RA, ERAF.1.47.38, 24–29; Information, 11 January 1949, RA, ERAF.1.14.19, 16–21. Punishment policy in matters of the population's obligations is a broad topic that cannot be enlarged upon in greater depth in this article. See for further information: Indrek Paavle, 'Sovietisation of Agriculture', *Estonia since 1945* (Tallinn, 2009) *Estonia since 1945: reports of the Estonian International Commission for the Investigation of Crimes Against Humanity*, eds. Toomas Hiio, Meelis Maripuu and Indrek Paavle (Tallinn: Estonian Foundation for the Investigation of Crimes Against Humanity, 2009), 37–78.

[41] First Department People's Court of Tartu registration cards of criminal cases, 1945–1950, RA, EAA.T-265.1.19a, 79, 149a, 223, 286. The number of people sentenced to imprisonment is probably not final because some registration cards are incomplete.

obligations, e.g. in Tartu County the smallest amount of debt for initiating court proceedings was 77 kg of hay.

Procurement as a Priority

After the re-establishment of the Soviet occupation in the autumn of 1944, the issue of procurement immediately became a priority. Half a dozen of the decisions made by the ECP(B) CC Bureau after returning to Estonia concerned the restoration of agriculture and procurement. Procurement issues predominated the minutes of the Bureau and henceforth, this accounted for the relatively strong power the ESSR government possessed in managing agriculture.[42] At the local level, the share of procurement was disproportionately large in comparison with the total set of tasks of the administrative body. Relevant issues were topical the whole year round but the peak of the procurement campaign was in the autumn when the collection of grain quotas commenced. Then the whole administrative body, the officials and the activists, got involved in the service of procurement, relegating all their other jobs to the background. The rural municipality Party organs and executive committees bore the main responsibility. Their minutes demonstrate that to a greater or lesser degree, the majority of the topical issues and decisions taken were related to procurement or general obligations of the population. Statistically, most of the decisions made by the executive committees were based on the people's application forms, the majority of which were appeals for lowering the quotas.[43] The local Party leaders and chairmen of executive committees had to take personal responsibility for successful procurement since their personal well-being depended directly on the farmers fulfilling their obligations. According to reports from Party leaders during campaigns, all their efforts were geared toward solving procurement issues. The goal was to extract the quotas from the farmers by any means necessary. Summoning farmers

---

[42]   Mertelsmann, *Searching for Reasons*.

[43]   Minutes of meetings of the Äksi Rural Municipality Executive Committee, RA, EAA.T-178.1.15, 41, 72, 73, 119, 151, 173, 174; Minutes of meetings of the ECP(B) Äksi Rural Municipality Committee, 1947–1950, RA, ERAF.1021.1.1; ERAF.1021.2.1; ERAF.1021.3.1; ERAF.1021.4. 1; Minutes of meetings of the ECP(B) Äksi Rural Municipality organisation, 1946–1948, RA, ERAF.207.2.1; ERAF.207.3.1; ERAF.207.4. 1.

to executive committees, persuasion, and more vigorous methods were used. Jaan Teplenkov, a Party organiser in Rõuge, kept a record of every single day of each month. According to his October 1946 report, 27 days were directly connected to procurement. In numerous meetings, procurement issues were discussed with procurement agents, village agents and activists. Among other things, he dismissed employees of the executive committee, and on three days he was solely engaged in 'coercive claims of debts' from farmers.[44] This meant that they went and took the grain by force. Quoting Ain Toompalu, a Party organiser in Saadjärve Rural Municipality: 'We need to conduct our explanatory work in the manner that we never leave a farm without making sure that the farmer delivers his grain.'[45] The memoirs of Party organisers describe breaking down barn doors, taking away grain reserves by force, and the involvement of destruction battalions (the latter being necessary due to the efforts of forest brothers to prevent coercive expropriation, often resulting in shooting and victims).[46] There was a fine line between persuasion and violence, and the problem of overstepping the limits of power was common all over the Soviet Union. In 1947, the USSR State Prosecutor Konstantin Gorshenin directed Andrei Zhdanov's attention to numerous incidences of violence in the procurement campaign, including examples from Estonia, e.g. Party representatives beating up farmers, locking them up in the cellar, threats to shoot them, etc.[47]

The priority of procurement became obvious in recruitment policy. In 1945–1947, 124 rural municipality Party organisers were dismissed for 'underperformance' (almost 1/3 of all dismissals), and 236 executive committee chairmen lost their jobs for the same reason from the autumn of

---

[44]   Activities of the Rõuge Party organisation secretary 1–31 October [1946], RA, ERAF.1175.1.1, 13.

[45]   Minutes of the ECP(B) Tartu County general meeting, 9 October 1946, RA, ERAF.12.6.3, 4.

[46]   Vambola Asper, 'Mälestusi Laiuse vallast aastatel 1946–1950' [Memoirs from Laiuse Rural Municipality in 1946–1950], undated manuscript, RA, ERAF.247.51.618, 6; 'Mälestusi partorgina töötamise ajast Kiidjärve vallas ja valla propagandistina töötamisest Kuuste vallas ajavahemikul 1945–1950' [Memoirs of the Years of a Party Organiser in Kiidjärve Rural Municipality and a Propagandist in Kuuste Rural Municipality in 1945– 1950], undated manuscript, RA, ERAF.247.53.23, 5.

[47]   Zubkova, *Pribaltika i Kreml'*, 176.

1944 to March 1947 (over 1/3 of all dismissals).[48] Underperformance was predominantly related to procurement. It was one of the few spheres in the responsibilities of local administrative and Party leaders that was actually measurable. In discussions of personal issues of rural municipality officials, 'a brief description' of the municipality in question was always drawn up by the Party committee using a special form with the core data, including indicators of procurement plans.

Procurement in the Context of Sovietisation

Why was procurement a priority? A major economic reason was to provide the state with the majority of its income. A clear economic aim of procurement was putting food at the disposal of the state. This was vital in 1944–1945 because of the war, but it retained its significance after the war as well. The sale quota system may not have been efficient but it worked and the state benefited from it. It is unknown to what extent procurement plans were actually fulfilled due to the lack of reliable data.[49] On the whole, farmers met their obligations and tried to avoid debts (even buying missing quantities on the market at extremely high prices) or quotas were seized by the courts.

The cause for implementing such sale quotas was probably the state's incapability to collect produce in any way other than coercive sale and collective farms. Rapid collectivisation was impossible for several reasons; first of all, the regime had to feel more secure in the countryside and active resistance had to be suppressed. The ESSR government's alternative suggestion to carry out procurement through a state buying-up system would not have fit in with the uniform system, since it would have granted too much decision-making power on the regional and local levels.

Elaborating on the economic consequences of sale quotas, Elena Zubkova has stated on the basis of Russian archival materials that as a con-

---

[48]   Data about the numbers of the soviet officials in the municipalities, 22 August 1947– 28 December 1947, RA, ERAF.1.48.158, 36, 53, 71, 81, 87, 89, 91, 92, 101, 108, 110; ERAF.11.8.150, 32; Report on the work of the Personnel Department of the ECP(B) CC for 1946, 19 January 1947, RA, ERAF.1.5.11, 111.

[49]   See also: *Eesti rahvastiku majandustegevuse näitarve XX sajandil* [Economic Indicators of the Population of Estonia in the 20th Century], eds. Martin Klesment and Jaak Valge (Tallinn: EKDK, 2007), 41–44.

sequence of hectare-based calculation, some of the land remained un-
cultivated, and the resistance of farmers became apparent in disclaiming
land and hiding grain.[50] Statistical data does not support this idea and
according to the available databases, the post-war reduction of sowing
areas only began in 1948–1949.[51] However, the land that had belonged to
farmers who gave up farming before 1948 was integrated into state farms
(as shown by decisions of executive committees) and thus remained in the
registry of arable land, although it may have been left fallow. Disclaiming
land was not at all easy with the movements of the population being monitored by a passport regimen and with mandatory registered addresses of
residence. Consequently, the majority of applications for disclaiming land
were rejected. Everybody who did not choose to hide in the woods had no
choice but to carry on farming. The scale of hiding livestock is hard to assess but it is necessary not to overemphasize it since accusations of hiding
livestock could involve other personal motives. For example, an inspection
conducted in the summer of 1947 showed that 3% of the cows had been left
out of the calculation. Still, smaller animals were hidden more frequently
because bigger animals were difficult to hide.[52] The size of livestock rose in
the second half of the 1940s and began to drop only in 1951.[53]

Failed procurement has often been considered to be a significant reason for launching the collectivisation of the Baltic countries. Relying on
the experience of the grain procurement crisis in the Soviet Union in
1928–1929, the authorities reached the conclusion that the only way to
acquire grain is to make the state the sole owner of the grain.[54] At the
same time, the post-collectivisation decline in production must have been
predictable. They may possibly have counted on the easier collection of
produce from collective farms in comparison with individual farms.

Besides economic arguments, the political reasons for the procurement
system, along with its consequences, must not be ignored. Firstly, coercive

---

[50] Zubkova, *Pribaltika i Kreml'*, 177.

[51] Feest, *Zwangkollektivierung*, 197; Mertelsmann, *Der stalinistische Umbau*,
196; *Eesti rahvastiku majandustegevuse*, 60.

[52] Ants Ruusmann, 'Eesti agraarajaloo allikad aastail 1945–1950: kasutatavus
uurimustes' [Source of Agrarian History in Estonia: Possibilities of the use at the
research], – *Ajaloolise tõe otsinguil*, I (Tallinn: Umara, 1999), 73–87.

[53] Mertelsmann, *Der stalinistische Umbau*, 190.

[54] Zubkova, *Pribaltika i Kreml'*, 176–177.

procurement created tensions that were necessary for the regime in order to break up the unity of society and thus contributed to the subjugation of the country. The system of differentiation and discounts created inequality which further incited animosity and tension. An ideological aspect was added in the form of implementing the whole tax system in an anti-*kulak* campaign, which was also a part of breaking up community ties by artificially creating an enemy figure. Expropriations of property resulting from betrayals and the failure to meet the quotas had a demoralizing impact. Farmers tried hard to postpone taking their last animals to the procurement centre at all costs but it was not always possible. The farmers' worst fear was falling into debt that could bring about imprisonment and deportation to Siberia.

Secondly, coercive procurement was quite possibly a means of suppressing active resistance. Depriving the farmers of the majority of their produce, including any prospective surplus, made it harder to help the forest brothers. According to judgements in historiography, the forest brothers had become less active by 1948 and by the time total collectivisation had been implemented, it had ceased to be a serious threat.[55]

The interrelation between the system of coercive procurement and the postponement of speedy administrative reform is probably what stands out the most. It was clear that the procurement system would only work through developed administrative structures and institutions. Hence attempts to launch another large-scale reform next to a new system were not an option. Famine might have been another aspect. Back then the authorities of the Soviet Union were implementing a harsh policy for acquiring grain wherever possible, and one of these regions was the Baltic countries.[56] Regardless of its relatively small total production, Estonia provided a remarkable share of food supplies to starving Leningrad. Therefore, it would have been too risky to change the system in a situation where reduced production in the Baltic countries would have caused severe consequences. The planned administrative reform had been abandoned before the famine but in that situation, it turned out to be the right decision, and therefore administrative reform kept being postponed. Administrative reform was embarked upon in May of 1949 immediately after it had become

---

[55] Mart Laar, *War in the Woods: Estonia's Struggle for Survival, 1944–1956* (Washington: Compass Press, 1992) 174.

[56] Zubkova, *Pribaltika i Kreml'*, 172.

clear that total collectivisation had begun, hence it was obvious that the old procurement system was going to become history.

In conclusion, we cannot ascribe greater significance to the political or economic impact of coercive sale. The unjust and exhaustive system of sale quotas had clear economic goals, and this played a significant role in destroying society and achieving the foreign regime's ultimate goal i.e. suppressing passive and active resistance. Through ruining the farming sector, it helped to prepare the final stage of Sovietisation – collectivisation.

Rumours of Impending Deportations as a Phenomenon Pertaining to the History of Mentalities

Hiljar Tammela[*]

Introduction. Sources

It is a known fact that many of the people who were to be deported in March of 1949 managed to hide and thus be spared that fate. Common sense would suggest that those who had heard talk of the impending deportations then went into hiding and were therefore not deported. In reality, the situation was somewhat more complex.

Archival records, diaries and memoirs from the decade following World War II reveal the slightly unexpected fact that rumours warning of impending deportations were circulating both before and after the deportations of March, 1949. This gives reason to consider the fear of deportation as a specific phenomenon. This article sets out to describe the reasons, extent and actual impact on people of that phenomenon.

When researching the preparation, execution, aftermath and other relevant aspects of the March deportations, I found a wealth of information in several eminent research papers published on the topic in recent decades.[1] Of note are several fascinating treatises on the mood among

[*] First published: Hiljar Tammela, 'Kuulujutud eelseisvast küüditamisest kui mentaliteediajalooline nähtus' – *Uuemaid aspekte martsikuuditamise uurimisest: Eesti Ajaloomuuseumi teaduskonverentsi materjale*, eds. Olev Liivik and Hiljar Tammela, Varia historica, no. 4 (Tallinn: Eesti Ajaloomuuseum, 2009), 117–129.

[1] For more, see: Aigi Rahi, *1949. aasta märtsiküüditamine Tartu linnas ja maakonnas* [The Deportations of March 1949 in Tartu City and County] (Tartu: Kleio, 1998); Aigi Rahi-Tamm and Andres Kahar, 'Deportation Operation *Pri-*

the people during the era in question, which also expound the prevailing mentality in more general terms.[2] I have based my research of the rumours circulating during the period in question and of the general mood of the people on archival records of the Estonian Communist Party kept at the Rahvusarhiiv (National Archives of Estonia), and on various published diaries and other private documents.

Regarding archival records, I mainly relied on the so-called informations, or reports that local Communist Party committees had to submit periodically to higher-level committees. In the context of the topic at hand, these reports are particularly fascinating for their examples of people's 'anti-Soviet sentiments', i.e. rumours, ironic verses, 'anti-regime statements', etc. registered by officials of the Estonian Communist Party. In addition to the reports compiled and disseminated within the Communist Party, the archives also contain reports drawn up by the state security organs on the sentiments of the people, which, while more detailed and elaborate, are unfortunately less intact.

Information from the period of the Estonian Soviet Socialist Republic have been published in diverse publications.[3] In recent decades, Western

---

boy in 1949' – *Estonia since 1944: reports of the Estonian International Commission for the Investigation of Crimes Against Humanity*, eds. Toomas Hiio, Meelis Maripuu and Indrek Paavle (Tallinn, Estonian Foundation for the Investigation of Crimes Against Humanity, 2009), 429–460; *Eestlaste küüditamine. Mineviku varjud tänases päevas. Artiklid ja elulood* [The Deportation of Estonians. Shadows of the Past in the Present Day. Articles and Biographies], eds. Ene Andresen et al. (Tartu: FP Kinnisvara, 2004); Pearu Kuusk, '1949. a. märtsisündmused küüditajate ettekannetes Tartu näitel' [The Events of March 1949 as Reflected in the Reports of the Deporters. A Case Study of Tartu], – *Tartu Linnamuuseumi aastaraamat*, VIII (Tartu: Tartu Linnamuuseum, 2002), 5–18, etc.

[2]   Eda Kalmre, 'Hirm ja võõraviha sõjajärgses Tartus. Pärimuslooline uurimus kannibalistlikest kuulujuttudest' [Fear and Hatred of the 'Other' in Post-War Tartu. A Folkloristic Study of Cannibalistic Rumours], – *Tänapäeva folkloorist*, 7 (Tartu: Eesti Kirjandusmuuseum, 2007); Indrek Jürjo 'Rahva reageeringud Stalini surmale KGB andmetel' [People's Reactions to Stalin's Death according to the KGB], *Tuna*, no. 1 (1998), 40–49. I myself have explored people's reactions to mainly foreign policy events in the following article: Hiljar Tammela, 'Estonians' Views on Events Abroad and in the Soviet Union 1944–1953' – *Estonia since 1944*, 151–162.

[3]   For more, see: *Eesti NSV põllumajanduse kollektiviseerimine. Dokumentide ja materjalide kogumik* [Collectivisation of Agriculture in the Estonian Soviet Socialist Republic: A Collection of Documents and Records], comp. Evald Laasi

researchers have also expressed an interest in Soviet reports on the sentiments of people, although their focus has been on records from the 1930s regarding the Russian Soviet Federative Socialist Republic.[4]

Of the various private documents, I have used published diaries, correspondence and memoirs. Given the context of the era, the diaries tend to either disregard the deportation campaign and the related rumours or mention them only in passing.[5] This further increases the value of the diaries of the educator and bibliophile Jaan Roos, with their multitude of fascinating facts.[6] In terms of published correspondence, of note are the letters that Helmut Tarand sent to his family from prison camp, which are a masterful example of the implicit criticism of the regime to be 'read between the lines'.[7]

---

et al. (Tallinn: Eesti Raamat, 1978), 311–312, 518–519, etc.; Evald Laasi, *Vastupanuliikumine Eestis 1944–1949. Dokumentide kogu* [The Resistance Movement in Estonia 1944–1949. A Collection of Documents], (Tallinn: Nõmm & Co, 1992), 16, 47, etc.; 'Dokumente metsavendlusest ja vastupanuliikumisest Eestis' [Documents on the Forest Brothers and the Resistance Movement in Estonia], eds. Viktor Boikov and Ants Ruusmann, *Akadeemia*, no. 10–12 (1991), no. 1–8 (1992), no. 3 (1993); *Märtsivapustused. Avaldamata arhiividokumente aastaist 1949 ja 1950* [March Turmoil: Unpublished Archival Documents from 1949 and 1950], ed. Mart Arold (Tartu: Tungal, 1995), 30–33.

[4]   Sarah Davies, *Popular Opinion in Stalin's Russia. Terror, propaganda and dissent, 1934–1941* (Cambridge: Cambridge University Press, 1999); Sheila Fitzpatrick, *Everyday Stalinism: Ordinary Life in Extraordinary Times: Soviet Russia in the 1930s* (New York, Oxford: Oxford University Press, 1999); Lynne Viola, *Peasant Rebels under Stalin: Collectivisation and the Culture of Peasant Resistance* (Oxford, New York: Oxford University Press, 1996).

[5]   E.g. see: Oskar Luts, *Viimane päevik (1944–1952)* [The Last Diary (1944–1952)] (Tartu: Virgela, 1996), 26 [20 April 1945].

[6]   Jaan Roos (1888–1965) was a renowned educator, scholar of literature and bibliophile who spent the period from 1944 to 1954 in hiding, in fear of being arrested. The indepth diary that he kept during those years (published under the title *Läbi punase öö* (*Through the Red Night*) in five volumes from 1997 to 2009, Publisher: Eesti Kirjanduse Selts, Tartu) is a unique source on the history of mentalities of the era.

[7]   Philologist Helmut Tarand (1911–1987), was sentenced in 1946, along with several of his colleagues, to serve ten years in prison camp as a result of the so-called History Museum trial, which unfolded from absurd charges made against employees of the History Museum for allegedly organising an armed rebellion, using the firearms in the museum's collection. Tarand returned to Estonia in

When working with references from the period in question (both archival records and private documents), one should be especially mindful of source criticism. We must not forget that a climate of political oppression limits freedom of expression and, conversely, boosts self-censorship among the population.

The Fear of Deportation: its Origins and Proliferation

The deportations of June, 1941 have been emphasised as a turning point in the way the Estonian population viewed the Soviet regime.[8] Although repressions and the dismantling of the existing social order had already begun the previous year, immediately after the Communist coup in June of 1940, the mass deportation perpetrated in June of 1941 served as a vivid demonstration of the kind of measures deployed by the new regime. The campaign, which saw close to 10,000 people deported from Estonia to Russia, three quarters of them women, children and elderly people, solidified a general anti-Soviet stance among the Estonian population. This also applies to people who had previously hesitated to take a stand regarding the new regime, whose numbers are estimated to have been quite large. The general opposition to the Soviet regime manifested in the subsequent Summer War and in 1944, when the German occupation regime succeeded in repeatedly drafting men to defend Estonia against the Red Army offensive.

When the Red Army re-occupied Estonia in the autumn of 1944, the people were justified in fearing subsequent mass deportations. Artur Vahter,[9] a soldier in one of the Estonian national military units of the Red

---

1956. For more, see: *Cassiopeia. Kirju kolmnurgast Vorkuta – Eesti – Krasnojarski krai* [Cassiopeia. Letters from the Triangle of Vorkuta – Estonia – Krasnoiarsk krai], ed. Andres Tarand (Tallinn: Hiiukoda, 1992).

[8] *Eesti ajalugu VI. Vabadussõjast taasiseseisvumiseni* [History of Estonia VI. From the War of Independence to the Restoration of Independence], ed. Sulev Vahtre (Tartu: Ilmamaa, 2005), 177–178; Olaf Mertelsmann, 'Stalinistlike repressioonide põhjustest' [On the Reasons behind Stalinist Repressions], *Sirp*, 7 November 2008, 14.

[9] Artur Vahter (1909–2004), a renowned conductor and music professor in later years, took part in the German-Soviet War in the ranks of the Red Army, mainly

Army, describes in his diary a telling scene from September of 1944, when he was stopping by a farm in Alatskivi Rural Municipality, Tartu County:

I was the first Estonian from our side to stop by there. There were many women who were afraid of what was going to happen to them: whether they were about to be told to get up and start walking towards Siberia, just as the Germans had predicted.[10]

The new leaders received hosts of similar questions that same autumn. In order to gauge the sentiments of the people and to mould them to the dictates of the regime, a tradition of question and answer evenings was immediately instituted. This meant organising regional meetings (e.g. at the local parish municipality centre) where a Communist Party lecturer would give a political talk and take questions from local people. Communist Party officials registered the questions and were to report them to higher levels. Depending on the event, questions were accepted in written form (submitted anonymously) as well as orally. In the latter case, the reports usually also include the names of the people who asked questions.[11] The records available at the National Archives indicate that one of the main topics of universal interest was that of deportations. People inquired about the fate of those deported in 1941 and about any forthcoming deportations. For example, in his report submitted to Tallinn, August Minne, Second Secretary of the Lääne County Party Committee, already makes a note of this type of concern in mid-October of 1944, i.e. only two weeks after the Red Army had reached the town of Haapsalu![12]

In most cases, party officials limited their reports to Tallinn from the counties to only the questions asked at the local meetings. However, we do have a record of a lecturer's answers from a question and answer even-

---

as conductor of various military orchestras. The diary that he kept from 1941 to 1945 was one of the few published diaries by Estonians who fought in that war.

[10]   Artur Vahter, *Kapellmeistri päevik* [Diary of a Bandmaster] (Tallinn: Olion, 1990), 116.

[11]   For more on question and answer evenings, see: Evald Laasi. '"Kas parteilastel on suuremad kõhud kui töölistel?" Noorsugu okupante küsitlemas' [Are the Bellies of Party Officials Bigger than Workers' Bellies? Questions from the Youth to the Occupiers], *Pilk*, no. 31 (1990): 1–2.

[12]   ECP(B) Lääne County Committee Secretary Minne, informational report no. 2, 4 October 1944, RA, ERAF.1.1.656, 5–5v.

ing held in Tartu County in July of 1946, which serves as an interesting example of the counter-propaganda tactics employed:

Question (citizen from Tartu): 'Can we continue working without fear and can we sleep soundly at night without having to worry that we might be deported?'

Answer (Comrade Kurvits[13]): 'The government has guaranteed and will do so in the future that every decent Soviet citizen is free and can work in peace, be they farmers or workers at a plant. These supposed deportation days have come and gone, today was even supposed to be one, and it has come and gone. These supposed days and predictions indicate quite clearly that there is no basis to them.'[14]

The case of the Armed Resistance League also bears mentioning here. The League was the most ambitious post-World War II endeavour of the Estonian Forest Brothers guerrilla fighters – it was to become an umbrella organisation of the resistance units.[15] According to its statutes, the guerrilla units of the League were to respond in case of a war between the Western countries and the Soviet Union and in case of deportations (!).[16] However, Soviet state security organs succeeded in impeding the organisation from getting off the ground by implementing efficient counter-tactics; neither could other resistance groups derail the deportations of March, 1949 in any significant way.

Party committee records and private documents of the era attest that Estonia was rife with deportation rumours since World War II until, at

---

[13] Richard Kurvits (1909–1967) was Secretary of the ECP(B) Tartu County Committee in 1946.

[14] ECP(B) Tartu County Committee Secretary Zaitsev to the ECP(B) Central Committee. Information from Tartu County Committee No. 262s, 8 July 1946, RA, ERAF.1.4.246, 137. Original quote. It bears mentioning that in addition to the above question, two other similar questions were asked at the same meeting.

[15] For more, see: Armed Resistance League – *Estonica web encyclopedia*, http://www.estonica.org/en/Armed_Resistance_League/, 1 June 2018.

[16] Mart Laar '1949. aasta märtsiküüditamine ja relvastatud vastupanuliikumine' [The Deportations of March 1949 and the Armed Resistance Movement], – *Eestlaste küüditamine*, 64.

least, the end of the decade.[17] Arguably, these constituted the most wide-spread type of rumour, alongside talk of the West obliterating the Soviet regime.[18] This raises the question as to what the basis was for the proliferation of such rumours.

Reasons for the Proliferation of Rumours

Firstly, we need to emphasise the general context. People considered the governing regime illegitimate and hostile towards the population, which is also suggested by innumerable documents in the archives of the Communist Party itself. The official media had very low prestige, as it was over-politicised, extremely ideological, lacking and selective in news, and almost completely devoid of any entertainment. This gave rise to the spread of so-called unofficial channels of information, including primarily all types of rumours.

The fact of the deportations of June, 1941 undoubtedly played a major role, as it had set a precedent. The June deportations had come as a great shock, altering the way people viewed the Soviet regime. From then on, it was logical to assume that what had happened once might very well come to pass again. Existing sources suggest that the fearful rumours climaxed in the spring, summer and autumn of 1949, i.e. immediately after the second wave of mass deportations.

In innumerable cases, the alarms of impending deportations were directly based on interpreting various daily events that had preceded deportations in the past. Such events included assembling larger train units at railway stations, passport checks in people's homes, summoning of local Party corps or destruction battalions, and so on.

There were also cases where the authorities themselves threatened people with Siberia. This has been recorded (and officially condemned) in Communist Party documents.

---

[17]   It bears noting that these messages also penetrated the Iron Curtain and reached the West through private letters, stirring up anxiety among Estonian refugees. For more, see: Voldemar Kures, *Seitsme lukuga suletud raamat* [The Book under Seven Locks], I (Tartu: Ilmamaa, 2006), 150 [22 May 1945], 237 [22 February 1947].

[18]   For more, see: Tammela, 'Estonians' Views', 151–162.

Detailed Rumours

Several rumours even provided specific dates for the impending deportations. For example, in the months following the March deportations of 1949, it was feared that subsequent deportations were to take place as early as 6 April, thereafter, for example, on 5 September, on 10 December, and so on.[19] People often attached magic beliefs to the numbers, i.e. they feared that new deportations would share the dates of the previous ones, e.g. around 14 June or 25 March.[20]

Often, the rumours also included the expected number of people to be displaced from Estonia in the near future. The suggested proportions tend to vary between 50% and 90%, while specific figures include 40,000 families, 120,000 people, etc.[21]

The rumours also speculated on the probable reasons for the feared events. Thus, there was a story circulating in Harju County in the winter of 1949 which suggested that the coast of the Estonian SSR had been declared a 'border protection zone' extending 100 km inland from the shoreline all along the coast, and that independent farmers living in the zone would be sent to Siberia and the collective farmers resettled farther inland.[22] On several occasions, deportations were associated with impending elections, whereas the description of the exact circumstances varied extensively. There were some who thought that deportations would

---

[19] Lääne County Committee Secretary Pruks, informer Neemsalu. Information No. 42s on the political mood among the population, 18 April 1949, RA, ERAF.15.5.367, 45; Jaan Roos, *Läbi punase öö* [Through the Red Night], III, Diary of 1948 and 1949 (Tartu: Eesti Kirjanduse Selts, 2001), 279 [5 September 1949], 317 [9 December 1949].

[20] Tarand, *Cassiopeia*, 162 [14 June 1948]; Joosep Reinholm, *Vanglakirjad. 1949–1954* [Letters from prison: 1949–1954] (Tartu: Ilmamaa, 2002), 197 [6 April 1951].

[21] Comrade Olin, head of the ECP(B) Organisation and Instruction Department to Comrade Senkevich, head of the Information Sector, Compilation of questions asked by workers, farmers and officials in the towns and counties of the Estonian Soviet Socialist Republic (questions posed to activists and written questions put into boxes, 18 February 1946, RA, ERAF.1.4.277, 69; Roos, *Läbi punase öö*, II, Diary of 1947, 22 [22 January 1947].

[22] From ECP(B) Harju County Committee Secretary Kelberg, informer Tomm, to the ECP(B) CC Department of Party, Trade Union and Komsomol Agencies, Information on the political mood among the population in Harju County in the period 23 November–31 December 1949, 4 January 1950, RA, ERAF.1.53.202, 6.

precede elections to decrease the numbers of potential opponents to regime candidates. Others feared deportations after the elections in retaliation for the presumably large percentage of opponents to the regime.[23] The rumours focused on various elections: the elections of the Supreme Soviets of both the Soviet Union and the Estonian SSR, but also of local Councils of Workers' Deputies, etc.

The rumours circulated in the spring of 1950 suggested a curious scenario. To tighten Moscow's control, the 8th Plenary Meeting of the Estonian Communist Party (Bolsheviks) Central Committee, held in March of the same year, had as a result of a Party power struggle replaced most of the leaders of the Estonian SSR. This gave rise to rumours that Nikolai Karotamm and other Soviet Estonian leaders had been removed from power because they had been excessively 'pro-Estonian' – as a penalty for refusing to sign a document whereby 90% of Estonians were to be deported from Estonia (!).[24]

The case of the Magical Calendar

In addition to the above rumours, which were, to some extent, based on logical reasoning, the period in question was also rife with talk inspired by dreams, astrology, predictions, visions and the like.[25] Difficult and critical times are likely to create emotional turmoil in people, making them more susceptible to various forms of esotericism.

A prime example is the case of the calendar for the year 1949. It was a large, roughly A3 or Tabloid format wall calendar published by the Ajalehtede Kirjastus (Newspaper Publishing House) in 90,000 copies, and dis-

---

[23]   From ECP(B) Tartu County Committee Secretary Laosson to the ECP(B) Central Committee, Tartu County Committee information no. 589, 7 September 1945, RA, ERAF.1.3.91, 195; ECP(B) Tartu County Committee Secretary Eihe to the ECP(B) Central Committee, Tartu County Committee information no. 27, 4 January–18 January 1946, January 1946, RA, ERAF.1.4.246, 20; Roos, *Läbi punase öö*, II, 44 [12 March 1947].

[24]   From ECP(B) Tartu City Committee Secretary Leede to the Information Sector of the ECP(B) CC Department of Party, Trade Union and Komsomol Agencies, Information no. 80s on the political mood among Tartu City officials, 7 April 1950, RA, ERAF.1.53.202, 55.

[25]   Tammela, 'Estonians' Views', 159.

tributed free of charge to the subscribers of central newspapers and also sold individually. The artist Jaan Jensen[26] had designed the calendar true to the style of the era – the list of calendar days was illustrated with a row of red flags, oak wreaths and ears of corn, and depictions of factory buildings and various vehicles from a train locomotive to a car. However, this innocent calendar created a flurry of outlandish rumours, spinning from one extreme to another.

Initially, the wall calendar was thought to feature omens of Estonia's imminent liberation; for example, the fact that the row of flags waned and disappeared completely at the month of May was interpreted as 'the disappearance of the Soviet regime from Estonia' by May.[27] Of special interest was a cross-shaped element depicted on the side of the train locomotive, which suggested that the train brought 'death to the Reds and Communists' and would transport 'the dead bodies of Communists eastward', away from Estonia.[28] Further positive interpretations were fuelled by a combination of blue, black and white found in the upper right corner of the calendar.[29]

Very soon, however, the calendar and in particular the cross-shaped element depicted on the train locomotive began to convey a completely opposite meaning. Jaan Roos made the following comment on this in his diary: 'All the people I know in Tallinn agree that the Estonian nation and country are doomed.'[30] This meaning ascribed to the calendar took further root in hindsight after the March deportations.

The reports arriving from the counties describing the anxiety generated by the calendar did not go unnoticed by Party officials. Since it was

---

[26] Jaan Jensen (1904–1967) was a professor at the Tallinn State Institute of Applied Arts and a prolific graphic artist, whose works from the period in question included political caricatures, posters, etc.

[27] ECP(B) Lääne County Committee Secretary Pruks, informer Masing. Information on the political mood among the population, 18 March 1949, RA, ERAF.15.5.367, 33.

[28] Roos, *Läbi punase öö*, III, 201 [12 March 1949]; ECP(B) Harju County Committee Secretary Torf, informer Tomm, to the ECP(B) CC Department of Party, Trade Union and Komsomol Agencies. Information no. 47/s on the political mood among the population in Harju County in the period 7 February–15 March 1949, 22 March 1949, RA, ERAF.1.28.86, 162.

[29] Roos, *Läbi punase öö*, III, 201 [12 March 1949].

[30] *Ibid.*, 203 [14 March 1949].

difficult to conceive any real counter-measures (considering the already ubiquitous propaganda, the aims of which included neutralising the rumours), a formal response was given by punishing the artist. The graphic artist Jaan Jensen, who was confounded by the meaning ascribed to the calendar,[31] was issued a serious reprimand at an Artists' Union board meeting for 'lack of vigilance'.[32] The penalty, however, was merely formal. The artist did not have to suffer any serious consequences, as is attested by a certificate issued to him the following year, stating that Jensen was 'an individual with a broad Soviet worldview and conviction' and 'one of our eminent contemporary caricaturists'.[33]

Deportations of March, 1949

In 1998, the Estonian National Museum sent to its network of correspondents one of its questionnaires, numbered KL 201 and containing 87 questions on the deportations of March, 1949. In response, the museum received close to 150 answered questionnaires, which have been archived in 17 extensive volumes and are available to researchers at the museum library.[34] The questionnaires were filled out 50 years after the events took place, which naturally raises the question of the reliability of human memory. However, when comparing the answers of the correspondents to archival records and private diaries recorded half a century earlier, we do not find significant discrepancies in reflecting on the topic at hand, which is why the questionnaires may be considered an entirely reliable source.

Most of the responders had in fact been deported during the deportations of March, 1949. The questionnaire topics also included questions on the signs pointing to impending deportations – whether the deportations had been preceded by any occurrences or situations that might have hinted at what was to come.

---

[31]   Rutt Eliaser, *Passita ja pajata* [No Passport, No Pot] (Tallinn: Abe, 1992), 159

[32]   Estonian Soviet Artists' Union, Board Report no. 12, 28 March 1949, RA, ERA.R-1665.1.92, 15v. I am grateful to Liivi Uuet from the National Archives for this reference.

[33]   Professional characterisation for Jaan Jensen, 28 February 1950, RA, ERA.R-1665.3.40, 7.

[34]   ERM KV, 867, 872–883, 917, 933, 962, 1058.

The signs of deportations mentioned by the respondents can be divided into four broad categories:
1) increased sightings of uniforms of all types (militia, security, military and other similar officials);
2) intensified road traffic, train units being assembled on the railway;[35]
3) (increased) rumours of deportations;
4) warnings from friends / colleagues / random people.[36]

A common theme, however, is that the warnings were usually not taken seriously. Many questionnaire responders note that they did not try to hide from potential deportation because they did not feel guilty of anything or believe that they might be deported. Others admit to the fear of deportation but add that they could not go into hiding for a longer period since they had to go to work. Somewhat typical is the way one woman recollects that she wanted to take her child to her friends' house and spend the night hiding there, but since those friends had a mean dog that was loose in the yard, she returned home.[37] The records at the Estonian National Museum suggest that although many responders had noticed signs of impending deportations, they were not that convinced that the operation would actually be carried out, and therefore also doubted the need to hide. To summarise, many people were not afraid enough of the deportations of March, 1949 to 'burn any bridges' for the sake of hiding, i.e. to risk missing work and the resulting problems, etc.[38]

However, we know from memoirs and Communist Party documents that at times, people took the rumours of impending deportations so seriously that they indeed went into hiding with their entire families for certain periods. In his diary, Jaan Roos describes similar instances that he had heard of, and also writes that he himself joined the families at whose

---

[35] Other sources also refer to the first two as the most recurrent signs of perceived danger; e.g. see: Meinhard Leetmaa, *Sõjas ja ikestatud Eestis* [In War and in Captive Estonia] (Stockholm: Välis-Eesti & EMP, 1979), 240; Margit-Mariann Koppel, 'Metsakohin toob ärevaid teateid' [The Woods Sing of Trouble], *Kultuur ja Elu*, no. 2 (1998): 54–57.

[36] Probably people who had learned of the deportation by coincidence or by indirect signs, since the operation was top secret. See also: Kuusk, '1949. a. märtsisündmused', 9.

[37] ERM KV, 877, 152.

[38] See also: Rahi, *1949. aasta märtsiküüditamine*, 46.

farms he was staying when they spent nights away from the farm's living quarters in fear of deportation (e.g. in August of 1945).[39]

By 1949, people had evidently heard so many 'prophecies' (that did not materialise) that they no longer really believed them. The constant fearful rumours regarding deportations ended up stultifying their alertness to the point that many no longer took them seriously by March of 1949 – and thus fell prey to the deporters.[40]

Those Who Escaped the March Deportations

Certainly, the exact opposite happened as well. Ants Käärmann, a guerrilla forest brother who was in hiding somewhere near the border of Valga and Võru counties, writes in his memoirs that after having been alerted to the impending deportations by several sources, he passed the warning on to the villagers and even allowed some people to hide out in his bunker for a while.[41] Communist Party documents report cases where rural municipality activists promoting collective farming arrived in villages during and immediately after the March deportations 'only to find abandoned farms'[42] (in Mahu Rural Municipality, Viru County). Obviously, there were many people who were alerted to the deportations in time and who were spared because they went into hiding.

According to available information, almost half of the 20,000 people selected for deportation in March of 1949 were not located! In order to reach the prescribed figure, the authorities resorted to so-called reserve lists, and by deporting the people on those lists they managed to reach the required quota – close to 20,000 people. In her monograph on the March

---

[39]   Roos, *Läbi punase öö*, I, 201 [16 August 1945].

[40]   The same view is expressed in: Laar, '1949. aasta märtsiküüditamine', 67.

[41]   Alfred Käärmann, *Surmavaenlase vastu. Eesti lõunapiiri metsavenna mälestusi* [Facing the Mortal Enemy: Memoirs of a Forest Brother from the Estonian Southern Border] (Tartu: Tartu Ülikooli Kirjastus, 1998), 165. See also: Rahi, *1949. aasta märtsiküüditamine*, 58.

[42]   From ECP(B) Viru County Committee Secretary Bolshagin to the ECP(B) CC Department of Party, Trade Union and Komsomol organs. Information on the work of local activists and on the attitude of the population towards the expulsion of kulaks, collaborators of the Germans, and other hostile elements, 28 March 1949, RA, ERAF.1.28.24, 35.

deportations in Tartu City and County, Aigi Rahi has identified several of the reasons why some of the people in the area managed to escape deportation. These main reasons can be summarised as follows:

1) bureaucratic mistakes (e.g. out-of-date addresses on the deportation lists, or using women's maiden names);
2) going into hiding from deportation (after having been alerted either before the deportations or during the operation);
3) being away from home by coincidence;
4) escaping from the deporters;
5) also, mercy shown by the deporters (e.g. in some cases where families had small children or bed-ridden family members).[43]

It is quite difficult to estimate which of the above reasons played a more decisive role. When comparing archival sources to individual memoirs, one is left with the impression that going into hiding and being away from home by coincidence played a more significant role in escaping deportation. However, our current knowledge does not allow for more specific conclusions.

The Aftermath of March

Just like the deportations of June 1941, the large-scale mass deportations that followed in March of 1949 had a devastating effect. What had been feared since 1944 had finally come to pass, and the unfolding of the events stirred up a frantic fear of a third mass deportation.

A Harju County Party Committee report from April of 1949 describes a situation in Rae Rural Municipality, where following a meeting of the village Party activists, a farmer woman supposedly remarked to a Party official: 'So, it's really true that there won't be a follow-up deportation. That's a weight off my chest. Now I can unpack my bags and tell the others as well.'[44] This episode was hailed as an obvious victory for Soviet propaganda efforts.

---

[43] Rahi, *1949. aasta märtsiküüditamine*, 57–61.

[44] From ECP(B) Harju County Committee Secretary Torf to the ECP(B) Central Committee. Information on the political mood among the population in Harju

In reality, the situation was not nearly as rosy for the authorities. The moods of the people alternated between anger and depression. All manner of deportation talk inundated the aftermath of the deportations of March 1949, from spring to the end of the year.[45] People everywhere were eagerly anticipating the outbreak of war, drawing obvious parallels between the events of the summer of 1941, when the Soviet-German War had erupted a week after the June deportations.[46] In Narva, the fear was that Estonians would launch pogroms against Russians after the deportations.[47] A rise in religious activities was also widely noted – this probably had to do with looking for emotional comfort.[48] A typical feature of the Party reports of 1949 is a decrease in voicing 'anti-Soviet statements'. Presumably, this does not reflect a more positive attitude towards the ruling regime, but is rather an indication of a deepening fear of expressing views openly.

It is difficult to accurately assess the extent and duration of the fear of deportation. Some families remember the image of packed luggage sitting in the corner waiting for an unexpected departure. This persisted for several years after the March deportations and the death of Stalin. Indeed, this information has been passed on mainly through family lore, since back then, people were afraid of expressing and writing down their thoughts – if arrested, their diaries and private letters could also serve as evidence of their guilt.

In his suggestions for periodising Estonian contemporary history, the Estonian historian Enn Tarvel has highlighted the period between 1956 and 1958 as one turning point. According to him, one of the distinc-

---

County in the period 15 March – 25 April 1949, 30 April 1949, RA, ERAF.1.28.86, 179.

[45]   E.g. see: Roos, *Läbi punase öö*, III, 219 [13 April 1949], 229 [6 May 1949], 258 [11 July 1949] etc., etc.

[46]   *Ibid.*, p. 211 [28.3.1949]; Jüri Kindel, *Vana mesipuu saladus. Metsavenna päevik* [The Secret of an Old Beehive. Diary of a Forest Brother] (Tartu: Hotpress, 2008), 140 [27 March 1949].

[47]   ECP(B) Narva City Committee Secretary Yeryomin. Information No. 030 on the political mood among city officials in relation to the expulsion of kulaks, criminals and their family members from the territory of the Estonian Soviet Socialist Republic, 4 April 1949, RA, ERAF.1.28.119, 31.

[48]   ECP(B) Lääne County Committee Secretary Pruks, informer Neemsalu. Information no. 93s on the political mood among the population, 19 August 1949, RA, ERAF.15.5.367, 100.

tive features of that demarcation line is the famous 20th Congress of the Communist Party of the Soviet Union, and specifically its achievement in soothing the atmosphere of fear and 'dispelling the ubiquitous fear of Siberia'.[49] We have to agree with Tarvel on this issue. It seems that the fear of deportation, along with the hope for a war that would liberate Estonia from Soviet occupation, gradually dissipated around the mid-1950s as the regime eased up somehow and people adjusted to the new situation.

In Conclusion

The fear of deportation was a phenomenon that affected people's minds in Estonia after World War II for almost ten years. To a large extent, it was based on a precedent – the deportations of June 1941, which were followed by another mass deportation in March of 1949.

Fearful rumours spread all over Estonia. This was made possible by people's opposition to the ruling regime and further fuelled by the low prestige of state media. The rumours were based on the misinterpretation of various daily occurrences, and support was also found in omens, dreams and other irrational signs.

When the deportations were finally carried out in March of 1949, the state security organs failed to track down a significant portion of the people who were to be deported. It is likely that many of them had found out about the threat and went into hiding deliberately. We can assume that the number of escaped people would have been even greater if people had not already been used to the background of endless rumours.

As talk of imminent expulsions (including specified dates and other details) was often heard but never materialised, people had grown apprehensive of such rumours. We may posit that this tendency culminated in 1949, when truthful rumours and warnings of an impending actual deportation were not taken seriously, as the constant rumour overload and misinformation had blunted people's alertness.

---

49   Enn Tarvel, 'Eesti lähiajaloo periodiseerimisest' – *Ajaloolise tõe otsinguil. 20. jaanuaril 1999 Tallinnas toimunud konverentsi 'Eesti lähiajaloo allikakriitilisi probleeme' materjalid* [On the Periodisation of Estonian Contemporary History – *In Search of a Historical Truth*. Conference catalogue: *Issues of source criticism in Estonian contemporary history*, Tallinn, 20 January 1999] (Tallinn: Umara, 1999), 113.

The mass deportation of 1949, however, fuelled fearful rumours and hearsay even further. These rumours seem to have dissipated only in the middle of the following decade, as the Soviet regime loosened its grip somewhat and the atmosphere of fear was toned down.

Forced Migration of Estonian Citizens to the East 1941–1951: Some Similarities with the Accounts of People Who Fled to the West

*Aigi Rahi-Tamm**

Introduction

As a result of the war and punitive policies of the occupations, thousands of Estonian citizens were sent out of their homes. In Estonian historiography, the narratives of war refugees and people deported to prison camps or exile have mostly been addressed separately, even though when we look at these accounts it is possible to delineate certain comparisons and correlations. These are stories of broken families who lived in the East and the West. This article focuses on what happened to the deportees, but issues concerning individual choices and their consequences, how people managed in unfamiliar situations, varied attitudes and adjustment for the refugees were also important.

Masses of people torn apart

In August and September of 1944, the roads in Estonia were busy with traffic – refugees, retreating Germans and advancing Soviet soldiers. While some Estonians were trying to escape, others, mostly those who had been mobilised into the German forces, were trying to make their

* First published: Aigi Rahi-Tamm, 'Eesti kodanike sundmigratsioon itta aastail 1941–1951: mõningaid võrdlusjooni läände põgenenute looga', *Acta Historica Tallinnensia*, no. 17 (2011): 72–94.

way home. What was the best course of action in this situation of war and change of power? Was it best to leave home and flee the war, to try to escape across the sea to Sweden, to retreat with the German Army and head for Europe, or to stay in Estonia and allow Red Army forces to imprison you, or to hide and put up a fight, or to try once again to blend into Soviet society and leave it all to fate?

In the autumn of 1944, the reinstated Soviet regime resumed its punitive operations against local inhabitants but by then it was too late to escape from Estonia; escape was successful only on rare occasions. The fear of deportation and violence at the hands of the Soviets during the summer months of 1941 had taken root and now people were even more fearful. The victorious end of the war did not herald a more peaceful period and the following years were filled with renewed campaigns against 'suspicious' and 'untrustworthy' citizens.[1]

In May of 1945, Europe was facing an enormous humanitarian crisis; millions had died and in addition to this there were all the wounded, exhausted, sick, outcast and homeless people who needed to be fed, housed and cared for. The Baltic people who had escaped from their homelands or been released from camps and the military formed but a small part of this mass of people waiting for a solution. The Soviet Union considered these Balts to be Soviet citizens and wished to bring them back, but this idea was far removed from the opinion held by those same people who had by now reached the West. Instead of returning home, most of them preferred to remain abroad, which clearly puzzled many Western officials. Yet as East-West relations cooled, this soon found increasing acceptance. According to the assessment of the repatriation department at the Estonian SSR Council of Ministers, on 1 September 1949 a total of 20,252 of the 74,200 Estonian citizens abroad had been brought back (this included prisoners-of-war).[2] This figure did not match Moscow's plans, which anticipated that

---

[1]   Alfred Rieber, 'Civil wars in the Soviet Union – Criticism', *Explorations in Russian and Eurasian History*, no. 4, 1 (2003): 158–162.

[2]   ESSR political-economic overview 1949, RA, ERAF.17/1SM.1.141, 59. Figures for repatriated see David Vseviov, *Kirde-Eesti urbaanse anomaalia kujunemine ning struktuur pärast Teist maailmasõda* [The development and structure of the urban anomaly in Northeastern Estonia after the Second World War] (Tallinn: Tallinn Pedagogical University, 2002), 80–83.

all citizens would submit to Soviet authority and be repatriated.[3] Those who were outside the Soviet Union's borders were automatically labelled 'traitors of the homeland' ('who had re-oriented from Nazi Germany to England, the USA and Sweden').[4] This established the attitude at the state level and contact with anyone in the West was considered an antagonistic act. Merely the fact that an individual had tried to escape from Estonia before the advance of the Red Army was sufficient for the Soviet security investigators to accuse them of being against Soviet rule. On being arrested they were often asked, 'Why did you want to escape abroad?'[5]

The Soviet state had its own solution for the post-war problems – rebuilding the country did not mean rebuilding homes, but instead destroying the homes of thousands of families and sending them out of their homeland.[6] On the one hand, the relocation of huge numbers of people after the war took place purely spontaneously – some left regions that had been devastated by war or gripped by famine, some returned after fleeing the war and others sought a place where they could make a living. On the other hand, there was also a clear political decision, which strongly affected the constituent population. This first struck the collectively guilty ethnic Germans living in the Soviet Union and in Central and Eastern European countries that were within the Soviet sphere of influence. This was then extended to include other nationalities – Poles, Ukrainians, Hungarians, Slovaks, etc.[7] A deportation of ethnic Germans took place

---

[3]   Repatriation policies see Indrek Jürjo, *Pagulus ja Nõukogude Eesti. Vaateid KGB, EKP ja VEKSA arhiividokumentide põhjal* [Exile and Soviet Estonia. Views based on archival documents of the KGB, the ECP and VEKSA], (Tallinn: Umara, Tallinn, 1996), 7–24; E. Kase, 'Repatrieerimine Eesti NSV-s' [Repatriation in the Estonian SSR] (Bachelor thesis, University of Tartu, 2005); Airi Kuusk, 'Repatrieerimispropaganda Eesti NSV-s repatriantide kaasamise näitel aastatel 1945–1953' [Repatriation propaganda in the Estonian SSR as illustrated by the involvement of repatriates in 1945–1953] (Bachelor thesis, University of Tartu, 2008).

[4]   ESSR political-economic overview 1949, RA, ERAF.17/1SM.1.141, 40.

[5]   In interrogations, many people were repeatedly asked this question, incl. e.g. to Professor Paul Ariste, RA, ERAF.130SM.1.3090.

[6]   Violent peacetime see: *Warlands: Population Resettlement and State Reconstruction in the Soviet-East European Borderlands, 1945-50*, ed. P. Gatrell and N. Baron (Basingstoke, New York: Palgrave Macmillan, 2009).

[7]   Ethnic cleansing see Gustavo Corni and Tamás Stark, 'Population movements at the end of the war and in its aftermath' – *People on the Move. Forced Popula-*

in Estonia on 15 August 1945. Of the 407 deportees, 261 were ethnic Germans – the remainder were of other nationalities, mostly family members who were Estonians and who went along voluntarily.[8]

Anyone who had 'been outside' the Soviet Union and had come in contact with Western influences was collectively under suspicion. According to an assessment by Viktor Zemskov, out of close to 4.2 million Soviet repatriates who had initially been placed in NKVD filtration camps and undergone 'screening',[9] 58% (2.4 million) were finally allowed home, 19% (801,000) were sent to serve in the armed forces, 14% (608,000) were sent to work battalions, and 7% (272,000) were handed over to the NKVD, which means they were sent to labour camps.[10] The monitoring of people who had been abroad and were initially allowed home (and who formed a separate category in the long list of arrestees from 1944–1953) could still end in imprisonment later on.[11]

People who had been re-evacuated to Estonia from the Soviet rear area were also under suspicion. Their views were assessed in a questionnaire, which together with their application for entrance to the ESSR, had to be sent to the ESSR Council of People's Commissars, where the decision was made regarding the return of evacuees to Estonia.[12] At the same time in 1945–1947, an uncontrolled 'element' streamed into Estonia – approximately 100,000 immigrants from the 'old Soviet republics'.[13]

---

tion Movements in Europe in the Second World War and its Aftermath, eds. P. Ahonen et al. (Oxford: Berg, 2008), 61-110.

[8]   Aigi Rahi-Tamm, 'Deportation of individuals of German nationality from Estonia in 1945' – *Estonia since 1944: reports of the Estonian International Commission for the Investigation of Crimes Against Humanity*, compiled by Peeter Kaasik et al., eds. Toomas Hiio, Meelis Maripuu and Indrek Paavle (Tallinn, Estonian Foundation for the Investigation of Crimes Against Humanity, 2009), 415-427.

[9]   Screening or suitablity checks in refugee camps where people had to answer questions about their past, views, etc.

[10]   Barbara Stelzl-Marx, 'Forced labourers in the Third Reich' –*People on the Move*, 185.

[11]   Jürjo, *Pagulus ja Nõukogude*, 10.

[12]   Siret Haller, 'Reevakueerimine ENSV-sse' [Re-evacuation to the ESSR] (Master thesis, University of Tartu, 2011).

[13]   Olaf Mertelsmann, 'Alatoitumuse tekitamine põllumajanduslikult rikkas piirkonnas: stalinistlik toiduainetega varustamise poliitika 1940. aastate Eestis'

Even though the loss of human life in the Soviet Union was great, in Stalin's eyes this did not increase the value of human life; imprisonment and deportations of individuals, families and ethnic groups continued until 1953. In addition to those people who were taken from their homes at gunpoint, there was another group that lived in constant fear of being deported. These people left their homes and in a sense lived voluntarily in exile. In some cases, these people continued to hide themselves and their families for years, running from one place to the next. These are ordeals that have often been overlooked.

For the whole Soviet period we lived a semi-illegal life. On hearing a rumour, we would find some friend at whose place we could to stay the night – this was not easy because who should we compromise in this way? How do we get there unnoticed with our family?[14]

By the time of the March deportations in 1949, many people were so exhausted from the constant hiding and changing locations that their attitude to the events that were taking place was one of resignation.

We had lived through a violent search when they were looking for our father. Things were thrown around for half the night, they brandished revolvers, they threatened us. We had hidden and stayed the night with friends, risking their safety. I had seen how my classmate Viive Vainola was arrested – she was taken from school during a break between lessons – two men holding each elbow and a third held a pistol to her back. Aldo Jürgen and the Kutsar brothers were arrested from the flat opposite ours – in the wave of arrests of Viljandi school students, boys I knew disappeared, and Aldo was a playmate of mine – the arrests had come very close to us. Arrests and deportations, this was norm of life. Now it was simply our turn.[15]

In the 1940s, Estonia was in the inescapable grip of varied processes and directions of migration due to people relocating due to the war, as well as

---

[Generating undernourishment in an agriculturally rich area: Stalinist policy regarding the supply of foodstuffs in Estonia in the 1940s], *Ajalooline Ajakiri*, no. 2 (2010): 201.

[14] ERM KV, Helle Viir.

[15] ERM KV, Helle Viir.

German- and Soviet-directed policies of repression, the results of which are still clearly visible in Estonian demographics today.[16]

In Estonian historiography, the fate of people in the 1940s has mostly been approached according to groups – arrestees, deportees, refugees, men at the front, etc. Even though their stories have many connections and overlaps, the search for similarities, differences and comparisons has been relatively circumspect.[17] The comparison of refugees and deportees who had become homeless may appear somewhat high-handed – is being removed from your home escorted by soldiers as part of a military operation in any way comparable with escaping, where people still had a certain degree of choice? In 1944, however, escape was generally a case of forced departure to flee the war, persecution and so forth, and this places Estonian refugees in a category of forced migration.[18] In reading the memoirs of these people over the long-term, certain attributes stand out, which might influence the reader to find similar traits. Whatever the reason for their departure from home, these stories share keywords that are typical of migration such as departure, luggage, journey, arrival, adjusting to new situations, relations with those left at home, etc. Strong emotions are also

---

[16]   Kalev Katus, Allan Puur and Asta Põldma, *Eesti põlvkondlik rahvastikuareng = Cohort population development in Estonia* (Tallinn: Eesti Kõrgkoolidevaheline Demouuringute Keskus, 2002), 46–50.

[17]   Here I will insert an example of one family's fate: 'Due to the occupation of Estonia by the Soviet Union, my oldest brother was mobilised (he was forced to, so as to protect his family). He died in Courland in 1944. My next brother joined the German Army, ended up in the West and from there went to Australia. As the war was ending, my third oldest brother was mobilised into the Soviet Army and wasn't discharged until after the deportations. Our father was arrested because he was member of the Home Guard and was released from prison after the deportation. My oldest sister was arrested for celebrating Estonian Independence Day (a group of young people hoisted the Estonian flag on the Tuulavere watchtower in Voore Rural Municipality, someone betrayed them) and she died in prison in 1947. In 1946–47, our mother was also arrested in a raid against the forest brothers. We five children were all alone. At the time we were deported our ages were – brother 17, sister 14, brother 11, myself 8 and 5-year-old brother.' See: ERM KV, Luule Porkanen (Karu).

[18]   Aivar Jürgenson, 'Vabatahtliku ja sunniviisilise migratsiooni dihhotoomiast migratsiooni makro- ja mikroteooriate taustal' [On the dichotomy between voluntary and forced migration on the background of macro- and microtheories of migration], *Acta Historica Tallinnensia*, no. 13 (2008): 101–116.

a part of it – death, pain of loss,[19] and suffering that bears no comparison, and may be present in the memoirs.[20] Without doubt this is a broad and complex topic. The experiences of deportees and refugees have previously been compared mostly with a sense of distance, for example by bringing together into one collection articles which describe aspects that are typical for both categories. According to Alfred Rieber, history professor at the Central European University, the research into deportations has until now concentrated primarily on the way punitive operations were conducted. The refugee issue has been treated more broadly, but even here there is a shortage of research which looks more deeply at integration processes. What was their position as 'foreigners' in the place that received them? How did the integration of 'foreigners' into society take place? How did they preserve (or lose) their identity? And so forth. These are just some of the common questions that should be asked of both refugees and deportees.[21] In today's multicultural society the mutual connections between migration and identity have become an important subject of research. Researching identity on the basis of individuals and national groups helps us to understand the effects that accompany migration generally on the global scale.[22]

---

[19]   The loss of homeland in the accounts of those deported to Siberia and those who escaped to the West have been analysed from a gender studies viewpoint by literature researcher Leena Kurvet-Käosaar, See : Leena Kurvet-Käosaar, 'Naistega juhtus teisi asju: Teine maailmasõda, vägivald ja rahvuslik identiteet Käbi Laretei teoses "Mineviku heli" ja Agate Nesaule teoses "Naine merevaigus"' [Different things happened to women: the Second World War, violence and national identity in Käbi Laretei's work *Sound from the Past* and Agate Nesaule's work *Woman in Amber*], *Ariadne Lõng*, no. 1/2 (2000): 84-96.

[20]   Meike Wulff has interviewed Estonians both in Estonia and the West and highlights the fact that the question of 'who suffered more' has come up in many interviews: Meike Wulff, 'Locating Estonia: perspectives from exile and the homeland' – *Warlands: Population Resettlement*, 249.

[21]   Alfred Rieber, 'Repressive population transfers in Central, Eastern and South-Eastern Europe: a historical overview' – *Forced Migration in Central and Eastern Europe, 1939–1950*, ed. A. J. Rieber (London: Frank Cass, 2000), 1-2.

[22]   Rina Benmayor and Andor Skotnes, 'Some reflections on migration and identity' –*Migration and Indentity. Memory and Narrative Series*, eds. R. Benmayor and A. Skotnes (New Brunswick: Transaction Publishers, 2005), 1-18; Thomas Pedersen, *When Culture Becomes Politics. European Identity in Perspective* (Aarhus: Aarhus University Press, 2008); *Collective Memory and European*

This article primarily looks at situations that were typical for people who were deported and digresses in-depth into connections with aspects of the Great Flight.

A selection of issues is covered that arise and form connections in the parallel reading of the stories of deportees and refugees and their analyses.

This article is based on general research[23], as well as published and unpublished memoirs, which are held in the Estonian National Museum[24] and in the collections of the Estonian Literary Museum.[25]

Identity. The Effects of Integration and Enlargement, eds. K. Eder and W. Spohn (Aldershot: Ashgate, 2005); for problems of Estonian identity see Aune Valk and Kristel Karu-Kletter, 'Rootsi eestlaste Eesti-identiteet' [The Estonian identity of Estonians in Sweden] –*Suur põgenemine 1944. Eestlaste lahkumine läände ja selle mõjud* [The Great Escape of 1944: The departure of Estonians to the West and its effects], eds. K. Kumer-Haukanõmm, T. Rosenberg and T. Tammaru (Tartu: University of Tartu Centre for Expatriate Estonian Studies, University of Tartu Press, 2006), 147-169; *Collection analysing issues of Canadian Baltic refugee identity: Home and Exile. Selected Papers from the 4th International Tartu Conference on Canadian Studies*, eds. E. Rein, K. Vogelberg, Cultural Studies Series, 7 (Tartu: Tartu University Press, 2006).

[23] Reporting on the issues of escaping is based on many general texts: *Suur põgenemine 1944*; *Rändlindude pesad: eestlaste elulood võõrsil* [Nests of migratory birds: life stories of Estonians abroad], ed. Tiina Kirss (Tartu: Estonian Literary Museum, University of Toronto Chair of Estonian Studies, 2006); *Sõna jõul. Diasporaa roll Eesti iseseisvuse taastamisel* [On the strength of words. The role of the diaspora in restoring Estonia's independence], eds. K. Anniste, K. Kumer-Haukanõmm and T. Tammaru (Tartu: University of Tartu Centre for Expatriate Estonian Studies Publications, 2008); *Eestlaste põgenemine Läände Teise maailmasõja ajal. Artiklid ja elulood* [The escape of Estonians to the West during the Second World War. Articles and life stories], eds. T. Hallik, K. Kukk, J. Laidla, R. Reinvelt (Tartu: Korp! Filiae Patriae, 2009); Aivar Jürgenson, 'Katkestatud paigaseosed: Argentiina eestlaste laagrimälestused' [Interrupted connections to place: camp memories of Argentina's Estonians], *Acta Historica Tallinnensia*, no. 15 (2010): 121-145; Aivar Jürgenson, *Vabatahtliku ja sunniviisilise*; the subject of deportations is mostly based on the author's earlier research.

[24] Estonian National Museum correspondent's collection, ERM KV. The material used in this article has mostly been gathered from interviews about the deportations (No. 201).

[25] KM EKLA, collection 350, Estonian life stories.

Broken Families: 'Did We Have a Choice?'

For part of the population, the social restructuring of the Baltic states meant elimination, being sent into exile and assimilation into a new environment.[26] In Estonia we speak of four main deportation operations – in 1941, 1945, 1949 and 1951, and in between those years there were other deportations (up to 100 people) which in total affected about 33,000 people. The decisions regarding the deportation process were made in Moscow, with regulations issued at the level of the USSR Communist Party, Council of People's Commissars, later the Council of Ministers, or with a directive issued by the USSR People's Commissar for Internal Affairs (NKVD), which determined the categories of people to be deported. The specific decisions about exactly who was to be deported were decided by the ministries of state security and internal affairs.[27] This was an imposed situation – there was no choice about whether to go or not. If you were caught, you were taken away.

To a certain extent, however, it is possible to speak of choice, even in the context of deportation. On the one hand there were those who managed to avoid deportation, whether by chance or by actively keeping away, and on the other there were those who voluntarily decided to resettle with their families, especially in 1945 and 1949. On the basis of these individual cases, we can also speak of individual decisions and the factors that determined these decisions in the context of forced exile.

In the Soviet Union, people were usually deported with their families – the 'guilt' of one person extended to all members of the family, and this included children. In August of 1945 during the period when people of German background were being deported, it was possible for children from mixed marriages (where one parent was not German) to remain with the parent who was allowed to stay in Estonia. It was left to the family to decide whether their children would be deported for resettlement with one parent or stay in Estonia with the other parent. Family members who

---

[26]   Norman Naimark, *Stalin's Genocides* (Princeton; Oxford: Princeton University Press, 2010), 88–98.

[27]   Aigi Rahi-Tamm, 'Küüditamised Eestis' [Deportations in Estonia] –*Kõige taga oli hirm* [Fear was behind everything], eds. S. Oksanen and I. Paju (Tallinn: Eesti Päevaleht, 2010), 63–94.

wished to voluntarily follow their family had to submit an application, which effectively meant an application to be deported. The instructions for carrying out a deportation operation included a secret note in the voluntary category, according to which the operative was to recommend that the whole family be resettled. The deportees were told that this would ensure better conditions for the family and the volunteer members of the family were also promised employment in their profession. These were empty promises because at the place of resettlement the volunteer was on equal footing with the other deportees and was registered in the same manner as people sent for resettlement. At this point we should also mention the people who went to Siberia voluntarily during the deportation operation in 1949 and later – for whom the deciding factor was to bear their fate together as a family, and who on arrival as special resettlers were also registered as deportees.

Õie's wedding day (2 April) was spent in a cattle car. For the love of her, her groom Ants, a free man, followed Õie to Siberia in the autumn to share her fate and raise a family.[28]

It is also intriguing to follow the stories of people who probably could have stayed in Estonia yet did not make use of their opportunities for avoiding or escaping deportation.[29] Here again the desire for the family to stay together and a sense of responsibility proved stronger.

'I too had the opportunity to escape deportation, but how could I send my mother and sister to an unknown fate and remain (in Estonia) as a forest brother', asks Uudo Suurtee, who was a 17-year-old schoolboy at the time.[30] This explanation is a common one.

At Jõgeva station, I could have left; I walked on the platform; I went to the shop. I had no money and nowhere to go. I was the oldest child in our fam-

---

[28]   ERM KV, Astrid Usin.

[29]   On avoiding deportation see Aigi Rahi, *1949. aasta märtsiküüditamine Tartu linnas ja maakonnas* [The deportation of March, 1949 in the city and county of Tartu] (Tartu: Kleio, 1998), 57-61.

[30]   ERM KV, Uudo Suurtee.

ily. My mother's health was poor. In Siberia, I was the breadwinner. If I had stayed in Estonia, my family would have died of hunger.[31]

In 1949 at the time of the March deportation, when rumours about the deportations spread quickly from region to region, many families remained at home because they were worried about their farm animals. And many who had gone into hiding soon returned home because their farming spirit would not allow their animals to starve or the cows to suffer from not being milked. But there were also those who allowed themselves to be deported in the fear that sooner or later they would be deported anyway and separately from their families; a shared fate is easier to bear.

In June of 1941, there was a raid. Our father resisted, and our family was able to escape. We hid in the woods until the Germans arrived. Now in the spring 1949, we didn't especially keep out of the way; the times were harsh.[32]

No one knew what would happen after the end of the deportation operations; would the people who had not been deported be subjected to follow-up deportations?[33] There were rumours that close to 90% of Estonians would be end up being deported.[34] For the authorities the issue of people who had not been deported remained a relevant subject until 1953. Erich Kõlar, who had been on the deportation list in 1941 but had at that time escaped, was arrested in 1950 when he was on tour as the conductor of the Philharmonic Variety Orchestra and sent into exile. His wife, Leelo Kõlar, whose father Riho Päts, a composer and choirmaster, was also arrested on 1 March 1950, decided to follow her husband with her one-year-old daughter to Kirov.

---

[31] Rahi, *1949. aasta märtsiküüditamine*, 51.

[32] ERM KV, Maie Kuusik (Kaldvee).

[33] Unlike Lithuania, where families that had avoided the March deportation were captured between 10–20 April and 2,927 people were taken away, there were no follow up deportations in Estonia in 1949, Arvydas Anušauskas, 'Soviet genocide and its consequences', *Lithuanian Historical Studies*, no. 4 (1999): 325.

[34] See article in this volume: H. Tammela, Rumours of impending deportations as a phenomenon pertaining to the history of mentalities.

...I was in Estonia in a stupid situation as an unskilled worker, outcast and hated, so I thought I'd go there too; at least our family would be together.[35]

People continued to fear deportation for decades and ready-packed suitcases stood in the corner of the room, just in case, until as late as the 1960s.

Recalling the deportations was a pivotal point in people's lives that brought back memories of other fateful moments when they had to assess their options in a matter of minutes. In this way the stories of the deportees also reveal the choices and assessments made during the Great Flight of 1944.

When the situation became critical again in 1944 and the Red Army started advancing, father also decided escape across the sea. Port of Salmistu was not far (7 km) and many people left from there (my sister's family included). But Hilda (mother) was against it. Firstly, she was afraid of water, especially the sea in autumn and secondly, she had small children, whose lives she did not want to endanger. So father gave up the idea, even though he had already reserved places on the boat. At that time there were also instances where people escaped without their family, but in this family that was not an option. So that is how I was taken to meet a different fate.[36]

In this example the emphasis is also on the desire to keep the family together and the sense of responsibility towards other family members. No matter how uncertain the future, it seemed that leaving home was an insurmountable task for many people.

I remember that it was night and we were travelling somewhere. Bright, clear stars shone in the sky. But by the morning we were home again. Our mother woke us up and she was crying. She was sorry to leave, we came back.[37]

---

[35]   Märt Kraav's interview with Leelo Kõlar, December 1997, http://www.temuki. ee/arhiiv/arhiiv_vana/ Muusika/0029.htm, 18 June 2011.

[36]   ERM KV, Hilda Sits.

[37]   Rahi, *1949. aasta märtsiküüditamine*, 46.

No doubt their mother hoped that the story about the deportations was just another one of many other rumours, and she turned back; they had to leave their home nevertheless.

Our father had a small motorboat ready at Käsmu, another family was in the boat with their luggage. [...] My brother Väino (born 1936) wasn't with us. He had been taken to our grandfather's in Tartu. Our father planned to go to Sweden by boat. Then some men came, there were about four of five of them. To mark the occasion, the men started drinking vodka until they decided not to go. They thought that they hadn't done anything wrong, each would go back to his own home. They were in their own country after all, what could they do anyway, these foreigners? But they did, and my father was arrested in December of 1944, [...] he died in 1948.[38]

Home had a hold on people – it provided a sense of security; the need for one's own home is an inseparable part of human nature and in essence very meaningful. The home has been attributed with social, psychological and emotional significance.[39] Home is where children are given all that we collectively call culture.[40] Aivar Jürgenson has analysed the motives of Estonians for leaving their homeland and he indicates a weakening of the home as a safe space and the sense of connection to place as a result of the events of World War II.[41] Tiiu Jaago has drawn attention to the continuing urbanisation in the 1930s, demographic behaviour and changes in family structure as a by-product or a weakening of intergenerational relations, which is clearly visible in Estonian stories of family traditions, where one's actions are no longer measured via those of one's family. The storytellers are no longer tied to their ancestors by a common home (farm) but home

---

[38]   KM EKLA, f. 350, 2358.

[39]   Tiina Peil, 'Kodu maastikus' [Home in the Landscape], *Vikerkaar*, no. 7/8 (2008): 146-147; for the effects of losing one's childhood home, changes in the experience of home and the lessening of the concept of home as a result of the critical events of 1940, see Katrin Paadam, *Constructing the Residence as Home: Homeowners and their Housing Histories*, Tallinn Pedagogical University. Social Science dissertations, 6, (Tallinn: Tallinn Pedagogical University, 2003), 119-140.

[40]   Katus, Puur and Põldma, *Eesti põlvkondlik rahvastikuareng*, 76.

[41]   Jürgenson, 'Vabatahtliku ja sunniviisilise', 111-114.

is more connected with oneself and one's individual identity.[42] The pain of leaving home and homeland (departing from stability) is expressed in the words of both refugees and deportees.[43] In the latter case it was unavoidable; refugees have over a long period of time had to come to terms with their drastic decision to leave their homes. To this day, this has remained part of the discussions about the Great Flight.[44]

Inevitably there have been a plethora of opinions that have accompanied the topic of escape. Those people who remained in Estonia have mixed feelings – a split stance, which has mostly been formed by their later life experiences and contact between local Estonians and expatriate Estonians, whose lives, compared with those lived in ESSR conditions, were considerably better.[45] There have been some very harsh viewpoints,

My father was a senior executive at Estonian Railways. He did not try to escape and persuaded his relatives to stay in Estonia. He was a volunteer in the War of Independence. To whom are we betraying our homeland? He despised those who fled in panic.[46]

This reveals a strongly encoded attitude that an unsuccessful attempt to escape was a positive outcome as far as the future of the Estonian people was concerned.[47]

---

[42]   Tiiu Jaago, 'Perepärimus ajaloo peegeldajana. Eesti materjali põhjal mõningate viidetega naabrite pärimusele' [Family tradition as a mirror of history. Based on Estonian material with some references to the traditions of neighbouring peoples] – *Pärimuslik ajalugu*, ed. T. Jaago (Tartu: University of Tartu Press, 2001), 264-280.

[43]   Maruta Pranka, 'Migratsioon *versus* kodu: vaateid ühele uurimisprojektile' [Migration versus home: views of one research project], *Mäetagused*, no. 43, (2009): 85-104.

[44]   Kaja Kumer-Haukanõmm, 'Teise maailmasõjaaegne eestlaste sundmigratsioon läände' [The forced migration of Estonians to the West at the time of the Second World War], *Acta Historica Tallinnensia*, no. 17 (2011): 95–110.

[45]   Rein Taagepera, 'Väliseestlus võrdlevas raamistikus' [The spirit of expatriate Estonians in a comparative framework], *Möte. Eesti Päevalehe ühiskondlikpoliitiline ajakiri*, 3 July 2007.

[46]   ERM KV, Arvo Puurand.

[47]   For more see the biographical interview *Sügis 1944* (Autumn 1944) conducted according to Merle Karusoo's method in: *Rändlindude pesad*, 662.

According to deportees, another aspect is discernible regarding escape. In 1949, compromising material was reputedly gathered about the people who were to be deported, which also included evidence about family members who had escaped from Estonia (mostly obtained from the Border Guard Department of Counterespionage) which was also the main evidence for the category of 'emigrated nationalists'.[48]

I was born in Andi village, Emmaste Rural Municipality in Hiiumaa. We worked on our farm – my father, mother, my three brothers and me. Our mother died in 1941 and my brothers managed to avoid being mobilised – they didn't join the Russian or German army. In 1944, my father and all three brothers fled to Sweden. I was left alone. I did the farm work. I satisfied all the quotas that were required, even the forestry quotas. [...] And then the 1949 deportation came. It was not until two years after I had been deported that I was read out the charge against me – I was guilty because my brothers had escaped abroad! [49]

A few people say that their escaped relatives were the direct reason for why they were deported. People mostly see the connection between the two events and the inevitable consequences that resulted.

It was on my 18th birthday that my uncle Rudolf, his wife and five children, and my grandmother Mari Tursk were deported to Siberia. My grandmother was supposed to go to Sweden in the autumn of 1944 ahead of the Russian invasion with her other son but she came back from the coast on her own. She asked who would make an old person like her go to Siberia. She went to live with Ruudi, her other son. [...] in 1949 the decision against my grandmother was read out to her – "Her sons' bad attitude towards the Soviet authorities" (two of her sons left for Sweden in 1944). [50]

---

[48]   Andres Kahar, 'Kuidas toimus väljasaadetavate kindlaksmääramine?' [How did the ascertainment of deportees take place?] – *Uuemaid aspekte märtsiküüditamise uurimisest*, eds. O. Liivik, H. Tammela, Varia Historica, IV (Tallinn: Estonian History Museum, 2009), 44–47.

[49]   ERM KV, Helje Metsalo.

[50]   ERM KV, Alja Saster. Mari Tursk, born in 1873, died in 1954 in Novosibirsk oblast, Tatarsk region.

It is only with great difficulty that we can nowadays reconstruct in detail situations that required people to come up with quick solutions. Many spontaneous decisions, influenced by the situation of the moment, have acquired meaning after reflection and discussion. The decisions were influenced by both personal characteristics and values,[51] as well as the opportunities presented by the overall situation, which some made use of and others did not.

The nature of the family relationships between those who remained in Estonia and those who left is an important question in the context of refugees and deportees, and one which emerges especially acutely in the descriptions of the separation of mothers and their children.

Maimo left when the German forces left and she said she was going to look for Toivo's father. [...] So she went to Germany and Toivo was left with us. He was something like a few months younger than a year.[52]

If any member of the family managed to stay behind during the deportations, it was the children as a rule, but there were also situations where small children ended up in Siberia on their own or with their grandparents. Not all mothers followed their deported children. This separation left wounds that have not healed even today.

[On my way back from Siberia] when I finally stepped onto the platform at Tartu railway station and stopped to wait there, a strange woman came up to me – it was my mother.[53]

In 1944 the decision to flee was complicated – one part of the family wanted to stay home, others wanted to leave – and on top of this there was great uncertainty.

But on Monday morning, 18 September, I received a phone call, "Aino, you are not needed at work at all at the moment. Take your son and go. One

---

[51] The unending process of understanding human values is referred to by Milton Rokeach, *Understanding Human Values. Individual and Societal* (New York: Free Press; London: Collier Macmillan, 1979), 1.

[52] KM EKLA, f. 350, 2330.

[53] Tartumaa County March deportations questionnaire answers No. 274 (in possession of the author).

day Estonia will need your son more." And to this day I don't know who
that was. I went on foot from Nõmme to Vastla to get my mother, sister
and son. I walked all through the night and we set off straight away. It was
heart-breaking how my son (born in 1940) did not want to leave. I begged
my father to come with us but he said he couldn't leave his household just
like that and said he would come later. He was killed in November of 1944.
[...] If we had known about the battle that the young Estonian soldiers waged
near Porkuni that day maybe we wouldn't have left...[54]

There were those for whom the determining factor was sharing their fate
as a family, while there were others who intentionally parted company – a
hidden aspect that stories in Tiina Kirss' *Rändlindude pesad* (*The Nests of
Migrating Birds*) reveal.[55] Here I recall the story of a pregnant woman who
was taken to Siberia because she was a family member of a 'public enemy'.
The rest of her family, her in-laws and their sons, managed to avoid deportation. The woman's mother could not bear to leave her daughter alone
in this situation and voluntarily went with her daughter. The husband
remained in Estonia, where he soon started a new family.[56]

Even though most families tried to help family members who had been
sent to camps or into exile – parcels were sent, they wrote letters and if
possible, they even visited them – the years spent apart changed people,
so the alienation after years of harsh suffering nevertheless ended in separation.[57] Miralda, whose husband was released by way of an amnesty in
1956, confessed that she could not find anything in common with her
husband.

---

[54]   KM EKLA, f. 350, 1573. Aino's husband, airman Second Lieutenant Martin
Terts, died on 13 July 1941 in an exchange of fire with units of the Soviet Border
Guard. On 27 June the Estonian Rifle Corps Air Squadron received an order to
evacuate to Soviet Russia, whereupon a number of the men fled into the woods.
Mass round-ups were organised to capture them.

[55]   *Rändlindude pesad*, 634-642.

[56]   Tartumaa County March deportations questionnaire answers No. 119 (in
possession of the author).

[57]   According to demographers, the causes for the high rate of marriage fail-
ures among those born in 1924–1928 lie in the years of war and terror, which
along with other horrors also destroyed families: Katus, Puur and Põldma, *Eesti
põlvkondlik rahvastikuareng*, 131.

When I think back on life, then I cannot understand how our family, so as-
piring, modest, honest and close, fell apart without any real reason, without
any effort, it just faded away, it didn't come to anything – as if it had never
existed. The war? Wrong choices?[58]
In the post-war years, the marriages of many men returning from the war
fell apart.[59]

It is difficult for these broken families to talk about this and other
'shadows', so they often remain invisible behind a wall of silence. Delicate
topics require a sensitive approach and the silence is understandable.[60]
And indeed, the shadowy aspects of life are an important component in
comprehending the times and the situations. Broken families are without
doubt one of the most painful outcomes that hit Estonian society in those
critical times.

Journey into the Unknown

There were many factors that shaped the lives of people who suddenly
found themselves in unfamiliar circumstances. As the operative group
entered the home they first conducted a search, identified the people who
were there and informed them of the deportation order, and then the people to be deported were ordered to pack their things. The time for this was
relatively short, ranging from a few minutes to an hour. There were also
those who were grabbed off the street. The amount of belongings and the
selection determined how well people managed in the early days. Here the

---

[58]   KM EKLA, f. 350, 462; for opportunities and impediments in the reunifica-
tion of families after imprisonment, see Nancy Adler, *The Gulag Survivor: Beyond
the Soviet System* (New Brunswick: Transaction Publishers, 2004), 139-146; for
family relations in men's biographies and for one arrested man's fight to keep his
family together, see Terje Anepaio, 'Heinrich Uustalu – between the cogwheels:
stigmatised family relations in the life story of a repressed man' –*Soldiers of
Memory. World War II and its Aftermath in Estonian Post-Soviet Life Stories*, ed.
E. Kõresaar (Amsterdam: Rodopi, 2011), 385-408.

[59]   Hester Vaizey, *Surving Hitler's War. Family Life in Germany, 1939-48* (Chip-
penham: CPI Antony Rowe, 2010), 98-101.

[60]   *Rändlindude pesad*, 642; Aigi Rahi-Tamm, 'Our untold stories: remembering
the Soviet time from a historian's viewpoint' – *Cultural Patterns and Life Stories*,
eds. K. Jõesalu and A. Kannike (Tallinn: Acta Universitatis Tallinnensis, Tallinn
University Press, 2016), 77–103.

difference between those deported before the war and after is noticeable. Each family deported in 1941 was only allowed to take 100 kilograms with them, and this constituted the minimum. In 1945 one tonne was permitted and in 1949 1.5 tonnes, but it is not known whether anyone succeeded in taking such amounts of luggage. The things they took with them helped people to stay alive in Siberia and they were exchanged for food with the locals. The deportees did not have fishing or hunting equipment and the freedom of movement necessary for obtaining extra food. The parcels and money sent from home were a big help and one that people deported in 1941 could not yet hope for.

For refugees the decision to set out was often also made in a very short amount of time. Of course, there were those who were thoroughly prepared for the journey, so alongside bare calves, summer dresses, a threadbare coat and feet stuffed into broken galoshes one might meet a lady with 15 suitcases of mink coats. The latter is undoubtedly the exception.[61] However it was also possible to lose these things very easily, especially when journeying on the roads in Germany, because of the war, difficulty in travelling (transport was provided for people, but with a minimum of luggage) and constant theft.

We certainly need to note the dangers that beset the refugees on their journey – stormy seas, poor vehicles and transportation, and attacks by Soviet and German aeroplanes and ships.[62] Like the trains that took people East, death threatened those that moved West by sea or land. It is just as disconsolate to read about the scenes on the beach at Gotland (small children dead from fatigue, bodies of drowning victims and people killed by bombs or in shipwrecks)[63] as it is to read the descriptions of the lorries and cattle cars overloaded with deportees, the corpses left by the road,

---

[61]   Raimo Raag, 'Eesti sõjapõgenike saabumine Ojamaale 1944. aasta sügisel kohaliku ajakirjanduse kajastuses' [The arrival of Estonian war refugees at Gotland in the autumn of 1944 as reported by the local press] – *Suur põgenemine 1944*, 93.

[62]   See also Captain Julius Laasi's description of escape and the attitude of German authorities towards escape: Kaja Kumer-Haukanõmm, 'Julius Laasi mälestusi 1944. aasta põgenemisest' [Julius Laasi's memories of his escape in 1944], *Tuna*, no. 3 (2009): 95-100.

[63]   Raag, 'Eesti sõjapõgenike saabumine', 88-90; see also: *Põgenemine kodumaalt 1943-1944*, ed. U. Eelmäe, *Harjumaa uurimusi*, 7 (Keila: Harju County Museum, 2005).

the distressed elderly, suffering infants and the sick, who in some cases were forcibly loaded onto the lorries by the operatives just so they could satisfy their quotas. Extraordinary cases intensified the already oppressive atmosphere and added to the general feeling of uncertainty. The deportees were not told of their destination, and the greatest fear was that children would be separated from their parents. On the one hand, it was perhaps a relief to know they were not behind prison walls but among Siberian villagers. On the other hand, the ideologically prejudiced attitude of local inhabitants intended to reduce sympathy towards the arriving 'contingent' was obvious,

... for their past and current behaviour, a large number deserve far more than official exile! [64]

Despite the punishments and threats, not all the local inhabitants lacked sympathy and courage to help those in need and they shared their food and shelter.

A leap into the unknown – this is how the start of the journey for many refugees should be described. They set off without knowing where or for how long.

My parents found someone, a family, to look after our farm. They were going to live there until the Russians were thrown out and we returned home. Most people who escaped to the West thought in the same way, that the time away from home was only temporary. [...] My father was convinced that the Western allies would not allow a new Russian occupation, that the invasion was temporary, recalls Eevi Tamm.

At the end of the war, her family was in Germany in the Soviet zone and they were sent back home via Poland and Ukraine.

...all I remember about this trip was arriving at Valga station. I read and re-read the name on the station building. Are we really back? It was a very

---

[64] Excerpts from the AUCP(B) Narym District Committee report to AUCP(B) Novosibirsk oblast Committee Secretary Kulagin about the reception of deportees, 19 July 1941 – Vadim Makšejev, *Narõmi kroonika 1930–1945. Küüditatute tragöödia. Dokumendid ja mälestused* [Narym Chronicle 1930–1945. The tragedy of the deportees. Documents and memoirs] (Tallinn: Varrak, 2011), 134.

special feeling. [...] It was autumn 1945. I was eleven years old. But I felt I had left my childhood behind.[65]

Very few returned to Estonia. Most people did their best to reach the US or British zones.

Even though most people who were trying to escape preferred neutral Sweden, some people who had started their journey had to go to Germany instead at the last minute. There they had to overcome the ordeals that were the lot of all homeless people. First, they went to a transit camp, where they had to give notice of their destination. There the refugees were also given food stamps for the days ahead. To avoid being sent to work camps or to work somewhere against their will, many people randomly said the name of a place without knowing if that place had work or a place for them to live. There was quite a large number of people who continued to travel around Germany on their own, stopping every now and again at some transit camp.[66]

From Gotenhafen harbour we were taken on to Berlin, where there was a distribution station. Finally, we reached the Sudetenland, and there were small villages there. At first, we were housed in a large hall in a schoolhouse and later separately as families in houses in the villages. There were coal mines close by, which were constantly being bombed. [...] One morning one of our German neighbours tapped on the window and told us that Hitler had died. Once again, the rumble of war sounded closer and closer. Our small community of Estonians set off towards the West. [...] But then on the road passing through a village we fell behind the rest of the group [...] and so together with my mother and sister we ended up in the midst of great confusion, [...] at some point the Russian army caught up with us. We were very afraid. We stopped in some village in a private house with a German woman. It was especially terrifying at night when you could often hear women's cries for help. It was said that doors should never be locked. And one night a Russian officer came into our room with his batman. Fortunately, the batman was so tired that he fell asleep immediately. The officer

---

[65]   KM EKLA, f. 350, 1802.

[66]   Erich Ernits, 'Põgenikud sõjajärgsel Saksamaal' (Refugees in post-war Germany) – *Eesti saatusaastad 1945–1960* [Estonia's fateful years 1945–1960], IV, eds. R. Maasing et al. (Stockholm: EMP, 1966), 9.

started harassing the German woman. But her daughter was so tough that she started to bite the officer. This officer was not so violent after all and that time it ended well. [...] In the autumn of 1944 at the same time that we were travelling to Germany, my aunt with her family managed to sail to Sweden in a boat.[67]

The end of the war brought changes but did not mark the start of peace. The millions of civilians who were on the move in fear of the invading Red Army were now concentrated into refugee camps, where fear of bombing raids and the advancing Red army was replaced by the fear of being forcibly repatriated.[68]

In Siberia they also hoped for the end of the war,

It was believed that when the war ended, death and fear would also come to an end, that cruelty would be replaced by compassion. Soldiers would come back from the front, those held in concentration camps and resettlers would be allowed to go home. During the four years of the war, nearly every second person in each "new contingent" sent to the Vasyugan region died. In some families everyone died. [...] But days went by, months went by and hope faded. Everything remained as it had been during the war – the "clean", the "unclean", the "kulaks", a "new contingent". The spring of 1945 did not become the spring of compassion.[69]

At the same time, new reprisals gained momentum in Estonia and thousands more people were sent into exile and imprisonment.

---

[67]   KM EKLA, f. 350, 1737.

[68]   Jürgenson, 'Katkestatud paigaseosed', 125-126, 130-131; for fears in Baltic refugee camps, see Thomas Balkelis, 'Living in the displaced persons camp: Lithuanian war refugees in the West, 1944-45' – *Warlands: Population Resettlement*, 28-31.

[69]   Makšejev, *Narōmi kroonika*, 226.

Reception of Foreigners

The immense flood of refugees produced by the war sorely tested the attitudes of Westerners. Refugees that reached Germany faced many years of moving from one place to the next (which at times took the form of panicky flight from the Red Army), until refugee policy became more clearly defined.

The reception of refugees in Sweden was organised differently. Refugees were received at the border by military personnel. A customs check was carried out at assembly points, where individuals were also registered, questioned, fed and medically examined, after which they were given a full sauna and provided with clothing. After a two-week quarantine period (the Swedes feared diphtheria and typhoid), the refugees were taken to more permanent camps,[70] which existed until the autumn of 1945 – unlike Germany, where the camp period for some refugees continued until 1951.

Mass migration has always been accompanied by problems, which could be more difficult or less so depending on the country in question. Estonians have recalled the Swedes and Sweden with a sense of gratitude. Preparations were made early in Sweden for receiving, housing and feeding the refugees (upon arrival they were offered cocoa and sandwiches), and integrating them into the local economy. Money was raised to help the refugees, donations of clothing, shoes and other such things were collected, Gotlanders gave the children fruit to improve their vitamin intake and then in October they started to pay them pocket money of 2 kroner a week.[71] However, there were complaints about the poor living conditions, lack of privacy and poor camp food in the Swedish camps,[72] and the attitudes of the locals is also mentioned in the memoirs. Nevertheless, the integration of refugees into everyday life in Sweden occurred more rapidly than in other places. Attempts were made to disperse them quickly, offer-

---

[70]   Raag, *Suur põgenemine 1944*, 176.

[71]   Raimo Raag, 'Eestlaste põgenemine Rootsi Teise maailmasõja ajal' [The escape of Estonians to Sweden during the Second World War] – *Eestlaste põgenemine Läände*, 59–62; Raag, 'Eesti sõjapõgenike saabumine', 94–104; Edgar Saar, 'Põgenemine Rootsi 1944. aasta hilissuvel ja sügisel' [Escaping to Sweden in the late summer and autumn of 1944], *Tuna*, no. 3 (2004): 65–78.

[72]   Jürgenson, 'Katkestatud paigaseosed', 123–124.

ing them work away from the big cities in small towns and settlements, in industry and agriculture (initially they were forbidden from staying in Stockholm, Gothenburg or Malmö). As work opportunities and language ability improved, the refugees increasingly started gathering in the larger centres, where there were more opportunities for meeting with other Estonians.[73] For most people who have lost their homeland, relating to their compatriots has been a determining necessity in creating at least some form of stability.[74]

Compared to Sweden, living conditions in the German camps and the opportunities for getting away from them were much worse. The overcrowded camps lacked privacy. Many people lived in barracks, storehouses, factories, and even former concentration camps, where sheets and blankets served as partition walls. These conditions are comparable to life in Soviet kolkhozes, where everything had to be public and visible for all to see. This increased tension between people and made life there relatively wearisome.[75] In Germany, it seems Estonians tended to trust the British zone more, hoping that the British would understand the Baltic situation better and that their attitude towards the Balts would be more favourable.[76] Although Great Britain was the first country to accept refugees, the prevailing attitude there towards the immigrants as a lower class did not tempt Estonians to settle there.[77]

---

[73] Raimo Raag, *Eestlane väljaspool Eestit. Ajalooline ülevaade* [Estonians outside of Estonia. A historical overview] (Tartu: University of Tartu Press, 1999), 70.

[74] Jürgenson, 'Katkestatud paigaseosed', 132-144; Tiina Kirss has stressed that Estonians who escaped to the West identified themselves as fellow sufferers right from the start, even though there were sometimes many differences of opinion. They started establishing their community at the very beginning, initially for gathering practical information to help them survive, to find relatives, entertainment and comfort. Later they started to identify themselves as part of the broader political community of refugees. A personal sense of being while living abroad was shaped by a community sense of belonging: *Rändlindude pesad*, 626. Balkelis, 'Living in the displaced', 32-35.

[75] *Ibid.*, 32-35.

[76] Ferdinand Kool, *DP kroonika. Eesti pagulased Saksamaal 1944–1951* [Displaced persons chronicales. Estonian expatriates in Germany in 1944 – 1951] (Lakewood: Estonian Archives in the U.S., 1999), 52.

[77] Kumer-Haukanõmm, *Eestlaste põgenemine Saksamaale*, 34.

The poor economic situation made the refugees a cheap source of labour. They were mostly used for heavy physical work in mines, industry, agriculture and in hospitals, which favoured young, fit, unskilled workers without families. Liberalisation of immigration laws providing opportunities for families and unemployable people did not occur until 1948.[78] Refugees regard the selection process for hiring labour to be one of the most humiliating experiences and one which made them fully aware of their inferior status. This is where the notion of 'slave market' comes into the refugees' stories,[79] which for Estonian readers is familiar mostly from the memoirs of deportees.

Then the local farmers came to select their day labourers. All the capable workers were lined up in front of the barracks – the local farmers came with their horse and cart, scrutinising the line as they selected suitable day labourers – they poked them in the stomach with their whip and the worker had climb onto the cart and was driven to some field somewhere.[80]

No doubt this kind of arrogant behaviour caused discontent, especially when compared to the person's previous life and work experience. Their 'value' was determined merely by their physical strength, and their education and intellectual ability could be nothing more than a hindrance. However, the 'slave market' described by the people who fled to the West and by those who had been deported are not comparable, even though presenting such texts in parallel might suggest that they are. Upon arrival, the deportees were met at the station by representatives of the sovkhozes and kolkhozes.

...they walked back and forth in the rooms carrying long bullock whips and wearing fur coats familiarising themselves with the goods. The directors traded or competed for the younger ones.[81]

---

[78] *Ibid*, 50; further migration to the USA, Canada, Australia etc. has symbolic meaning in the lives of refugees: Jürgenson, 'Katkestatud paigaseosed', 139.

[79] Aivar Jürgenson has also referred to the accusation by Eastern Bloc countries that Western countries were using refugee camps as a slave market: Jürgenson, 'Katkestatud paigaseosed', 137.

[80] *Ibid.*, 124.

[81] ERM KV, Helle Viir.

We were herded with all our luggage into a large room where the slave market began. There is no other way to describe this procedure. They were like gypsies at a horse market – looking into your mouth and patting you. No compassionate glances at the weak or infirm – they are unnecessary ballast. They wanted young, strong labourers. Builders and technicians were in demand – drivers, tractor drivers, blacksmiths and so on. No one needed a "bookworm", a useless good-for-nothing like me. The only reason I had any value was because I was young, big and strong. The women were ogled quite lecherously until it became clear that they had two or three children in tow and then even the boss's glance became quite harsh.[82]

But women with children and the elderly had to be accommodated somewhere. This collection of deportees was clearly a disappointment for the local leaders.

No one wanted single women with children. I awaited my fate together with two women from our truck – Vaike and Helmi. Vaike had given birth to a son in May and Helmi in the autumn. Evening fell. It was clear that we would have to sleep the night right there under the open sky. So, we three women put our possessions together. We made a bed for the children on the bags. They rested there.[83]

These are excerpts describing how the deportees were received in Siberia in April of 1949. They had no options to choose from, no opportunities to seek better employment or places to live. It was good if one could get any work to all to be able to feed oneself and one's family. Eleonore Kivi, who was deported in 1941, recalls her employment options in the following way,

We worked the whole summer at the bridge and filled the dam with soil. [...] We got bread from the shop on the basis of a list of names. In the beginning I got 1.2 kg of bread – 400 g for my daughter (born 1940) and 800 g for myself. In October, most of us were sent to the forest to do logging work. Only those with small children stayed in the village. I wasn't able to do much work in the summer. In mid-July, my daughter got sick once again. She had

---

[82]   *Ibid.*, Uudo Suurtee.

[83]   *Ibid.*, Helmi Übius.

stomach problems and the nursery would not take her. [...] The wind was piercing, and it was minus 20 degrees. My feet were cold and I didn't have any work clothes. Then one Sunday I went to the market and bought myself some birch bark shoes and toerags. I had a pair of men's woollen socks with me. In this way I was able to get warm footwear for myself. It was strange to go around wearing a coat with a silver fox collar and birch bark shoes. [...] We got bread from the factory shop. While we sawed wood, the bread quota was 600 g and 400 g for children. The bread was not pure rye. It also contained unpeeled potatoes and coarse oat and barley flour. We were able to saw wood until 10 November. One day we were told there would be no more work for us. We had to find work for ourselves. I sold my skirt, blouse and dress. I bought potatoes from the market and worked out how long they would last if I ate two potatoes a day.[84]

In 1941, the local leaders in the oblasts of Siberia did not regard the living and working conditions of the deportees as their responsibility. They thought that it was the task of the security officials. The recollections of the deportees confirm the attitude of the authorities,

...we were sent here not to live but to die.[85]

It was not until the spring of 1944 that a separate department for deportees began to take responsibility for the employment of these exiles. In comparison to the previous account by Eleonore, the complaint by the refugees in Sweden that the camp food and living conditions were poor and the food monotonous seems outright inappropriate.[86] In comparing the situations we need to point out possible dangers – we must not forget the context and we must not give accounts at the individual level the power of generalisation.[87] Many researchers of identity and memory have identified how people reconstruct their stories based on different experi-

---

[84] Eleonore Kivi's memoirs. Manuscript in possession of the author.

[85] Makšejev, *Narōmi kroonika*, 163.

[86] Jürgenson, 'Katkestatud paigaseosed', 124, 128-129.

[87] Alun Munslow, *Narrative and History* (Basingstroke, New York: Palgrave Macmillan, 2007), 101-102.

ences and how these are constantly changing.[88] When discussing specific events the person compares them with better and worse times, and during their lifetime they can re-think the same event.

Siberian village life was a true shock for Estonians. The poverty, and the living and working conditions were so unfamiliar, compared to Estonia, that some people were driven to the edge of despair. The mental and physical fatigue caused by the way they were treated made them susceptible to illness and this is clearly evident in the high death rate of those deported in June of 1941 (approximately 60% of deportees died). The situation of the deportees started to improve to some extent in 1946. According to accounts from deportees, improvement in conditions began in 1951. In the latter half of 1949, it can be seen how the central authorities more forcibly pushed the responsibility for the working and living conditions of the deportees onto the shoulders of the local oblast authorities by threatening the managements of the kolkhozes and sovkhozes that lagged behind that if they did not improve conditions, the deportees would be relocated somewhere else.[89] The better kolkhozes and sovkhozes were promised that they would be supplied with a new 'contingent'. For example in the winter of 1949–1950, the leaders of the Omsk oblast were given hope that they would receive new deportees from Latvia.[90]

As general conditions improved, we must not overlook the struggles of specific groups, for example single elderly persons, disabled persons and mothers with small children,[91] because their lives could continue

---

[88]   Stuart Hall, 'Who needs identity?' – *Identity: A Reader*, eds. P. du Gay, J. Evans and P. Redman (London: Thousand Oaks, 2003), 15-19; Vieda Skultans, *The Testimony of Lives: Narrative and Memory in Post-Soviet Latvia* (London: Routledge, 1998); Ene Kõresaar, 'Elu ideoloogiad' [Life ideologies], – Estonian National Museum series, 6 (Tartu: Estonian National Museum, 2005), 8-16; *Rändlindude pesad*, 623-624.

[89]   Centre for Documentation of Contemporary History of Omsk Oblast, f. 955, o. 9, d. 5, 9-10.

[90]   State Archive of the Russian Federation (GARF), f. R-9479, o. 1, d. 464, 91p. Nevertheless, a new deportation in Latvia did not take place, but people were continually brought from Lithuania until 1952.

[91]   Mara Lazda, 'Women, nation and survival: Latvian women in Siberia', *Journal of Baltic Studies*, no. 1 (2005): 1-12; Tiina Kirss, 'Survivorship and the Eastern exile: Estonian women's life narratives of the 1941 and 1949 Siberian deportations', *Journal of Baltic Studies*, no. 1 (2005): 13-38.

to be just as difficult in the later period. A fair number of deportees lived in conditions that made the lives of people sent to prison camps appear more bearable.

...that girl who ran away writes and is quite satisfied with her life there in the camp. They have no shortage of food and their clothes are fine and they even get a wage. She is more worried about us here, us exiles.[92]

The deportees had to find accommodation and a job on their own to take care that they earned their living. In the camps, food was distributed on a quota basis (the quantity of food was determined by the amount of work done). When reading the memoirs of deportees, we inevitably reach the conclusion that even though these people were all sent to suffer, the conditions and people's opportunities differed. The same applies to refugees. Certainly, the struggles were not easy for single women, who set out on their journey alone with children and had to establish themselves in new situations – work was physically draining and poorly paid, they had little time for their children and little hope of a better life. That these women had to be both strong and brave is the conclusion of Anu-Mai Kõll, based on a survey of how Estonian women managed in Sweden in 1953.[93] World War II and the reorganisation of society changed the role of women in the community, making many of them the main breadwinner and, as the head of the family, responsible for taking care of everyone.[94]

In retrospect, the way Estonians were received abroad can be assessed through various factors. General descriptions of the way people managed and of the living and working conditions in the region are interwoven, while on the other hand, the contacts at the level of single individuals are clearly discernible. The situation in terms of prejudice is the most com-

---

[92]   Deportation file of the family of Aino Tross, RA, ERAF.3-N.1.1601.

[93]   Anu-Mai Kõll, 'Eesti põgenike toimetulekust Rootsis naiste perspektiivist' [On how Estonian refugees coped in Sweden from the perspective of women], – *Eestlaste põgenemine Läände*, 82.

[94]   Katus, Puur and Põldma, *Eesti põlvkondlik rahvastikuareng*, 253; Anu Narusk, 'Eesti naised ja ratsionaalsed valikud' [Estonian women and rational choices], *Ariadne Lõng*, no. 1/2 (2000): 52; Mie Nakachi, 'Gender, marriage, and reproduction in the postwar Soviet Union' –*Writing Stalin Era. Sheila Fitzpatrick and Soviet Historiography*, eds. G. Alexopoulos, J. Hessler and K. Tolmoff (Palgrave Macmillan, 2011), 101-116; Vaizey, *Surving Hitler's War*, 150-155.

plicated. In many places, propaganda work had been done before the deportees arrived and animosity towards them had been clearly stirred up. Estonians were reviled as robbers, killers and fascists. Over time, relations with the locals improved, as a rule. Fairly soon, local people realised that they were not criminals but instead, unfortunate people. Yet attitudes at the official level, as it were, could remain hostile for a long time. Tepliakov, one of the directors of a factory in Omsk oblast, who was chastised in 1950 because he had failed to repair the factory's barracks, wrote the following in response to the report, 'I agree that it is uncomfortable for families to live in such places but, fascists that they are, they have brought much greater discomfort to the Soviet people'.[95] Compassion for the deportees was clearly an indicator of anti-Soviet views, and one could be harshly punished for this.

The label of fascist was not unfamiliar for refugees either. DPs (displaced persons) from the Baltics were constantly accused of having Nazi sympathies.[96] 'Screening' tests to determine political compatibility, the return of Latvian and Estonian soldiers who had escaped to Sweden back to the Soviet Union in 1946, and other such things are connected to the weight of suspicion on Baltic refugees, intensifying fear among the refugees that they would handed over to the Soviet Union. This unleashed a strong desire to leave Europe for some safer place that could provide better material opportunities and a more positive attitude towards refugees, places like the USA, Canada, Australia, and others.[97] The continuation journey became symbolic in itself. With this journey they left the past behind and started a new life in a new homeland that would replace Estonia.[98] Memories from this early period of exile focus mainly on descriptions of the escape, while camp-life, with its negative undertone as one of the most problematic periods in their lives, was often overshadowed by

---

[95]   GARF, f. R-9479, op. 1, d. 464, 114.

[96]   Jürgenson, 'Katkestatud paigaseosed', 129-132; Carl Göran Andrae, *Rootsi ja suur põgenemine Eestist 1943-1944* [Sweden and the Great Flight from Estonia in 1943-1944] (Tallinn: Olion, 2005), 148-166.

[97]   Over 27,000 Estonians went to overseas countries from German DP camps, up to 4,000 Estonians remained in Germany: Ernits, 'Põgenikud sõjajärgsel Saksamaal', 8-9; By end of 1952, 8,000 Estonians had left Sweden, 15,500 Estonians remained: Alur Reinans, 'Eesti põgenikud Rootsi statistikas' [Estonian refugees in Swedish statistics] – *Suur põgenemine 1944*, 144.

[98]   Jürgenson, 'Katkestatud paigaseosed', 139.

other events. Yet it is this period which would provide more extensive opportunities for comparative analysis of the experiences of people, who for
various reasons have found themselves in an unfamiliar country.

There was no escape from Siberia because the deportees were quickly
bound to their new location. While those who were deported in 1941 were
sent out for an indeterminate length of time, starting from 1948 exile
became a life sentence. This was done because the authorities wanted to
remove any hope of ever returning home and minimise the number of
escape attempts, of which there were many in 1946–1947. They made the
punishment harsher – one could be punished with up to 20 years of forced
labour for escaping or helping someone else escape. But as described in
various reports and memoirs, the hope of someday returning to Estonia
held a dominant position in the survival strategy of deportees. Even before arriving in Siberia in 1949, many of them sincerely believed that the
Western nations would not allow a new injustice to take place.

*There were rumours that America would not allow us to be taken to Siberia,
soon the lorries would turn around and we would move back home. At one
station there were lorries with a row of tanks and machine guns on them. It
was believed that the war had already begun. People believed in the "white
ship" which was going to come from America to save us.*[99]

This hope was slow to abate even later. Stories such as this – '*We wouldn't
be staying long in Siberia; no doubt America and the Western countries
would demand that Russia stop occupying the Baltic states and independence would be restored*' – were circulating even in the 1950s.[100] Reports on
the deportees indicate the special expectations of the Balts – the outbreak
of war between the Soviet Union and the British/Americans, and plans
for what to do in the event of war (escape to the taiga to organise partisan
activities).[101] Though this was utopian, it was part of the attitude of the
exiles to not surrender to the situation. They sought moral support from
those who had fled to the West, hoping that their compatriots would do
something to protect them.

---

[99] ERM KV, Ilmar Paunmaa.

[100] *Ibid.* Arne Välja.

[101] Rahi-Tamm, 'Küüditamised Eestis', 85.

Adjusting to the reality of Siberia did not take place in a uniform manner. During the first years, belief in their imminent release was so strong that people did not hasten to establish homes or acquire farm animals, clinging instead to an expectant wait-and-see position for a long time, which they later regretted when cold and hunger came. Sooner or later they inevitably reached the understanding that in Siberia, one could only rely on oneself, and that as a deportee their first priority was to do everything to stay alive.

People's actions in critical situations is certainly an important research topic, which would help us to understand the various management strategies in the context of refugees and deportees. How could apathy be overcome,[102] and what role did the help of companions and meeting with others have?[103] In Siberia, opportunities to meet other Estonians was limited and under supervisory control. How is it possible to maintain hold on one's homeland and culture when you are forced to forget it?[104] What were the behaviour patterns that reflected the Estonian identity, home and people, which each nationality took with them, whether in the East or the West?[105] There is an abundance of factors that shaped people's futures abroad, and their significance is more varied than we see when we make quick generalisations. Even though Siberia signifies suffering and pain to the deportees, they are also able to see other aspects in this period of their lives.

We each have our own Siberia, with differing emphasis. For the elderly it meant leaving their homes, declining life, away from children, support and medical aid. For what? Adults. Single mothers. What will happen, what will become of my children if I break? Will I manage? Harsh, stupid oppression – this too is unfamiliar, hard work, a foreign land – but we have

---

[102] Peter Gatrell and Nick Baron, 'Violent peacetime: reconceptualising displacement and resettlement in the Soviet-East European borderlands after the Second World War', –*Warlands: Population Resettlement*, 259.

[103] Valk and Karu-Kletter, 'Rootsi eestlaste Eesti-identiteet', 147-169.

[104] Norman Naimark, 'Ethnic cleansing between war and peace', – *Landscaping the Human Garden. Twentieth-Century Population Management in a Comparative Framework*, ed. A. Weiner (Stanford: Stanford University Press, 2003), 233-235.

[105] Anthony Smith, *The Ethnic Origins of Nations* (Oxford: Basil Blackwell, 1986), 22-24; a special subculture has developed in Siberia, which was influenced by local Siberians and the cultural heritage of various repressed peoples.

no access to their memories. It was easier for the young. They had strength, simple physical strength. Though their lives were destroyed, their education unfinished, their world restricted – but they still had the optimism of youth. Sometimes I wonder if we gained something too. Maybe we are able to differentiate between basic values and false gloss and superficiality. And maybe we know what one's own people and homeland means. Maybe we are better able to withstand the trials of today, which our generation endures, and resist them. Maybe this is not such a small thing?[106]

In Conclusion

The forcible relocation of people is varied as a topic. It conceals thousands of personal tragedies, and both those who were taken East and those who fled to the West became homeless. Though their lives unfolded in quite different ways, upon arriving in a foreign land they both stood face-to-face with similar situations and emotions such as exile, not knowing what was going on, difficulty in managing, negative attitudes, all manner of restrictions, etc. These reflect the typical processes of migration. We often use the same words when we describe the situations (of both refugees and deportees), but the deeper significance is not transferable from one category to the other.

During the last 20 years, research on deportations has been fruitful. The first deportation stories that were released from behind the wall of silence reflected freedom from Soviet prohibition – the desire to tell all, which had until now been condemned to silence. These were stories full of pain and suffering (death, disease, hunger, constant shortage of food, humiliating treatment, unjust accusations, overly difficult work in the harsh climate of Siberia, harsh living conditions). Over time other aspects began to creep into the stories – relating between themselves, education, general welfare, participation in local life, the Siberian landscape, adjusting to the situation, varied strategies for survival, coming to terms with the past (even today), etc. which were more optimistic in tone. Naturally all the readings have been affected by the specific situations that people experienced, their life experience, personality and so on.[107] An open and

---

[106] ERM KV, Helle Viir.

[107] Many migration researchers, psychologists, sociologists and others have written about the connections between the new location and people, as well as

more varied approach makes it possible to analyse the fate of forcibly deported people in different stages and situations, and in comparison with the narratives of other people who have been caught up in migration, to better understand the trials of others. The stories of deportees, refugees and those who have been in camps do not form a unified whole. Because of their background, underlying values, descriptions of life, how people coped, and their opportunities vary considerably in regard to individuals, stages, and regions.

The variety of human fates, the aftereffects of different events, the multitude of viewpoints, the variety of interpretations[108] and pluralistic ways[109] of approaching the past could inspire more involvement from contemporary, as well as future, generations. The accounts of deportees and refugees are often linked. They are the stories of broken families, one occurring in the West, the other in the East. The lives of separated people, one group in the closed-off Soviet Union, the others in the free West, and the resulting restrictions and opportunities have strongly affected our attitudes – they have caused a sense of guilt, accusations and estrangement. Sometimes lack of knowledge has been replaced by incomprehension, and unfortunately, overcoming this may be trapped in the shackles of time. Or it is time to start creating a dialogue between these separate stories?

---

the factors that affect people's values: Jürgenson, 'Vabatahtliku ja sunniviisilise', 99-100; Robin Williams Jr., 'Change and stability in values and value systems: a sociological perspective' – *Understanding Human Values*, 15-46; Vivien Burr, *The Person in Social Psychology* (Psychology Press, Taylor & Francis Group, 2002), 133-151; Jonathan Turner and Jan Stets, *The Sociology of Emotions*. (Cambridge: Cambridge University Press, 2009), 261-283; *The Self and Others. Positioning Individuals and Groups in Personal, Political, and Cultural Contexts*, eds. R. Harre and F. Moghaddam (Praeger Publishers, 2003); Aigi Rahi-Tamm, 'On the Borderline between Tears and Laughter: Changes of Tonality in the Life Histories of Estonian Deportees' – *Life Writing and Politics of Memory in Eastern Europe*, ed. S. Mitroiu (New York, Palgrave Macmillan, 2015), 144–164.

[108] Interpretation as an underestimating link does not negate the general rule in historical research in which unreliable sources and accounts about past events cannot be used: see Mart Kivimäe, 'Kirjandus ja teaduslik objektiivsus ajaloos' [Literature and scientific objectivity in history], *Sirp*, 23 September 2005.

[109] On Peter Burke's suggestion when combining alternative memories (family, locational, class and national memories, etc.), it would be useful to take a pluralistic approach: Peter Burke, *Kultuuride kohtumine. Esseid uuest kultuuriajaloost* (Tallinn: Varrak, 2006), 65.

How Was the Decision to Carry out a Joint Deportation Operation in the Soviet Baltic Republics in the Spring of 1949 Adopted in the Kremlin?: Nikolai Karotamm's Notes on his Meeting with Joseph Stalin on 18 January 1949

*Meelis Saueauk, Tõnu Tannberg**

The decision issued on 29 January 1949 by the USSR Council of Ministers names the central committees of the Lithuanian, Latvian and Estonian communist parties, and the councils of ministers of the Lithuanian, Latvian and Estonian SSR's as the initiators of the mass deportation carried out in March of 1949.[1] It is, however, extremely likely that the governments of the Soviet republics, or their central committees, did not discuss such collective initiatives or propose them to Moscow. Instead, the decision to

---

[*]   First published: Meelis Saueauk and Tõnu Tannberg, 'Kuidas võeti Kremlis vastu otsus ühise küüditamisoperatsiooni läbiviimiseks Balti liiduvabariikides 1949. aasta suvel?: Nikolai Karotamme ülestähendus kohtumisest Jossif Staliniga 18. jaanuaril 1949', *Tuna: ajalookultuuri ajakiri*, no. 3 (2014): 92–97.
[1]   USSR Council of Ministers Decision no. 390-138ss dated 29 January 1949 'Concerning the expulsion from the territory of Lithuania, Latvia and Estonia of kulaks and their families, the families of illegally residing or convicted bandits and nationalists and of those killed in armed combat, legalised bandits who continue active resistance and their families, as well as the families of those who have assisted repressed bandits' – *Eestlaste küüditamine: mineviku varjud tänases päevas: artiklid ja elulood* [The Deportation of Estonians: Shadows of the Past in the Present: Articles and Life Stories], eds. E. Andresen et al. (Tartu: FP Kinnisvara, 2004), 181.

carry out this mass deportation was made by a narrow circle of decision-makers in Moscow within the top-ranking leadership of the USSR. Karo-tamm's notes on his joint visit together with his Latvian and Lithuanian colleagues to Joseph Stalin and the leadership of the Soviet Union in January of 1949 exist as exceptional material on how the decision was made to carry out the March deportation. These notes include information on how a formal initiative was obtained from the Communist Party leaders in those Soviet republics.

Karotamm had been in Stalin's office at the Kremlin only once before in 1944.[2] They had also met at large-scale Party or state events in Moscow: during demonstrations and parades, at receptions, at sessions of the USSR Supreme Soviet, etc.[3] Thus being summoned to see Stalin was quite a special event for Karotamm. He arrived in Moscow in January of 1949 to discuss the establishment of collective farms, and he was also invited to the memorial session at the Bolshoi Theatre on 21 January commemorating the 25th anniversary of Lenin's death. Antanas Sniečkus, the First Secretary of the Lithuanian Communist Party Central Committee, and Jānis Kalnbērziņš, the First Secretary of the Latvian Communist Party Central Committee, were also invited to Moscow at the same time.

Karotamm signed a statement in Moscow on 15 January addressed to the Secretary of the All-Union Communist Party (Bolsheviks) (hereinafter the AUCP(B)) Central Committee Georgy Malenkov and others regarding the collectivisation of the Estonian SSR. In the last clause of this statement, he proposed to the AUCP(B) Central Committee 'to expel kulaks, their families and some elements hostile towards the Soviet regime (18,000–20,000 people in total)' from the Estonian SSR and to hand their property over to the collective farms. Karotamm nevertheless left

---

[2]   In August of 1944, N. Karotamm was with the same group, meaning the leaders of the communist parties of the Baltic Soviet republics, in a meeting with J. Stalin to settle the forthcoming changes in their borders and the post-conquest sovietisation programme in the Baltic region. It is worth mentioning that at that time, N. Karotamm was not yet officially the First Secretary of the ECP Central Committee. It was not until September of that same year that he was appointed to that post. See further: Tÿnu Tannberg, *Politika Moskvy v respublikakh Baltii v poslevoennye gody (1944–1956). Issledovaniia i dokumenty* (Moscow: Rosspen, 2010), 43–44.

[3]   Karotamm's notes on Stalin, not dated (1945–1948?), RA, ERAF.9607.1.86.

the final decision in this matter to the Soviet leadership. Additionally, if the question of the expulsion of the kulaks was not decided 'positively' in the near future, he proposed as an alternative option to implement passport regimen restrictions against them, residence restrictions in certain regions, etc.[4]

Yet Karotamm completed a new letter to Stalin as the Chairman of the USSR Council of Ministers already on 17 January, which left out the other options and requested permission from the AUCP(B) Central Committee and the USSR Council of Ministers for expelling the kulaks. The letter states:

Regarding the kulaks, we have hitherto carried out a policy of restricting and ousting them. The time has come to make a turnaround in this policy and to liquidate kulaks as a class in the Estonian SSR by sending kulaks and their families together with the families of the henchmen of the German invaders out beyond the borders of the republic. This banishment has to be carefully prepared and carried out before the spring sowing of 1949. It is very important that this operation be carried out simultaneously in the Estonian, Latvian and Lithuanian SSR's.[5]

What forced Karotamm to correct his positions and to use Stalin's longstanding quote about liquidating the kulaks as a class? Karotamm has himself admitted that he proposed the deportation of the kulaks after the discussion of the kulak question at the AUCP(B) Central Committee.[6] This may, in fact, explain Karotamm's change of heart. By then, Karotamm had most likely not yet received Stalin's answer from Moscow to the proposals for relocating kulaks within the borders of Estonia that he and Arnold

---

[4]   Information on the status and next tasks of the construction of collective farms in the Estonian SSR, 15 January 1949, RA, ERAF.1.14.66, 1–6.

[5]   'On the Progress in Establishing Collective Farms in the ESSR', Report from the First Secretary of the ECP(B) Central Committee to USSR Council of Ministers Chairman J. V. Stalin, 17 January 1949 –*Eesti NSV põllumajanduse kollektiviseerimine: dokumentide ja materjalide kogumik* [The Collectivisation of the Agriculture of the Estonian SSR: Collection of Documents and Materials], eds. E. Laasi et al. (Tallinn: Eesti Raamat, 1978), 489–494, 492.

[6]   *Märtsivapustused. Avaldamata arhiividokumente aastaist 1949 ja 1950* [March Turmoil. Unpublished Archival Documents from 1949 and 1950], ed. Mart Arold (Tartu: Tungal, 1995), 61.

Veimer, the Chairman of the Estonian SSR Council of Ministers, had submitted in October of 1948. Now, however, he was persuaded on the spot (probably by Malenkov himself or his subordinates) to submit a proposal to Stalin for 'liquidating the kulaks as a class' in the traditional Stalinist way, meaning by repressing the kulaks.

At 22:05 on 18 January, the Latvian, Estonian and Lithuanian Communist Party leaders Kalnbērziņš, Karotamm and Sniečkus entered Stalin's office. Alongside Stalin, members of the Soviet Union's leadership, that is the Party's Central Committee Politburo, Georgy Malenkov, Lavrentiy Beria, Vyatcheslav Molotov, Aleksei Kossygin, Anastass Mikoyan and Nikolai Voznessenski were also present.[7] Thus Kliment Voroshilov, Nikolai Bulganin, Lazar Kaganovitch, Andrei Andreyev and Nikita Khrushchev were the Politburo members not in attendance. According to Karotamm's notes, the conversation with Stalin reportedly took place in quite a 'comradely', informal manner. Karotamm asserts that he is the one who made the proposal to Stalin for deporting the kulaks. Unfortunately, Karotamm has not noted if the Lithuanian and Latvian Party leaders made any proposals for deportation and what those proposals were. All that can be discerned from the notes is that deportation was the position of all three Party leaders. Thereat, only the deportation of kulaks was mentioned, but not of other categories of enemies. Karotamm noted that it was he in particular who emphasised to Stalin that the property of the kulaks had to be given free of charge to the collective farms. It is also important that Stalin assigned the preparation of questions regarding the deportation of the kulaks to his security marshal Lavrentiy Beria and the preparation of questions regarding agriculture to Malenkov. From this it appears that these leading figures in the Sovietisation of the Baltic states were already operating in the first rank of power in Stalin's inner circle, even though the AUCP(B) Central Committee Secretary Aleksei Kuznetsov was still officially supposed to be in charge of the state security organs. According to the notes, Stalin also touched on the question of reorganising the administrative division of the Baltic region into a system

---

[7]   *Na prieme u Stalina. Tetradi (zhurnaly) zapisei lits, priniatykh I.V. Stalinym (1924—1953 gg.). Spravochnik*, ed. A. Chernobaev (Moscow: Novyi Hronograf, 2008), 515. Instead of Karotamm, the name I. T. Norotamm is erroneously in this publication and in the alphabetical register, he is erroneously identified as a Lithuanian political figure.

that divides those territories into *rayons* (this is missing in the recorded notations).

At this point, it is advisable to take the power struggle in the Kremlin's power elite into consideration. The struggle basically lay in the competition for key positions in J. Stalin's inner circle that had already been in progress since 1946 with varying degrees of success between the so-called Leningrad grouping (Andrei Zhdanov, Aleksei Kuznetsov, Andrei Voznessenski, and others) on the one hand, and Georgy Malenkov and Lavrentiy Beria on the other. This struggle had reached its decisive phase by the outset of 1949, which ultimately proved to be fateful for the above-mentioned Leningrad grouping. L. Beria and G. Malenkov, whom J. Stalin made jointly responsible for preparing the forthcoming deportation operation in the three Baltic Soviet republics, also worked very actively at the same time to neutralise the positions of power of their competitors. Precisely in January of 1949, they launched their decisive attack on their competitors, the fabricated 'Leningrad Affair'. This ultimately culminated with the physical destruction of the figures belonging to the Kremlin's highest-ranking power elite who were associated with Leningrad (A. Kuznetsov, A. Voznessenski, and others), and more broadly with the repression of Party leaders throughout the Soviet Union whose background was tied to the City on the Neva.[8] This same time period also became fateful for Vyatcheslav Molotov, whose 'personal question' J. Stalin dealt with personally in January of 1949. V. Molotov lost his position as Minister of Foreign Affairs in the spring and thereafter he was no longer included in decision-making regarding the more important questions.

N. Karotamm's notes on his meeting with J. Stalin are an important source not only regarding the mass deportation of March, 1949, but also in comprehending the mechanisms by which late-Stalinist cultural policy functioned in the Estonian SSR. Karotamm's notes from 18 January 1949 provide us with the key to understanding why Hans Leberecht became

---

[8]   See further concerning the 'Leningrad Affair' and the power struggle in the post-war Soviet Union: Yoram Gorlitzki and Oleg Khlevniuk, *Cold Peace: Stalin and the Soviet Ruling Circle, 1945–1953* (Oxford; New York: Oxford University Press, 2004); Aleksandr Danilov and Aleksandr Pyzhikov, *Rozhdenie sverkhderzhavy: SSSR v pervye poslevoennye gody* (Moscow: ROSSPEN, 2001), Elena Zubkova, *Poslevoennoe sovetskoe obshchestvo: politika i povsednevnost'. 1945–1953 gg.* (Moscow: ROSSPEN, 2000); Rudolf Pikhoia, *Moskva. Kreml'. Vlast': Sorok let posle voiny. 1945–1985* (Moscow: Rus'-Olimp, 2007).

one of the top writers in the Estonian SSR – the calling card of the Soviet republic at that time. A noteworthy circumstance in this meeting was the fact that according to N. Karotamm, J. Stalin 'praised Hans Leberecht' at least 'twice' and accentuated his considerable skill in writing. The mention of a second-rate writer in such a context was surely unexpected for N. Karotamm, especially since the jury of the Ilukirjandus ja Kunst Publishing House novel-writing competition (P. Viiding, P. Rummo, F. Kõlli, E, Männik) of 1948 had declined to award a prize to Leberecht's manuscript[9] and instead awarded first prize to Osvald Tooming's novel *Ainus võimalus* [The Only Chance]. According to Paul Rummo, a member of the jury, Leberecht's result would have been better if 'the work's basically correct idea development would have been accompanied by greater skill in artistic figuration and, what is important in this case, a more thorough knowledge of factual details'.[10] Thus in the sense of literature, this work was weak in the jury's opinion.

Stalin was surely unaware of the details of the novel-writing competition. He was thinking about ideological justification of the wholesale change that awaited Estonian villages – mass collectivisation – and H. Leberecht's work was suitable in every respect for this task. Karotamm admittedly mentioned Mart Raud's poem *Maa kasvab* [The Land Grows] at the meeting, but this surely did not speak meaningfully to the lord of the Kremlin. For Karotamm, the 'great leader's' glorification directed at H. Leberecht was naturally a guideline for action. Upon his return to Estonia, he immediately had a new jury assembled (J. Semper, D. Rudnev, L. Remmelgas, P. Kuusberg, O. Urgart), which denounced the previous jury, the members of which 'did not base their evaluation of the work on Party standpoints, but rather on those of formalist aestheticism'. The new jury annulled the decision of the previous jury and naturally awarded first prize to the work *Valgus Koordis* [The Light in Koordi]. No work was fond to be worthy of the second prize, and the original winner – Oskar

---

9   H. Leberecht submitted a manuscript in Russian of his story *Valgus Koordis* [Light in Koordi] to the novel-writing competition, in which only hitherto unpublished works could be entered. Yet most of his story had already been published in the magazine *Zvezda*.

10   Paul Rummo, 'Romaanivõistluse ülevaade' [Overview of the Novel-Writing Competition], *Sirp ja Vasar*, 11 December 1948.

Tooming – was awarded with the third prize.[11] An edition of collected literary works glorifying life on collective farms was published very quickly, including excerpts of Leberecht's story and also Raud's poem.[12] Lembit Remmelgas translated Leberecht's manuscript with dispatch into Estonian and the work was already published as a book in the spring of 1949, as if in mockery of the thousands of people who had been deported to Siberia. Yet in the autumn of that same year, the work was awarded the Stalin Prize as an 'outstanding example of the synthesis of Soviet ideology and socialist realism'.[13] In order to understand the context of the course of events described above, it is appropriate to recall that domestically within the Estonian SSR, this was a time when the struggle against 'bourgeois nationalism' was gathering steam, and the power struggle within the leadership of the Estonian SSR was intensifying, culminating with the Communist Party's plenary session in March of 1950 and the removal of Nikolai Karotamm from his position.

The audience of the Party leaders from the Baltic Soviet republics lasted about 45 minutes in total and they left together at 22:50. Nikolai Bulganin and Kliment Voroshilov later joined the group gathered in the office. The guests left Stalin's office 20 minutes past midnight. Thus the fate of about 100,000 Lithuanians, Latvians and Estonians was sealed. Hans Leberecht, however, need not ever have found out why and how his initially rejected work suddenly was unexpectedly raised to the centre of attention and he himself became a famous writer overnight.

---

[11]   Sirje Olesk, *Tõdede vankuval müüril. Artikleid ajast ja luulest* [On the Teetering Wall of Truths. Articles on Time and Poetry] (Tartu: Eesti Kirjandusmuuseum, 2002), 78–79.

[12]   *Uued sihid: koguteos* [New Aims: a Collected Work], ed. Paul Rummo (Tallinn: Ilukirjandus ja Kunst, 1949).

[13]   Rein Veidemann, 'Eesti-vene kirjandusliku kommunikatsiooni kurioosum: Hans Leberechti jutustus "Valgus Koordis" (1948–1949)' [A Curiosity of Estonian-Russian Literary Communication: Hans Leberecht's Story *Valgus Koordis* (1948-1949)] – *Blokovskii sbornik XVIII. Rossiia i Estoniia XX veke: dialog kul'tur*, ed. L. Pild (Tartu: Tartu Ülikooli Kirjastus, 2010), 304–305. *Valgus Koordis* was translated from Russian into 23 languages. This work was the most widely translated literary work of the Estonian SSR until the mid-1960s.

Appendix 1

N. Karotamm's Notes on his Meeting with J. Stalin at the Kremlin on 18 January 1949

[...][14] At 21:15, C[omrade] Sukhanov telephoned[15] to say that the 3 Central Committee secretaries (Baltic) should be at C[omrade] Poskrebyshev's office at 21:45.[16] We went (Kalnb[ērziņš][17] and me [Karotamm]) there. At the right time. C[omrade] Malenkov came to us there and advised us that we should only talk about the main questions (kulaks, mechanisation) with C[omrade] St[alin]. We'll resolve other matters then already. C[omrade] Sniečkus came 4–5 min[utes later].[18]

We stepped into C[omrade] St[alin's] office at exactly 22:05. C[omrades] St[alin], Molotov, Kossygin, Malenkov, Beria, Mikoyan and Voznessenski sat around a table beside the left wall.

We all greeted one another by shaking hands. We sat down at the table. C[omrade] St[alin] asked, 'So what questions do you have?' Kalnberzinš spoke first. Then me and then Sniečkus.

I stressed 3 questions: speeding up the tempos of collectivis[ation] and the liquid[ation] of the kulaks as a cl[ass]; improvement of the technical base of a[gri]cult[ure]; prep[aration] of the cadres of the col[lective] farms.

When I started speaking, then C[omrade] Stalin said: '*A vy popravilis*'! [But you've gotten well!]' I replied that '*Eto khorosho, togda mozhno naibol'she*'! [That's good, then I can work more!]'. St[alin] himself smiled at this.

---

[14]   N. Karotamm's notes on his meeting with J. Stalin at the Kremlin were put in writing immediately after the meeting. To make them easier to read, abbreviations have been written out in squared brackets, and translations and brief commentaries of Russian sentences and phrases have also been added.

[15]   Apparently Georgy Malenkov's assistant Dmitri Sukhanov is being referred to here.

[16]   Stalin's secretary and head of the CPSU Central Committee Special Sector Aleksandr Poskrebyshev.

[17]   Latvian Communist Party Central Committee First Secretary Jānis Kalnbērziņš.

[18]   Lithuanian Communist Party Central Committee First Secretary Antanas Sniečkus.

We spent the most time on the kulak question. At first C[omrade] St[alin] said that your collectivisation % is small, so isn't it premature to liquid[ate] the kulaks, that if it would be 30–40%. During our exchange of views, he checked a couple of times to see if this really is our firm opinion or if we're just saying so '*dlia nas tut* [for us here]', as he said. We insisted that this really is our opinion. I added that there were also opinions in the [ECP] Central Committee Bureau that the most hostile kul[ak] elements could be deported initially. But – this wouldn't solve the problem. Finally, St[alin] said – let's deport them. But this has to be done quickly so that it wouldn't make the villages nervous for a long time.

Regarding mechanisation, he asked how many tractors were needed. I said 550 in 1949. Together with all other machines. C[omrade] Stalin especially insisted that together with tractors, threshing machines have to be provided because threshing has to be done when times are busy. '*Traktory dadim! Dadim!* [We'll give you tractors! We will!]' he said in conclusion.

Then C[omrade] St[alin] directed our attention to the particular importance of soil improvement in Estonia, Latvia and probably also in Lithuania. I said that there are 680,000 [ha] of cultivatable marshland in Estonia, 350,000 ha of that is partially already provided with drainage ditches, and that yields 500,000 tn of rye or 35,000 [?] per year. Yet we need equipment for this. Excavators etc. St[alin] ordered that a soil improvement plan be drawn up '*po etapam* [in stages]' and submitted.

St[alin] praised Hans Leberecht twice, his story *Zvezda*. That man knows how to see! He knows how to write! He asked if he [Leberecht] knows Estonian, if he writes in Estonian, etc. I replied that he doesn't write in Estonian. But surely he can learn that as well. Then he asked if you have had literary works published on collective farms. I told him about M[art] Raud's *Maa kasvab* [The Land Grows].

Then he asked if the intellectuals were warming up to the Soviet regime. We replied that they were. Admittedly not quite all of them, but definitely the majority.

We also discussed the question of cultivating flax. C[omrade] Mikoyan raised the question that flax cultivation wasn't making headway in the Baltic lands. I replied that the ESSR's a[gri]culture had abandoned flax cultivation over the past 30–40 years and had switched to livestock farming, that flax wasn't held in esteem as a source of income. St[alin] said: '*Konechno, narod ved' umnyi. On zhe vidit, chto iavliaetsia dokhodnym* [Of course, the people are smart. They see what is profitable]'. Then we stressed that much more favourable conditions than have hitherto existed have to be created for flax cultivators, and that flax processing has to be mechanised (factories). St[alin] asked us to work out our proposals on this matter, what kinds of conditions would be appropriate in our opinion for fostering flax cult[ivation], and then we'll consider what to do.

Then we spoke further about the idea that the property of the kulaks who were to be liquidated was to be given free of charge to the collective farms (I insisted on this). St[alin] said that this was correct: '*Nado i krest'iaanstvo vputat' v eto delo protiv kulaka!* [It is necessary to drag the peasantry into this anti-kulak thing as well!]'. He repeated this idea twice.

In conclusion, C[omrade] St[alin] assigned C[omrade] Malenkov to resolve all questions regarding agriculture. He assigned C[omrade] Beria to resolve questions regarding the deportation of the kulaks and to make the necessary preparations with the *MGB* and *MVD*.

We bid farewell by shaking hands and left.

Recorded on the night before 19 January 1949 in Moscow at the ESSR Council of Ministers representation at 2:30.
N. Karotamm

Source: Manuscript, RA, ERAF.9607.1.302, 1–3.

Estonia and the Communist Century: an Essay

Toomas Hiio

I

In November of 2017, 100 years passed since the Bolsheviks seized power, in other words the Great Socialist October Revolution, as was the official name for this event during the Soviet era. The October Revolution was the most important of the historical events that had to be written as a grammatical exception in Estonian with every word in its designation capitalised during the era of Soviet occupation in Estonia. Another such event was the Great Patriotic War. The establishment of its own grammatical rules, the newspeak coined by George Orwell in actual practice, was only one of the methods by which the totalitarian regime tried to saturate all of society with the regime's identity.

Estonia's middle-aged people of today still remember communist holidays. Nine and ten-year-old pupils in city schools were already forced to stand for hours on end at demonstrations on both 7 November and 1 May, waiting for their turn, and then to march through the city's central square under slogans in praise of the Party and government, its wise domestic and foreign policy, or other things that the propaganda and agitation departments had selected for that particular occasion, for instance 'Zavershaiushhemu godu pjatiletki – nash udarnyi trud! [For the final year of the Five-Year Plan – Our Shock Work!]', and all those others. The more important local Party and Soviet figures and military leaders stood on the tribune. Loudspeakers shouted out those same slogans that the demonstrators carried on red sheets alongside pictures of communist saints affixed to wooden poles: mostly state leaders and the classics of

Marxism-Leninism. The marchers were expected to respond with cheers. While insufficient zeal in responding could cause problems in the Stalin era, the excessive exuberance of many cheers of greetings in the Brezhnev era of the 1970s was already pure sarcasm. Tallinn's temporary tribune in the city's central square was built in front of the building in which the Russian theatre had operated since the end of the 1940s. A rumour spread that the theatre's sign – Russian Theatre – had to be taken down for the November and May demonstrations because it could be interpreted as a characterisation of the entire group that stood on the tribune built under the sign. While processions with flags and the pictures of saints led by the cross were part of the orthodox tradition of church holidays that the Bolsheviks took over with their compulsory demonstrations of 7 November and 1 May, then this was all the more 'Russian stuff' and a humiliating obligation for Estonians.

II

The 200th anniversary of the birth of Karl Marx was celebrated in many parts of the world in 2018. The President of the European Commission personally referred to him as one of the thinkers who has influenced European history the most. This is not expressly wrong because the consequences of the affected wisdom of philosophers and political economists are rarely millions of victims, unprecedented suffering, economic collapse and backwardness. Or was there a grain of sarcasm in this message as well? Hardly. But from here we arrive back at processions led by the cross. One of the most important components of totalitarian ideologies is populism. The poor and the sufferers of the entire world, or at least the Aryan race, were promised redemption almost during the lifetime of those people themselves, in return for selfless work and struggle. Thus at the outset of the 1960s, Nikita Khrushchev also promised to build up communism by the 1980s. There was not much in this that differed compared to the paradise, resurrection, rebirth and eternal bliss that the great religions of the world promise, only the deadlines were shorter. Both totalitarian ideologies treated religions as their opponents and enemies in the struggle for the hearts and minds of the people. 'Religion is the opium of the people', taught Marx and Lenin, but this sentence already originated from at least the era of the French Revolution, when the Marquis de Sade used it. During World War II, necessity forced both totalitarian ideologies to admit, if not defeat, then certainly at least a stalemate in this struggle. Stalin allowed the Orthodox Church to once again operate more actively and even released some priests from Gulag camps. Himmler, on the other hand, had to tolerate army chaplains – Lutheran and Orthodox clergymen, Islamic mullahs and Buddhist priests – even in Waffen-SS units recruited from occupied areas.

Political ideologies do not usually claim to be scientifically grounded because they represent the interests and will of one or another stratum of society, or at least they claim to do so. Yet the common denominator of totalitarian ideologies, both communist and national socialist, was their pretension to being the only correct form of society and government, which was allegedly justified by their scientific grounding. The most important component of science is open scientific discussion and debate. The communist movement already tried to prevent all manner of debate in the 19th century. The persecution of Jews, Bolsheviks and plutocrats alone was sufficient in and of itself for the national socialists. It was not arguments but rather votes at congresses, conferences and meetings that mattered. Scientific arguments are not needed for collecting these votes, rather it is propaganda and political-technological proficiency that counts. Debate within the Party became life-threatening for those on the losing side in Soviet Russia in the 1920s already.

Yet Marx, Engels and Lenin had supposedly discovered the laws of how society functioned and for this reason, the arrival of communism, as they predicted, was inevitable. At the same time, this justified the displacement, imprisonment and destruction of everyone who stood in the way of the proletariat as the only progressive class, and its vanguard, the Communist Party, on the road to the predestined communist future. The theory of communism was taught at all levels of education from kindergarten to doctoral studies and it was impossible in the Soviet Union and the Eastern Bloc to acquire higher education without passing exams in 'Red subjects'. Even as late as the 1960s and 1970s, millions of people in Western liberal democracies also took communist doctrine completely seriously in its very diverse forms of expression starting with Stalinism and ending with Eurocommunism. Lenin is said to have already referred to numerous intellectuals among them as useful idiots in his day.

Defiance of the generation of their parents was their impetus, along with their belief that the communist system is capable of liquidating social inequality and establishing an absolutely just polity. This belief was supported by propaganda from the Eastern Bloc in the media, and conveyed by communist parties in the Western countries, and also by secret services from the Eastern Bloc, the agents of which provided support and financing here and there when necessary. Most of these believers and people who took this doctrine seriously had never been to a single Eastern Bloc country.

The ambition of political ideologies to be scientific, along with the desire to preordain mankind's future has not disappeared nowadays either. Recall the claim made by Francis Fukuyama of the 'end of history', and the people who believed in that claim about 30 years ago. This nevertheless mostly characterises various extremists, whose science marches hand in hand with the conviction of mankind's original sin and future paradise. The first that come to mind are ecological fascists, vegan extremists, and others. If democracy were scientific, elections would not be needed because science would have determined the outcome in advance already. Such was the custom in society striving towards communism – elections were admittedly held, because the 'most perfect democracy' required elections, but there was no competition between candidates. The Party had selected them in advance and there could be no doubt concerning the results. The Party had a monopoly over declaring social scientific truth, which was not found through academic discussion, but rather in the Party apparat and according to need.

III

Fanatics, naïve fellow travellers, opportunists and careerists carry the totalitarian ideologies. Their blind faith allows fanatics to commit the most violent acts upon the incitement of ideology, and they are redeemed in advance by the inevitability of predestination. Fanatics are not born, they are indoctrinated. Even as early as the Middle Ages, the Janissary elite units were formed in the Ottoman Empire, consisting entirely of boys who had been kidnapped from among Christians and converted to the Islamic faith. Post-civil war Soviet Russia provided Party soldiers with a large pool of human resources for indoctrination – millions of orphaned children, whom the state cared for within the limits of its meagre resources in orphanages, colonies and other institutions, and eradicated illiteracy, channelling these children to selected reading matter that was the only literature allowed. Later history also knows of various kinds of forces of revolutionary guards. It was not only unfortunate orphans who fell victim to total brainwashing in Soviet Russia – educating the entire succeeding generation in the communist spirit was one of the regime's most important priorities. The brighter ones of these young people were sent to workers' faculties to prepare them for enrolment in institutions of higher education. The gaps in their general education were compensated for, but ideological training was provided first and foremost. The aim was the education of a new generation of intellectuals that would be free of 'bourgeois vestiges' and completely loyal to the communist idea. In the mid-1920s, about 40% of students enrolling in institutions of higher education were alumni of the workers' faculties. In terms of its idea, the workers' faculty resembled the tsarist era orthodox ecclesiastic seminary, which was a chance for the sons of countless village clerics and other boys of simple origin to acquire a level of education that was equated with secondary education. In the era of intensified perpetuation of the Russian identity – tsar, faith and fatherland – during the reign of Tsar Alexander III, alumni of the orthodox seminaries accounted for an ever-increasing proportion of university students. They no longer became priests, but rather the progeny of Russia's academic intellectuals, in whose spirituality Great Russian chauvinism had played a major role.

The proletariat was to be the leader and bearer of communist society. The status of one's parents – worker, employee and intellectual or peasant – was entered in forms and other documents until the end of the Soviet Union and was one of the indexes of population statistics. Thus the derivative of the Russian social estates, which had been abolished by the Provisional Government that had come to power as a result of the February Revolution of 1917, was turned upside down. Tsarist Russia classified its subjects according to religion and estate. The conviction that every person has their place in society predetermined by God according to their extraction in the form of estate, and that only the most capable can proceed to the next level, was now replaced by the assertion from communist theory of the proletariat's inescapable privilege to lead social progress to its predetermined finale.

The Soviet educational system had its biographies of saints. Self-sacrifice was stressed in struggle and in building up communism. Nikolai Ostrovsky's (1904–1936) autobiographical novel *How Steel was Tempered* was compulsory reading matter for pupils in Estonian basic schools as well after the occupation of Estonia in 1940. Nine editions of this book have been published in Estonian. The book tells the story of a simple young man who fought in the Russian Civil War in the ranks of the Red Army, and after that fought against kulaks. Thereafter the young man ruined his health completely by working on building a railroad of national importance under harsh and difficult conditions.

In the early 1970s after a dormant interval, construction work resumed on the Baikal-Amur Mainline (BAM), which had originally started out as a Komsomol shock work project. The Trans-Siberian Railroad from the tsarist era, which connected Russia's European part to the coast of the Pacific Ocean, passed too close to the Chinese border. Relations with China had rapidly worsened after Khrushchev's speech in 1956, where he accused Stalin of a personality cult and the illegal repression of hundreds of thousands of people, and this led to armed conflict in 1969. Now the authorities were again counting on the enthusiasm of young people. One of the examples set for them was Ostrovsky's novel. Recruitment was carried out in Estonia as well and quite a few young people joined the campaign. The command economy had already demonstrated their incapability to cope with flexibly solving the problems facing the state and society. One of the ways to compensate for this was the mobilisation of young people for so-called shock work construction projects, as has been mentioned above. Now mobilisation was voluntary, even though attempts were made, for instance, to tempt young men whose term of compulsory military service in the Soviet Army was drawing to an end by offering them various benefits.

The biographies of heroes of the Soviet Union who had fallen on the battlefield were examples of self-sacrifice. The author of this essay studied at a secondary school in Tallinn that was given the name of Jakob Kunder (1921–1945) in 1975. Lieutenant Kunder was a platoon leader in the Red Army Estonian Rifle Corps who repeated Aleksandr Matrosov's heroic deed in the battles in Courland in March of 1945 – he blocked the embrasure of an enemy fortified machine-gun nest with his body. Becoming a hero could only be the logical result of the hero's lineage and the preceding course of his life. The Soviet Union lost millions of soldiers in World War II and thus had plenty of potential heroes from which to choose. Kunder qualified as a hero because he came from a simple family, joined the communists after the occupation of Estonia, served in the militia (Soviet police) starting in 1940 and fought as a member of an NKVD destruction battalion in 1941. Nothing could be left to chance.

The most violent NKVD interrogators, and men and women who clearly enjoyed torturing their victims did not necessarily have to be fanatics. Leaving aside possible psychic degeneration, violent strength of purpose and willingness to employ all means in the name of achieving their objective were precisely among the virtues that the NKVD expected of its personnel. Additionally, Stalin himself personally gave permission to apply all means for obtaining confessions. Older men were hardened in the trenches of the Great War and in the Russian Civil War, while younger men were hardened by seeing and causing cruelties and appalling human suffering in arrests, deportations and prisons. Violence, obedience and alcohol were the content of these men and women, with assistance from the slogan repeated from time to time that everything they were doing was only in the name of a brighter future. The guilt of the persons being interrogated and tortured was already proven by the fact of their arrest, and their confession and subsequent punishment was the only possible result of this due process.

IV

No society is absolutely just. This also applies to tsarist Russia as well as Estonia under authoritarian rule in 1934–1940. The Bolsheviks who seized power in Russia in 1917, and the Estonian Bolsheviks who were installed in power after the occupation of Estonia, promised a turnaround to a better future. There was no shortage of believers and people who went along with the change. This is illustrated in Estonia by the number of Estonians who were arrested and executed on the orders of the subsequent terror regime, that of the national socialists beginning in 1941. If we leave aside the innocent victims who were imprisoned and murdered for the sole reason of their race (Jews and Romani), mental illness or some other serious disability, several thousand people were executed in Estonia on the orders of the SS and the police during the first year of German occupation. Estonia is one of the few European countries where the national socialists and their henchmen murdered more members of the country's native nationality than Jews.

A dilemma emerges in the case of the victims of terror regimes – if the regime itself is criminal, then it could be assumed that all the victims of that regime are innocent sufferers. This does not hold true. There was a significant number of people among the victims of the national socialist terror in

1941–1944 who really had actively participated in the preceding communist terror. And vice versa: among the several thousand men and women who were murdered, and the tens of thousands who were arrested by the Soviet Union's state security organs starting in 1944, there were also people who had participated in the national socialist terror and had shed blood during the German occupation. But both of them should nevertheless have had the right to a just and fair trial instead of the procedures carried out by secret services and the decisions handed down by secret tribunals.

It is unjust that an entire nation should be criminalised because of the actions of some of its citizens; but it is equally unjust that its criminals should be able to shelter behind a cloak of victimhood, is how the Max Jakobson Commission formulated its response to this contradictory question in 2001 according to the Estonian experience.

The motivations of collaborators differed, starting from revenge for humiliations and insults and ranging to careerism and avarice, or the actual naïve belief in the justness of the cause that they were serving. It soon turned out that it was no longer possible to get off that train, even though the acts of the occupying regime soon horrified many collaborators as well. The most malicious crimes were admittedly committed under the direction of officers of the Soviet Union's state security organs and their subordinates, who received their orders directly from central agencies in Moscow, which received their orders in turn from Stalin and his inner circle. Part of the responsibility, however, lies with those Estonian men and women who actively collaborated with the occupying regime and unquestioningly implemented Party policy.

Like elsewhere, there were many intellectuals among the fellow travellers, the 'useful idiots', in Estonia. Post-publication censorship in authoritarian Estonia and the 'arrogance of moneyed men and Pro Patria movement members', which supposedly had oppressed them, and liberation from which the more naïve among them initially saw in the 'June coup' of 1940, were immediately replaced by the bridle bit of Marxist-Leninist censorship. Estonian intellectuals could not have been unaware of the absence of freedom of thought, expression and of the press in the Soviet Union. Did they consider this an inevitable side-effect of total world reform? George Orwell, Ernest Hemingway, and others have described, in the light of their own personal experiences, the disappointments of those intellectuals who believed in the possibility of communist world reform and complete overall equality, and who had fought in the international brigades in the Spanish Civil War in the name of these ideals. The writer Paul Kuusberg (1916–2003), who was himself a simple construction worker from a poor family, stood at the steering wheel of Soviet Estonian literature for a quarter of a century. He revealed the background of his going along with the occupying regime in 1940 and his later disappointments rather more cautiously in his memoirs published in 1996:

I guess we thought that we could finally succeed in achieving the end of the persecution of the labour movement and of democratic thought, that we wouldn't have to register our meetings with the police [anymore], that cops or snitches would no longer sit in on our meetings, that we would achieve complete freedom of speech, thought, the press, assembly and association. Unfortunately, yes unfortunately many and many of the labour activists who supported the June coup were unable to foresee the harsh consequences of the events that were taking place. This applies to me as well among the others.[1]

Estonia's hundred or so 'prison communists', most of whom were released from prison in the spring of 1938 by the amnesty declared by President Konstantin Päts, and the couple of thousand so-called June communists who went along with the coup – more properly those from these two groups who survived World War II – believed after the end of World War II that they could start building up communism Estonian style. This, too, is no unique Estonian trait. A large number of communists in the future Eastern Bloc shared the same hopes. But Stalin's state held all of its dependents in an iron grip and communists of the native nationality were needed only for creating the impression for the subjugated peoples as if the seizure of power and the communist coup originated from among their own people according to their own most fervent wishes. Famous defectors, like the former East German Wolfgang Leonhard (1921–2014), and Milovan Djilas (1911–1995), who was part of the Yugoslavian leadership, have described the experiences and disappointments of communists of the native nationality.

Estonia's own 'prison communists' and 'June communists' were like the proverbial Moors who had done their duty and could thereafter go by

---

[1]   Paul Kuusberg, *Rõõmud ja pettumused* [Joys and disappointments] (Tallinn: Kupar, 1996), 240–241.

the end of the 1940s. The experienced NKVD foreign intelligence agent Karl Säre (1903–1945) was sent to lead Estonia's communists in 1940 but was caught by the Germans in 1941. Nikolai Karotamm (1901–1969), a spy who had similarly received his training in underground subversive activities among others at the Communist University for Western Minority Peoples in Leningrad in the 1920s, inherited Säre's position. Johannes Lauristin (1899–1941), Oskar Sepre (1900–1965) and Arnold Veimer (1903–1977) headed the government of the ESSR in the 1940s. All three had been serving sentences of forced labour for communist subversive activity in 1924–1938. The positions connected to domestic state security also belonged to the 'prison communists' – Boris Kumm headed the People's Commissariat for State Security, while Andrei Murro, and later Aleksander Resev, headed the People's Commissariat for Internal Affairs. Both the government members and the Estonian state security chief were the marionettes of their deputies, the actual leaders sent from Moscow. Estonia's deputy ruler in 1940–1941 was Vladimir Bochkarev, the representative of the All-Union Communist Party (Bolsheviks) CC and the Council of People's Commissars in the Estonian SSR. In 1944–1947, the heads of the AUCP(B) CC Estonian Bureau Nikolai Shatalin, Georgy Perov and Viktor Yefremov filled a similar role.

A number of Estonian intellectuals and left-wing socialists who had gone along with the communists in 1940 were also initially promoted to high-ranking positions. NKVD foreign intelligence had selected them in advance and they themselves had accepted their selection for various reasons. The more renowned from among them were the doctor and poet Johannes Vares (1890–1946), who became Chairman of the ESSR Supreme Soviet Presidium, the former history professor Hans Kruus (1891–1976), who was appointed People's Commissar for Foreign Affairs and President of the Academy of Sciences, the writer Johannes Semper (1892–1970), appointed People's Commissar for Education, the educator and man of letters Nigol Andresen (1899–1985), who was initially Deputy Chairman of the Council of People's Commissars and later the First Deputy Chairman of the Supreme Soviet Presidium, the naturalist Harald Haberman (1904–1986), who became the chief of internal defence in 1940 and passed the NKVD's orders on to the marionette government, the former private lawyer and member of the Riigikogu (Estonian parliament) Aleksander Jõeäär (1890–1959), who was promoted to People's Commissar for Justice, and others. Some of them had belonged to left-wing political parties in

1917–1920 but had thereafter given up politics for more sensible activities. They had not forgotten their left-wing sympathies and this is probably one of the grounds from which NKVD recruiters approached them. A certain generational aspect can also be noticed, on which the Great War and the Estonian War of Independence left their imprint. Most of the young communists sentenced to prison in the Trial of the 149 in 1924, who were raised to the top-level leadership of occupied Estonia in the 1940s, were born in the last years of the 19th century or the outset of the 20th century, for which reason they were too young to be involved in the Great War and had, in many cases, already chosen the opposing side by the time of the War of Independence. On the other hand, many prominent left-wing Estonian socialists were 10 years older, for which reason they had managed to enrol in university during the tsarist era. They were conscripted into Russian ensign schools in 1916 and even made it to the front. Most of them had also fought for the Republic of Estonia in the War of Independence. Johannes Vares, the leader of the marionette government, had been decorated with a high-level military medal, the Estonian Cross of Liberty, for his services in that war against Soviet Russia.

They were all removed from power in 1950. The most prominent of them were arrested, confessed to what they were accused of, mostly 'bourgeois nationalism', and were sent to prison camps. Yet Stalin already died three years later and compared to thousands of other victims who survived the Soviet terror, their imprisonment ended up being much shorter. Most of them applied for reinstatement as members of the Communist Party, not so much out of conviction, but rather to restore the rights and privileges that they had been deprived of. In the years of Gorbachev's perestroika, they were among the first to be raised to prominence as examples of the victims of Stalin's personality cult. This was part of the justification for the claim that communism was a project that could potentially be realised, but that Stalin, by his brutality, and Brezhnev, by letting things take their course, had ruined this otherwise noble venture. This claim remains suitable for salon discussions to this day among Western European Marxists and circles that reflect their views back to Estonia.

V

New people were promoted in place of those that had been removed in 1950: apparatchiks who had already been sent from the Soviet Union to

Estonia earlier, including a large number of Estonians from Russia. These were men and women who had themselves, or whose parents had decided to stay in Soviet Russia in 1917–1920, or who had remained there through the twists of fate. They had been trained there and had survived Stalin's purges of the 1930s, one of the target groups of which had been the elite of national minorities. They had been 'tempered' in World War II, and were now sent to Estonia to continue its Sovietisation. Ivan Käbin and Karl Vaino, who headed the ECP in 1950–1988, Johan Eichfeld, Aleksei Müürisepp, Artur Vader and Käbin, who served as chairmen of the Supreme Soviet Presidium in 1958–1983, and Müürisepp and Valter Klauson, who had headed the Council of Ministers in 1951–1984, all belonged to this category. Their younger partners were men selected from among those who were mobilised from Estonia into the Red Army in 1941 who had proven their trustworthiness in the rear area and at the front. The situation was no different in the Eastern Bloc countries as well. They were similarly led by men and women, many of whom had received their preparation in the 1920s and 1930s in Party schools in the Soviet Union and had fought in World War II in the Red Army or in national military units subordinated to the Red Army. Ho Chi Minh as well as Josip Broz Tito, likewise Erich Honecker, Imre Nagy, and many others had all studied in Moscow.

The top leadership of the Estonian SSR consisted almost without exception of the above-mentioned 'cadres' until the outset of the 1960s. Then men whose place and date of birth were in 'bourgeois' Estonia started being promoted to leading positions in the executive branch, yet at least their biographies included going along with the coup in 1940 and 'tempering' in the ranks of the Red Army Estonian Rifle Corps in 1941–1945. Of the 16 men who served in the top leadership of the Estonian branch of the CPSU in positions as secretaries in 1950–1978, only four had been born and raised in Estonia: Otto Merimaa and Dmitri Kuzmin (1908–1998), a representative of the younger generation of 'prison communists', and starting in the 1970s, Vaino Väljas, one of the heroes of the 'Singing Revolution' of 1988, and Arnold Rüütel, who was elected the President of Estonia in 2001. The occupation continued and locals were still not trusted. Nevertheless, by 1975, men and women born in Estonia already formed the majority in the leadership of the executive branch among the members of the ESSR Council of Ministers.

VI

By the end of the 1950s, when most of the surviving deportees and political prisoners in forced banishment and in the Gulag had been released and had returned to Estonia, and armed resistance (the forest brothers movement) had been suppressed, it was clear to the majority that the Soviet occupation in Estonia would not end soon. A third world war between East and West, which many of the inhabitants of occupied countries were hoping for, did not break out. The nuclear balance brought relaxation of tensions and peaceful coexistence instead. The two opposing sides tolerated each other. Yet the Western countries still did not recognise the incorporation of the Baltic states. Occupation and annexation were violations of international law and contradicted justice in general, yet also provided the opportunity for applying pressure to the opposing side and for internal subversion by preserving hopes for liberation among occupied or subjugated peoples. The democratic governments of the Western countries had to take all of their voters into consideration. Here the members of exile communities of the Baltic refugees who had escaped abroad ahead of the advancing Red Army during the Second World War played an important role, since they did not allow the politicians of their countries of residence to forget the fate of the Baltic states for the sake of some deal with the Soviet Union that may appear to be favourable. Gough Whitlam (1916–2014), the Prime Minister of Australia and leader of the Labour Party, made just such an attempt in 1974, when he announced that Australia was abandoning the non-recognition of the annexation of the Baltic states. One of his justifications was cynical – there was nothing for him to lose because the Baltic expatriates always vote for the liberals anyway. A year later, the liberals did indeed come to power and nullified Whitlam's decision. History is pitiless:

Like fellow leftists around the world, Whitlam liked to take pride in being on the right side of history. [...] [W]hen the Soviet Empire collapsed in 1991 and Lithuania, Latvia and Estonia regained their independence, Gough Whitlam was left stranded on the wrong side of history.[2]

---

[2]   Christopher Carr, 'Saint Gough's unmentioned sin', *Quadrant Online*, June 2013, https://quadrant.org.au/opinion/qed/2013/06/saint-gough-s-unmentioned-sin/, 1 June 2018.

Great empires rely first and foremost on officialdom – bureaucracy and the army. This was the case in imperial Germany, Austria-Hungary and also tsarist Russia. Bureaucracy prefers obedience and capability over original ideas. This ensures stability, but also sows the seeds of stagnation and decay. Careers progress through service ranks and every Russian collegiate registrar had the staff of an actual privy councillor in his briefcase, like every ensign had a marshal's baton. The Soviet state, which was more centralised than any earlier empire, also needed the virtues of bureaucracy, obedience and capability. The Communist Party's apparat and its executive organs were closely intertwined. The declarative principle of the one and only party was democratic centralism, which in actuality meant the concentration of absolute power in the hands of the Party's top leadership. This was one of the many reasons for the collapse of the system. Not a single more important decision was made without approval from the highest level. Marxist-Leninist theory and its derivatives and developments right through to scientific communism and developed socialism, to which all had to regularly swear loyalty, yet which was long since outdated with its 19th century ideas, also hamshackled the top leadership. The continuation of the process of worldwide revolution was still being mentioned in the Party congress speeches of the 1970s, even though now the export of revolution launched by the Comintern in its day was continuing in the Third World with an eye to the Soviet Union's strategic objectives.

No society whatsoever is capable of living for decades in either the heat of revolution or the fight for independence. Sooner or later, the time of careerists and opportunists will arrive. A new generation had in the meantime grown up in Estonia. All that it knew about life in the Republic of Estonia was only what their parents and grandparents had told them and what they had read in books from the period of Estonia's independence. The standard of living had gradually improved because Nikita Khrushchev's wish to catch up to and pass the USA also included improving the people's living conditions, ahead of which the development of heavy industry had been preferred in the Stalinist era. Conformation began. More and more Estonians joined the Communist Party as members, more out of careerism than conviction. Advancement to positions in the nomenklatura, those positions of public power that were filled through decisions by the Party, which firmly held on to this decision-making privilege, mostly also required membership in the Party. In the 1980s, over 100,000 inhabitants of occupied Estonia belonged to the CPSU, and over half of them were Estonians. Yet there were even more people who on principle refused to give the devil their little finger merely in return for tiny Soviet benefits. By that time, the Komsomol communist youth association had developed into a mass organisation that was long since no longer as organisation that one joined, but rather one that simply took people on as members. We are not proud of this, but we went along with it.

New generation communists gradually manned the positions freed up by the old cadres. In the 1960s during the years of Khrushchev's thaw, the hope for 'socialism with a human face' was their self-justification. Even this slender hope disappeared after the Prague Spring was crushed. In 1990, the absolute majority of those 50,000 Estonian communists renounced their Party membership cards without much regret. Some presented their activities over the course of the past era as either 'undermining the system from within' or as 'advancing the Estonian cause regardless of everything'. The capacity for adaptation of most of them was entirely sufficient for getting involved in the new politics, but the new politics itself also shaped itself according to the contours of those who were entering that politics. The scant base of support in Estonia for the idea of communism is also demonstrated by the fact that unlike many other Eastern European countries, the remnants of the Communist Party of 1991 have not been successfully reanimated here into a functioning political party over the nearly 30 years that have passed since the restoration of independence, and neither has a single new political party been successfully launched that would proclaim a communist future. Politicians who proclaim altogether more utilitarian values have taken over the sentiments of the target group that always exists for populist politics.

VII

Communism is first and foremost a political ideology with worldwide ambitions. Yet like every political ideology, communism must also take as its point of departure the local environment in which it uses its power. There is a certain parallel here with the anecdote about how Christian missionaries in Greenland had to explain to the Inuit that Hell is a terribly cold place. In Estonia, Soviet propaganda made anti-German sentiment prominent during and immediately after World War II. Anti-German sentiment had been one of the pillars of Estonian nationalist ideology as well since the mid-19th century. More broadly speaking, the serfdom of Estonians that had lasted for 700 years under the arbitrary action of Baltic German manorial lords, and especially the uprising of Estonians against the conquerors on the eve of St. George's Day in 1343, the 600th anniversary of which was commemorated in 1943, were also put to use as tools of Soviet propaganda.

Like every kind of violent seizure of power, revolution is first and foremost a question of power, the removal of the former elite and its replacement with a new elite. The Soviet Union's occupying regime was exceptionally violent in removing Estonia's elite. A total of nearly two percent of Estonia's population was imprisoned or deported in 1940–1941, and only a small fraction of these people made it back to their homeland after 15–20 years. In addition to these people, over 30,000 men were hauled away to NKVD labour battalions under the aegis of mobilisation into the Red Army in the summer of 1941. The men who survived there were formed into Red Army Estonian national units in 1942, and a heavy blood sacrifice was exacted from them at the front. After the war, human material was recruited from among them for Sovietising Estonia in addition to the 'prison communists', the 'June communists', but primarily the thousands of men and women sent from the Soviet Union to Estonia. The new Soviet elite never got over its inferiority complex regarding the former elite and the West until the end of the Soviet Union. They craved the material benefits of the former elite, starting with the manor houses of the large Baltic German landowners and ending with luxury apartments, mostly in modern apartment houses or villas from the era of independent Estonia in the 1930s, the owners of which had been sent to the Gulag or deported. Starting in the 1960s, Western clothing and other consumer goods, and tourist trips to 'capitalist' countries, became status symbols. The gulf separating the standard of living of a member of the top-level nomenklatura from that of an ordinary worker or collective farm worker was sometimes many times deeper in the workers' state than it was between employers and employees in the 'degenerating' Western democracies.

Replacing the elite is nevertheless not enough for bringing the entire country and society into line. The Soviet Union and its Communist Party lost the struggle for the hearts and minds of Estonians from the very beginning. The Soviet Russian regime was treated like the Russian regime, just as had been the case in the tsarist era. Most Estonians continued to identify themselves with their own land and people. They did not consider themselves as subjects of a so-called state of the whole people (*obshchenarodnoe gosudarstvo*) that was being built up in the period of developed socialism starting in the 1960s and 1970s, a state populated by many nations, who were gradually becoming Russian-speaking 'Soviet people'. Estonians had become a society of smallholders in the 1920s and the communist ownership policy requiring liquidation of private property was something that was actually never forgiven. The enthusiasm of Estonians in taking back the land property and farms that once belonged to their parents or grandparents during the period of restitution in the early 1990s amply demonstrates this. Secondly, Estonian nationalist ideology that had been developed since the latter half of the 19th century, which placed the Estonian spirit in opposition to the German and Russian empires, was already too strong to be replaced by communist ideology. In the present-day era of individual values, it may even seem unexpected that the sturdy walls of the Estonian spirit were erected by the policy for creating a national identity, which was implemented, at times in the form of campaigns, in Estonia's authoritarian era in the latter half of the 1930s. This policy ranged from the Estonianisation of first names and surnames to culture, art, architecture and nature conservation, and not least in terms of importance, the national campaign for placing 'the Estonian flag in every home'. These blue, black and white flags, banned by the Soviet regime in 1940 and then carefully hidden, were brought out of their hiding places in 1988, and that early summer 30 years ago was the time when the communist regime had to start admitting its defeat.

Authors

Toomas Hiio is the Head of Research of the Estonian Institute of Historical Memory and simultaneously (since 2005) in the same position in the Estonian War Museum – General Laidoner Museum. Graduated as historian at the University of Tartu in 1991, since 2007 PhD student. From 1993 to 1998 at the University of Tartu (deputy head of an research project, head archivist of the university and university historian), 1998–2003 in the public service (adviser to the President of Estonia and to the former President of Estonia). 1998–2008 executive secretary of the Estonian International Commission for the Investigation of Crimes Against Humanity and 2008-2016 member of the board of Estonian Institute of Historical Memory. Editor-in-chief of the Estonian Yearbook of Military History (since 2011). Has published more than hundred articles and author, compiler or editor of a number of books. Main topics of research: university history 19th and 20th century), history of World War II and Estonian history of the 19th and 20th century.
toomas.hiio@mnemosyne.ee

Dr. Ivo Juurvee (PhD in history, University of Tartu) is the Head of the Security & Resilience Programme and a Research Fellow at the International Centre for Defence and Security since 2017. He is also a part time researcher at the Estonian National Defence College. Previously he has been a practitioner in the field of security for more than 13 years. Among other positions in Estonian public service, he has been an adviser at the National Security and Defence Coordination Unit of the Estonian Government Office and head of the Internal Security Institute of the Estonian Academy of Security Sciences. Juurvee has also taught security related topics at the University of Tartu, the NATO School at Oberammergau and in the EU Border Guard Agency FRONTEX master's programme on border man-

agement. He has worked as an Honorary Research Fellow at University College London's School of Slavonic and East European Studies. Juurvee's professional and academic areas of interest have been information warfare and intelligence services. In addition to a number of academic articles, he has authored two monographs on the history of intelligence services.
ivo.juurvee@icds.ee

Dr. Peeter Kaasik is a researcher at the Estonian Institute of Historical Memory and researcher at the Estonian War Museum - General Laidoner Museum. He received PhD in history from Tallinn University. Main topics of research: history of the World War II and Estonian history of the 19th and 20th century.
peeter.kaasik@esm.ee

Dr. Olaf Mertelsmann is Associate Professor in Contemporary History at the University of Tartu, Estonia. Among his monographs are *Zwischen Krieg, Revolution und Inflation: Die Werft Blohm & Voss 1914–1923, Der stalinistische Umbau in Estland,* and *Everyday Life in Stalinist Estonia.* He has edited for example *The Sovietization of the Baltic states, Central and Eastern European Media under Dictatorial Rule and in the Early Cold War,* and *The Baltic states under Stalinist Rule.*
omertelsmann@yahoo.co.uk

Dr. Norman M. Naimark is the Robert and Florence McDonnell Professor of East European Studies at Stanford University, a Professor of History and (by courtesy) of German Studies, and Senior Fellow at the Hoover Institution and the Freeman-Spogli Institute for International Studies. Naimark is interested in modern Eastern European and Russian history and his research focuses on Soviet policies and actions in Europe after World War II and on genocide and ethnic cleansing in the twentieth century. Professor Naimark is a Member of the Learned Committee of the Estonian Institute of Historical Memory.
naimark@stanford.edu

Aivar Niglas (BA in history, University of Tartu) is a researcher at the Estonian Institute of Historical Memory. His primary themes of research are: Estonians in the German Army during the Second World War, So-

viet military bases in Estonia in 1939–1941, release and rehabilitation of repressed persons of Estonian origin after Stalin's death.
aivar.niglas@mnemosyne.ee

Dr. Indrek Paavle (1970–2015, Phd in history (University of Tartu)), was a senior researcher at the Estonian Institute of Historical Memory. His main research topics were the history of 20th century institutions and the repressive policy of occupying regimes in Estonia. He wrote the monograph 'Õiguse ja omariikluse eest. Otto Tief (1889–1976)' [In the Name of Justice and Independent Statehood. Otto Tief (1889–1976)], which was published in 2014.

Eli Pilve (MA in history, Tallinn University) is researcher and project manager at the Estonian Institute of Historical Memory. Her main research topics include: Land reform in Estonia 1919, Estonians opting for citizenship after the Tartu Peace Treaty, persecution of the so-called exploiters and enemies of the people during the Soviet regime in Estonia and ideological upbringing in the Estonian SSR school system.
eli.pilve@mnemosyne.ee

Dr. Aigi Rahi-Tamm is an Associate Professor and Head of Archival Studies at the University of Tartu. Her main field of research is 20th century history with particular emphasis on mass violence and social history in the Soviet period. She is the author or co-author of several articles and two monographs.
aigi.rahi-tamm@ut.ee

Dr. Meelis Saueauk (PhD in history, University of Tartu) is senior researcher at the Estonian Institute of Historical Memory. His main research topics include: Stalinism, political history, intelligence and counter-intelligence agencies in the Baltic Sea region. He is the author of monograph 'Propaganda and terror', and author or co-author of several articles.
meelis.saueauk@mnemosyne.ee

Hiljar Tammela received an MA in history from the University of Tartu. He is researcher at the Estonian Institute of Historical Memory and PhD student at the University of Tartu. Main research topics include political history from the first half of the 20th century and mass repressions. *hiljar.tammela@mnemosyne.ee*

Dr. Tõnu Tannberg is Academician at the Estonian Academy of Sciences, Professor of Estonian History at the University of Tartu, Research Director at the Estonian National Archives and Co-Founder and Member of the Council of the Estonian Institute of Historical Memory. His main research fields are: 1) Political history of the Estonian SSR; 2) Baltic military history from 1710 to 1917, 3) History of Russia in 19th and 20th century.
tonu.tannberg@ra.ee